Butterworths
Questions and Answers

Administrative Law

2nd edition

Jeffrey Barnes

BJuris LLB (UNSW), MPubLaw (ANU)
Senior Lecturer, School of Law, La Trobe University
Director, Learning & Teaching, School of Law,
La Trobe University

Roger Douglas

BA, LLB (Melb), MPhil (Yale), PhD (La Trobe)
Associate Professor, School of Law, La Trobe University
Director, Honours, Research & Graduate Studies,
La Trobe University

LexisNexis Butterworths
Australia
2007

LexisNexis

AUSTRALIA	LexisNexis Butterworths
	475–495 Victoria Avenue, CHATSWOOD NSW 2067
	On the internet at: www.lexisnexis.com.au
ARGENTINA	LexisNexis Argentina, BUENOS AIRES
AUSTRIA	LexisNexis Verlag ARD Orac GmbH & Co KG, VIENNA
BRAZIL	LexisNexis Latin America, SAO PAULO
CANADA	LexisNexis Canada, Markham, ONTARIO
CHILE	LexisNexis Chile, SANTIAGO
CHINA	LexisNexis China, BEIJING, SHANGHAI
CZECH REPUBLIC	Nakladatelství Orac sro, PRAGUE
FRANCE	LexisNexis SA, PARIS
GERMANY	LexisNexis Germany, FRANKFURT
HONG KONG	LexisNexis Hong Kong, HONG KONG
HUNGARY	HVG-Orac, BUDAPEST
INDIA	LexisNexis, NEW DELHI
ITALY	Dott A Giuffrè Editore SpA, MILAN
JAPAN	LexisNexis Japan KK, TOKYO
KOREA	LexisNexis, SEOUL
MALAYSIA	Malayan Law Journal Sdn Bhd, SELANGOR DURAL EHSAN
NEW ZEALAND	LexisNexis, WELLINGTON
POLAND	Wydawnictwo Prawnicze LexisNexis, WARSAW
SINGAPORE	LexisNexis, SINGAPORE
SOUTH AFRICA	LexisNexis Butterworths, DURBAN
SWITZERLAND	Staempfli Verlag AG, BERNE
TAIWAN	LexisNexis, TAIWAN
UNITED KINGDOM	LexisNexis UK, LONDON, EDINBURGH
USA	LexisNexis Group, New York, NEW YORK
	LexisNexis, Miamisburg, OHIO

National Library of Australia Cataloguing-in-Publication entry

---

Barnes, Jeffrey Wilson.
Butterworths questions and answers: administrative law.
2nd ed.
ISBN: 978 0 409 323689.
1. Administrative law — Australia. I. Douglas, Roger (Roger Neil). II. Title.
342.94

© 2007 Reed International Books Australia Pty Limited trading as LexisNexis
First edition, 2003.

Inquiries should be addressed to the publishers.

Typeset in Optima and Sabon.

Printed by Percetakan Anda Sdn Bhd (Malaysia).

Visit LexisNexis Butterworths at www.lexisnexis.com.au

Contents

Preface

Administrative law is a remedial subject which intersects with many areas of society. It focuses on the availability of remedies for securing a measure of accountability in respect of decisions of government and related actions. The core remedial avenues are judicial review, merits or tribunal review, and ombudsman investigation.

While certain other law subjects are remedial in nature, a distinctive aspect of administrative law is the way the remedial avenues are *not* in practice freestanding areas of law. Administrative law is a kind of meta-law. The rights to seek review by a body, such as a court, tribunal or an Ombudsman, and the controls such bodies provide, generally operate *on* particular statutory regimes in which the powers of government officials are set out and in which primary or first-instance decision-making takes place. Therefore, in administrative law, it is always necessary to bear in mind that the statutory and common law remedies have a general application to incidents purportedly occurring under particular governmental regimes.

In this work the primary decision-making occurs under a Commonwealth regulatory scheme neatly found in a single regulation: reg 4A of the Customs (Prohibited Imports) Regulations 1956 (see p xiii). This regulation has been chosen as the vehicle for primary decision-making because the legal framework is reasonably challenging, while at the same time the length and the subject matter of the regulation make it a highly accessible piece of legislation.

The legislation and some of the problems in this book were the subject of a past administrative law examination at La Trobe University, so we write with the advantage of direct experience of student answers. References in our problems to the incumbents of particular offices are inevitable, but they should be read, of course, as relating to fictitious incumbents and not to those people who actually occupy the positions in question.

The second edition of this work has made possible a number of changes and improvements to this work.

Significant legal developments which have occurred since the first edition and which are reflected in the present work include:

- the publication of a survey of outcomes for applicants who have succeeded in judicial review proceedings: see Chapter 1;
- the enactment of the Legislative Instruments Act 2003 (Cth): see Chapter 2;
- developments in relation to the relevance (or otherwise) of 'legitimate expectations': see Chapter 5;
- the establishment of discretionary compensation schemes for compensation by the Australian government: see Chapter 9;
- the expansion in the implied statutory duty to give reasons for a decision: see Chapter 14.

The available sources have altered also. The answers for this work draw heavily on primary sources represented in the main casebooks. An important new entrant in the field of administrative law since the book's first edition is R Creyke and J McMillan, *Control of Government Action: Text, Cases and Commentary*, LexisNexis Butterworths, Sydney, 2005. The other casebook frequently drawn upon is Roger Douglas, *Douglas and Jones's Administrative Law*, 5th ed, Federation Press, Sydney, 2006.

These developments in the law and available sources have necessitated changes to a number of the questions. We have also taken the opportunity to improve all the answers by sharpening and clarifying the argument. Readers who diligently mastered the first edition may realise that we have sometimes changed our mind as to what constitutes the correct or preferable answer to particular questions. Various lessons could be drawn from this, but the one we would like you to draw is that administrative law does not necessarily yield uniquely correct answers to particular questions.

The 'Examiner's Comments' sections have also frequently been developed. We have been more attentive to articulating the skills required to answer a question well. This is reflected in the table, set out in the Introduction (see p x), giving a guide to the skills which are illustrated and discussed in this work. We think this guide to the skills employed in administrative law adds a significant and useful dimension to this work.

The original 'Makepeace Scenario' was written by Roger Douglas, the legislation having been chosen by Jeffrey Barnes. While the authors of this work each contributed to every answer, we wish to point out that Jeffrey Barnes is the primary author of Chapters 1, 2, 9–11 and 13–15, and Roger Douglas is the primary author of Chapters 3–8, 12 and 16.

On a personal note, we thank the publishers for their encouragement and assistance. We would also like to thank our spouses, Jane Barnes and Robin Burns, for their encouragement and forbearance while we worked on the second edition of this book.

We hope the book will continue to be stimulating and deliver insights to all students of administrative law. We encourage readers to email us if they can offer constructive feedback on the book:

J.Barnes@latrobe.edu.au;

R.Douglas@latrobe.edu.au.

Jeffrey Barnes
Roger Douglas
July 2007

Introduction

This book is an aid to your study of administrative law topics and a guide to developing legal skills particularly used in administrative law. Some general remarks follow about the make-up of the work, the principles underpinning it, and how to use it productively.

Make-up

Each topic contains problem questions and essay questions. The problem questions are based on reg 4A of the Customs (Prohibited Imports) Regulations 1956 (Cth): see p xiii.

In keeping with other works in the Questions and Answers series, the book provides explanatory material to increase understanding of the exercises. 'Key Issues' provides a handy introduction to each topic. In the sections 'Examiner's Comments' and 'Common Errors to Avoid', students will find comments on the questions and the answers, as well as many practical tips.

Design principles

Essay writing in administrative law is important for all students. Even if you are not examined by essay questions, you will benefit by attempting the essay questions for yourself. The essay questions lay bare the concepts of administrative law, a good understanding of which is assumed when you come to problem-solving.

In most cases the answers in the book are *not* intended to represent, in their entirety, an answer a student might reasonably achieve in an examination, or even an A-grade answer. We readily acknowledge that the answers are too detailed for students to achieve in practice, especially within the time limits stated. They might nevertheless be described as 'model' answers, in that they are the kind of answers students ideally should aim for. In other words, the answers illustrate the general *approach* you ought to take. At the same time the answers and the accompanying commentary attempt to provide instruction on the distinctive techniques required to answer questions in administrative law.

Students need to remember that the answers to the problem questions, including statements of general principle, were written for a particular set of facts arising under particular legislation. It would be extremely unwise for any student reader, in his or her own answer to a question under different legislation, to incorporate unthinkingly an answer or part of an answer from this work, word for word.

The 'model' answers are also less than perfect or complete. This is due not only to the word limits, but also because, when discussing disputed or controversial issues, a number of different responses can be made and not all can be included in a work of this size and nature. Where possible, the 'Examiner's Comments' sections assist students in pointing to alternative, acceptable approaches.

Where the answers draw on cited materials such as cases or legislation, they are generally materials which are readily available to students in casebooks and other prescribed sources. We have done this deliberately for the important reason that it shows students how to handle the materials generally available to them. However, note that a particular answer may have drawn simultaneously on a number of casebooks of Australian administrative law (particularly Roger Douglas, *Douglas and Jones's Administrative Law*, 5th ed, Federation Press, Sydney, 2006 and R Creyke and J McMillan, *Control of Government Action: Text, Cases and Commentary*, LexisNexis Butterworths, Sydney, 2005), even though students would normally be expected to access only one of them.

In some instances sources have been drawn upon even though they are not referred to in the standard casebooks. They may be of very recent origin. Or the sources may have come to light from our own scholarly researches of the law, whether for teaching purposes or in the course of wider research. We have drawn upon such sources because they are useful illustrations for the points we are making. Students should not be concerned at the occasional appearance of cases or other references that are not prescribed for them; they should remember that their examiner knows what material has been prescribed in their particular unit, and it is the way this material is handled by which students are primarily assessed.

As we are writing for a national audience, and with due regard for the kind of supplementary assistance which a work of this kind provides, we have concerned ourselves almost exclusively with federal law and the relevant common law. Students need to bear in mind that, additionally, legislated state administrative law and the precedents on such law are usually examinable.

Finally, but not least, a further design principle for this work has been to illustrate legal skills commonly encountered in administrative law. The following table is a guide to a number of such skills. The table is not a complete listing for each skill; many of the skills are evident in a large number of the answers. The table focuses on answers in which the examiners' comments highlight the skill or where we believe the answer to be a particularly good illustration of the skill.

General skill	Facet of the skill	Illustrative example: Question; (Chapter)
Essay writing	Analysing a statement	7(2), 15(5)
	Interpreting a statement	28(9)
	Approaching 'Discuss' questions	1(1), 44(14)
	Defining key terms	1(1), 21(7)
	Using dictionaries to assist interpretation of the question	3(1), 7(2), 35(11), 41(13)
	Working out a methodology	46(15)
	Critically analysing statements	4(1), 15(5), 24(8), 35(11)
	Comparative approach to the law	46(15), 47(15)
	Analysing theories	4(1)
	Using a case study as a methodology	5(1), 44(14)
	Applying constitutional and general legal knowledge	1(1), 24(8), 39(13)
	Demonstrating operational understanding of the law	3(1), 18(6), 21(7), 41(13)
	Structuring answers clearly	3(1))
	Discussing issues in a dialectical manner	18(6), 24(8), 27(9)
	Giving examples	7(2)
	Writing conclusions to essays	30(10))
Analysing legislation	'Navigating' one's way through complex legislation	42(14)
	Reading together several provisions of an Act	6(2)

General skill *cont'd*	Facet of the skill	Illustrative example: Question; (Chapter)
Analysing legislation *cont'd*	Structuring complex legislative requirements by means of an algorithm or a step-by-step approach	8(2)
	Using the law of statutory interpretation	8(2)
	Setting out legislative requirements clearly and logically	42(14)
Case analysis	Determining the weight of a non-binding 'precedent'	14(4), 34(11)
Problem-solving	General approach to problem-solving	32(10), 48(16), 49(16), 50(16)
	Ascertaining facts and handling factual uncertainty	6(2), 19(6), 23(7), 34(11), 37(12)
	Recognising red herrings	45(15)
	Raising issues	45(15)
	Setting out the legal framework	33(11), 43(14)
	Writing answers where there is uncertainty	6(2), 12(4), 16(5), 19(6)
	Combining more than one area of administrative law	13(4), 23(7), 33(11), 48(16), 49(16), 50(16)
	Handling ethical dilemmas	40(13), 49(16)
	Marshalling the law to achieve the objectives of the 'client'	29(9), 37(12), 48(16), 49(16), 50(16)
	Performing various 'clinical' legal tasks	40(13)

Using this work

Before attempting any of the questions in a topic read the 'Key Issues' section of the topic to ensure you have enough background knowledge to attempt the questions.

Before attempting a problem question be sure you have carefully read or are familiar with the primary decision-making legislation: reg 4A of the Customs (Prohibited Imports) Regulations 1956 (Cth). Then, read or re-read 'The Makepeace Scenario' (see p xvi), as this sets out background facts for a number of the problem questions.

Customs (Prohibited Imports) Regulations 1956 (Cth) Reg 4A

4A Importation of objectionable goods

(1) In this regulation, unless the contrary intention appears:

computer game means a computer program and associated data capable of generating a display on a computer monitor, television screen, liquid crystal display or similar medium that allows the playing of an interactive game.

computer generated image means an image (including an image in the form of text) produced by use of a computer on a computer monitor, television screen, liquid crystal display or similar medium from electronically recorded data.

film includes a cinematograph film, a slide, video tape and video disc and any other form of recording from which a visual image, including a computer generated image, can be produced, but does not include a computer game.

interactive game means a game in which the way the game proceeds and the result achieved at various stages of the game is determined in response to the decisions, inputs and direct involvement of the player.

publication means any book, paper, magazine, film, computer game or other written or pictorial matter.

(1A) This regulation applies to publications and any other goods, that:

    (a) describe, depict, express or otherwise deal with matters of sex, drug misuse or addiction, crime, cruelty, violence or revolting or abhorrent phenomena in such a way that they offend against the standards of morality, decency and propriety generally accepted by reasonable adults to the extent that they should not be imported; or

(b)   describe or depict in a way that is likely to cause offence to a reasonable adult, a person who is, or who appears to be, a child under 18 (whether the person is engaged in sexual activity or not); or

(c)   in relation to a computer game — are unsuitable for a person under 18 to see or play; or

(d)   promote, incite or instruct in matters of crime or violence; or

(e)   promote or incite the misuse of a drug specified in Schedule 4.

(2)   The importation of goods to which this regulation applies is prohibited unless a permission, in writing, to import the goods has been granted by the Attorney-General or a person authorized by the Attorney-General for the purposes of this subregulation.

(2AA)In considering whether to grant a permission under subregulation (2), the Attorney-General or the person authorised by the Attorney-General is to have regard to:

(a)   the purposes for which the goods are to be imported; and

(b)   the extent to which the person to whom any permission to import the goods would be granted conducts activities of an artistic or educational, or of a cultural or scientific, nature to which the goods relate; and

(c)   the reputation of the person referred to in paragraph (b), both generally and in relation to an activity referred to in that paragraph; and

(d)   the ability of that person to meet conditions that may be imposed under subregulation (3) in relation to the goods; and

(e)   any other relevant matters.

(2A) The Attorney-General may, by instrument in writing, appoint a person to be an authorized person for the purposes of subregulation (2).

(3)   A permission under this regulation shall be subject to such conditions imposing requirements or prohibitions on the person to whom the permission is granted with respect to the custody, use, reproduction, disposal, destruction or exportation of the goods, or with respect to accounting for the goods, as the Attorney-General or a person authorized by the Attorney-General for the purposes of subregulation (2) thinks necessary to ensure that the goods are

not used otherwise than for the purpose for which he grants the permission.

(4)   Application may be made to the Administrative Appeals Tribunal for review of a decision of the Attorney-General under subregulation (2):

(a)   refusing to grant a permission; or

(b)   granting a permission subject to conditions by the person to whom the permission was granted subject to conditions.

(5)   The Attorney-General may certify in writing that in his or her opinion it is in the public interest that responsibility for a permission or a refusal of a permission specified in the certificate should reside solely with the Attorney-General and should not be reviewable by the Administrative Appeals Tribunal.

(6)   The Attorney General is to give a copy of a certificate to the person to whom permission was refused or given subject to conditions under subregulation (4).

(7)   A certificate must include a statement of the grounds on which the certificate is issued.

(8)   While a certificate is in force in relation to a permission or a refusal of a permission, subregulation (4) does not apply to that permission or refusal.

(9)   The Attorney-General is to cause a copy of a certificate to be laid before each House of the Parliament within 15 sitting days of that House after the day on which the certificate is issued.

(10)   Subject to subregulation (6), if the Attorney-General:

(a)   refuses to grant a permission to a person; or

(b)   grants a permission to a person subject to conditions;

he or she is to inform the person of the decision by notice in writing within 30 days after making the decision.

(11)   A notice under subregulation (10) must include:

(a)   a statement to the effect that application may be made to the Tribunal under the *Administrative Appeals Tribunal Act 1975* for review of the decision to which the notice relates; and

(b)   except where subsection 28 (4) of that Act applies — a statement to the effect that a person who is entitled to apply to the Tribunal for review of the decision may, under section 28 of that Act, request a statement that includes the reasons for the decision.

(12)   A contravention of subregulation (11) in relation to a decision does not affect the validity of the decision.

The Makepeace Scenario

Caledenia is a large and militarily powerful State occupying a number of islands in the southern Indian Ocean. Its dominant religion is Mindu, a polytheistic version of Gha. Arachnorchis is a Caledenian intellectual, noted for his radical criticisms of corruption in Caledenia. In 2000 he wrote and illustrated a book, *The Night of a Thousand Shames* ('the book'). This described an attack by a platoon of drunken Caledenian soldiers on a Catholic convent on the outer island of Burdettia, and its aftermath. One scene features a 15-year-old boy forcing a nun to feed the convent's supply of communion wafers to a group of hungry monkeys. (Reports of this incident had aroused a denunciatory address from the Catholic Archbishop of Parramatta, Cardinal Virtue.) In addition to its vivid prose, the book included numerous drawings portraying the atrocities committed by the soldiers, and photographs of the burnt-out convent and the charred remains of several nuns. In 2001, Arachnorchis accidentally fell out of a ninth-floor window while being interviewed by police attached to Caledenia's much-feared National Socio-Legal Research Centre.

Makepeace, an Australian Christian organisation, made arrangements to import copies of the book for general distribution in Australia as part of its ongoing campaign against the Caledenian government. This campaign has strained relations between Caledenia and Australia. On a recent visit to Australia, the Caledenian Minister for Culture and Aircraft Production warned the Australian government that allowing importation of the book might be treated as an act of cultural warfare which could severely demoralise the police responsible for the protection of the Australian embassy, and which might encourage chauvinist members of the Caledenian Politburo to reject Telstra's tender for the reconstruction of the Caledenian telecommunications system.

The Australian Cabinet discussed what it should do, and decided that Customs should be asked to treat the book as a prohibited import. The

Attorney-General was asked to refuse any request that Makepeace might make to be allowed to import the book, but said:

> This is a matter for me and me alone. I will not be dictated to. If I think the book should be allowed in, I shall allow it in, even at the cost of my political career. But I probably won't allow it in.

PART 1
Introduction

Chapter 1

Concepts, Context and Critical Appraisal

Key Issues

This chapter deals with general concerns of administrative law. These concerns are initially raised usually at the outset of an administrative law unit. But they are not purely introductory. As the unit progresses, students are expected to relate the concerns to the various topics. Accordingly, the questions below require students to demonstrate an understanding of these matters in the context of the unit as a whole.

The general concerns are interrelated. For convenience they are considered under three broad headings:

1. concepts;

2. context; and

3. critical appraisal.

1. Concepts

It has been said that 'The starting point for any consideration of administrative law is a realisation that it is a species of adjective [procedural] law rather than substantive law': D Bennett QC, 'The Assimilation of Judicial Review to Review on the Merits', *Canberra Bulletin of Public Administration*, vol 58, 1989, p 94. While the author was considering only judicial review, the statement holds up well for administrative law broadly understood. Judicial review is adjectival, as in this description by Kirby J (in *Minister for Immigration and Ethnic Affairs v Guo* (1997) 191 CLR 559 at 598–9):

> Whereas on appeal a court will often enjoy the power and responsibility of substituting its decision for that under appeal, judicial review is designed, fundamentally, to uphold the lawfulness, fairness and reasonableness (rationality) of the process under review.

Mr Bennett's observation also holds true for the parliamentary Ombudsman, whose brief is to examine complaints about maladministration. And one can see the adjectival side to merits review in the legal framework of merits review tribunals. Under the Acts which establish them, tribunals are given *powers of review*, even though at the end of the day a merits review tribunal can exercise the same substantive powers which are available to the primary decision-maker whose decision is being reviewed.

The adjectival character of administrative law is, however, just one of a number of useful conceptual starting points. What are others?

Constitutional concepts and doctrines are probably the most important set of concepts underlying and supporting administrative law. Textbooks and casebooks commonly review these concepts and discuss their relevance for administrative law. The concepts include the rule of law, the separation of powers, representative government and democracy, parliamentary sovereignty, ministerial responsibility and federalism.

The public–private distinction is another important conceptual basis of administrative law. Public law writs (*certiorari*, prohibition and *mandamus* and their statutory equivalents) control the exercise of public power, whether it has a purported statutory or common law source: *R v Criminal Injuries Compensation Board; Ex parte Lain* [1967] 2 QB 864. Merits review tribunals such as the Administrative Appeals Tribunal (AAT) have at the core of their business a public element, as the decisions they review must be made under an enactment: see, for example, s 25 of the Administrative Appeals Tribunal Act 1975 (Cth) (the AAT Act). And although the Commonwealth Ombudsman can investigate some Commonwealth service providers under contract (Ombudsman Act 1976 ss 3(4B), 3BA), the office's main business is in investigating administrative action by public bodies: government departments and 'prescribed authorities': s 5(1).

2.   Context

The wider context of administrative law takes in an extensive range of matters including:

- the institutional framework of government (including the Cabinet and the executive council);
- the administrative process, which includes the different ways in which delegated legislation is made and administrative discretion is exercised;
- the origins and rationale of administrative law remedies;
- the underlying interests at stake; and
- the effects and impact of administrative law.

3.   Critical appraisal

Administrative law is in an imperfect state. As elsewhere in their legal studies, students are expected to use and develop their critical faculties. Evaluation and criticism in administrative law needs to be on an informed basis, accompanied by rigorous analysis and defended against opposing arguments that may foreseeably be made. Critical analysis often benefits by being theoretically informed: a theory of administrative law or a more general legal or social theory. The limitations of a theory, perspective or standpoint brought to bear on a topic always need to be analysed and acknowledged. Students should also be aware of key social and political debates about administrative law, such as to what extent judges are 'political actors' in administrative law cases and the appropriate level of independence of tribunals.

Before attempting the questions, check that you are familiar with the following issues:

✓ the general scope of administrative law, including the roles of the courts, merits review tribunals and the Ombudsmen as mechanisms of review, and the purposes of the related mechanisms of reasons for decision and freedom of information;

✓ the distinction between procedure and substance and how this is reflected in judicial review and the other administrative law remedies;

✓ the constitutional concepts and doctrines which underpin administrative law;

✓ the wider context of administrative law, including the institutional framework of government, the administrative process, the underlying interests, and the effects and impact of administrative law;

✓ theories and debates about administrative law;

✓ the extent to which each of these issues is reflected in administrative law cases and legislation.

QUESTION 1

> Underlying legal doctrine governing the parliament, the executive and the courts is a constitutional ideal — an ideal separation of powers. This ideal has had a striking and profound influence on the scope of judicial review exercised by federal courts, but the same cannot be said with respect to the AAT's statutory functions.
>
> Discuss this statement.
>
> **Time allowed: 1 hour**

Answer Plan

(i)   Introduction:

  • Defining the separation of powers ideal.

- Introducing the notion of a partial separation of powers in practice.
- Approach to answering the question.

(ii) The federal courts.
- Prohibition on merits review: *Quin's* case.
- Other evidence of the influence of the separation of powers ideal.

(iii) The AAT.
- Executive powers.
- Overlaps with common ingredients in the exercise of judicial power.
- Lack of enforcement powers.

(iv) Conclusion.

 Answer

(i)   Introduction: defining the separation of powers ideal

The separation of powers ideal postulates a government divided into three departments: the legislature, the executive, and the judiciary. Each exercises its own function: 'the legislature makes, the executive executes, and the judiciary construes the law': Marshall CJ, cited in *New South Wales v Commonwealth* (the *Wheat* case) (1915) 20 CLR 54 at 90 per Isaacs J. And each is composed of its own distinctive personnel. Thus, for instance, any interference by one branch in the work of another is a breach of the ideal. This is the 'pure' version of the separation of powers: M Vile, *Constitutionalism and the Separation of Powers*, Clarendon Press, Oxford, 1967, p 13.

As the name implies, the separation of powers ideal is not directly enforceable in the courts. Rather, the ideal acts as an influence on the development of constitutional, statutory and common law doctrines which may be enforced by claimants bringing actions before the courts. This doctrine evidences a partial or incomplete separation of powers.

The remainder of this essay elaborates on the statement. Examples are given of how the ideal has differentially influenced the capacity of federal courts to undertake judicial review and the capacity of the AAT to undertake merits review. Brief consideration is given as to why this is the case.

(ii)   The federal courts

There are many common law restrictions on the courts which are the product of the influence of the separation of powers ideal, or which are certainly consistent with it. Probably the most important of these is the acceptance that the merits of a decision (and related issues such as reviewing government policy) belong to the executive. An oft-cited statement is that of Brennan J in *Attorney-General (NSW) v Quin* (1990) 170 CLR 1, a case in which the High Court considered whether the common law ought to recognise a substantive ground of review based on 'legitimate expectations'. In his Honour's judgment there are clear limits on the courts' jurisdiction in administrative law (at 35–6):

> The duty and jurisdiction of the court to review administrative action do not go beyond the declaration and enforcing of the law which determines the limits and governs the exercise of the repository's power. If, in so doing, the court avoids administrative injustice or error, so be it; but the court has no jurisdiction simply to cure administrative injustice or error. The merits of administrative action, to the extent that they can be distinguished from legality, are for the repository of the relevant power and, subject to political control, for the repository alone.

The High Court agreed with this statement in *Corporation of the City of Enfield v Development Assessment Commission* (2000) 199 CLR 135 at [43]–[44].

In *Quin*, Brennan J explained the prohibition on merits review by courts. One rationale arose from the need for public acceptance: 'If judicial review were to trespass on the merits of the exercise of administrative power, it would put its own legitimacy at risk': at 38. But the justification was not limited to 'political' considerations. He also explained the prohibition on merits review in terms redolent of the separation of powers (at 37 and 38):

> ... the court needs to remember that the judicature is but one of the three co-ordinate branches of government ... The courts have a duty to uphold and apply the law which recognises the autonomy of the three branches of government within their respective spheres of competence and which recognises the legal effectiveness of the due exercise of power by the Executive Government and other repositories of administrative power.

In *Quin's* case the rejection of the substantive protection of 'legitimate expectations' was, in the judgment of some members of the court, partly based on regard to the separation of powers ideal: per Mason CJ at 23 and Brennan J at 34–9. *Quin* is but one of a number of cases in which a suggested ground of review has been rejected because of separation of powers concerns. In these cases, the separation of powers ideal has been used in a 'gatekeeper' role to reject suggested grounds which would effectively allow merits review. Another is *Minister for Immigration, Local Government and Ethnic Affairs v Kurtovic* (1990) 21 FCR 193, where one member of the Federal Court, Gummow J, rejected the suggested ground of 'substantive unfairness' for the reason that 'the question of where the balance lies between competing public and private interests in the exercise of a statutory discretion goes to the merits of the case, and is thus one for the decision-maker, not the courts, to resolve': at 221.

The influence of the ideal is also strongly evident at the remedial stage of judicial review proceedings. The courts cannot stand in the shoes of the repository. If the decision-maker is left with a 'residual discretion', in the sense that the decision-maker can 'decide the ultimate question favourably or unfavourably to the successful applicant' before the court, the court 'usually, if not invariably ... remits the matter for further consideration according to law': *Minister for Immigration and Ethnic Affairs v Conyngham* (1986) 11 FCR 528 at 541.

Although the courts' judicial review powers are in these ways profoundly influenced by the separation of powers ideal, the courts' functions and powers necessarily go *against* the separation of powers ideal in its pure form. The most important of these lies at the very root of judicial review: the idea of checking and balancing. It will be recalled that the 'pure' version of the separation of powers doctrine forbids *any* interference by one branch in the workings of another. But another important constitutional ideal, the rule of law, *requires* 'the courts to grant whatever remedies are available and appropriate to ensure that those possessed of executive and administrative powers exercise them only in accordance with the laws which govern their exercise': *Corporation of the City of Enfield v Development Assessment Commission* (2000) 199 CLR 135 at 158 per Gaudron J. Judicial review therefore necessarily involves the court in examining the legality of an administrative decision and, where appropriate, striking it down. Even though judicial review extends to interference by the court in a purported exercise of power by the executive, this examination (and hence interference) is *limited* to the general principles of law explained by Brennan J in *Quin*. In this way, the checking and balancing carried out under the banner of judicial review can be reconciled with the separation of powers (at least a partial separation of powers) — for checking and balancing still leaves 'the ultimate functions committed by law to the decision-maker': *Minister for Immigration and Ethnic Affairs v Guo* (1997) 191 CLR 559 at 599 per Kirby J.

(iii) The Administrative Appeals Tribunal

By comparison, the AAT is much less restricted by separation of powers concerns.

On the one hand, the AAT is vested with a plenitude of executive powers; powers the federal courts do not have. The tribunal reviews administrative decisions on the merits: AAT Act s 43(1). It can take into account and review government policy: *Drake v Minister for Immigration and Ethnic Affairs* (1979) 24 ALR 577. It is not bound by the rules of evidence: AAT Act s 33(1)(c). It can exercise a power that was open to the decision-maker although not actually exercised: *Fletcher v Commissioner of Taxation* (1988) 19 FCR 442. It can substitute a decision for that of the primary decision-maker: AAT Act s 43(1)(c)(i). Membership of the tribunal does not bring judicial tenure (s 8), although a few members are Federal Court judges.

On the other hand, the AAT's powers overlap with the federal courts' in several ways. The tribunal is adjudicative. A federal executive body is not impermissibly exercising judicial powers simply because:

... it gives a final decision; nor because two or more contending parties appear before it between whom it has to decide; nor because it gives decisions which affect the rights of subjects; nor because it is a body to which a matter is referred by another body: *Brandy v Human Rights and Equal Opportunity Commission* (1995) 183 CLR 245 at 256 per Mason CJ, Brennan and Toohey JJ.

Nor does the formation of an opinion as to legal rights and obligations by a tribunal involve the exercise of federal 'judicial power': at 258. In short, in the powers it is allowed to exercise the AAT does to a great extent resemble a court. As the High Court itself has acknowledged, 'common ingredients in the exercise of judicial power ... may also be elements in the exercise of administrative ... power': *Precision Data Holdings Ltd v Wills* (1991) 173 CLR 167 at 189, cited in *Brandy* by Deane, Dawson, Gaudron and McHugh JJ at 267.

What restrictions flowing from the separation of powers ideal are there then on administrative tribunals? Acknowledging that 'It is hard to point to any essential or constant characteristic' of exclusive judicial power (*Brandy* at 267), the High Court has held that the power of enforcement (the power to carry a judgment into effect between the contending parties) is the most important indicator: *Brandy* per Deane, Dawson, Gaudron and McHugh JJ at 268. Therefore, it has been said that tribunals cannot 'make final and enforceable decisions on questions of law': R Douglas, *Douglas and Jones's Administrative Law*, 5th ed, Federation Press, Sydney, 2006, p 31. In other words, the decisions of tribunals are 'not directly enforceable': R Douglas, *Administrative Law*, 2nd ed, LexisNexis Butterworths, Sydney, 2004, [1.2.6]. Thus, in the unlikely event that the government refuses to implement a decision of the AAT, the tribunal could not order the executive government to carry its decision into effect; nor, even more so, could it punish an official or person for failing to do so. In such a case the courts could be called upon to make appropriate orders — provided that a federal court is not asked merely to rubber stamp the tribunal's decision with the court's imprimatur: *Brandy*.

(iv) Conclusion

In theory (the ideal or pure version of the separation of powers) each branch of government and its constituent institutions is supposed to enjoy complete separation from other branches. In practice the separation of powers works differently in separating 'judicial' from 'executive' power. At the federal level of government in Australia, the ideal has had much greater influence on the federal courts than it has on the AAT. It is because judicial and executive powers are inherently different and do different things in the real world that the influence of the ideal is differently felt.

Examiner's Comments

The question requires a 'constitutional' perspective of administrative law yet it must be acknowledged that the extent to which administrative law lecturers include constitutional material in their units varies. In other words, the question might not be typical of one asked in a three-hour examination. Nevertheless, the question is worth asking here because the study of administrative law assumes a knowledge of basic constitutional considerations, such as the separation of powers and the rule of law, and students cannot truly understand it without making the constitutional connection.

The answer is strong in defining the separation of powers ideal and in distinguishing it from its enforceable legal manifestation in practice. As the statement in the question referred to the 'ideal', students would be expected to take up this distinction. The answer is also strong in giving specific instances of how the ideal affects, or alternatively does not affect, the operation of the federal courts and the AAT.

Other cases could legitimately have been mentioned. For instance, separation of powers concerns explain why the court refrains from entering a 'political field': an 'area of ministerial policy giving effect to the general public interest', to quote Brennan J in *South Australia v O'Shea* (1987) 163 CLR 378 at 411.

The major limitation of the answer is in the way it approaches the requirement to 'discuss'. 'Discuss' is not an easy academic requirement in that it (quite deliberately) does not map out a clear strategy for the examinee. Examinees have to do that themselves. The strategy taken in this answer was to *elaborate* on how the statement is true. While this clearly falls within the scope of 'discuss', the answer is short on other strategies. In the last sentence we glimpse an explanation of *why* the separation of powers works differently depending on whether we are looking at the federal courts or the AAT.

The answer glosses the ways in which the courts do seem to exercise executive power: the power to review 'jurisdictional facts' on their merits on the evidence before them: *Corporation of the City of Enfield v Development Assessment Commission* (2000) 1999 CLR 135 at [38]; the power to review on the ground of unreasonableness appears to stray into the merits somewhat (cf *Quin* at 36 per Brennan J); and the elasticity (or is it manipulability?) of the grounds of review especially the grounds of relevant and irrelevant considerations.

The answer also glosses the ways in which the AAT is constrained by separation of powers concerns, that is, does not have judicial power. The power to determine binding precedents could have been mentioned. Also, a person may not obtain relief from the tribunal upon the ground that the statute purportedly empowering the challenged administrative action is *ultra vires* the parliament: *Re Adams and the Tax Agents' Board* (1976) 1 ALD 251 at 257 per Brennan J. If more space were available, as in an assignment, the implications for the AAT of the decision of *Wilson v Minister for Aboriginal and Torres Strait Islander Affairs* (1996) 189 CLR 1 (the *Hindmarsh Island* case) could be discussed. But this decision only affects the use of Ch III judges in the performance of non-judicial roles, so it is relatively marginal in terms of the above question.

Common Errors to Avoid

- Not stating what the separation of powers ideal stands for. Alternatively, confusing it with a distribution of powers (the powers institutions enjoy in practice under a partial separation of powers).

- Confusing the courts' checking and balancing role with the separation of powers — assuming that that role is evidence of the pure form of the separation of powers ideal, rather than the reverse.

- Not providing evidence, backed up by references to legislation and case law, of the influence of the separation of powers ideal.

- Incorrect usage: employing 'legislative' as a noun when the correct term is 'legislature'.

QUESTION 2

'[I]n the shadow of the legal rights [is] the concrete reality of human interests.' Taking Roscoe Pound's definition of an interest as 'a demand or desire which human beings either individually or in groups seek to satisfy' the realist legal philosopher Professor Julius Stone propounded that:

> ... law along with other social mechanisms seeks such a degree of adjustment among the chronically conflicting interests as will allow social ordering to maintain itself: *Social Dimensions of Law and Justice*, Maitland Publications, Sydney, 1966, p 166.

Discuss Stone's view in the context of administrative law, giving at least three examples of how administrative law seeks to adjust conflicting individual and social (that is, collective) interests.

Time allowed: 1 hour

Answer Plan

(i)   Introduction: main issues the statement by Professor Stone raises.

(ii) Illustrative areas of administrative law:

- *Carltona* doctrine.
- Procedural fairness: the hearing rule.
- Extension of time to make application for judicial review.

- Powers of the AAT in relation to government policy.
- The Ombudsman's jurisdiction.
- Freedom of information.

(iii) Conclusion.

 ## Answer

(i)   Introduction: main issues the statement by Professor Stone raises

Upon analysis it would appear that the statement of Professor Stone makes three general claims:

1. that underlying law there are 'chronically conflicting interests';

2. that law seeks an adjustment to maintain the social order; and

3. that the adjustment is a limited one: it is only 'such' an adjustment as is necessary for those ends.

In this answer I take several areas of administrative law and investigate those claims.

(ii)   Illustrative areas of administrative law

Carltona doctrine

The *Carltona* doctrine is a common law doctrine which permits *some* repositories of statutory powers to authorise subordinates to act as agents of the repository. In *Minister for Aboriginal Affairs v Peko-Wallsend Ltd* (1986) 162 CLR 24 at 38 Mason J stated the rationale of the principle and the criteria which are to be applied to determine whether a repository has such a power:

> The cases in which the principle has been applied are cases in which the nature, scope and purpose of the function vested in the repository made it unlikely that Parliament intended that it was to be exercised by the repository personally because administrative necessity indicated that it was impractical for him to act otherwise than through his officers responsible to him.

Underlying the *Carltona* doctrine is an interest in the statute law being observed according to its terms. Observing the law in this manner supports the rule of law. But there is also an interest in powers held by repositories with 'multifarious functions' being able to be exercised by subordinates. Otherwise the effective working of government would be threatened. The *Carltona* doctrine adjusts these interests. It does not allow repositories to authorise subordinates on a whim (vindicating the rule of law to some extent). But neither does it prohibit a repository from authorising another; it does not require a decision-maker to go to the lengths of employing an instrument of delegation if they wish to spread the decision-making burden. The concept of 'administrative necessity' is the vehicle for this trade-off — this adjustment of conflicting interests.

The cases on the *Carltona* doctrine accordingly demonstrate that some executive demands for a 'Carltona' authority will be supported by the law, while others will not. In the first category is the *Carltona* case itself (*Carltona Ltd v Commissioners of Works* [1943] 2 All ER 560): a ministerial war-time power to requisition private property was held to be subject to the power to authorise an experienced official. So too is *Ex parte Foster; Re University of Sydney* (1963) 63 SR (NSW) 723 (power of governing body of university to authorise others, depending on the importance of the subject matter), and *O'Reilly v State Bank of Victoria Commissioners* (1983) 153 CLR 1 (power of Deputy Commissioner of Taxation to authorise departmental officer to act for him). In the second category is *Tickner v Chapman* (1995) 57 FCR 451 where the Federal Court ruled that the Minister was duty bound to consider personally the evidence of 'women's business' and could not rely on the opinion of a female staff member who had read a report reviewing the evidence. See too *Minister for Aboriginal Affairs v Peko-Wallsend Ltd* (1986) 162 CLR 24 at 37–9: a Minister, the repository of a power to grant land to Aboriginal claimants, could not, without executing an instrument of delegation, leave his staff to decide what facts or matters would be taken into account.

Procedural fairness: the hearing rule

Underlying the hearing rule are a number of individual and collective interests. On the one hand, there is the individual interest in 'being afforded [an] opportunity to influence the course of events': *John v Rees* [1969] 2 All ER 274 at 309 per Megarry J. As the judge said in that case, individuals resent not being included in decision-making which affects them. They have an interest in being involved and in being respected. It is not only individuals with special interests who demand to participate in decision-making. There is a general desire for quality decision-making and it is assumed that ensuring relevant information is before the decision-maker will promote better decisions: R Creyke and J McMillan, *Control of Government Action: Text, Cases and Commentary*, LexisNexis Butterworths, Sydney, 2005, [10.1.9]. And once decisions are made there is a desire that they be respected; this objective is assisted by participation. However, there is another side to the story. There is a social interest in not overjudicialising the administrative process: *Kioa v West* (1985) 159 CLR 550 at 629 per Brennan J. There are costs involved in affording participation. It is trite to observe that the public demands that governments use their resources wisely and only where needed.

How are these conflicting interests adjusted? Partly through the implication test as to whether the hearing rule applies at all, but also through the content test: the test by which the particular requirements are determined. A commonly cited passage is that of Mason J in *Kioa* where he pointed out some of the key considerations: the circumstances of the case, the nature of the inquiry, the subject matter, the rules under which the decision-maker is acting; the interests of the individual; and the interests and purposes, whether public or private, which the statute seeks to advance or protect or permits to be taken into account as legitimate considerations: at 584–5.

An example of a case in which the demand for participation was strong is *Re Macquarie University v Ong* (1989) 17 NSWLR 113. A university committee recommended that the position of the Head of the law school be declared vacant without giving notice to the Head of one of the grounds. Here the interest was livelihood and the procedural flaw was basic — a lack of notice of a fundamental ground for acting.

But compare *Krstic v Australian Telecommunications Commission* (1988) 20 FCR 486. The applicant had had her employment with Telecom terminated and she was upset about several things including the refusal of legal representation before a review tribunal. The court did not find that the former employee had been denied procedural fairness. She was only a probationary employee and had been afforded a hearing of sorts. Her main complaint was being refused legal representation. The court was seemingly mindful of not wasting public resources. In its view the applicant was quite able to stand up for herself. The court could not see the need for a lawyer to participate in a decision about whether an officer should be appointed permanently after a period of probation. It also noted the implicit public demand in the statute that the lay tribunal proceed informally.

Extension of time to make application

The Administrative Decisions (Judicial Review) Act 1977 (Cth) (ADJR Act) states that applications to the Federal Court or Federal Magistrates Court must be made within a prescribed time period of certain events occurring. For instance, if reasons have been given in writing, the period is 28 days from the time reasons were given. This time limit, is however, subject to a discretion to allow a late application 'within such further time as the court concerned (whether before or after the expiration of the prescribed period) allows': s 11(1)(c).

Provision for this discretion is the result of an adjustment of conflicting interests. On the one hand, there is the interest in the finality of decision-making and the quick resolution of disputes: *Hunter Valley Developments Pty Ltd v Cohen* (1983) 3 FCR 344 at 348. On the other hand, there is the interest in being 'fair and equitable' to the applicant if that interest is sufficiently pressing in the circumstances of the case: *Hunter Valley* at 348. The law adjusts these interests by making a prima facie rule that proceedings commenced outside the prescribed period will not be entertained, and by laying down non-exhaustive principles to guide the exercise of the court's discretion: *Hunter Valley* at 348.

Powers of the AAT in relation to government policy

The AAT is not bound by government policy: *Drake v Minister for Immigration and Ethnic Affairs* (1979) 24 ALR 577. The Federal Court noted that it was for the AAT 'to frame any general statement of the precise part which government policy should ordinarily play in the determinations of the Tribunal': at 590. The tribunal did so in the consequential rehearing: *Re Drake and Minister for Immigration and Ethnic Affairs (No 2)* (1979) 2 ALD 634. The President, Brennan J, set out what the tribunal's general practice should be:

> When the Tribunal is reviewing the exercise of a discretionary power reposed in a Minister, and the Minister has adopted a general policy to guide him in the exercise of the power, the Tribunal will ordinarily apply that policy in reviewing the decision, unless the policy is unlawful or unless its application tends to produce an unjust decision in the circumstances of the particular case: at 645.

This formulation was arrived at after a careful analysis of the underlying interests. As Brennan J acknowledged, 'a balance may have to be struck between the achieving of [an objective of public significance] and the interests of an individual': at 643. There are powerful interests which support the tribunal ordinarily following ministerial policy: the tribunal's independence might be affected by it exercising what is essentially a political function; it also lacked the desire to develop policy because its membership was not appropriate and it was 'unsupported by a bureaucracy fitted to advise upon broad policy': at 644. But there is a countervailing interest: the avoidance of an injustice in a particular case if a ministerial policy were to be applied. An 'injustice' is not evidenced by a mere objection to applying a policy but by a detriment to an individual which outweighs the benefits of applying the policy: at 645.

The Ombudsman's jurisdiction

The Ombudsman has been given a general jurisdiction to investigate complaints about a matter of administration by a government department or by a prescribed authority: Ombudsman Act 1976 (Cth) s 5. Excluded is action taken by a Minister: s 5(2)(a). Action taken by a delegate of a Minister is not excluded: s 5(3). These provisions represent the adjustment of conflicting interests. On the one hand, there is the interest in individuals being able informally and cheaply to complain about government maladministration:

> What every form of government needs is some regular and smooth-running mechanism for feeding back the reactions of its disgruntled customers, after impartial assessment, and for correcting whatever may have gone wrong: *Re British Columbia Development Corp and Friedmann* (1984) 14 DLR (4th) 129 at 139.

On the other hand, there is the interest in preserving the system of ministerial responsibility to the parliament as part of the system of responsible government. In theory a Minister is responsible not only for his or her own actions but for the entire portfolio: *Egan v Willis* (1998) 195 CLR 424 at 452 per Gaudron, Gummow and Hayne JJ. In excluding the personal actions of Ministers from the Ombudsman scheme the law recognises the special importance of allowing Ministers to be responsible to parliament for their own actions; a system which could well be undermined if the Ombudsman were to be empowered to review ministerial action across the board.

Freedom of information

Within the Freedom of Information Act is a mechanism for adjusting conflicting interests. On the one hand, there is the public interest in accountability of government and in public participation in government. On the other hand, there is the competing interest in secrecy for the purpose of preventing prejudicial effects to essential public interests such as the workings of Cabinet, deliberation by government, and so on: *Re Eccleston & Department of Family Services and Aboriginal and Islander Affairs* (1993) 1 QAR 60 at 74. The Act resolves the competing interests differently according to the category of documents at stake. In some instances, the dice is loaded in favour of government as in the case of Cabinet documents (s 34), but it is much less so in the case of 'internal working documents' where to be exempt disclosure must be 'contrary to the public interest': s 36(1).

(iii) Conclusion

When applied to administrative law, Stone's thesis that law is an instrument for adjusting chronically conflicting interests focuses attention on the adjustment which occurs in that area of law. Sometimes, as in determining the content of the duty to accord procedural fairness, the balance is struck by providing general indicative criteria. The provision for allowing late applications for judicial review is similar. In other cases the balance is struck by clear rules, as in the Ombudsman's jurisdiction over the exercise of ministerial powers. A further type of adjustment mechanism is the use of a broad term. In freedom of information we saw the use of 'the public interest'. The AAT also has a broad rule of practice to determine whether ministerial policy is to be applied. And the *Carltona* doctrine for determining the power of a repository to act through others depends on the concept of 'administrative necessity'.

Across the breadth of administrative law, courts, tribunals and the legislature all negotiate the need to 'balance' conflicting interests.

Examiner's Comments

This is a well-constructed answer. The answer began strongly by analysing the claims of the question, effectively setting out the main themes to be addressed. This was followed up in the main body of the answer by several illustrations of each of the claims. By paying close attention to the claims the answer did not depart from the question. While a satisfactory answer might have ended at this point, the conclusion to the answer proceeded to reflect on the benefits of analysing administrative law in the way suggested by Stone. This gave the answer a thoughtful and satisfying ending.

Another strength of the answer is the way it is able to show how even blanket rules can reflect processes of adjustment. So, for instance, in the case of the exclusion of personal ministerial actions from the Ombudsman scheme, this is seen as an adjustment when viewed in the context of complaints about governmental action.

A limitation of the answer is the way in which the examples are given one after each other in the main body of the answer. Ideally, the examples should be linked to each other by a narrative. However, a perfect essay is not expected.

Also, it was not necessary for the answer to give more than three examples. But the fewer the examples, the more depth would be required.

Common Errors to Avoid

- Not analysing the statement by Stone to determine precisely what claims are being made.
- Giving examples of areas of law without pointing out the underlying conflicting interests.
- Not referring to the precise way in which the law adjusts the conflicting interests.

QUESTION 3

> 'Judicial review of administrative action is inevitably sporadic and peripheral': S de Smith, extracted in R Creyke and J McMillan, *Control of Government Action: Text, Cases and Commentary*, LexisNexis Butterworths, Sydney, 2005, p 70.
>
> Is judicial review peripheral?
>
> (*Hint*: consider the various senses in which judicial review may or may not be peripheral.)
>
> **Time allowed: 45 mins**

Answer Plan

(i) Introduction.
- Definition of 'peripheral'.
- Approach to answering the question.

(ii) Senses in which judicial review is peripheral.

(iii) Senses in which judicial review is not peripheral.

(iv) Conclusion.

 Answer

(i) Introduction

Peripheral: *adj* 1 of minor importance; marginal. 2 of the periphery; on the fringe: *The Australian Concise Oxford Dictionary.*

The question whether judicial review is peripheral depends on the context. Judicial review is peripheral in some senses but not in others.

(ii) Senses in which judicial review is peripheral

The courts are peripheral in the sense of governing; that is, if one compares what courts do to the executive government whose decisions they periodically review. Moreover, they are *necessarily* peripheral in this sense. This is the point essentially being made by de Smith extracted in Creyke and McMillan, p 70, from which the quotation in the question is drawn. De Smith points out that 'Public authorities are set up to govern and administer' and it necessarily follows that it is not the function of courts to carry out the day-to-day administration of the law (even if that were possible).

A related sense in which courts are peripheral is that courts look at the pathology of administration (when things go wrong); but this (it has been argued) is not the typical occurrence. According to Douglas, 2006, p 1 'bureaucrats are inveterate rule obeyers'. We can agree with this observation, noting that 'rules' in this sense includes administrative rules, and also that in high-volume decision-making areas mistakes appear to be common: Douglas, 2006, pp 10–12.

Judicial review is also peripheral as an avenue of resort both in absolute numbers and relative to other avenues of redress. The volume of applications is helpfully reviewed by Douglas: 2006, pp 653–7. He points out that, putting aside migration cases, there have been only about 150 ADJR Act applications to the Federal Court each year. Other federal courts, including the Federal Magistrates Court, do not change the picture much. Douglas also considers the State scene to be similar although the author only considers published law reports.

Judicial review applications in non-migration cases pale beside applications to other forums. Applications to tribunals vary between 3,000–12,000 each year (Creyke and McMillan, p 115), the AAT receiving about 6,000 appeals each year: Douglas, 2006, p 653. The Commonwealth Ombudsman is even more popular: more than 16,000 complaints were made during 2003–4: Douglas, 2006, p 215.

To a great extent the law, buttressed by constitutional principle, enforces this marginality. It confines judicial review to the review of questions of law and to the making of orders which go no further than correcting legal error. Further, the law subordinates judicial review by requiring aggrieved persons to opt for tribunal or Ombudsman review if that form of redress is more suitable. Section 10 of the ADJR Act allows a court to refuse to grant an application for the reason that adequate provision is made by a law for the review of the decision, conduct or failure to perform a duty. This provision can be invoked at an interlocutory stage: Douglas, 2006, p 779. The common law also empowers courts to decline to grant relief on the basis that 'a more convenient and satisfactory remedy exists': *R v Commonwealth Court of Conciliation and Arbitration; Ex parte Ozone Theatres (Aust) Ltd* (1949) 78 CLR 389 at 400, as cited in *Re Refugee Review Tribunal; Ex parte Aala* (2000) 204 CLR 82 at [56]. Further, there are cases in which courts have exercised their discretion against the applicant at least partly for the reason that a tribunal was a more satisfactory avenue: *Bragg v Department of Employment, Education and Training* (1995) 59 FCR 31 at 33–4; *Anderson v Commissioner for Employees' Compensation* (1986) 12 ALD 612. The mere fact that an applicant prefers to opt for judicial review over tribunal review is not enough: *Whittaker v Child Support Registrar* (2000) 106 FCR 105.

There is good reason for this preference for a 'satisfactory and convenient remedy' to be availed of. As Sweeney J said in *Anderson*:

> If the court were [to undertake judicial review in relation to questions of law], and that opinion proved to be unfavourable to the applicant, he could then seek a review of the facts by the Tribunal, which might lead to a finding of facts which would render the court's opinion academic: at 613.

(iii)   Senses in which judicial review is not peripheral

So far we have seen a number of senses in which judicial review is peripheral or marginal. But there are two important senses in which judicial review is *not* peripheral. The first applies to plaintiffs who *do* apply for judicial review and are not refused relief in the court's discretion. In a substantial minority of non-Migration Act cases applicants enjoy success before the federal courts: Douglas, 2006, p 655. Further, it is *not* true that court-ordered reconsideration 'may result infrequently in a different decision': Mason, as cited in Douglas, 2006, p 796. An empirical survey of outcomes in judicial review cases by Creyke and McMillan found that most cases were ultimately resolved in favour of the successful party; in only 17% of cases was reconsideration adverse to the successful applicant: Douglas, 2006, p 796.

The second sense in which judicial review is not peripheral stems from the way in which courts lay down 'the fundamental principles which govern the legality of administrative behaviour': Douglas, 2006, p 656. These principles include the duty to accord procedural fairness, the principle of acting within the powers conferred; and the various prohibitions on abuse of power. Section 5 of the ADJR summarises the principal heads of illegality, most of which reflect the common law. Although in a review sense the grounds are more important for courts than they are for tribunals engaged in merits review or for the Ombudsman, they are also important in the work of these other avenues. This is particularly the case with the Commonwealth Ombudsman.

The Ombudsman must form an opinion within s 15(1) of the Ombudsman Act before making a formal report recommending remedial action. The grounds for the opinion mirror in most cases the grounds of judicial review. The AAT relies less on judicial review grounds. The tribunal is *not* required to find there has been an illegality before it makes any decision to set aside or substitute the decision under review. Some illegalities in the primary decision-making process such as denial of procedural fairness are of no relevance to the tribunal's review. On the other hand, if the primary decision-maker lacked the power to act, so too will the tribunal (except to confirm that fact). Further, the tribunal will be concerned that its own processes are lawful; it will need to observe the duty to accord procedural fairness, ensure it takes account of relevant considerations, does not take account of irrelevant considerations, acts on probative evidence and for proper purposes, does not make errors of law in interpreting the law, does not act at the direction of another person, does not rigidly follow a policy without regard to the merits of the case, does not act unreasonably in the *Wednesbury* sense, and so on.

The fundamental principles which have been described above apply not only to the work of other review mechanisms in important ways; they apply to primary decision-makers. The point which is being made here is that, even without review being sought, one cannot say that judicial review is peripheral in an educative and guiding sense. While it would be optimistic to assume that primary decision-makers routinely apply the law (cf Douglas, 2006, pp 10–12) one cannot assume to the contrary either, given the nature of bureaucracies. At the very least we need to acknowledge that the very legislative schemes with which administrators work or are supposed to work have been designed in the light of the fundamental principles. Provisions excluding judicial review principles such as the duty to accord procedural fairness (Douglas, 2006, pp 506–7) are the exception. More typical are legislative schemes such as the Health Insurance Act 1973 (Cth) in *Edelsten v Health Insurance Commission* (1990) 27 FCR 56 which, the court found, 'provides a statutory code governing the requirements of natural justice': at 71 per Northrop and Lockhart JJ. Granted, there are also Acts which provide minimal codification of procedure (as in *Krstic v Australian Telecommunications Commission* (1988) 20 FCR 486) but in such a case the legislation is read against the background of the common law. It is not only procedures which may be codified. Legislation commonly includes 'details of the matters which the decision-maker may or must take into account' (Douglas, 2006, p 432);

see, for example, *City of Botany Bay Council v Minister for Transport and Regional Development* (1999) 58 ALD 628.

(iv) Conclusion

The question whether judicial review is peripheral depends, as the question hinted, on the sense of peripheral one has in mind. While it is true in some senses, including the primary sense intended by de Smith, it is not true in other senses. One ought not easily dismiss the utility of judicial review.

 ## Examiner's Comments

This answer is well constructed. The beginning and the conclusion are succinctly expressed. The main body is clearly structured by looking first at the ways in which the statement might be true before looking at ways in which it is not.

The answer teased out well various senses of the key word in the question — 'peripheral'. It is strong in the number of senses it discusses. It made good use of the dictionary for general support. It maintained a close connection with the question throughout.

Statistics were referred to but this is a matter of detail and certainly not expected in a three-hour examination. The broader theme of the effects of administrative law and judicial review in particular is well within the reach of good students at least. At the risk of stating the obvious, law students should be aware of the way administrative law operates; otherwise students risk acquiring a narrow black letter understanding only. It is pertinent to note that all the information on the operation of judicial review was gathered from the two leading casebooks.

 ## Common Errors to Avoid

- Not appreciating that the effects and impact of administrative law, and judicial review in particular, are part of the understanding of administrative law.
- Writing a general unfocused essay on judicial review instead of addressing the particular issues raised.
- Writing an essay on the limitations of judicial review. The actual question is narrower.
- Not taking up fully the hint in the question. It suggests students consider a number of senses to 'peripheral' and not just the one which de Smith may have been referring to.

QUESTION 4

'No-one believes any more the "fairy tale" that judges simply declare the law', said Lord Reid some time ago. An extreme view is that judges are simply political actors, 'strict and complete legalism' being an untenable theory of judging on this view. Between the extremes of 'strict and complete legalism' and 'judges are political actors', theories about judicial politics in administrative law now abound; so much so that the politics of judicial review is in danger of being over-theorised.

Discuss. In addition to a discussion of legalism, refer to two or more theories of judicial review in your answer.

Time allowed: 1 hour

Answer Plan

(i)   Introduction.

(ii)   Legalism.

(iii) Theories of the state generally.

(iv)   'Judicial merits review'.

(v)   'Judicial imperialism'.

(vi)   Managerialist perspective.

(vii) Postmodernism

(viii) Conclusion.

 Answer

(i)   Introduction

A person looking for theories about administrative law and judicial politics encounters a minefield. The theories are vaguely defined, are often advanced with minimal support, and conflict with each other. None are completely satisfactory, but this does not mean that they lack validity or utility. Below I examine in turn legalism, red light or green light theories of the state, 'judicial merits review', 'judicial imperialism', the managerialist's perspective of administrative law, and finally postmodernism.

(ii)   Legalism

An initial problem for any 'political' theory of administrative law is the orthodox theory of judging. Judges have often put forward the theory that what underlies their judgments in the public law area is a 'strict and complete legalism' (Sir Owen Dixon's famous phrase, uttered at his swearing-in as Chief Justice of the High Court).

In a talk entitled 'Judicial Legitimacy' (included in an Appendix to *The Rule of Law and the Constitution*, Boyer Lectures 2000, ABC Books, Sydney, 2000), the present Chief Justice of the High Court of Australia, the Hon Murray Gleeson, gave a brief account of this time-honoured legal conception. His Honour stated that legalism entails 'fidelity to the Constitution and to the techniques of legal methodology' (p 137), and interpreting and applying 'the values inherent in the law': p 134. His Honour readily acknowledged the law-making capacity of the judiciary (p 129), but pointed to 'the ordinary day-by-day application of statutory rules and settled legal principles' as occasions when legalism and hence judicial legitimacy is most easily seen: p 129. His Honour also acknowledged the role of judicial discretion within the limits of the principles governing the exercise of such discretion.

Many administrative law cases seem to be straightforward, non-contentious *applications* of legal principle, and hence offer clear support for the theory of legalism. Importantly, they do not then support any *opposing* theory, such as the view that judges are 'political actors' deciding on purely political grounds. Cases supporting legalism include: *London County Council v Attorney-General* [1902] AC 165 (a bus is not a tram); *Green v Daniels* (1977) 51 ALJR 463 (no three-month waiting period mentioned in the statute; also no basis to argue that applicant did not have standing to sue); *Thorpe v Minister for Aboriginal Affairs* (1990) 26 FCR 325 (effect of Acts Interpretation Act read off the statute); *SAT FM Pty Ltd v Australian Broadcasting Authority* (1997) 75 FCR 604 (all the considerations pointed to the broadcasting plan being of a legislative, not administrative, character); *Minister for Aboriginal Affairs v Peko-Wallsend Ltd* (1986) 162 CLR 24 (implication in statute made by Mason J compelling on all counts); *NSW v Canellis* (1994) 181 CLR 309 (witness at inquiry clearly outside scope of *Dietrich* ruling); and *R v Magistrates' Court at Lilydale; Ex parte Ciccone* [1973] VR 122 (magistrate arriving with one party at house declared unfit for human habitation, a clear instance of reasonable apprehension of bias).

Other cases support legalism in that the *values* which are applied are orthodox constitutional or common law values protected by the courts. They include *Golden-Brown v Hunt* (1972) 19 FLR 438 at 449–51 (democratic value in parliamentary law-making, not executive law-making); *Watson v Lee* (1979) 144 CLR 374 at 381 (rule of law value that citizens can access the law); *Ainsworth v Criminal Justice Commission* (1992) 175 CLR 564 (value of protecting individual reputation); *Foley v Padley* (1984) 154 CLR 349 (individual privacy, freedom of movement and environmental values); and *Attorney-General (NSW) v Quin* (1990) 170 CLR 1 (value of maintaining element of separation of powers in judicial review).

However, there are also cases — far from aberrations — in which the courts have taken into account considerations which do not easily fit within the set of traditional constitutional or common law values.

Examples include *Project Blue Sky Inc v Australian Broadcasting Authority* (1998) 194 CLR 355 at [97] ('public inconvenience'); *O'Reilly v State Bank of Victoria Commissioners* (1983) 153 CLR 1 at 32 (judgment as to what amounted to 'administrative order and efficiency'); *Minister for Immigration and Ethnic Affairs v Teoh* (1995) 183 CLR 273 at 291 (nature of statement resulting from ratification of an international convention); *Onus v Alcoa of Australia Ltd* (1981) 149 CLR 27 at 42 and *Australian Conservation Foundation v Minister for Resources* (1989) 19 ALD 70 at 74 (community values, beliefs and expectations); and *R v Hickman; Ex parte Fox and Clinton* (1945) 70 CLR 598 at 616 (manufacturing of compromise enabling limited judicial review in face of a 'total' privative clause). This is not to suggest these cases are wrong; merely that legalism, as defined, is not an entirely adequate theory.

(iii) *Theories of the state generally*

From a theory of judicial review which tends to paint the judiciary as neutral and autonomous, we now turn to overtly political theories. 'Behind every theory of administrative law there lies a theory of the state', say C Harlow and R Rawlings, *Law and Administration*, Weidenfeld and Nicholson, London, 1984. More specifically, they put forward an overarching theory that judges are under the influence of a 'red light' or 'green light' theory of the state. In the first, the judge or commentator sees the function of administrative law as 'to control the excesses of the state': Douglas, 2006, p 33. In the second, 'the function of administrative law is to facilitate the operations of the state rather than curb them': p 32. It is not difficult to see particular judgments as either red light (for example, *Ansett Transport Industries (Operations) Pty Ltd v Commonwealth* (1977) 139 CLR 54 per Mason J) or green light (for example, *Krstic v Australian Telecommunications Commission* (1988) 20 FCR 486). However, in so far as a judge's approach (red or green light) may vary from case to case (Douglas, 2006, pp 34–5), it is not clear how red light and green light characterisations can be anything more than a label for a particular approach or a description of the practical effect of a decision in a particular case.

It may be more constructive to examine particular (alleged) red light or green light approaches. 'Judicial merits review' and 'judicial imperialism' are two critical theories charging judges with taking impermissible or inappropriate red light approaches. Managerialist perspectives tend to accuse the courts of giving insufficient attention to green light approaches.

(iv) *'Judicial merits review'*

Parties sometimes see the courts as the pursuit of politics by other means: Douglas, 2006, p 56. It has become common to assume that there is no clear boundary between merits review and judicial review: Douglas, 2006, p 56. Courts therefore have some leeway to pursue a particular policy of their own making and trespass into the merits: Douglas, 2006, pp 423–4. A clear example is the Federal Court's decision, reversed by the High Court in *Minister for Immigration and Ethnic Affairs v Guo* (1997) 191 CLR 559. The High Court criticised the Federal Court for granting a declaration that the applicants were entitled to the appropriate entry visas, for in so doing the court had, in the High Court's finding, intruded on the merits and 'allowed their decision to be influenced by their own views of the state of affairs in the People's Republic of China': Douglas, 2006, p 737. And the same casebook author has pointed out that if, after very careful analysis of the facts, a court finds a decision unreasonable, it is difficult to think that the same decision could be made again: Douglas, 2006, p 56.

The debate about judicial merits review suggests the means by which some judges occasionally act under a red light theory. However, it does not indicate the specific policies red light judges act under, other than perhaps a felt need to arrive at a just outcome in the case at hand. A deeper problem for the judicial merits review theory is that it fails to recognise the forces which constrain judges: Douglas, 2006, pp 56–7. They include the requirement to observe the separation of powers; the fact that the court's legitimacy is tied up with their legal expertise; and the pressure on judges to dispose of matters expeditiously. And, moreover, the rarity of cases which turn solely on a finding of error of jurisdictional fact or unreasonableness suggests that these analogues of merits review (if this is what they are) are atypical.

(v)   'Judicial imperialism'

Arthurs (extracted in Douglas, 2006, p 24) has advanced the theory that judges take another 'red light' approach in cases dealing with tribunals. The theory can be summed up as 'judicial imperialism'. The author is critical of Dicey's analysis of the rule of law which, as he reads it, makes the ordinary courts supreme and the ordinary law all-pervasive. Arthurs is critical of the assumption that tribunals must act judicially and must be rendered subject to the review of judges, when in fact tribunals perform quite different tasks or perform them in quite different ways.

Arthurs' theory is plausible to the extent that courts and tribunals do perform different functions and the courts ought to be sensitive to that — but is it the case that courts are imperialistic? Is *Australian Postal Commission v Hayes* (1989) 23 FCR 320 evidence of this theory? In this case, the Federal Court held that the AAT was bound to afford an effective right of cross-examination to each party (including the government respondent), which meant that a video the respondent wished to show in the course of cross-examination did not have to be shown to an applicant before the latter gave evidence-in-chief. In later AAT cases, 'ambush' tactics were criticised on fairness and efficiency grounds (*Re Prica and Comcare* (1996) 44 ALD 46) and were labelled 'confrontationist' and 'opposed to openness and co-operation': *Re Taxation Appeals No NT94/281–NT94/291* (1995) 30 ATR 1279.

Another case in which the Federal Court has been criticised for going too far in imposing judicial standards on tribunals is *Sullivan v Department of Transport* (1978) 20 ALR 323. It is criticised for not requiring the tribunal to give a 'helping hand' to an unrepresented applicant: M Allars, *Introduction to Australian Administrative Law*, Butterworths, Sydney, 1990, [7.46].

Even if the courts are 'imperialistic' on occasions, there are certain doctrines which mitigate any tendency to judicial imperialism with respect to tribunals. These include: doctrines of deference when review of jurisdictional facts is sought (see *Enfield City Corporation v Development Assessment Commission* (2000) 199 CLR 135 and *Attorney-General (Cth) v Queensland* (1990) 25 FCR 125); and the ruling in the *Bond* case (*Australian Broadcasting Tribunal v Bond* (1990) 170 CLR 321) that an 'intermediate decision' is not reviewable as a decision under the ADJR Act unless the statute expressly provides for the making of a finding or ruling on that point.

(vi) Managerialist perspective

Managerialism is more a perspective than a full-blown theory of judicial politics in administrative law. The managerialist conception of accountability emphasises three factors:

1. accountability of officials, primarily to the political branch of government (Bayne, extracted in Douglas, 2006, p 73);

2. speedy production of outcomes (Allars, extracted in Douglas, 2006, p 72); and

3. saving of money (Bayne, extracted in Douglas, 2006, p 75).

Managerialism entails a view of the state which, while it does not reject legalism, nevertheless questions whether managerial values, such as efficiency, should always be subordinated to administrative law values such as fairness and openness. As Sir William Cole, an eminent public administrator, lamented: 'accountability devices "ensure that efficiency cannot be taken as an end in itself but has to be subordinated to other ends"': cited by Bayne, extracted in Douglas, 2006, p 74. To the lawyer, legalism is a basic assumption; but from the perspective of the administrator, legalism is viewed as an older conception of accountability which overly concentrates on correct procedures: Allars, extracted in Douglas, 2006, pp 71–2.

It is not clear that administrative law can be so easily theorised as simply subordinating claims of efficiency to correct procedure as some managerialists claim. In the area of procedural fairness, on grounds of practicality, courts have tailored rights of fairness in relation to decisions of the executive council (*FAI Insurances Ltd v Winneke* (1982) 151 CLR 342); have been reluctant, on practical grounds, to impose procedural duties in respect of Cabinet decisions (*South Australia v O'Shea* (1987) 163 CLR 378; *Minister for Arts, Heritage and*

Environment v Peko-Wallsend Ltd (1987) 15 FCR 274); have taken account of limited resources in migration cases (*Zhang v Minister for Immigration, Local Government and Ethnic Affairs* (1993) 45 FCR 384); and have grafted the defence of necessity onto the bias rule to ensure 'that the rules of natural justice cannot be invoked to frustrate the intended operation of a statute which sets up a Tribunal and requires it to perform the statutory functions entrusted to it': *Laws v Australian Broadcasting Tribunal* (1990) 170 CLR 70 at 89 per Mason CJ and Brennan J. More generally, the value of preventing fragmentation of the processes of administrative decision-making was recognised in *Australian Broadcasting Tribunal v Bond* at 336–7 per Mason CJ.

(vii) Postmodernism

Postmodernism offers a general position so far as the meaning of 'texts' is concerned. Administrative law texts within its scope would include administrative law legislation and case law as well as commentaries. A sample claim is that 'We cannot extract any one component of this hermeneutic process, such as an understanding of a text, and treat it as an uncontested, stable, or non-contingent starting point': S Feldman, extracted in T Blackshield and G Williams, *Australian Constitutional Law and Theory: Commentary and Materials*, 4th ed, Federation Press, Sydney, 2006, p 368. The implicit claim about meaning being contested seems to suggest that if one reads a text one cannot ever say that the meaning is clear or beyond dispute at least to someone. The claim about meaning being unstable and contingent suggests that meanings can and are prone to change. The latter claim seems trite.

What of the former claim that it is wrong to see the meaning of a text as uncontested? We should recall the myriads of routine applications of the law referred to by the Chief Justice in the discussion of legalism above. Almost no-one would argue that the Minister for Social Security has the power to refuse benefits to Presbyterians or that the Minister for Immigration has the power to order an asylum seeker to be taken to an island without food or water. And even though cases normally go to court because the law is a little unclear, what about the cut-and-dried cases of law which were referred to in the discussion of legalism above? For instance, can it really be said that there was a real doubt about whether the bus operated by London County Council was a tram? Only in a trivial and formal sense — that there was a case (*London County Council v Attorney-General* [1902] AC 165) — was the question contested. But the case did not reveal any real doubt about the meaning of 'tramways' *in the circumstances of the dispute*. This is not to say that the text 'tramways' in the relevant statute might not fit the postmodernist description if one viewed the text as a work of literature. Perhaps the point to be made about the postmodern position is not that it is wrong; but that it is not all that relevant to interpretation by lawyers and judges (legal interpretation). The question of legal interpretation is not — is this legal text *in all its possible applications* 'uncontested'. Legal interpretation is not concerned with constructing a general theory of meaning; it is concerned with the meaning of particular texts having regard to particular facts: Lord Justice Sedley, 'This Beats Me' *London Review of Books* Vol 20(7) 2 April 1998. It may or may not turn out that the meaning is uncontested on those facts.

Of course, legal interpretation in particular cases is often contested, and texts often later appear to be non-stable and contingent, but these are trite observations so far as law is concerned.

(viii) Conclusion

The politics of administrative law is over-theorised, for all the theories surveyed have a monopolistic tendency; that is, they tend to exaggerate their ability to explain the complexities of administrative law and judicial politics. Nevertheless, each of the theories has some merit. Indeed, legalism is satisfactory in many cases, and it appears to be the leading theory when one takes into account its ability to explain routine cases or applications of the law — as the Chief Justice of the High Court has pointed out. At least for routine cases, alternatives to legalism may be less convincing, but they offer a partial and at times insightful explanation of less routine cases.

 # Examiner's Comments

The question is a challenging one, in that it required students to demonstrate more than a knowledge of administrative law doctrine; a knowledge of a number of theories was additionally required. Of course, the range of theories provided here could not easily be achieved in a three-hour examination. A take-home examination might be different.

The answer drew on a work by the Chief Justice of the High Court which students may or may not have read. Some other source could have been used to describe legalism.

Some students may not have come across one or more of the theories. That would not matter so long as two or more theories were discussed.

Some of the theories were only sampled. This is clearly acceptable in the context of an examination or an assignment with a word limit, particularly if, as here, the writer does not claim the example covers the field.

The answer is strong in four ways. First, the answer provides a crisp response to the question at the outset (and at the conclusion) to ensure the overall response is simple and clear. Second, the answer is knowledgeable in that the author addresses a range of theories. Third, by looking for evidence on both sides (that is, evidence which tends to support a theory *and* evidence which tends to contradict it), the theories are critically analysed, not just described. Fourth, it is well constructed:

the theories are related to one another and not just discussed independently, devoid of narrative.

The discussion of postmodernism is contestable. If one goes to some more recent descriptions of postmodernism and the law one finds the admission that there *are* plain cases. (See, for example, M Davies, 'Authority, Meaning, Legitimacy' in J Goldsworthy and T Campbell (eds), *Legal Interpretation in Democratic States*, Ashgate/Dartmouth, Aldershot, England, 2002, pp 123–4; M Davies, *Asking the Law Question: The Dissolution of Legal Theory*, 2nd ed, LawBook Co, Sydney, 2002, pp 325–6.) Indeed, the source of postmodernism used in the above answer (Feldman) goes on to say 'An interpreter is never a radically free subject who arbitrarily imposes meaning on a text; we are always limited by the prejudices that we inherit from our interpretive community and its traditions': p 1065.

The answer could have legitimately discussed other theories, for instance, economic or feminist theories (M Aronson, B Dyer and M Groves, *Judicial Review of Administrative Action*, 3rd ed, Lawbook Co, Sydney, 2004, p 8); and see generally M Allars, *Introduction to Australian Administrative Law*, Butterworths, Sydney, 1990, [1.5]–[1.31]; M Loughlin, *Public Law and Political Theory*, Clarendon Press, Oxford, 1992.

The answer is also limited in its discussion of the ways in which administrative law might be thought to be over-theorised — for instance, it might also be over-theorised if theories are put forward without it being clear how they afford assistance in addressing practical problems or in illuminating a legal text.

 ## Common Errors to Avoid

- Not showing a knowledge of any theories concerning the role of the judiciary in administrative law.
- Not discussing the theory of legalism as required.
- Not giving the sources of particular theories.
- Not being critical: assuming that all theories should be taken at their word simply by being in print, rather than looking for evidence which supports, and evidence which contradicts, each theory discussed.

 ## QUESTION 5

'*Green v Daniels* (1977) 51 ALJR 463; 13 ALR 1 was decided in the early days of the "new administrative law", but the broad issues it raised still resonate today.'

Discuss.

Time allowed: 1 hour

Answer Plan

(i)   Introduction.

- Major issues outlined.
- The *Green v Daniels* story in brief.

(ii) The tension between governmental and legal dictates and between administrative and legal rules.

(iii) The adequacy of judicial review remedies for making administrators accountable.

(iv) Conclusion.

 # Answer

(i)   Introduction

Two major issues which *Green v Daniels* raised were, first, the related tension between governmental and legal dictates, and between administrative and legal rules; and second, the adequacy of judicial review remedies for making administrators accountable.

Before elaborating on these issues, it is helpful if the material facts and holdings of the case are first outlined. *Green v Daniels* involved a 16-year-old fourth form (Year 10) school leaver, Karen Green, who sought unemployment benefits in December 1976. No general discretion was bestowed on the Director-General of Social Security and his or her delegates under the relevant Act, the Social Services Act 1947 (Cth). Instead, in s 107 of the Act, specific criteria were laid down. If an applicant met them the Act provided that the applicant 'shall be qualified to receive an unemployment benefit'. Relevantly, the Act provided that a person would so qualify if the Director-General was satisfied that he or she was 'unemployed' (s 107(c)(i)) and had 'taken reasonable steps to obtain work' which, in the opinion of the Director-General, was suitable to be undertaken by that person: s 107(c)(iii). Ms Green had made out a declaration that she would not be undertaking full-time education or training in the following year (1977), and she had made efforts to seek employment. But she was denied the benefit she sought following the application of an administrative rule in the departmental *Unemployment and Sickness Benefit Manual*. It stated that 'as a general rule' school leavers would not be eligible until the end of the school vacation. The manual had been written in the light of a concern that the Act was open to abuse from 'school leaver claimants' who 'for one reason or another have returned to their studies' after the end of the vacation.

Ms Green challenged the decision in the original jurisdiction of the High Court. At the time there was a right of appeal to the Director-General personally (s 15), but there was no right to seek review by an independent merits review tribunal with determinative powers; nor was judicial review available in any other federal court. Her application for judicial review succeeded to the extent that the court ordered the Director-General to reconsider her application according to the requirements of s 107(c) of the Act as interpreted by the court. However, on reconsidering Karen Green's case, the Director-General found that she was not entitled to benefits as at the date of her original application in December 1976. After unsuccessfully complaining to the Ombudsman, some applicants in Karen Green's position were awarded ex gratia compensation. According to Douglas, Ms Green received nothing: Douglas, 2006, p 395.

(ii) The tension between governmental and legal dictates and between administrative and legal rules

In the first place, the case raised a tension between governmental and legal 'dictates'. It was clear that the department was under pressure to respond to the perceived problem of abuse by 'school leavers' of the unemployment benefit regime: getting the benefit over the summer vacation and then 'changing their minds' and returning to school for Year 11 or 12. We know this because the departmental manual referred to instances of this occurring (at 466) and the court noted the department seeing it as 'an abuse of the Act': at 468. However, note the court's expression: 'the quite understandable desire to prevent what is seen as an abuse of the Act'. The court's standpoint is different: it is not involved in the routine administration of the Act and is not responsible to the Minister for any perceived problem.

Relatedly, there was a tension between administrative and legal rules. The department's perception that there was a major problem with the administration of the Act led to the development of the 'general rule' referred to above whereby school leavers were subsequently routinely denied the benefit. Ms Green was told, simply, that 'school leavers were not getting it'.

However, this is not to say that administrative rules or policy statements necessarily give rise to legal problems. In his reasons in the case Stephen J emphatically supported the development and use of administrative rules (or instructions or policy), saying (at 467):

> [The Director-General] must, no doubt, for the benefit of his delegates and in the interests of good and consistent administration, provide guidelines indicating what he regards as justifying such a state of satisfaction.

Nevertheless the fact that as a matter of practical reality administrative rules need to be and are made creates the potential for conflict with legal rules (in this case, the Social Services Act). Administrative rules are only lawful if:

> ... the policy [statement] is consistent with the statute under which the relevant power is conferred, and provided also that the policy is not, either in its nature or in its application, such as to preclude the decision-maker from taking into account relevant considerations, or such as to involve the

decision-maker in taking into account irrelevant considerations: *Neat Domestic Trading Pty Ltd v AWB Ltd* (2003) 198 ALR 179 at 186 per Gleeson CJ.

Thus, as Stephen J held in *Green v Daniels*, if the instructions are 'inconsistent with a proper observance of the statutory criteria' and the delegates observe those instructions, the decisions will be invalid: at 467.

In the case at hand, the manual was not totally inconsistent with the Act. Stephen J observed that the fact that the instruction required a decision-maker to take account of a person being a school leaver in assessing whether he or she is truly an intending entrant into the work-force was *not* an error in itself. It did not involve 'the introduction of irrelevant factors into a decision-making process': at 467.

But, crucially for how the case was to be disposed, the court found on closer analysis that the instruction was not consistent with the Act in the way it operated to determine the criteria of intention (s 107(c)(i)) and the taking of steps to obtain work: s 107(c)(iii). With regard to the former, the instruction determined intention at the cost of being wrong in the case of all those applicants who had truthfully told the department that they had ended their school days. The instruction produced 'unacceptable' and 'erroneous results': at 467. With regard to s 107(c)(iii), Stephen J found that the instruction imposed a 'quite arbitrary time of almost three months' before the criterion was to be regarded as having been complied with — the length of the vacation being an extraneous circumstance. His Honour also found that it was discriminatory to impose on the class of students who leave within 28 days of the end of the school year a requirement which was not imposed on other school leavers: at 468.

Although *Green v Daniels* was perhaps the first instance of judicial review in so far as the relevant department was concerned (Creyke and McMillan, [7.2.6]), and much has changed since then including the government's awareness of the requirements imposed by statute law and administrative law, it is fair to say that the basic tensions evident in *Green v Daniels* are still with us today. Governments and courts work from different standpoints in the legal system and there is still a need for administrative rules in many areas of decision-making. As Clark notes (in an article extracted in Douglas, 2006, p 383), 'Administrative policies are developed in response to problems faced by administrators especially where the agency is engaged in high volume decision-making'.

(iii) The adequacy of judicial review remedies for making administrators accountable

As noted above, Karen Green was successful before the court to the extent that the court ordered the department to consider her application afresh according to law. When they did, she was knocked back again — on different grounds. So, ultimately she was not successful as a result of her judicial review application, except in establishing the law which ought to have been followed. *Green v Daniels* is still good law in this respect. It remains a basic principle of judicial review that the court is able to make an order which corrects the legal error but is not able to stand in the shoes of the decision-maker. The question which this case therefore raises is this: how worthwhile an avenue of redress is judicial review from the point of view of applicants with meritorious cases? Karen Green's case throws some doubt on the utility of judicial review in that respect, but we should not, of course, treat one case as necessarily representative. *Green v Daniels* was an early administrative law case and it may be that, with considerable experience of administrative law, the executive is now less prone to find against an applicant on any court-ordered reconsideration.

(iv) Conclusion

The immediate aftermath of the 1977 *Green v Daniels* case suggests an intransigent department unfamiliar with the rigours of administrative law accountability. *Green v Daniels* resonates today not for this reason but because it raised basic issues of administrative law: the tensions between government and legal dictates and between administrative and legal rules; and the utility of judicial review remedies.

Examiner's Comments

The object of this question is to enable students to demonstrate, through the vehicle of a case study, their general understanding of basic aspects of administrative law and judicial review in particular. *Green v Daniels* is a classic case on the legality/merits distinction, but there are others that might have been picked for this role: see Creyke and McMillan, [7.5].

So far as it goes, this is a fairly sophisticated answer, referring as it does not only to the administrative rule but to the context in which the rule arose: the political problem of perceived abuse of the Act. However, it should be noted that *Green v Daniels* raises other significant issues which could legitimately have been mentioned if time permitted. They include the following:

(i) *The appropriate discretion to confer on administrative decision-makers* Are more and more detailed Acts the answer, or is a more general discretion preferable?

(ii) *The accessibility of the courts* While 16-year-old Karen Green made it to the High Court, how do the less fortunate fare today?

(iii) *Implications drawn by the courts* Stephen J made implications from the statute in finding that the instructions were arbitrary and discriminatory. To what extent should the courts, as unelected bodies, draw implications in legislation in the course of judicial review?

(iv) *The elastic nature of the ground of irrelevant considerations* The court held that treating a person's status as a school leaver as a conclusive test was not the introduction of an irrelevant factor: at 467. On the other hand, it held that the duration of the school holidays was 'an extraneous circumstance': at 468.

(v) *The objectivity of judicial reasoning* Sometimes the law is so plain there can be no doubt about its objectivity. For instance, the question of standing was held to be 'clear': at 469. At other places, the reasoning is less objectively based, as in the assumption that 'surely only a small proportion' of school leavers were dishonest: at 467.

(vi) *The relevance of alternative avenues of redress* In Karen Green's case, the only alternative avenue of redress was an appeal to the Director-General of Social Security. While this hardly posed an adequate alternative in the circumstances of the case, the subsequent establishment of the AAT and other independent review bodies can pose a dilemma for courts as to whether they ought to accept an application for judicial review.

(vii) *Alternatives to judicial review* To what extent has the emergence of merits review overcome the limitations of judicial review?

Finally, a comment on the suggestion in the answer that the apparently intransigent attitude displayed by the department in *Green v Daniels* is not typical of government nowadays. If a student were not restricted by the time constraints of a three-hour examination, reference could have been made to the empirical study of judicial review outcomes by Creyke and McMillan: see Douglas, 2006, p 796. This study suggests that reconsideration following judicial review usually results in a decision more favourable to the successful applicant.

 # Common Errors to Avoid

- Describing the facts and holdings of the case at excessive length without devoting sufficient space to analysis.
- Summarising the case, rather than highlighting particular issues which the case raises.
- Discussing what particular law the case established, rather than the more general issues it raised.

PART 2

Administrative Rule-Making

Chapter 2
Administrative Rule-Making

Key Issues

The topic of administrative rule-making covers such processes concerning administrative rules as: consultation prior to their making; 'professional vetting'; notification, publication and registration; parliamentary tabling; parliamentary scrutiny; parliamentary disallowance; and sunsetting.

There are a number of reasons why administrative rule-making finds a ready home in most administrative law units and textbooks. First, administrative rules, like administrative decisions, are usually made by the executive. Second, administrative rules and administrative decisions are not always distinct opposites — rather, they shade into each other, with some administrative rules having an ambiguous status (for example, by-laws, as mentioned in *Minister for Industry and Commerce v Tooheys Ltd* (1982) 4 ALD 661). Third, the various statutory, non-judicial controls over administrative rule-making complement judicial review of administrative rules under the rubric of *ultra vires*. Fourth, as judicial review of administrative action includes the review of rules which have been made, it is a short step to examine the process of creating them. This is particularly the case since the exercise of some of the controls, or the failure to observe certain procedural obligations, can affect the validity or enforceability of particular rules (and to similar effect decisions made purportedly made under them).

Administrative rules may be categorised in different ways:

- *By their source* We can examine their scope of operation and distinguish between those which have a federal source and apply nationally, and those which have a State or Territory source and apply only to that State or Territory.
- *By their form* We can examine what a rule is called, such as whether it is expressed to be a regulation made under an Act.
- *By their character and effect* We can distinguish between rules which are legislative and those which are not.

- *By their status* We can examine their enforceability and distinguish between rules which are legally binding and those which are not. Government policy instructions are classic illustrations of non-binding rules (*Green v Daniels* (1977) 51 ALJR 463), and statutory 'guidelines' are also not binding if a court finds that is the intention of parliament.

The statutory, non-judicial controls over administrative rule-making are the central concern of this topic. Both State and federal controls apply. In keeping with the scope of this work, this chapter will concentrate on the applicable federal law.

Until 2005 the Acts Interpretation Act 1901 (Cth) governed the rule-making process of 'regulations' and 'disallowable instruments'. The principal current sources of law at the federal level are now the Legislative Instruments Act 2003 (Cth) (LIA) and provisions bearing upon legislative instruments in the Acts Interpretation Act 1901 (Cth), especially s 15AE (inserted by the Acts Interpretation Amendment (Legislative Instruments) Act 2005 (Cth)). In summary those provisions:

- determine the scope of administrative rules which are subject to the controls laid down by the LIA: LIA Pt 1; Acts Interpretation Act s 15AE;
- determine when, and the conditions under which, legislative instruments take effect: LIA ss 12, 31, 32;
- require the Secretary to the Attorney-General's Department to cause steps to be taken to promote the effectiveness, clarity and intelligibility of legislative instruments: LIA Pt 2;
- require a rule-maker to consult before making a legislative instrument: LIA Pt 3;
- require a legislative instrument, and the Explanatory Statement that relates to the instrument, to be registered on the Federal Register of Legislative Instruments: LIA Pt 4;
- require a legislative instrument to be tabled in both Houses of Parliament: LIA ss 38, 39, 45;
- provide for disallowance of a legislative instrument by a House of Parliament: LIA ss 42, 44, 45;
- provide for 'sunsetting' of legislative instruments: LIA Pt 6.

The LIA commonly sets out the consequences (if any) of the exercise of a control or of any failure to comply with a particular rule-making obligation. In addition, students need to be aware of the scrutiny and reporting role of the Senate Regulations and Ordinances Committee established under Senate Standing Order No 23: <http://www.aph.gov.au/Senate/pubs/standing_orders/b05.htm#23>.

Before attempting the questions, check that you are familiar with the following issues:

✓ the general reasons for the making of administrative rules;

✓ the rationale for controlling the making of administrative rules, especially those which are legislative in character;

✓ the history of regulation of administrative rule-making;

✓ the scope, nature and effect of the controls on the making of administrative rules under the LIA (together with the relevant case law).

 # QUESTION 6

> On 15 October, a regulation is made under the Customs Act 1901 (Cth). (Assume the regulation is lawfully made and registered.) The regulation commenced on the day it was registered: 16 October. The regulation states that the book titled *The Night of a Thousand Shames* (see 'The Makepeace Scenario', p xvi) is a prohibited import. (Assume it is not otherwise a prohibited import.) The regulation has been tabled in the Senate, but not in the House of Representatives. Makepeace seeks to import a copy of the book on 2 November of the same year.
>
> Advise it as to whether the failure to table the regulation in the House of Representatives has any legal consequences, and, if so, what they are. In giving that advice assume today is 2 November.
>
> **Time allowed: 15 mins**

Answer Plan

(i)   Outline of answer and approach.

(ii) Relevant law.

(iii) Application of law to the facts.

(iv) Conclusion.

 # Answer

(i)   *Outline of answer and approach*

In short, the failure to table the regulation in both Houses of Parliament may have legal consequences, depending on the facts. However, at the moment there are insufficient facts to answer the question definitively. The relevant law under the LIA is applied to the facts as fully as possible.

(ii) Relevant law

The law governing the tabling in parliament of Commonwealth regulations is set out in the LIA s 38. The Act applies because regulations are legislative instruments: s 6(a). The Act sets out the consequences of any failure to table a legislative instrument. If an instrument that is required to be laid before each House is not so laid, 'the legislative instrument ceases to have effect immediately after the last day for it to be so laid': s 38(3).

The phrase 'the last day for it to be so laid' means six sitting days of the relevant House after the registration of the instrument. In reckoning the days, the day of registration, if it was a sitting day, is not counted: Acts Interpretation Act 1901 (Cth) s 36(1).

The phrase 'ceases to have effect' entails the same effect as a repeal: s 45(1). This in turn does not involve a retrospective change in the law: s 15. In other words, the legal operation of the instrument prior to the time it ceases to have effect is not affected. For an example, see *Thorpe v Minister for Aboriginal Affairs* (1990) 26 FCR 325.

(iii) Application of the law to the facts

In the problem concerning *The Night of a Thousand Shames*, there has been a failure to table the regulation in a House of the parliament (the House of Representatives). This means that the regulation would cease to have legal effect immediately after the period when it was required to be tabled. This period is six *sitting* days after the registration of the instrument (16 October). Since the relevant day for importation purposes is 2 November, and since this day is more than six days after the date of registration, it is possible that the sitting-day period has elapsed. However, we do not know this for certain, and further research is required. We need to check the official records of parliament for the relevant period.

(iv) Conclusion

On the current information, my advice is that, if there have been six sitting days by and including 1 November, then the regulation prohibiting the book would have ceased to have effect immediately after that day. If the regulation has ceased to have effect, there is no prohibition in force on 2 November and the book may be lawfully imported on that day.

If, on the other hand, there have not been six sitting days by and including 1 November, then the regulation prohibiting the book has not ceased to have effect. If the regulation has not ceased to have effect, then it continues to have effect, at least on 2 November and until the end of the prescribed sitting-day period.

Finally, it may be noted that the government would not be able, by a later regulation, to alter retrospectively the rights of Makepeace: see s 12(2) of the LIA.

Examiner's Comments

This problem was designed to test students' understanding of the provisions relating to the tabling of legislative instruments in the LIA (formerly the Acts Interpretation Act 1901). As the answer shows, several provisions of the Act need to be read together for a full and proper understanding. This is not unusual in working out the meaning and effect of a statutory provision.

Specifically, students need to show they understand the meaning of 'sitting days' and to be aware that parliament does not necessarily sit every day.

The problem was deliberately set without giving students the crucial information of when the sitting-day period had elapsed (if it had). This ensures the problem is not identical with *Thorpe*. Also, students would be required to show they understand the significance of *finding* facts in administrative law problems. The proper handling of facts is an important legal skill. As Sir Robert Megarry said in a classic legal article emphasising the importance of learning how to handle facts, a good problem for law students should call for an answer which begins with the words 'It Depends': 'Law as Taught and Law as Practised', extracted in S Bottomley and S Bronitt, *Law in Context*, 3rd ed, Federation Press, Sydney, 2006, p 9.

Common Errors to Avoid

- Not being aware of the LIA. Citing the Acts Interpretation Act as a result of relying on an out-of-date textbook or set of notes.
- Not being aware of the difference between six days and six sitting days in s 38(1) of the LIA.
- Stating the general provisions of the law (s 38 of the LIA) but not applying them to the facts.
- Not giving the advice on an 'It depends' basis.
- Making the assumption that the sitting-day period had lapsed. There is no warrant for this assumption on the information given.
- Not indicating how one might find out whether the sitting-day period had elapsed.

QUESTION 7

'The Commonwealth approach [to regulating which rules are subject to the Legislative Instruments Act] represents the triumph of substance over form': R Douglas, *Douglas and Jones's Administrative Law*, 5th ed, Federation Press, Sydney, 2006, p 309.

Discuss. Answer on the basis of the current law.

Time allowed: 1 hour

Answer Plan

(i) Introduction: matters for discussion.

(ii) What is meant by 'form' and 'substance' in the regulation of rule-making?

(iii) Does the Commonwealth approach represent the triumph of substance over form?

(iv) To the extent the Commonwealth approach represents a 'triumph' of substance over form, is it a worthy one?

 Answer

(i)   Introduction: matters for discussion

The statement by Douglas gives rise to three matters for discussion. First, what is meant by 'form' and 'substance' in the regulation of the area of rule-making? Second, is it true that the Commonwealth approach represents the triumph of substance over form? Third, to the extent that the Commonwealth approach does represent a 'triumph' of substance over form, is that a worthy one?

(ii)   What is meant by 'form' and 'substance' in the regulation of rule-making?

Form and substance refer to different ways to control the threshold requirements concerning the regulation of rule-making. The threshold question is — what is the scope of the field to be regulated? Which rules are subject to rule-making controls?

A regulatory approach which relies on 'form' is one that looks to what a rule is called to determine whether a particular rule is caught by the controls over rule-making. For instance, under the Commonwealth scheme which existed until 2005, if a rule was in form a 'regulation' it was subject to the controls laid down in Pt XII of the Acts Interpretation Act 1901 (Cth). These included the requirement to table the regulation in both Houses of Parliament and the provision for the regulation to be disallowed by either House (in practice the upper House).

In contrast, a regulatory approach which relies on 'substance' rejects what a rule is called as the threshold requirement, and looks to the operation of a rule — its character or effect — as the test. The LIA lays down a test of substance when it defines a legislative instrument as an instrument 'that is of a legislative character': s 5(1)(a). The partially definitive, but non-exhaustive definition of 'legislative character' in s 5(1) and (2) of the Act underlines that what is significant is how the rule operates, for a rule is taken to be of a legislative character if 'it *determines* the law or *alters* the content of the law ... and it has the direct or indirect *effect* of affecting a privilege ...'.

(iii) Does the Commonwealth approach represent the triumph of substance over form?

I think there is much truth in this claim at the point when the LIA took effect on 1 January 2005, but it is less convincing after the amendment to the Acts Interpretation Act assented to in November 2005.

Immediately before the LIA took effect, the regime which controlled rule-making at the federal level of government was contained in Pts XI and XII of the Acts Interpretation Act 1901 (Cth) and in the Statutory Rules Publication Act 1903 (Cth). The Acts Interpretation Act regime applied to 'regulations' and to 'disallowable instruments'. If a rule was called a regulation it was automatically caught by the regime. Part XII provided for notification of the making of the regulation, the commencement of a regulation, parliamentary tabling of regulations, and parliamentary disallowance of a regulation. If a rule was not called a regulation, prima facie it was not subject to the operation of Pt XII. However, Pt XI added to the scope of Pt XII for it provided that, if a provision of an Act conferred power to make an instrument *however described*, and the enabling provision expressly provided that the instrument was a disallowable instrument for the purposes of the relevant section of the Acts Interpretation Act, then the Pt XII controls applied to the instrument. For instance, if in an Act a Minister had the power to make a 'determination' and in that Act parliament treated a 'determination' as a disallowable instrument, then the determination became subject to the same controls as a regulation. On the surface, Pt XI was a regime based on form since if a rule other than a regulation was not treated as a 'disallowable instrument' it was not caught by the Acts Interpretation Act controls. But fundamentally it was a regime based on politics since whether a non-regulation was treated as a disallowable instrument was a decision for government and the parliament.

The other federal regime which controlled rule-making until 2005 was the Statutory Rules Publication Act 1903 (Cth). It governed the printing, sale and availability of 'statutory rules' which were rules, regulations or by-laws, made under any Act by certain public authorities. Like Pt XII of the Acts Interpretation Act the scope of this regime was based on the rule having a certain form and being made by certain authorities. In summary, immediately before the Legislative Instruments Act came into force the Commonwealth approach to the regulation of rule-making was largely one of form, but was also dictated by political considerations operating in particular areas of substantive regulation.

The LIA altered this approach. The 2003 Act followed a report by the Administrative Review Council on the Commonwealth approach which criticised it as 'patchy, dated and obscure': R Creyke and J McMillan, *Control of Government Action: Text, Cases and Commentary*, LexisNexis Butterworths, Sydney, 2005, p 273. It was the council's idea that the new regime apply across the board to instruments of a legislative character unless excluded by the enabling Act: R Douglas, *Douglas and Jones's Administrative Law*, 4th ed, Federation Press, Sydney, 2004, p 325. The 2003 Act repealed the previous regimes and laid down the basic threshold rule that the Act would apply to a 'legislative instrument', defined as 'an instrument in writing that is of a legislative character': s 5(1). As explained above this is a test of substance not of form. The Act applies not only to legislative instruments made after the commencing day (1 January 2005). Instruments made before the commencing day and still in force must be lodged on the Federal Register of Legislative Instruments: s 28.

However, the extent to which the Act overall provides for a substance test needs to be gauged after other provisions of the Act are taken into account. First, s 5(3) provides that an instrument that is registered is taken, by virtue of that registration, to be a legislative instrument. This indicates that a rule-making authority has a discretion to add to the register a rule which is not of a legislative character. If it does it will presumably do so on political grounds, not according to the substance of the rule. The main use of this provision may come about where a rule-making authority is in doubt about the character of a rule; the provision effectively allows the authority to extend the scope of the Act by its own actions.

Second, the LIA automatically treats certain instruments as legislative instruments:

- an instrument made before, on or after the commencement of the Act and described as a 'regulation' by the enabling legislation: s 6(a);

- an instrument, other than a regulation, made before the commencing day and falling within the description of a 'statutory rule' under s 5(1) of the Statutory Rules Publication Act 1903 (Cth): s 6(b);

- an instrument made before the commencing day and declared to be a disallowable instrument: s 6(d);

- a proclamation made before, on or after the commencing day: s 6(e).

In these ways the Act is using a test of form to define the scope of the Act. It should be noted that, although s 6(b) and (d) relate to instruments made before 2005, s 6(a) and (e) have an indefinite operation into the future.

Third, an instrument is not a legislative instrument for the purposes of the LIA if it is included in the table of general exclusions set out in s 7 of the Act: s 7(1)(a). Similarly it is not a legislative instrument if a later Act provides otherwise: s 7(1)(b). Further, the LIA also provides exceptions for particular categories of legislative instruments in relation to the scope of the power to disallow (s 44) and of the sunsetting regime: s 54.

In summary, the LIA was a mix of regulatory strategies. Its starting point was a 'substance' approach: s 5(1). However, in significant respects the Act adds to the previous regulatory approach based on form, rather than replacing it. This is evidenced by the continued capture of regulations: s 6(a). It must also be noted that the emphasis on substance is weakened by the numerous general exemptions from the Act in s 7(1), notwithstanding the statement in s 7(2) that 'The inclusion of an instrument in the table in subsection (1) does not imply that an instrument of that kind would, if it were not so included, be a legislative instrument unders subsection (1)'.

But the regime provided by the LIA was dramatically altered by an amendment to the Acts Interpretation Act 1901 in late 2005: the Acts Interpretation Amendment (Legislative Instruments) Act 2005 (Cth). The amendment inserted s 15AE into the Acts Interpretation Act. The amendment is taken to have commenced on the commencing day of the LIA, that is, 1 January 2005: s 2(1). Section 15AE provides that, if a provision of an Act requires or permits an instrument that is described as a legislative instrument to be made, then an instrument made under that provision is a legislative instrument for the purposes of the LIA: s 15(1). Subsection (2) makes clear that subs (1) is a deeming provision as it provides that the description of an instrument as a legislative instrument does not imply that the instrument is of a legislative character. Taken together, what these provisions provide for is a wholly alternative approach to the LIA for instruments made after the amendment took effect.

While the LIA starts with the basic proposition that it is the substance or character of an instrument that matters, the 2005 amendment to the Acts Interpretation Act makes clear that it is the form or description that matters. Since the Acts Interpretation Act contains basic provisions about Acts — a drafting template of sorts — it seems likely legislative drafters will routinely describe an instrument as a legislative instrument, or not as the case may require: s 15AE(3). Thus, it is likely that entrance to the LIA in the future will not depend on the test of 'legislative character' under the Act, as elaborated on by the common law and as qualified in detail by the Act. With the backing of the Acts Interpretation Act, entrance to the LIA will depend in practice on the description in the enabling Act of the instrument as a legislative instrument or as an instrument that is not a legislative instrument. I say 'in practice' because the operation of s 15AE does depend on the practice of legislative drafters. If in the unlikely event drafters do not describe an instrument as a legislative instrument or as not a legislative instrument, then the main tests would remain those set out in the LIA.

In conclusion, it would seem that the statement by Douglas, which in fairness was based on the law as at 1 November 2005, was broadly accurate when made since it reflected the 2003 Act. However, the insertion of s 15AE into the Acts Interpretation Act on 15 November 2005 promises a return to the form approach for instruments made after

1 January 2005. Even so, the statement by Douglas concerning the LIA will *not* cease to be true, but it is likely that it will be limited to the instruments made before the 2003 Act took effect.

(iv) To the extent the Commonwealth approach represents the 'triumph' of substance over form, is it a worthy one?

The statement by Douglas seems to suggest that the use of a substance approach is a worthy achievement. The word 'triumph' means 'the state of being victorious or successful'; 'a great success or achievement'; 'joy at success; exultation': *The Australian Concise Oxford Dictionary*. Also the idea of substance being preferred to form has a long history in the law; formalism being associated with earlier and out-of-date ways of governing. Should we, with Douglas, support the use of a substance approach in the LIA? I think we should, though with some reservations. A substance test was the only way in which a comprehensive register of delegated legislation could have been mandated given the multitude of names by which rules have been described in the past (for example, determination, order, direction, notice, plan, proclamation and declaration: Creyke and McMillan, 2005, p 269) and the difficulty of searching the Commonwealth statute book for all the possible names used in the past. However, we should not see a substance test as 'the victor', for two reasons: in the long term it is likely to be eclipsed by the form approach under s 15AE of the Acts Interpretation Act; and a substance approach is much less convenient than a form approach. If there is an available alternative a government department should not be forced to ascertain the character of a rule to determine whether a rule is caught by the controls of the LIA. The *prior* determination by the drafter that a category of instrument is or is not subject to the LIA provides clarity to parliamentarians, the Senate Scrutiny of Bills Committee and the ultimate users of the eventual Act.

Although the LIA and the attendant provision in the Acts Interpretation Act make for a complex way of drawing the boundaries around the LIA, the combination of substance and form-based approaches ensures both convenience and wide coverage, something neither approach could achieve on their own.

Examiner's Comments

This question is aimed at a fundamental part of the rule-making topic — the threshold issue of determining which rules are caught by the LIA. Students commonly have initial difficulty with the idea of a form-based approach. They assume law catches what in their view ought to be caught (and what ought to be caught should not in their view depend on name-calling). They are surprised therefore by the extent to which the law has relied, and continues to rely, on a form-based approach, and have difficulty also with the multiple approaches taken by the Act. This question therefore tests how well students understand, at a conceptual level, the approaches to regulating rule-making at the Commonwealth level.

The answer has a number of strengths. The answer is a model of clarity in that it found the statement by Douglas to involve three claims and proceeded to discuss each. Explaining and giving examples of the key concepts gave the answer a solid basis. Copious, precise and detailed references to the Act added much authority. And it made good use of the humble dictionary, an underrated resource in examinations.

The answer is up to date, revealed by the discussion of the amendment to the Acts Interpretation Act in 2005: the insertion of s 15AE. Further, the answer was sound in predicting that s 15AE would in practice contribute to a predominantly form-based approach to defining the ambit of the controls over Commonwealth rule-making, rather than a substance approach which relied on the concept of 'legislative character' in s 5(1) of the LIA. Examination of Commonwealth Acts passed since the amendment took effect shows that, rather than continue with the former practice of using a host of ad hoc terms, drafters of Bills regularly use the term 'legislative instrument' in providing for the making of administrative rules — thus attracting the controls of the LIA. Drafters continue to use the conventional form of 'regulations' in providing for the making of administrative rules by the Governor-General. The First Parliamentary Counsel of the Commonwealth Office of Parliamentary Counsel has issued a drafting direction to ensure that a form-based approach is used in future provisions of Bills providing for the making of 'subordinate instruments': 'Drafting Direction 3.8: Subordinate Instruments' (2006), [16] at <http://www.opc.gov.au/about/drafting_series/DD%203.8.pdf> Under the direction, drafters are required to deal expressly with the status of every subordinate instrument by one of the following techniques: using a term which attracts s 6 of the LIA (automatic inclusion); using s 7 of the LIA which provides for automatic exclusion by regulations; or by attracting s 15AE by stating that the instrument concerned either is a legislative instrument or is not a legislative instrument.

The answer refers to the previous Commonwealth regime to highlight the difference between 'form' and 'substance' approaches. An alternative approach might have been to refer to a State regime as an example of a form-based approach.

 # Common Errors to Avoid

(i)   Not analysing the statement to derive the main issues to be discussed.

(ii)   Not limiting the answer to the threshold matter of which rules are caught by the LIA — writing instead a general essay on the Act in the hope that something might be relevant.

(iii) Not defining and giving examples of the key concepts in the statement.

(iv) Not closely analysing the LIA to identify every possible relevant provision.

(v) Not being up to date on the law: not showing awareness of the amendment to the Acts Interpretation Act in 2005.

QUESTION 8

The Attorney-General issues a certificate under reg 4A(5) of the Customs (Prohibited Imports) Regulations. The certificate states, in part:

> In my opinion it is in the public interest that responsibility for a permission to import, or a refusal of a permission to import, the film *Caledenia: the Untold Story* should reside solely with the Attorney-General and should not be reviewable by the Administrative Appeals Tribunal.

Advise the Attorney-General whether the certificate must be lodged on the Federal Register of Legislative Instruments.

Time allowed: 40 mins

Answer Plan

(i) Relevant law.

(ii) Application of the law.

- Step 1: ascertain whether the certificate is automatically caught (or excluded) by the terms of the LIA.

- Step 2: if neither, ascertain whether the certificate is automatically caught (or excluded) by relevant provisions of the Acts Interpretation Act 1901 (Cth).

- Step 3: if neither, ascertain whether the certificate falls within the conclusive definition of 'legislative instrument' in s 5(1) and (2) of the LIA.

- Step 4: if not, ascertain whether the certificate falls within the general definition of 'legislative instrument' in s 5(1) of the LIA.

(iii) Conclusion.

Answer

(i) Relevant law

A legislative instrument made on or after the commencing day of the Legislative Instruments Act 2003 (LIA) (1 January 2005) must be lodged on the Federal Register of Legislative Instruments: LIA s 24. Hence the certificate must be lodged on the Federal Register of Legislative Instruments if it is a 'legislative instrument' within the meaning of that section. Whether it is depends on tests supplied by the Act, and other law bearing upon the term 'legislative instrument'. The procedure adopted here is:

- Step 1: ascertain whether the certificate is automatically caught (or excluded) by the terms of the LIA;

- Step 2: if neither, ascertain whether the certificate is automatically caught (or excluded) by relevant provisions of the Acts Interpretation Act 1901 (Cth);

- Step 3: if neither, ascertain whether the certificate falls within the conclusive definition of 'legislative instrument' in s 5(1) and (2) of the LIA;

- Step 4: if not, ascertain whether the certificate falls within the general definition of 'legislative instrument' in s 5(1) of the LIA.

(ii) Application of the law

Step 1

Some instruments are automatically caught. These are the instruments declared to be legislative instruments under s 6. The certificate is not in this category.

Some instruments are automatically excluded by the LIA: ss 7, 9. The certificate is not excluded.

As the certificate's status is not clear, we proceed to Step 2.

Step 2

Some instruments are automatically deemed to be legislative instruments by s 15AE of the Acts Interpretation Act 1901. They are deemed if the enabling Act describes the instrument as a legislative instrument: s 15AE(1). Conversely the instrument is not subject to the LIA if the enabling Act describes the instrument as not being a legislative instrument: s 15AE(3). The certificate is not caught by either provision.

As the certificate's status is not clear, we proceed to Step 3.

Step 3

The next step is to determine whether the certificate is caught by the specific definition of 'legislative instrument' in s 5(1) and (2) of the LIA. Section 5 provides:

5 Definition — a legislative instrument

(1) Subject to sections 6, 7 and 9, a *legislative instrument* is an instrument in writing:

    (a) that is of a legislative character; and

    (b) that is or was made in the exercise of a power delegated by the Parliament.

(2) Without limiting the generality of subsection (1), an instrument *is taken to be* of a legislative character if:

(a) it determines the law or alters the content of the law, rather than applying the law in a particular case; and

(b) it has the direct or indirect effect of affecting a privilege or interest, imposing an obligation, creating a right, or varying or removing an obligation or right. (emphasis added)

Section 5 contains a *definitive* test of legislative instrument. If one combines s 5(1) and (2), an instrument will be a legislative instrument if it meets the test of legislative character in s 5(2) and it is or was made in the exercise of power delegated by the parliament.

The first question is then — is the certificate caught by the definition of legislative character in s 5(2)? There is no doubt that it falls within s 5(2)(b).

What of s 5(2)(a), which requires that the instrument 'determines the law or alters the content of the law, rather than applying the law in a particular case'? Consider, first of all, the initial part of s 5(2)(a). Regulation 4A(8) provides that 'While a certificate is in force in relation to a permission or a refusal of a permission, subregulation (4) does not apply to that permission or refusal'. Regulation 4A(4) enables applications to be made to the AAT for review of the decision to refuse importation of a prohibited import. Is the effect of reg 4A(8) to alter the content of the law? Two arguments may be made that it does have that effect. One, the law on appeals to the AAT is altered because that law no longer applies to the particular permission. 'The law' includes its operative effect. It is not necessary that there be a formal alteration to the terms of the law. Second, it is sufficient that the law is altered in a single case. This gains support from the case law on the meaning of 'administrative character' under s 3(1) of the Administrative Decisions (Judicial Review) Act 1977 (Cth) (ADJR Act). The courts have had to decide whether an instrument is of administrative or legislative character; if the latter, the making of the instrument is not directly reviewable under the Act. In *Queensland Medical Laboratory v Blewett* (1988) 84 ALR 615 at 634–5 Gummow J pointed out that it was not necessary that a 'law' or an instrument of a 'legislative character' be a rule of general application. His Honour instanced laws which apply to the action of a single person on a single occasion.

Let us now consider the second part of s 5(2)(a). This provision *excludes* instruments 'applying the law in a particular case'. Can it be said that the certificate operates in this way? In *Minister for Industry and Commerce v Tooheys Ltd* (1982) 4 ALD 661 the character of a ministerial determination under s 273 of the Customs Act was examined. It was argued by the Minister that the determination altered liability to duty and changed the relevant law. Nevertheless, the court found that a refusal to make a determination (and, semble, the decision to make a determination) was of administrative, and not legislative, character. This is because determinations involve the application of a general rule to a particular case. The determination in *Tooheys'* case is analogous to the certificate in the present case. This is because, while the certificate alters the law, it *also* involves the application of a general rule to a particular case. The general rule in the present case is reg 4A(5): the power of the Attorney-General to issue the certificate.

Unfortunately, it is not clear from s 5(2)(a) whether the certificate is of legislative character in the defined sense. The legislation has posited a dichotomy (altering the content of the law, rather than applying the law in a particular case) but, as apparent in this case, it is not always a true dichotomy. In the present case, arguments can be made that the certificate *both* applies the law in a particular case and alters the content of the law.

It is therefore necessary to proceed to the more general definition of 'legislative instrument' in s 5(1).

Step 4

The question is whether the certificate is (a) of legislative character and (b) is or was made in the exercise of a power delegated by the parliament: s 5(1).

As para (b) is more straightforward it shall be dealt with first. Section 8 of the LIA is clearly directed to widening the meaning of 'power delegated by the Parliament'. It refers to two levels of delegation of authority: to a 'power delegated by the Parliament' and then to a power 'under the authority of the Parliament, further delegated'. Almost certainly the second delegation is intended to be a reference to an authority arising in a rule made under an Act. However, the LIA does not say so explicitly and the reference to 'under the authority of the Parliament' is a little ambiguous. Recourse to the Explanatory Memorandum is permitted: s 15AB of the Acts Interpretation Act 1901 (Cth). The Explanatory Memorandum to the Legislative Instruments Bill 2003 (Cth) states in relation to cl 8:

> This clause defines power delegated by the Parliament to include a further power of delegation authorised by the Parliament. This ensures that the definition of legislative instrument, which is set out in subclause 4(1), covers instruments that are made under enabling regulations or other legislative instruments.

The Explanatory Memorandum has confirmed the tentative interpretation that was formed from an initial reading of s 8. Hence, the certificate, which is made under regulations, satisfies s 5(1)(b) of the LIA.

We come to the remaining question raised by s 5(1)(a): is the certificate an instrument in writing that 'is of a legislative character'? With the lack of direct precedent on the interpretation of this phrase we turn for guidance then to the interpretation of 'a decision of an administrative character' in s 3(1) of the ADJR Act. The cases have established that administrative character is distinguished from legislative character and judicial decisions: *Minister for Industry and Commerce v*

Tooheys Ltd (1982) 4 ALD 661 at 665. The cases have made it clear there is no single indicator. Several indicators have been suggested. Comprehensive lists appear in *SAT FM Pty Ltd v Australian Broadcasting Authority* (1997) 75 FCR 604, and also in *Central Queensland Land Council Aboriginal Corporation v Attorney-General (Cth)* (2002) 116 FCR 390 at 408 per Wilcox J, drawing upon the full Federal Court in *RG Capital Radio Ltd v Australian Broadcasting Authority* (2001) 113 FCR 185. The factors, and whether they are apparent in the case of the certificate, are set out in columns 1 and 3 of the table below. Note that some of the pointers are expressed in the negative.

1 Pointer to legislative character	2 Case authority	3 Whether the pointer exists in the case of the Attorney-General's certificate
The decision creates new rules of general application	*SAT FM; Central Qld Land Council*	No
The decision determines the content of a law or has the effect of changing the content of a law	*Minister for Industry and Commerce v Tooheys Ltd; Queensland Medical Laboratory v Blewett*	Yes; see answer above
The decision is *not* the application of the law to a particular case	*SAT FM; Central Qld Land Council*	No; see answer above
Notification is required as a means of publicising the decision, eg, in the *Gazette*	*SAT FM*	Yes, parliamentary tabling provided for: reg 4A(9)
The decision has a binding legal effect	*SAT FM; Central Qld Land Council*	Yes: reg 4A(8)
No provision for AAT review	*SAT FM; Central Qld Land Council*	Yes
Requirement of public consultation	*SAT FM; Central Qld Land Council*	No

In making the decision the decision-maker must have regard to wide policy considerations	*SAT FM*	No (?)
Provision for parliamentary control	*Central Qld Land Council*	Not formally, but parliamentary tabling provided for: reg 4A(9)
The power to amend the decision, say by notice in writing, is analogous to the legislature's power to amend legislation	*SAT FM*	Yes: Acts Interpretation Act 1901 s 33(3)
Once the decision is made, it is *not* subject to executive variation or control	*SAT FM*	No; the Attorney-General may revoke it, etc: Acts Interpretation Act 1901 s 33(3)

Column 3 of this table shows that there are competing indications as to whether the certificate is of legislative character. But the considerations are not of equal weight: *SAT FM* at 309. How important is the generality (or lack thereof) of a rule? The generality of a rule is not essential: *Federal Airports Corporation v Aerolineas Argentinas* (1997) 76 FCR 582. However, in their study of the cases Creyke and McMillan (2005, [2.4.29]) conclude that it remains an important consideration. What are other more important considerations? Although we are considering s 5(1) of the LIA it ought to be remembered that s 5(2)(a) highlights two particular considerations: whether the rule alters the content of the law, as oppposed to applying the law in a particular case. Because they have been singled out by the legislature, they ought to be considered to be more important in this context. As shown above, the certificate does alter the law (legislative pointer), but it also applies the law to a particular case (administrative pointer). If one considers the lack of generality of the certificate and the way it applies the law to a particular case, it is more likely than not that the certificate would be considered to be *not* of legislative character, notwithstanding that there are some indications of its legislative character in the regulation.

(iii) Conclusion

After a detailed study of the law, it is concluded that it is more likely than not that the certificate is not required to be lodged on the Federal Register of Legislative Instruments. However, at the rule-maker's discretion, an instrument may be lodged for registration whether or not it is of legislative character: LIA s 5(3).

Examiner's Comments

An understanding of particular legislation is often assisted by methodically analysing it in the form of a 'logic tree' or an algorithm, see: W Twining and D Miers, *How to Do Things with Rules: A Primer of Interpretation*, 4th ed, Butterworths, London, 1999, App II; J Erasmus and D Elliott, 'Tips and Techniques for Drafting Complex Law', *Legislative Drafting in Perspective* (2004) at <http://www.ciaj-icaj.ca/english/publications/J-Erasmus&D-Elliott-Tips&techniques%20-%20JE%20and%20DE.pdf>. In a like vein, the answer arranges the relevant law on determining whether an instrument is a 'legislative instrument' under four major steps and then applies the law step by step.

It is an interesting fact that the broad legislative statement of what is a legislative instrument in s 5(1) of the LIA is the first statement on that topic in the Act, but the last to be treated in our step by step approach. This is because the model rightly prefers deeming provisions to be examined before broader legislative tests are invoked if necessary. It is efficient to consider simple deeming provisions first. It is also wise to do so, since a deeming provision can cut across a substantive provision — a deeming provision can effect a result which is not apparent from applying the general principle. The Commonwealth Government's handbook on the LIA also advises users to apply the deeming provisions first: *Legislative Instruments Handbook* (2004) para 3.9 at <http://www.ag.gov.au/www/agd/agd.nsf/Page/Legislativedrafting_BackgroundtotheLegislativeInstrumentsAct2003>.

Is it necessary in an examination to go through each and every step? Mentally you should take each step as far as it is necessary. If the answer at a step makes it clear one way or the other whether the instrument is a legislative instrument, it is not necessary to go further. It is also probably not essential to *write out* steps which have not advanced the discussion except to move us immediately to the next step. So, in the above answer, an answer would not be unsatisfactory for omitting a reference to Steps 1 and 2. But a student is likely to be rewarded for referring to these steps nevertheless. What is very important in an examination is to head for the law which raises issues for discussion. In the case of the above problem, it is Steps 3 and 4.

As is common in the present work, the answer goes beyond what is expected of an A answer; it is a model answer to provide students with guidance. The cases are drawn from the standard casebooks: R Douglas, *Douglas and Jones's Administrative Law*, 5th ed, Federation Press, Sydney, 2006; R Creyke and J McMillan, *Control of Government Action: Text, Cases and Commentary*, LexisNexis Butterworths, Sydney, 2005. Although the compilers have chosen different cases, in an examination students would not be expected to have a knowledge of both casebooks. Students should note how the answer drew on other sources: the law of statutory interpretation (s 15AB of the Acts

Interpretation Act) and the Explanatory Memorandum to the Legislative Instruments Bill 2003. It is debatable whether an A paper would need to discuss the interpretation of s 8 as a student may not see any ambiguity.

Despite the confident reference in the answer to 'a detailed study', the answer is not perfect. It may be that, in applying s 5(1) of the LIA, the answer places too much reliance on the general criteria of 'legislative character' in the ADJR Act case law. The case of *Federal Airports Corporation v Aerolineas Argentinas* (1997) 76 FCR 582 downplays the use of such critera:

> If there is anything that the authorities make plain ... it is that general tests will frequently provide no clear answer. ... There is no escape, in my view, from the need to examine closely the particular provisions and the particular circumstances: at 591 per Lehane J.

However, with respect, it is not clear how this approach adds anything other than factoring in the impression of the interpreter gained from considering the Act and the circumstances.

The meaning of 'legislative character' can be a difficult concept to apply when there are competing indications. It is noteworthy that, in its review of the ADJR Act cases on the meaning of 'administrative character', the editors of the *Australian Administrative Law Service* observe that 'The difficulties inherent in the legislative/administrative dichotomy has resulted in individual cases tending to be decided upon their particular facts': [312B]. Perhaps after the present problem students will appreciate the lengths the drafter has gone to in providing deeming provisions in the LIA and in s 15AE of the Acts Interpretation Act!

 # Common Errors to Avoid

- Not being aware that the certificate alters the law, on the (mistaken) assumption that law and legislation are and must always be general in character.
- Not considering the ADJR Act case law on the meaning of 'decision of an administrative character'.
- Merely stating the competing indications as to whether the certificate is of legislative character; not attempting to judge whether, on balance, the instrument is of legislative character.

PART 3

Limitations on Government Action and Judicial Review

Chapter 3

Powers to Act: Threshold Requirements

Key Issues

The most fundamental principle of administrative law is that administrators may do only what they are empowered to do: *Entick v Carrington* (1765) 95 ER 807; 2 Wils 275. This principle should come as no surprise. Any other principle would be inconsistent with the rule of law.

Difficulties arise, however, as soon as one attempts to apply the principle. The starting point will normally be the relevant legislation. (The exceptional cases will be those where the immediate source of the power is either the Constitution or common law.) Legislation is both the source of powers and a determinant of the extent of those powers. However, legislation must be interpreted.

Interpretation proceeds on a variety of assumptions. One is that it is a means of achieving particular results. It should, if possible, be interpreted on that basis. An interpretation which would mean that there were no circumstances in which the legislation could ever operate is therefore normally to be rejected in favour of an interpretation which would give some efficacy to the legislation. Courts act on the basis that the legislature is presumed not to have intended to abridge common law rights unless this is clear from the language of the legislation. This is a reasonable assumption, if only because drafters will be so familiar with the principle that they will know that the only way to ensure that legislation does abridge common law rights will be to make this clear. Legislation will also be interpreted on the basis that the drafters of the legislation are familiar with administrative law and that they must be taken as intending that ordinary administrative law reasoning will govern the exercise of the relevant powers unless it is clear that the legislature does not intend these rules to apply.

This facilitates the drafting of legislation. It means that legislators do not have to state that powers are to be exercised in a procedurally fair manner, or that they are not to be used for the personal enrichment of the repository of the power, or that they are to be exercised according to whether the day in question is a propitious one for Librans, assuming

Pluto to be in the ascendant. It also means that one can understand legislation only if one knows what those shared assumptions are. Sometimes assumptions are such that, if one put them to the traveller on the 67 tram, the traveller would agree that the legislature could not have intended that the assumption should be violated. Others are less obvious — which is just as well, since otherwise there would be no point in studying administrative law, which would be a bad thing.

Issues which can give rise to difficulties can be conveniently divided into two categories: threshold questions, which relate to whether an administrator has the power to act; and questions which relate to whether powers have been exercised properly. Examples of threshold questions include:

- When a power is conferred upon a particular official, what are the boundaries of that power? (Does a power to administer posts and telegraphs permit the establishment of symphony orchestras? Does a power to prohibit noxious industries allow the tolerance of noxious industries, provided that they comply with certain conditions?)

- When powers are conferred on a particular official, can that official arrange to have them exercised by someone else?

- Where a decision-maker has purported to make a decision, can the decision-maker subsequently reconsider the matter and make a different decision?

- Where legislation prescribes a procedure for making a decision, is following the procedure a condition precedent to the validity of the decision?

In relation to the proper exercise of powers, questions include:

- Are there circumstances in which a decision-maker has the power to base a decision on an erroneous interpretation of the law?

- Where an administrator possesses a discretion in relation to the making of a decision, may the administrator formulate de facto rules to govern the exercise of the discretion?

- Where an official has a discretionary power, may (or must) the official defer to a hierarchical superior in deciding how to exercise that power?

- Do administrators have the power to make decisions which appear to be irrational?

- How far do administrators have the power to base their decisions on mistaken findings of fact?

The boundary line between threshold questions and proper exercise questions can be a vague one, and for administrative law purposes it is not necessary to make this distinction. However, for the purposes of this book, it is convenient to spread our coverage of powers issues over two chapters; in this, the first of the two, we present questions which arise from 'threshold' issues.

Before attempting the questions, check that you are familiar with the following issues:

✓ the circumstances in which repositories of powers may delegate those powers to others, and the procedures by which they can do so;

✓ whether a person who has exercised a power is empowered to change his or her mind and exercise the power in a different way; and

✓ the effects of failure to follow procedures which have been laid down in relation to the making of particular decisions.

QUESTION 9

On 1 December 2006, pursuant to reg 4A(?A) of the Customs (Prohibited Imports) Regulations (Cth), the Attorney-General appointed Dr Bowdler to act as an authorised person for the purposes of handling requests for permission to import prohibited goods. In January 2007, Dr Crippen, a lecturer at Higgins University, sought permission to import *50 Fun Things to Do with Heroin*. His reason was an interest in the attractions of drugs, and his own belief that there are no more than nine fun things to do with heroin (one being adding it to the Vice-Chancellor's sandwiches). In April 2007, Dr Bowdler considered the application and formed a provisional view that permission should not be granted. Before making a final decision, however, she received a letter from the Attorney-General, dated 15 April, stating that, pending a review of the regulation, authorised persons were to refuse all applications for permission to import books which promoted or incited the use of Sch 4 drugs, regardless of their merits. On 22 April, Dr Bowdler wrote to the Attorney-General, complaining about the letter, arguing that it constituted an unlawful attempt to fetter the discretion of authorised persons. However, on 1 May 2007, she wrote to Dr Crippen advising him that she had decided to reject his application on the grounds that it was the Attorney-General's policy not to accede to any applications, regardless of their merit. She signed the letter in the Attorney-General's name. As she said to a colleague: 'If he's going to give me orders, he can bloody well take responsibility for my decisions.' On 1 June 2007, the Attorney-General wrote to Dr Bowdler as follows:

Dear Dr Bowdler,

Withdrawal of Authority to Act as Agent: Customs (Prohibited Imports) Regulations

It is clear from your recent letter in which you challenge the legality of my instruction of 15 April that you are out to undermine me. In the circumstances, it would be intolerable that you should continue to act as my agent in relation to the granting of permissions, for it would be absurd if you were ever to allow your unfounded qualms to overcome you to the point where you were to sign in my name a permission of a kind that I have in fact expressly forbidden. I am therefore withdrawing my appointment of you to act as my agent, dated 1 December 2006. This will take effect as from 2 June 2007.

Attorney-General

On 1 July, Dr Crippen wrote to Dr Bowdler asking her to reconsider her decision and on 1 August, Dr Bowdler wrote to Dr Crippen, saying that she had reconsidered the matter and that, despite the instructions in the Attorney-General's letter of 15 April, she had decided to permit the importation of the book, as requested. This time, she signed the letter in her own name. On 1 September, police raided Dr Crippen's office and found him reading about the ways in which heroin can make watching soccer exciting. Was he impermissibly in possession of prohibited goods?

Time allowed: 40 mins

Answer Plan

Three issues arise:

(i)   Did the letter of 1 June revoke the delegation of 1 December 2006?

(ii) Did Dr Bowdler have the power to revoke her initial 'decision'?

(iii) Could Dr Crippen be said to be in possession of prohibited goods?

 Answer

(i)   Did the letter of 1 June revoke the delegation of 1 December 2006?

The letter of 1 December appointed Dr Bowdler to act as an authorised person. Though not in name, Dr Bowdler was effectively a delegate because, by virtue of the instrument of appointment, she had the power to grant permissions as that enjoyed by the Attorney-General: subregs (2), (2A). There can be no doubt that the Attorney-General had the power to revoke Dr Bowdler's appointment: Acts Interpretation Act 1901 (Cth) s 33(3). There is no contrary intention in the Customs (Prohibited Imports) Regulations. The question is whether his letter of 1 June 2007 did this. It is likely that the Attorney-General intended that it should. However, on its face, the letter does not revoke the appointment. Rather, it purports to revoke an authority which Dr Bowdler never possessed — and which the Attorney-General may never have been in a position to confer — an authority to act as agent. The two forms of authorisation are quite different: see *O'Reilly v State Bank Commissioners* (1983) 153 CLR 1. A delegate is a person appointed pursuant to statute who, for the duration of the appointment, is empowered to exercise the powers conferred on the delegator. A delegate acts in their own name: *Re Reference Under s 11 of the Ombudsman Act 1976 for an Advisory Opinion; Ex parte Director-General of Social Services* (1979) 2 ALD 86 at 94 (Brennan J); *O'Reilly v State Bank of Victoria Commissioners* (1983) 153 CLR 1, 30–1 (Wilson J); but note Acts Interpretation Act 1901 (Cth) s 34AB(c). An agent is someone who acts in the principal's name. The power to appoint agents is an implied power, and the willingness of courts to imply that power depends on matters such as the importance of the power and the degree to which the nominal repository of the power could perform his or her functions in the absence of a power to act through agents: *O'Reilly v State Bank Commissioners* (1983) 153 CLR 1, but cf *Carltona v Commissioner of Works* [1942] 2 All ER 560, 563 where Lord Greene MR suggested that the power to act through agents may be regulated politically rather than judicially.

One construction which could be placed on the letter is that it was intended as a revocation of Dr Bowdler's authority, whatever the basis for that authority might be. Consistent with this is the fact that otherwise the purported revocation would achieve nothing, given that Dr Bowdler had never been appointed as the Attorney-General's agent. An alternative interpretation would be that the Attorney-General should be presumed to know the law, and that official letters should be given their literal interpretation. Policy considerations are of only limited assistance here. On one hand, it might be argued that all instruments which confer powers should be given an interpretation which limits the conferral of powers. On the other hand, it might be argued that powers of revocation should be strictly interpreted so that only by unambiguous revocations can a revocation be affected. One might, perhaps, be able to argue that the power to revoke has not been exercised in like manner to the power of appointment (cf Acts Interpretation Act s 33(3)), and that therefore the revocation has not been effective. One might also note that the Attorney-General's concerns about Dr Bowdler acting in his name, as expressed in the letter, might not apply in relation to Dr Bowdler's exercise of powers as a delegate. On the basis of these arguments, I am inclined to the view that the purported revocation may not have been effective.

(ii) Did Dr Bowdler have the power to revoke her initial 'decision'?

Assuming that the revocation was ineffective, Dr Bowdler would probably have had the power to make the decision to permit importation. The position could, however, depend on whether the initial decision was lawful or not. If the initial decision had been lawful, Dr Bowdler's powers to make a second decision in relation to the issue would depend on whether the legislation permitted the making of multiple applications. The regulations are silent in relation to this issue, but it is at least arguable that an intention can be evinced to the effect that, subject to appeals, intra vires decisions should be final. The alternative would be that applicants for permission could make repeated requests for permission, and repeated appeals to the AAT in the event of permission being refused. Finality can be a virtue, and this might be taken as suggesting that the decision-maker's powers would be exhausted once the decision had been made. However, the position is different if the decision is flawed by jurisdictional error. When that is the case, there is no legally operative decision, and the decision-maker is free to reconsider the matter: *MIMA v Bhardwaj* (2002) 209 CLR 597.

At first sight, it might seem that Dr Bowdler lacked the authority to make the relevant decision. Because Dr Bowdler signed in the Attorney-General's name it purported to be a decision made by Dr Bowdler as agent for the Attorney-General. But Dr Bowdler had never been appointed as agent. Therefore, it might seem, she had no power to make the decision in this capacity. The decision is, therefore, arguably a legal nullity.

Against this is a counter-argument. Dr Bowdler undoubtedly possessed the power to make the decision in her role as delegate. Does it matter that she purported to make the decision as agent? The mere fact that a decision-maker with particular powers acted on the basis of an erroneous assessment of the source of those powers is not fatal to the validity of a decision: see *Mercantile Mutual Life Insurance Co Ltd v Australian Securities Commission* (1993) 40 FCR 409. But if the nature of the power and the conditions for its exercise depend on its source, a mistake as to its source may be fatal to its purported exercise. If Dr Bowdler's powers relevantly varied according to whether she was agent or delegate, an erroneous assumption as to their source might mean that their purported exercise had miscarried. Here the source of the power has some implications. Error has meant that the purported decision has been signed as agent rather than delegate. A delegate is personally responsible; an agent is not. But these may not be relevant differences. Failure to sign in the correct capacity is arguably an intra-jurisdictional error rather than a jurisdictional one. And in *Carltona* at least, Greene MR's argument that Ministers would be politically responsible for the choice of their agents would seem to imply that they would also be politically responsible for their choice of delegates. Dr Bowdler's comments to her colleague suggest that she saw a difference between acting as delegate and acting as agent, but this seems to go not to whether she possessed a power to grant permissions but rather to whether she exercised that power properly.

If I am correct in assuming that Dr Bowdler had the power to make the permission decision regardless of her perception of the source of the power, and that her powers were substantially the same regardless of their source, her apparent belief to the contrary suggests error of law on her part. In any case, as a repository of a discretionary power, she has exercised that power in a manner inconsistent with her beliefs as to how the power should be exercised. She has therefore constructively failed to exercise the power, and is therefore (if still empowered to act as a delegate) free to make a second purported decision.

(iii) Could Dr Crippen be said to be in possession of prohibited goods?

If, contrary to what I have argued, the letter of 1 June terminated Dr Bowdler's powers as delegate, and if the book falls within the regulation, Dr Crippen is in possession of a prohibited import. This is because Dr Bowdler would not have had the power to reconsider the matter on 1 August. If charged with a criminal offence, Dr Crippen would be able to argue that, given his understanding of the facts, he was entitled to import the book, and in my opinion this argument would succeed. Even if lack of mens rea is not a defence under the legislation (and I do not know whether it is or not), he would be able to rely on the fact that his belief involved an honest and reasonable mistake of fact.

Examiner's Comments

This question requires an examination of the difference between delegation of a power and the appointment of a person to act as an agent, together with an examination of the circumstances in which a repository of a power becomes *functus officio*.

Each of these issues is handled carefully. Given the large number of facts and the key relevance of the dates, handling the facts accurately would be assisted by writing out a chronology (a listing of the material facts in date order).

The answer recognises the ambiguity of the 1 June letter, and discusses matters which point to one construction rather than another being placed on the letter. Its tentative conclusion seems to me to be the correct one, but it would be open to someone answering the question to conclude that the letter would probably be construed as a withdrawal of the authority to act as a delegate. The only conclusion which would not be open would be the conclusion that the issue was so clear-cut as to admit of no debate. For this reason, it is necessary to consider the validity of Dr Bowdler's subsequent decision, assuming she had the authority to make it.

The answer recognises that an exercise of power is not necessarily flawed by a mistake on the part of the decision-maker as to its source, and likewise recognises that in this situation what matters is the practical relevance of the mistake. It is not dogmatic as to whether the differences between delegates and agents are such that a mistake as to one's status amounts to jurisdictional error. In this respect, it is prudently cautious: there appears to be no authority directly in point.

The analysis of the circumstances in which a decision-maker loses the power to reconsider a decision is consistent with authority, as is the analysis of the circumstances in which a repository of a power may reconsider the decision.

The answer concludes that, even if Dr Bowdler was found to have acted as delegate in making the decision of 1 May, the decision would nonetheless be invalid. This, however, anticipates issues to be discussed in the next chapter. Students who had not yet familiarised themselves with those issues could be forgiven for overlooking them.

The answer does not discuss whether Dr Crippen could have relied on the 'de facto officer' doctrine in the event that Dr Bowdler was found to have been stripped of her powers as delegate. The position appears to be that the doctrine applies only to the apparent occupants of particular offices, and not to those who might appear to be the delegate or agent of an office: see E Campbell, 'De Facto Officers' (1994) 2 *Australian Journal of Administrative Law* 5 at 7. I do not consider that there was any need to discuss the issue, although an answer which did so, and got the law right, would deserve credit for doing so.

Given that this is an administrative law question, it is not necessary to consider whether Dr Crippen would be guilty of a criminal offence if the permission decision was invalid, although it would be essential to advert to this issue if a real, live Dr Crippen were to consult you in your professional capacity. The answer correctly identifies relevant issues and wisely refrains from attempting a definitive statement of the law in this area.

Common Errors to Avoid

- Not recognising that the appointment of an authorised person is equivalent to the power to delegate.
- Not being clear about the differences between the powers of a delegate and the powers of an agent.
- An analysis of the revocation of an instrument which does not refer to s 33 of the Acts Interpretation Act will be incomplete. Sometimes, in order to fill a gap left by power-creating legislation, it is necessary to look not only at common law, but also at other statutes.
- Do not simply assume that the letter of 1 June was unambiguous.
- Be sensitive to the need to recognise that, for some purposes, purporting to make a decision is not the same as making what the law regards as a 'decision'. Recognising this requires considerable mental gymnastics, since in some legal contexts the term 'decision' includes 'purported decisions', while in others it doesn't.

QUESTION 10

Following an application by Makepeace to import *The Night of a Thousand Shames* (see 'The Makepeace Scenario', p xvi), the Attorney-General decided to issue a certificate under reg 4A(5) of the Customs (Prohibited Imports) Regulations (Cth). He tabled a copy of the certificate in the Senate, but forgot to arrange to have a copy laid before the House of Representatives. He later refused to permit the book's importation. Twenty sitting days after he issued the certificate, Makepeace made an application to the AAT for review of the Attorney-General's decision to refuse permission. The AAT proceeded with the hearing. The Attorney-General applied to the Federal Court for an order to stop the AAT hearing. Would his application be likely to succeed? Assume that a certificate is not a legislative instrument for the purposes of the Legislative Instruments Act 2003 (Cth).

Time allowed: 30 mins

Answer Plan

(i)   The effect of a valid certificate.

(ii) The general effect of failure to table.

(iii) Arguments that failure to table means that the certificate ceases to be operative.

(iv) Arguments suggesting that the certificate continues to be operative.

(v)   Conclusions.

Answer

(i)   The effect of a valid certificate

A valid certificate bars a person from appealing to the AAT against a decision to refuse permission to import: reg 4A(8). A certificate having been issued, Makepeace may seek AAT review only if the certificate is invalid or inoperative. In this case, the only basis on which Makepeace might challenge the decision lies in the Minister's failure to table the certificate.

(ii) The general effect of failure to table

In failing to table the certificate within 15 sitting days, the Attorney-General has clearly failed to comply with a requirement under the regulations: reg 4A(9). Failure to comply with a procedural requirement associated with the exercise of an administrative power is not necessarily fatal to the validity of that exercise of power: *Australian Broadcasting Commission v Redmore Pty Ltd* (1989) 166 CLR 454; *Project Blue Sky Inc v Australian Broadcasting Authority* (1998) 194 CLR 355:

Whether it is depends upon whether there can be discerned a legislative purpose to invalidate any act that fails to comply with the condition. The existence of the purpose is ascertained by reference to the language of the statute, its subject matter and objects, and the consequences for the parties of holding void every act done in breach of the condition: *Blue Sky* at [91] per McHugh, Gummow, Kirby and Hayne JJ.

Here there is no reason to believe that the procedures associated with the making and issuing of the certificate were not followed. The certificate therefore began life as a valid certificate. The question is whether it ceased to be operative after the period for tabling the certificate elapsed. There is, however, no reason to believe that the High Court's observations do not apply equally to this latter question. Failure to table does not necessarily mean that the certificate does not continue to operate, but may do so if a legislative purpose to that effect can be evinced from the wording, subject matter and objects of the regulation, and from the consequences for the parties of holding that the certificate ceased to operate.

(iii)   Arguments that failure to table means that the certificate ceases to be operative

Several considerations suggest that failure to comply with the tabling requirement means that certificates cease to be operative. First, one can compare the regulation's silence in relation to the effects of failure to table with its express reference to the effects of failure to notify of the right to AAT review and to reasons: reg 4A(12). This can be taken as indicating a legislative intention that the former failure should be fatal to the ongoing effectiveness of the certificate. Had the legislators' intention been otherwise, they would have made the same kind of express provision for the consequences of failure to comply with the tabling requirement as they made in relation to failure to comply with the obligation to notify as to the right to reasons. Conversely, however, one might compare the lack of any reference in the regulations to the effects of failure to table with the express provision in the Legislative Instruments Act 2003 (Cth) s 38(3), which states that failure to table a statutory instrument renders it inoperative as from the day by which it must be tabled.

Second, certificates have the effect of depriving people of a right to appeal which they would otherwise have enjoyed. This is a serious consequence, and the legislature envisages that the Attorney-General should be politically responsible for taking this step. It is not unreasonable to suggest that the continued operation of the certificate should be conditioned upon the activation of the accountability mechanism.

(iv) Arguments suggesting that the certificate continues to be operative

That said, it is at least arguable that the certificate continues to operate. Failure to advert to the consequences of non-compliance could be taken to reflect an assumption that such a failure would not be fatal to the continuing validity of the certificate. The fact that express reference is made to procedural failure in subreg (12) is not conclusive, since it relates to the validity of the certificate and not to the question of its continued operation.

Second, if it is in the public interest that a certificate be issued, it is arguable that appeals to the AAT should not become feasible simply because of the Attorney-General's failure to comply with a procedural requirement. However, since the condition for issuing a certificate is the Attorney-General's perception of the public interest, rather than an independently verified assessment of the public interest, this last argument is not particularly compelling.

(v) Conclusions

In my opinion, it is not clear whether failure to table the certificate means that the certificate ceases to operate as from the time by which tabling was required. That said, in my opinion, the arguments in favour of the certificate ceasing to be operative are somewhat stronger than those to the contrary. I would also note that, while Makepeace's application was almost certainly out of time (it is rare for parliament to sit for 20 days during a four-week period), there is no suggestion that the Attorney-General is relying on this as a ground for his application. This probably reflects a well-founded belief that such an argument would be doomed to fail.

In my opinion, the Attorney-General's application would *probably* fail.

Examiner's Comments

The question requires you to assume that a certificate is not a legislative instrument. In our opinion, this assumption is probably correct: see Question 8). This question requires consideration of the effects of failure to comply with a procedural requirement associated with the exercise of a power. This case involves a slightly different issue to that which arose in *Project Blue Sky*, since this case relates, not to the initial validity of the certificate, but to its subsequent force. The answer treats this as an immaterial difference, I think with justification.

The question requires an attempt to apply the *Blue Sky* criteria, and the answer performs this task well. It addresses both arguments which suggest that the certificate ceases to operate, and arguments which might be advanced in favour of its continued operation. It attempts to assess the persuasive force of different arguments, and does so reasonably well. Its caution in assessing the likely outcome of the Attorney-General's application seems warranted.

The question does not call for a discussion of whether Makepeace's application could be successfully challenged on the basis that it was out of time — as it almost certainly was. An answer would therefore not be marked down for failing to raise the issue. This answer recognises that the application was probably out of time, but that this was unlikely to matter. In doing so, it does more than I think is necessary, but the examinee could not be sure that the question would be given a narrow construction. In briefly addressing the issue, the examinee insured against the possibility that the examiner would expect the issue to be addressed, and also demonstrated awareness of a potential issue which most examinees did not notice.

 # Common Errors to Avoid

- Equating the effect of failure to table a certificate with the effect of failure to table a legislative instrument.
- Assuming that the question related to the validity of the certificate *ab initio*.
- Failing to recognise arguments both for and against the conclusion that the certificate ceased to operate prior to the application to the AAT.

 # QUESTION 11

Among the National Libertarian Party's election promises was that, if elected, it would abolish all forms of censorship. Somewhat to its surprise, the party won a majority of seats in the House of Representatives, but faced a hostile Senate. A regulation repealing reg 4A of the Customs (Prohibited Imports) Regulations was disallowed, and legislation intended to achieve the same effect was also defeated in the Senate. Following these defeats, the Attorney-General caused the following notice to be printed in the *Gazette*:

Customs (Prohibited Imports) Regulations, reg 4A(2)

Pursuant to this subregulation, I hereby permit any person to import any item to which the regulation applies.

Now answer the following questions:

(i) The Victorian Attorney-General responded by applying to the Federal Court for a declaration that the permission in question was invalid. Would the application be likely to succeed?

(ii) Could the Attorney-General grant permission to a class of people in respect of a class of what would otherwise be prohibited imports?

Time allowed: 20 mins

Answer Plan

(i) Was the blanket 'permission' a valid exercise of power?

- Inconsistency with the purposes of the regulation.
- Inconsistency with reg 4A(2AA).

(ii) Is there a power to grant 'class' permissions?

- Inconsistency with the decision-making process envisaged by reg 4A(2AA).
- The regulations appear to envisage that permissions be given only to persons.

 Answer

(i) Was the blanket 'permission' a valid exercise of power?

In my opinion, the purported permission to import is invalid. Although the Attorney-General clearly possesses a power to grant permission to people to import what would otherwise be prohibited imports (reg 4A(2)), this does not, in my opinion, warrant the granting of blanket permissions. My reasons are as follows.

Inconsistency with the purposes of the regulation

The purported exercise of power is almost totally inconsistent with the purpose of the regulation. While it is not always easy to assess the purpose of a legislative provision, it is clear that the purpose of reg 4A is to provide for the general exclusion of the goods listed in reg 4A(1A). The fact that there is a power to grant permission to import is not inconsistent with this interpretation. All it suggests is that the regulation-maker recognised that some circumstances might exist in which importation should be permitted. If it had been the regulation-maker's intention that all of the 'prohibited' goods should be able to be imported, there would have been no need to make the regulation.

Inconsistency with reg 4A(2AA)

In any case, reg 4A(2AA) makes it clear that the power to permit is not to be exercised by granting blanket permissions to import. It requires a person who is considering whether to grant permission to import to take account of certain matters. In purporting to grant a global permission to import, the Attorney-General could not take account of the matters listed in the subregulation. Since the identity and attributes of many potential importers would be unknown to the Attorney-General, he or she could not know why they would be importing the goods, their relevant activities, nor their reputation.

(ii) Is there a power to grant 'class' permissions?

Inconsistency with the decision-making process envisaged by reg 4A(2AA)

In general, the considerations discussed above would mean that the Attorney-General could not grant permission to a class of people to import a class of imports, since it would almost invariably be the case that there would exist at least one member of the class whose attributes would not be known — especially if the class included people who were not yet, but who might subsequently become, members. If the only relevant criteria were those set out in paras (a)–(d) of reg 4A(2AA), it might be possible to define a class by reference to attributes which would ensure that all current or future members of the class would be people to whom permission might appropriately be given. The requirement that the decision-maker have regard to all other relevant matters would, however, preclude the granting of permission to a class defined by criteria such that people might subsequently become members of the class. In relation to such members, the Attorney-General could not know whether relevant matters existed or would exist. Only if the class was defined in a manner such that the Attorney-General knew all that he or she needed to know about all the members of the class, might it be possible to grant permission to a class of people.

The regulations appear to envisage that permissions be given only to persons

A similar conclusion might be reached by another route. Paragraphs (b), (c) and (d) of reg 4A(2AA) envisage that permission be given to persons (which would include corporate entities, these being legal persons). While permission to members of a class might be treated as involving permission to persons who are members of the class, it is arguable that the reference to persons means that permission may be given only to specific individuals. For the reasons I have given in the preceding paragraph, it would rarely matter which interpretation was adopted. The only situation in which the issue would arise would be the rare situation where the Attorney-General was aware of the relevant attributes of all members of the class. In that case, however, the class would almost certainly be small and, given the ambiguity surrounding this issue, the Attorney-General would be advised to give separate permissions to each member of the class personally.

Examiner's Comments

This is a relatively straightforward question designed to test the capacity to apply and interpret legislation. The first part of the question requires awareness of two considerations which bear on the breadth of power conferred by this regulation:

1. the constraints posed by the need to reconcile the exercise of a power with the purposes of the regulation which confers it; and

2. those which follow by virtue of the need to reconcile a purported exercise of power with the various provisions of the legislation.

The answer recognises this, and argues persuasively that the purported permission is inconsistent both with the general purposes of the regulation and with the decision-making scheme created by the regulation. Either of these arguments would have been a sufficient basis for concluding that the purported grant of permission was invalid, but it is nonetheless preferable to discuss both of them.

The discussion about circumstances in which 'class' permissions could be granted is persuasive, if a bit laborious. Nonetheless, while the issue could probably be disposed of by arguing simply that reg 4A(2AA) envisages grants to persons, that conclusion is not so self-evident as to preclude a discussion premised on the possibility that the regulation could also apply to classes of persons, in the event that this could be reconciled with the requirement to take account of the considerations set out in subreg (2AA).

 # Common Errors to Avoid

- Assuming that because there is a power to grant permission to import, anyone can be permitted to import anything.

Chapter 4
Improper Exercise of Power

Key Issues

Even if an administrator can act in particular circumstances, that administrator can err if he or she does not exercise his or her powers properly. If a discretionary power is conferred on an administrator, the administrator must normally consider the exercise of that power upon being asked to do so by someone in a position to benefit from a favourable exercise of that discretion. Repositories of discretions must make up their own minds. They may not make a particular decision simply because someone tells them to do so, or because there is a policy which appears to require them to do so. They may not act on misinterpretations of the law. They may not use their powers for purposes other than those for which the power was conferred. They may not take into account matters which are legally irrelevant, and they must take into account matters which are legally relevant. If their decisions are based on findings of fact, there must be some evidence to support their final decision. They err if their decision is so unreasonable that no reasonable person acting according to law could have reached it. If they do any of these things, and if this affects their decision, then their exercise of power will be treated as having miscarried.

Not all mistakes are grounds for judicial intervention, however. The fact that an administrator makes a mistake of fact is not normally sufficient to warrant the decision being overturned. Other errors must be material in the sense that they are such that the decision might have been different had the error not been made. They are immaterial, they do not affect the validity of the decision.

It is relatively easy to set out these principles. It is much harder to apply them. Doing so requires an awareness of what is entailed by these requirements. What is an error of law as opposed to an error of fact? What makes a consideration one which must (or must not) be taken into account? When is an 'error of fact' fatal to the validity of a purported exercise of power? It may also require familiarity with a sizeable body of case law so that one can have a sense of the circumstances in which courts will find that administrators have made particular mistakes.

Before attempting the questions, check that you are familiar with the following issues:

✓ How much weight may an administrator give to the views of superiors and to policy?

✓ What makes a consideration a 'relevant' or an 'irrelevant' consideration, and what makes a purpose an 'unauthorised purpose'?

✓ In what circumstances may a decision be struck down on the grounds that it is unreasonable?

✓ In what circumstances are decision-makers permitted and not permitted to make erroneous findings of fact?

QUESTION 12

Assume for the purposes of this question that the regulations have been amended by the addition of the words '(f) the drug MBA and its variants' to subreg (1A).

MBA is a chemical which was initially developed as a possible taste-enhancer, to be used in a line of 'adult' chocolate drinks marketed by Moonshine, an American cocoa-house chain. Research suggested that the chemical produced soothingly hallucinogenic effects, and tended to be associated with enhanced performance of intellectual tasks. The demands it made on the body were mitigated by virtue of its tendency to prolong sleep, once a person had actually gone to sleep, but it did not itself produce sleepiness. Prisoners who used the drug tended to become less aggressive and more industrious. Its only negative effect was that it produced impaired sexual performance, and this tended to reduce its appeal to those who took sexual performance seriously. A variant on the drug, MBA-LTU, largely overcame this problem. Both drugs were banned by the United States Government on the ground that they were believed to cause pleasure, and the Australian Government followed suit.

Goldenyears, an Australian aged-care provider, is anxious to import quantities of the drug from the Netherlands, claiming that its use would enhance the quality of life of its 'customers'. On 1 July, it commissioned Kelly University's National Centre for Hallucinogenic Studies (Kelly) to conduct research into this question, subject to necessary permissions being obtained.

Kelly University has a somewhat tarnished reputation. Its Deputy Vice-Chancellor (Research and Hospitality) was reprimanded and fined $30 by the University Council last year after it was revealed that he had encouraged researchers to cut costs by reporting research results without actually doing the research for which they had been funded. The government has also had concerns about the university's inability to account for 2kg of plutonium which had been entrusted to its Centre ➤

for the Study of Friendly Forms of Nuclear Energy. The Hallucinogenic Studies Centre, however, is well regarded.

On July 15, the Kelly research director wrote to the Attorney-General, seeking permission to import a quantity of MBA-LTU for use in trials to determine its effect on the quality of life of a sample of volunteer customers. She explained that the National Centre for Hallucinogenic Studies was highly regarded, and detailed its research in related areas. The letter also set out the precautions that would be taken to ensure that the drug was used only for its intended purposes. The letter was delivered to the Attorney-General's office the following day. It was read by a work-experience student, who wrote a memo for the Attorney-General stating that, in her opinion, the application was without merit. On 19 July, after reading the student's memorandum and glancing quickly through the letter of 15 July, the Attorney-General wrote to Kelly stating that he had decided to refuse permission.

His stated reasons were as follows:

1. The proposed safeguards were inadequate.

2. He had some reservations about the propriety of granting the requisite permission to a centre in a university whose response to academic fraud had been to do no more than reprimand the senior administrator responsible.

3. The message he had been getting from the community was that a lot of hypocrisy surrounded calls for the legalisation of MBA, since the proponents of MBA had shown no interest in the legalisation of other kinds of drugs. He personally regarded this criticism as misplaced, but his government naturally took public opinion into account both because, as a democratic government, it was morally obliged to do so, and because as an electorally vulnerable government, it was prudent to do so.

On 2 August, he was asked in the Senate by Senator Greenleaf whether it was true that his decision to refuse importation had also been influenced by fears that the granting of permission would give Goldenyears a competitive advantage over Qualitycare, a chain currently under Commonwealth control. He stated:

> In contrast to the Honourable Senator and the government in which he once served, I am always mindful of the need to ensure that Commonwealth enterprises are run as profitably as possible. I would certainly not act in a manner detrimental to this fine enterprise. But I can assure the Honourable Senator that our advice was that, even if we granted Kelly's request, it would have made little difference to Qualitycare's commercial viability. So if my decision was influenced by this consideration, the degree of influence was minimal and certainly no greater than fiscal responsibility would dictate.

A certificate of the Attorney-General precludes AAT review. A freedom of information request yielded evidence of the role of the work-experience student. The Attorney-General's personal assistant is a person of utmost integrity and is willing to give evidence that the Attorney-General only glanced at the letter.

Advise Kelly whether the Attorney-General's decision to refuse permission to import a quantity of MBA-LTU is invalid.

Time allowed: 45 mins

Answer Plan

This question gives rise to these issues:

(i)   Has the Attorney-General failed to take account of relevant considerations?

(ii) Did the Attorney-General take account of irrelevant considerations?

(iii) Unauthorised purpose.

(iv) Unreasonableness.

 # Answer

In my opinion, an application for judicial review of the Attorney-General's decision would succeed.

(i)   Has the Attorney-General failed to take account of relevant considerations?

A consideration is a relevant consideration if it is one which the decision-maker is obliged to take into account. The factors which a decision-maker is bound to take into account are determined by construction of the statute which confers the decision-making power. Matters to be taken into account include both those which the statute expressly requires be taken into account and matters to be determined 'by implication from the subject matter, scope and purpose of the Act': *Minister for Aboriginal Affairs v Peko-Wallsend* (1986) 162 CLR 24 at 39 per Mason J.

A decision-maker is obliged to take material into consideration so long as the material is actually or constructively before the decision-maker: *Peko-Wallsend*. Taking a matter into consideration requires 'proper, genuine and realistic consideration of the merits of the case': *Khan v Minister for Immigration and Ethnic Affairs* (unreported, FC, Gummow J, 11 December 1987, noted (1987) 14 ALD 291).

Here, subregs (2AA) and (2A) make it clear that the Attorney-General is to take account of a number of specified considerations. He appears not to have done so.

Kelly's letter of 15 July raised a number of relevant arguments to support its contention that permission should be granted. These included the purpose of the research (subreg (2AA)(a)) and Kelly's fitness to conduct it: subreg (2AA)(b), (c). These matters also bore on whether Kelly would be likely to be able to meet such conditions as the

Attorney-General might place on a permit to import, as did the safeguards proposed by the university: subreg (2A). The Attorney-General was therefore required to consider those issues before granting or refusing to grant permission. While there might be circumstances in which a repository of a power could be said to have given consideration if a subordinate has given the matter proper consideration, this is not one of them. The *Carltona* doctrine does not assist the Attorney-General. There are strong arguments to the effect that here the decision-maker may not act through an agent: the fact that the regulations provide for a form of delegation (reg 4A(2A)); the fact that no administrative inconvenience would be occasioned by limiting decision-makers to the Minister and delegates (cf *O'Reilly*); and the fact that the decision is one of some importance. Further, even if the decision-maker were permitted to act through an agent, this does not mean that the decision-maker can act through *any* agent; the legislation cannot be taken as evidencing an intention that the power to grant permission should effectively be informally exercised by a temporary, junior, non-employee. While the arguments against allowing the Minister to act through a subordinate are not as strong as those in *Peko-Wallsend*, they are nonetheless considerable. (It is therefore not necessary to consider whether the work-experience student took account of all relevant matters.)

Nor can it be said that the Attorney-General gave 'proper, genuine and realistic' consideration to the matters set out in the letter. 'Glancing' at a letter is not enough. Fortunately, in this case, there is evidence to prove both the role of the student and the cursory nature of the consideration. In addition to this evidence, the cursory nature of the reasons for refusal would constitute evidence suggesting failure to consider relevant matters. The reasons in the letter make no reference to the purposes of importation. They barely address the centre's reputation. They do not indicate why the proposed security arrangements are defective.

Failure to take account of a relevant consideration is not necessarily fatal to an administrative decision. If the Attorney-General's decision would have been the same, even if he had considered the relevant matters, his failure to do so would not be fatal to the validity of his decision: *Peko-Wallsend*. In this case, however, it cannot be said that the failure to consider the relevant matters was immaterial to the decision. It is clear that some of the matters raised by Kelly were matters which, if properly considered, might have made a difference to the permission decision. The failure to consider those matters was therefore material.

In my opinion, there can be little doubt that the Attorney-General has erred by virtue of having failed to take account of relevant considerations. He could and would be ordered to reconsider the matter.

(ii)   Did the Attorney-General take account of irrelevant considerations?

Irrelevant considerations are considerations which the decision-maker is bound *not* to take into account. Whether a consideration is an irrelevant consideration requires attention to the language and to the scope, subject matter and purpose of the legislation. Here there is no express reference to matters which may not be taken into account. Whether matters are irrelevant considerations often depends on implications to be drawn from the legislation. The impaired ethics of Kelly University's Deputy Vice-Chancellor and their treatment by the council are clearly not irrelevant considerations. Indeed, in my opinion, they are clearly relevant considerations. It could, however, be argued that two irrelevant considerations were taken into account: the political implications of granting permission to import; and the Commonwealth's economic interests. The former consideration is clearly not a 'relevant' consideration in the sense that it *must* be taken into account, but it is not clear whether it is a consideration which may not be taken into account. In my opinion, there are arguments which can be made both ways. In favour of the proposition that political considerations can be taken into account is the fact that it is a decision which the Attorney-General is empowered to make. The fact that the repository of power is a senior member of the government can be taken as suggesting a relatively unfettered discretion: *Peko-Wallsend*. Moreover, the regulations themselves are predicated on the assumption that an important rationale for the prohibitions in the regulations is their propensity to arouse strong, emotional responses from members of the public. It does not seem inconsistent with the spirit of the regulations for the Attorney-General to take account of those feelings.

There are, however, contrary arguments. While the Attorney-General is empowered to make the decision in question, there is also provision for a form of delegation. This envisages that the decision may sometimes be made by people who are not senior politicians, and this in turn could suggest that the regulations are predicated on the assumption that political considerations are not to be taken into account. Second, subreg (2AA) suggests that decisions are — to a considerable degree — to be based on the merits of the request, and that decisions should be 'technical' rather than 'political'. These last two arguments are not conclusive, but in my opinion, they suggest that political considerations *may* be irrelevant considerations.

A stronger case can be made for arguing that the interests of competing, government-controlled institutions are irrelevant considerations. They have nothing to do with the achievement of the purposes of the regulations and there is almost nothing in the scheme of the regulations to suggest that they may be taken into account.

It appears that Qualitycare's interest was small, but material, in the sense that, had it not been taken into account, the decision might have been different. The Attorney-General's statement to parliament does not rule out the possibility that Qualitycare's interests influenced his decision. It certainly does not amount to a claim that his decision would have been the same even if Qualitycare's interests had not been taken into account.

(iii) Unauthorised purpose

It is not necessary to consider whether the Attorney-General has acted for an unauthorised purpose, since it is hard to see how he could have acted for an unauthorised purpose without thereby taking an irrelevant consideration into account. (The converse does not necessarily apply.) For the sake of completeness, however, I shall consider whether the ground could be made out. Powers conferred for one purpose may not be exercised to achieve an ulterior purpose: *Thompson v Randwick Municipal Council* (1950) 81 CLR 87. An assessment of the purpose for which powers are conferred requires construction of the relevant legislation: *Padfield v Minister for Agriculture* [1968] AC 997; *R v Toohey (Aboriginal Land Commissioner); Ex parte Northern Land Council* (1981) 151 CLR 170. In this case, it is arguable that the Attorney-General acted for an unauthorised purpose in so far as he based his decision on its contribution to the Commonwealth's economic interests.

Here the purposes of the regulation are not specified. They must be inferred from the scope and subject matter of the regulations. In my opinion, the purpose of the regulations is both to prohibit the importation of objectionable goods, and to allow for the exceptional case where importation might be in the public interest. The regulations do not appear to be designed to enable the government to play favourites among enterprises engaged in service delivery. If the decision had been made for the purpose of protecting Qualitycare, it seems to me that it was for an unauthorised purpose. This would clearly be the case if Qualitycare were a private body owned, say, by relatives of the decision-maker. It is not so clearly the case when Qualitycare is a government responsibility but, even then, it is strongly arguable that it is not a purpose of the regulations to protect the economic interests of other agencies of government. The Minister's motives may not have been base, but that does not matter; neither were those of the councillors who made the decision which was struck down in *Thompson's* case.

The fact that a decision has been made for an unauthorised purpose is not necessarily fatal to the validity of the decision. The unauthorised purpose must have been a 'substantial' reason for the decision. A purpose can be a 'substantial' one so long as the decision in question would not have been made but for the purpose in question: *Thompson v Randwick Municipal Council*. This test appears to be more rigorous than the test for the materiality of relevant and irrelevant considerations, which seems counter-intuitive. It should be noted that in

Thompson it was not necessary to consider whether a decision could be quashed if the improper purpose *might* have been responsible for its having been made.

If a decision is flawed by virtue of unauthorised purpose only if it *would not* have been made but for the unauthorised purpose, it is arguable that the decision here is not flawed, since one cannot be sure whether the interests of Qualitycare were pivotal. If the materiality test were the same as that which applied in relation to relevant and irrelevant considerations, it follows from my earlier analysis that I think it would probably be satisfied.

In my opinion, the unauthorised purpose ground has been made out.

(iv) Unreasonableness

A decision can be struck down on the grounds of unreasonableness if it is so unreasonable that no reasonable decision-maker acting according to law could have made it: *Associated Provincial Picture Houses Ltd v Wednesbury Corporation* [1948] 1 KB 223. There are aspects of this case which suggest that the decision was unreasonable. The Minister's cavalier attitude to the purpose of the importation seems unreasonable. In a sense, too, the Minister acted unreasonably in assuming that the way to protect a Commonwealth enterprise from competition from another enterprise was to reduce the latter's capacity to offer attractive services, rather than increasing the capacity of the Commonwealth enterprise to do so. However, to establish unreasonableness requires more than a sense that the logic underlying the decision was flawed. If the Attorney-General's decision had otherwise been lawful, I do not think that, given what we are told about the corruption which seems still to characterise Kelly University, the Attorney-General's decision was so unreasonable that no reasonable decision-maker acting according to law could have reached it. The problem here is not that the Attorney-General was unreasonable, but that he did not act according to law.

Examiner's Comments

This answer correctly identifies the legal issues raised by the problem and handles them well. Relevant authorities are referred to and applied. The analysis of irrelevant considerations recognises the need to determine these by reference to the relevant legislation. (This is relatively easy in relation to the regulations, given subreg (2AA).) It also recognises that it is not always necessary for the nominal decision-maker to be the person who does the considering. Having done so, it argues persuasively that material submitted in support of permission applications should be considered by the decision-maker personally, and certainly not a work-experience student. It recognises that *Peko-Wallsend* did not involve the question of whether 'consideration' could ever be 'delegated', but rather the circumstances in which the repository of a power could delegate the consideration of all or some relevant issues to someone else.

The discussion of irrelevant considerations is not supported by authority, although it follows logically from *Peko-Wallsend*, and constitutes a correct statement of the law. In relation to the issue of whether a decision-maker may take account of political considerations, I think that the answer correctly identifies the arguments for and against. Given these arguments, it would be open to students to reach a variety of conclusions in relation to the question of whether the political considerations were 'irrelevant'. The only conclusion which would not be warranted would be a dogmatic conclusion one way or the other.

A student who concluded that Qualitycare's interests were an irrelevant consideration might well conclude that there was no point in discussing whether seeking to advance those interests could also constitute an unauthorised purpose. Different examiners could fairly differ in relation to whether students should address the unauthorised purpose issue. My view is that students should err on the side of caution and at least mention that this issue could arise. The answer we are given here does more than this; it states the law, applies it, and provides authority. In discussing when an improper purpose is enough to invalidate a decision taken for a variety of purposes, the answer only partly addresses the variety of ways in which the relevant test has been formulated. However, it does discuss the test as expressed in *Thompson* and also recognises that this test should be understood in terms of the context in which it was formulated. Given that the validity of the Attorney-General's decision did not turn on whether it could be said to have been made for an unauthorised purpose, I do not think it is seriously flawed by its failure to discuss the full range of possible materiality tests and their implications — especially given that there appear to be no cases which have actually turned on this issue.

The analysis of unreasonableness again states the relevant law, and provides authority. Its application is, I think, correct.

Common Errors to Avoid

- Failure to relate assessments of relevance to the regulations.
- The assumption that any consideration which is not a 'relevant' consideration is an 'irrelevant consideration'.
- Failure to recognise the rigorous demands of the *Wednesbury* unreasonableness test.

QUESTION 13

The ancient religion of Gha is practised in the San Sycotico valley of California. Gha emphasises humanity's essentially triadic nature. According to Gha, the universe is governed by a committee of three super-gods. Gho is an amiable, drug-using hedonist, and is hermaphroditic. Ghu is a rational, self-denying entity whose self-denial is reflected in a desire to deny others the pleasures it denies itself. Ghi, the god of volcanoes, nuclear wars, plague and famine, acts arbitrarily and with cruelty. It is definitely not a good idea to pass into the spiritual world when Ghi is the god on duty, and many of the teachings of Gha are oriented towards choosing auspicious days for one's death. The practitioners of Gha make money (which is what Ghi urges them to do) by selling exquisitely carved statues of the super-gods engaged in their preferred pursuits.

Wycliffe is a pastor in the Church of the Free Spirit in Camberwell, a Melbourne suburb. While visiting California, he buys three Gha carvings. One shows Ghu creating the accounts of the universe. A second shows Gho, lips around a hookah, while simultaneously being engaged in a variety of other apparently pleasurable activities. Ghi is shown eating a baby (which appears to be dead). On his arrival at Tullamarine, the carvings are seized by Customs. Wycliffe applies to the Attorney-General for permission to import them, saying that they would be kept in a private museum which he has set up in a crypt under his house. He wants the statues for private devotional purposes. A person authorised by the Attorney-General (the 'authorised person') advises that permission should be refused. Prior to the decision being communicated to Wycliffe, the Attorney-General issues a certificate precluding AAT review. Wycliffe seeks reasons. The authorised person's reasons for refusing importation are as follows:

1. I accept that Wycliffe wishes to import the carvings for devotional purposes. I do not think, however, that devotion to cocaine smoking, fornication, cannibalism and child abuse is the kind of devotion which the Attorney-General's department should be facilitating.

2. Wycliffe does not appear to engage in artistic, educational, cultural or scientific activities of a nature to which the goods relate. As far as I can judge, the only relevant activities in which Wycliffe engages are of a purely superstitious nature.

3. To judge from the inquiries I have made from his neighbours, Wycliffe is a harmless enough character, albeit one who would be the better for a bit more Ghu and a bit less Gho. However, it is a well-known fact that exposure to carvings of the kind that he seeks to import could change all that. If I were otherwise inclined to grant permission to import, this would cause me some concern.

4. If the statue of Ghu is a prohibited import (which I doubt), I
    consider that Wycliffe should not only be allowed to import it,
    but to do so unconditionally. I would hate to see the other statues
    destroyed. They are disgusting, but in their way they are also
    exquisite. I think we should keep them in the large display
    cabinet in the erotica room in the George Knowles building.

Reasons are furnished on 24 December. On 25 January of the following
year, Wycliffe's solicitor seeks your advice in relation to whether the
decision could be overturned, and if so, how. She says that her
instructions are that 'everyone knows that you don't smoke cocaine'.
Gho is probably smoking either marijuana or opium. By 'devotion',
Wycliffe had meant admiration of the craftsman's skills. If the baby was
dead, how could Ghi's activities be called child abuse? Wycliffe was
planning to write a book on the art of cruelty, but he was worried that if
the authorised person knew this, she would urge the confiscation of
some of the other works he kept in the crypt. As to why he did not seek
advice earlier, he had said: 'Christmas is my time off.'

Now answer the following questions:

(i)   Would the AAT, the Federal Court, or the Federal Magistrates
      Court be likely to hear the application?

(ii) Have any errors of law been made in the decision to refuse
      importation?

(iii) Aside from judicial review, are there possible alternative courses
      of action by which Wycliffe may press his claim to be allowed to
      import the statues?

Time allowed: 45 mins

Answer Plan

Wycliffe is attacking decisions in relation to the Ghi and Gho carvings.
It is not necessary to discuss the Ghu carving. The answer addresses the
following issues:

(i)   Avenues of review.

(ii) Possible errors of law.

 • 'Smoking cocaine' was not a reviewable error.

 • Misunderstanding of 'devotion' was not a material error.

 • Child abuse.

 • Artistic reasons.

 • Well-known fact.

(iii) Alternative courses of action.

The answer will address each of these issues, with a view to
determining whether they constitute grounds for review.

Answer

(i) Avenues of review

The decision cannot be reviewed in the AAT, since a certificate has been issued precluding this. We have no information to suggest that the certificate is defective. We must therefore assume that it would achieve its intended effect.

An application could be made for judicial review, either under the Judiciary Act 1903 (Cth) or under the Administrative Decisions (Judicial Review) Act 1977 (Cth) (ADJR Act). Since more than 28 days have elapsed since the giving of reasons, the time has passed for the making of an application under the ADJR Act as of right: ADJR Act s 11. Wycliffe would therefore need an extension of time if he wished to proceed under the ADJR Act. He has not given a particularly good reason for his delay but, in my opinion, he would be granted the extension he seeks. First, the delay has only been for three days. Second, and because of this, it is hard to see how the Commonwealth's capacity to present an effective defence to the claim could in any way have been impaired by the delay. Counting against the granting of an extension of time is the fact that his case is one which, on its face, is not particularly strong, but if a court were to share that opinion, there would be little to be gained by being granted an extension. I think that an extension would almost certainly be granted.

There are no time limits for bringing an action under the Judiciary Act, although failure to make a timely application might constitute grounds for the discretionary denial of relief. In this case, there would be no question of relief being refused if Wycliffe were to make out his claim. However, while proceeding under the Judiciary Act would be non-problematic, it would be preferable to proceed under the ADJR Act, notwithstanding the need to apply for an extension of time. The reason is that an application for review on the 'no evidence' ground appears to be more easily made out when made under the special provisions of the ADJR Act (s 5(1)(h), (3)) than when made under the general law.

(ii) Possible errors of law

'Smoking cocaine' was not a reviewable error

It is not clear that a court could take judicial notice of the fact that cocaine is not smoked. Expert evidence to this effect might be needed, but it would, in my opinion, be to no avail. The decision would be bad if it was 'irrational, illogical and not based upon findings or inferences of fact supported by logical grounds': *Re Minister for Immigration and Multicultural Affairs; Ex parte Applicant S20/2002 (2003) 198 ALR 59* at [34] per McHugh and Gummow JJ. The finding that Gho was smoking cocaine is arguably not supported by logical grounds, both because there is no basis for knowing what drug the god was supposedly smoking, and because it is almost certain Gho would not be smoking cocaine. But *S20* requires that the decision be 'based on' the finding. This is unlikely. If the decision-maker believed that cocaine, when smoked, was a particularly dangerous drug, and that Gho was smoking cocaine, such an argument might be tenable, but a more plausible interpretation is that the language is careless and intended simply to state that the decision-maker regarded it as relevant that Gho appeared to be smoking an illicit drug.

Under the ADJR Act s 5(1)(h) and (3)(b), a decision is reviewable if it was based on the existence of a particular fact, and the fact did not exist: *Minister for Immigration and Multicultural Affairs v Rajamanikkam* (2002) 210 CLR 222. But an applicant can succeed on this ground only if the fact which did not exist was 'critical' to the decision in the sense that it be possible to say 'on a proper analysis of the decision, the reasons for decision or the decision-making process that, had [the] particular finding not been made, the decision in question would not have been reached': *Rajamanikam* [58], McHugh and Gaudron JJ. This casts a heavy burden on the applicant and one which, in my opinion, Wycliffe would be unable to discharge.

Misunderstanding of 'devotion' was not a material error

While the authorised person has misunderstood what Wycliffe meant by 'devotion', this is not necessarily a ground for review. The meaning of everyday language is not a question of law, but a question of fact: see, for instance, *Collector of Customs v Agfa Gevaert Limited* (1996) 186 CLR 389. On review, a court is therefore concerned, not with whether the interpretation was correct, but whether it was open to the 'interpreter'. In my opinion, the interpretation the authorised person placed on Wycliffe's language was an interpretation which was open to her. Indeed, it was probably the most reasonable interpretation. Thus, even if she misunderstood Wycliffe, she has not erred in law. Nor could her error ground review on the grounds of unreasonableness. It is clearly not unreasonable in the narrow *Wednesbury* sense.

Nor, I think, could Wycliffe argue that the decision fell foul of s 5(1)(h) coupled with s 5(3)(b). First, Wycliffe would have to establish that the authorised person erred in concluding that Wycliffe was using 'devotion' in its popular sense. Second, Wycliffe would have to demonstrate that the error was critical. Third, there are passages in three of the five judgments in *Rajamanikam* which suggest that the no evidence ground is not made out if there is evidence which warrants the decision-maker's (erroneous) finding of fact. If so, the decision-maker has not erred, since there was clearly evidence to support her finding, notwithstanding that her finding was incorrect.

Obviously, if the matter were to be reconsidered, Wycliffe could make his interpretation more explicit. If so, his chances of receiving a favourable outcome would be enhanced. The authorised person clearly shares his assessment of the aesthetic merits of the statues (see Question 13, point 4).

Child abuse

There is little merit to the argument that the decision was flawed on the ground that the baby was dead, which meant that Ghi's activities could not be called child abuse. Even assuming the baby to be dead, it would be open to the authorised person to make the inference that it has recently been killed, and quite possibly by Ghi. The inference of abuse is therefore warranted. In any case, it was open to the authorised person to make a finding that the statue portrayed the eating of a living baby. The finding does not seem to involve a finding of fact, but the formation of an opinion. It could therefore not be classed as a fact which did not exist and could not ground review under s 5(1)(h), (3)(b). Even if the finding were not warranted, it would be unlikely to constitute material error, whether at common law or for the purposes of the ADJR Act. Developing the 'child abuse' argument would, in my opinion, alienate the court unnecessarily and possibly even counter-productively. If this were the only argument on which Wycliffe could succeed, his case would, I think, be doomed.

Artistic reasons

The authorised person failed to take account of Wycliffe's artistic and cultural reasons for wanting to import the statues, but she cannot be said to have thereby erred. The requirement that one take account of a relevant consideration arises only when the decision-maker is actually or constructively aware of the possible existence of that consideration. She took account of Wycliffe's apparent reasons for wanting to import the statues. She was not required to read his mind as well. In the absence of anything to suggest that Wycliffe intended to use the material for a book, the decision-maker was not obliged to take this consideration into account. Obviously, if the matter were to be reconsidered, Wycliffe could draw the authorised person's attention to his real reasons, in which case the authorised person would be required to take his submissions into account. The authorised person would not, however, necessarily be required to believe Wycliffe. Nor does taking a consideration into account necessarily mean a favourable outcome.

Well-known fact

The corruptive effect of the portrayal of evil is not 'well known'. It is asserted, and it underlies calls for censorship, but a rejection of this assertion underlies arguments against censorship, and — given that these have generally prevailed — we must treat the 'well-known fact' claim with scepticism. It is not a 'fact' of which courts could or would take judicial notice.

This, however, is not necessarily fatal to the validity of her decision. First, in order to satisfy the requirements of s 5(1)(h) and (3)(b), Wycliffe would have to show that the alleged 'corruptive effect' was indeed a fact which did not exist. For methodological reasons, this would be difficult, even assuming that there was in fact no such effect.

Second, he would have to show that this conclusion was critical in the sense that the adverse decision could or would not have been made without it. If the arguments set out in Question 13, point 1 of the authorised person's reasons were sufficient conditions for the decision, errors in Question 13, point 3 would not be fatal to the decision. The authorised person's statement suggests that she did not 'base' her decision on this matter in the sense required by *Rajamanikkam*.

An alternative argument which Wycliffe might rely on proceeds from Burchett J's decision in *Fuduche v Minister for Immigration, Local Government and Ethnic Affairs* (1993) 45 FCR 515. In that case, in deciding whether the applicant was a 'special needs relative' the delegate made assumptions about the origins of her depression. In making such a decision (which, his Honour considered, required medical qualifications), the delegate was found to have acted irrationally and therefore unreasonably. Here, the authorised person might be treated as having made a decision which required psychological expertise which she may not have possessed. (We do not know this.) I do not regard this as a strong argument. It is possible to distinguish *Fuduche* on the grounds that there were other aspects of that case which meant that the decision was unreasonable. Moreover, the impugned finding in *Fuduche* was central to the delegate's finding. Here, the authorised person's reasons suggest that it simply reinforced her in her decision.

I therefore doubt that Wycliffe would be successful if he were to seek judicial review of the decision refusing his application for permission to import the two statues.

(iii)) *Alternative courses of action*

There are, I think, two courses of action open to Wycliffe. One would be to use the machinery provided by the Customs Act 1901 (Cth) for challenging seizure of the statues as prohibited imports. It is at least arguable that they do not fall within subreg (1A). The other would be to ask the authorised person to reconsider her decision, drawing her attention to the matters which should have been drawn to her notice earlier. Strictly speaking, she would neither be obliged nor empowered to reconsider the matter, given that she does not appear to have exceeded or failed to exercise her powers. However, the regulations do not expressly rule out a second application and, in any case, she might prove receptive if she thought the new material was relevant. It is possible that a challenge to the Customs' decision could be settled on the basis of a limited permission to import.

 # Examiner's Comments

This is a difficult question which requires an understanding of the circumstances in which decisions can be reached on the grounds that they are based on erroneous factual assumptions. This requires recognition of both the common law rules and the more liberal statutory provisions which apply where decisions are reviewable under the ADJR Act. These provisions have been the subject of the High Court's frustratingly inconclusive decision in *Minister for Immigration and Multicultural Affairs v Rajamanikkam*.

This answer handles these issues reasonably well. It recognises that Wycliffe is out of time and must seek an extension of time if he is to make an ADJR Act application. It recognises that such an application would almost certainly be successful, but it also recognises the significance of being able to proceed under the ADJR Act rather than the Judiciary Act.

Its handling of the 'fact' issues is reasonably good. Its handling of the common law basis for review on the basis of errors of fact/inadequate evidence is a little superficial in that it does not discuss the variety of tests which have been applied in this context in England and Australia. However, since I doubt that the answer turns on which of these tests applies, I do not regard this as a serious error. The use of the *Agfa-Gevaert* case as authority for the proposition that the error was one of fact rather than law assumes that a distinction drawn for one purpose may be applied in a somewhat different context, and *S20/2002* contains warnings against this assumption. Nonetheless, I do not think that the answer has thereby fallen into error.

Otherwise, the handling of the 'factual error' issues was good. The examinee appears to have a good understanding of *Minister for Immigration and Multicultural Affairs v Rajamanikkam*. (It is wisely cautious as to what the case actually decided.) The handling of *Fuduche* demonstrates awareness of the need to recognise that superficially relevant cases may not be conclusive.

The answer also makes reference to the Customs Act and to the possibility of negotiating with the primary decision-maker. Students would not be expected to consider the former possibility, since there is nothing in the materials to indicate that there are in fact procedures for challenging the seizure of alleged prohibited imports. Nor is it necessary to consider the possibility of further negotiations. I do, however, consider that this answer is strengthened by reference to these matters.

 # Common Errors to Avoid

- Do not assume that administrators commit a legal error simply because they make erroneous findings of fact. They are obliged to act only on the basis of the evidence before them. They are also normally required to do no more than make findings of fact which are open to them on the basis of the evidence.

- The absence of evidence to support a decision-maker's finding of fact does not necessarily mean that the decision is legally flawed. Even under the ADJR Act (which almost certainly applies in this case), the absence of evidence for a particular fact is grounds for review only if the finding of the fact in question was a legal prerequisite to the making of the decision in question and was not reasonably open to the decision-maker, or if the applicant can show both that the fact did not exist and that the decision-maker based the decision on that finding of fact.

QUESTION 14

Following several cases in which different authorised persons made apparently inconsistent decisions in relation to applications for permission to import prohibited publications, the Attorney-General prepared a set of guidelines for them. The guidelines stated:

1. Final responsibility for decisions under subreg (2AA) (permission decisions) lies with the authorised person.

2. In exercising powers under the subregulation, authorised persons should consult the department's 'list of permissions'.

3. An authorised person should not normally make a permission decision which is inconsistent with a prior permission decision by the Attorney-General or an authorised person unless:

    (a) the prior decision was, in the opinion of the authorised person, contrary to law;

    (b) there are prior decisions which, in the opinion of the authorised person, are inconsistent with each other;

    (c) the prior decision was, in the Attorney-General's opinion, wrong; or

    (d) the authorised person consults with the Attorney-General before making a permission decision.

In litigation under the Customs Act 1901 (Cth), Lovely Ladies' Chatter was found to be a prohibited publication, but controversy surrounded the decision. There were several applications for permission to import the book for particular purposes. Some were granted and some were not.

One of the most recent applicants is your client, Dr Jeckyll. She is anxious to explore the degree to which reading the novel is accompanied by increased hostility to, and contempt for, women. She also wants to examine the degree to which those found to score high on her anti-F(emale) scale gain greater pleasure from reading the novel. Her proposal received the approval of the Hans Eysenck Clinic where she works with anti-social adolescents, and she has a large grant for the project. Her request for permission to import was rejected. In explaining his decision, the authorised person wrote:

I have considerable reservations about aspects of your research. In particular, I am profoundly uneasy about research which will apparently involve the book being read by large numbers of testosterone-charged students, in circumstances where you say you have grounds for anticipating that it will produce a statistically significant increase in anti-female sentiments. On the other hand, if this is indeed its effect, I can see why you should think that it is as well that we know this.

In making my decision I have been guided by several similar applications. In each case, permission was denied. Some of these cases were weaker than yours, but one was, if anything, even stronger. I have also spoken to the Attorney-General who has made his views only too apparent, and who has regularly issued certificates precluding AAT review of refusals of permission to import books like this.

I would add that, in my opinion, there is no reason why you should not conduct your eminently valuable research using similar, and equally objectionable, locally published books which freely circulate within Australia.

Dr Jeckyll wants to know whether she has any legal redress. She also says in the course of your conversation:

I've got another dispute over a similar issue. I want to import *Me and Ewe* in order to calibrate a Pruriometer. I told that authorised person that several of my colleagues had already been given permission to import the book, but the authorised person said that wasn't relevant. How come I lose both times?

What advice do you give Dr Jeckyll regarding (i) the validity of the decision to refuse permission for *Lovely Ladies' Chatter* to be imported, and (ii) the authorised person's stand in relation to the importation of *Me and Ewe*? Assume that the Attorney-General has issued a certificate precluding AAT review.

Time allowed: 25 mins

Answer Plan

This question involves four issues.

(i)   Are the guidelines illegal?

(ii) Inflexible application of policy.

(iii) Acting under dictation.

(iv) Did the other authorised person err?

 # Answer

In my opinion an application for judicial review would probably fail.

(i)   Are the guidelines illegal?

In so far as the guidelines are illegal, the authorised person has no power to apply them. Here, I do not think the guidelines are illegal, although I am by no means confident in this conclusion.

The guidelines correctly begin with an acknowledgement that final responsibility for decisions lies with the authorised person.

In suggesting in Question 14, point 2 that authorised persons *should* consult the list, it is, in my opinion, simply requiring authorised persons to observe sound administrative practice. Other things being equal, consistency is an element of good administration: *Re Drake and Minister for Immigration and Ethnic Affairs (No 2)* (1979) 2 ALD 634.

Point 3 comes close to imposing an impermissible fetter on the discretion of authorised persons. The term 'normally' means that the policy does not purport to fetter authorised persons' discretion completely. Moreover, the provision relating to 'illegal' precedents (3(a)) means that the policy does not purport to preclude the consideration of legally relevant considerations nor to mandate the consideration of legally irrelevant considerations. In this respect, it differs from the policy which was held illegal in *Green v Daniels* (1977) 51 ALJR 463. It limits the exercise of discretion, but not much more than the policy which was upheld and taken into account in *Drake (No 2)*. Point 3(b) simply states the obvious: where previous decisions are mutually inconsistent, they cannot all be followed. Point 3(d) is simply good practice. However, in so far as 'authorised persons' are delegates, point 3(c) seems inconsistent with Acts Interpretation Act s 34A which envisages that delegates are to act on the basis of their own beliefs rather than those of others.

But even if point 3(c) is unlawful, it is unlikely that this would be fatal to the validity of the decision. There is nothing to suggest that the decision might have been different if point 3(c) had not been present in the guidelines, although it is conceivable that its presence encouraged the authorised person to treat the presumption in favour of consistency as stronger than he might otherwise have treated it.

(ii) Inflexible application of policy

The repository of a discretionary power may take account of government policy, but must consider the unique circumstances which arise in each case, and be prepared to depart from policy if the circumstances of a case warrant this: *Drake (No 2)* at 640–1.

Whether the authorised person applied the policy inflexibly is not altogether clear from the facts as presented. This is not a case where the authorised person opted for a decision which he regarded as wrong (but mandated by the policy), in preference to one which he regarded as right. Rather, it is one where he took the policy into account. He addressed the merits of the application, and carefully considered whether Dr Jeckyll's application was caught by the policy. He took the matter sufficiently seriously to consult the Attorney-General (obviously anticipating that the case was one where it might be appropriate to depart from precedent). However, as far as I can see, he did not address the question of whether this was a case which warranted a departure from the policy. He does not seem to have considered whether the 'stronger' case was one in which permission should have been given (even if it did not have to be given). I think, therefore, that he may have applied the policy inflexibly. I could not, however, rule out the possibility that at trial he would say that he had in fact considered whether to depart from the policy, but had decided that the circumstances of Dr Jeckyll's case were not such as to outweigh the advantages of maintaining consistency across decisions.

(iii)   Acting under dictation

In general, the repository of a power is responsible for its exercise and must act independently of others, including hierarchical superiors: *R v Anderson; Ex parte Ipec-Air Pty Ltd* (1965) 113 CLR 177. The degree of independence expected of a decision-maker may, however, vary according to the degree to which the decision in question involves political as opposed to technical issues: *Ansett Transport* per Aickin J. If the authorised person made his decision because he felt obliged to give effect to the Attorney-General's wishes, his purported exercise of discretion would arguably have miscarried. While it might be argued that the authorised person's decision should be treated as a political decision, the structure of the regulations envisages decisions which involve judgments which have what one might call a 'technical' element. The decision seems to be less 'political' than the decisions which provoked the *Ipec* and *Ansett* cases.

However, these cases also make it clear that decision-makers may allow themselves to be influenced by arguments advanced by their hierarchical superiors. This is not a clear-cut case of acting under dictation. The authorised person had independently formed the view that the arguments for and against granting permission were evenly balanced, and then, having taken into account precedential cases, took the Attorney-General's views into account.

If he regarded the Attorney-General's views as conclusive, he could, I think, be said to have acted under dictation. If, however, he merely gave them considerable weight, this could not, I think, be said. Here, the authorised person is not performing a *highly* specialised technical role, but rather one which the Attorney-General himself is equally competent to perform. It also seems relevant that the authorised person's powers are powers which could also be exercised by the Attorney-General and powers which the Attorney-General could reserve to himself if he so chose. For these reasons, I think that such acting under dictation as has occurred here is considerably less unacceptable than that which took place (and was upheld) in *Ansett Transport (Operations) Pty Ltd v Commonwealth* (1977) 139 CLR 54.

(iv)   Did the other authorised person err?

I do not think the other authorised person erred in refusing to take into consideration other cases dealing with the importation of *Me and Ewe*. There is no express legislative requirement to do so. The duty could arise only if it fell within the category of '(e) any other relevant matters': subreg (2(AA)(e). This provision means that categories (a)–(d) are not exhaustive, but it is to be read in the light of authority to the effect that relevance is nonetheless to be inferred from the 'nature, scope and purpose of the power': *Peko-Wallsend* at 38. It is not clear how guidelines made outside the legislation can constitute or give rise to considerations which the decision-maker is *bound* to take into account. While consistency may be consistent with good government, and while it might be desirable that decisions reflect a commitment to good government, there is High Court authority to the effect that the content of previous administrative decisions does not constrain administrators from making different decisions in subsequent cases: *Attorney-General (NSW) v Quin* (1990) 170 CLR 1. At most, departure from a policy or practice may affect the content of the duty to afford procedural fairness.

Not does it follow from the existence of two apparently inconsistent decisions that one must be flawed. Inconsistency is inherent in the existence of discretion. Moreover, even if inconsistency did imply that one decision must be flawed, it would not follow that it would be the latter decision which was flawed.

Examiner's Comments

This answer correctly identifies the issues raised by the question, and handles them well. It recognises the need to distinguish between the legality of guidelines, and the question of whether they have been applied improperly. Answers may vary according to the way in which the facts are interpreted, and students would be marked not on the basis of a 'correct' interpretation of the facts, but on whether their answer reflected an interpretation which was reasonably open to them. One of the strengths of this answer is that it recognises the uncertainty surrounding the 'facts'. Both in exams and practice, this is wise. 'The facts' of a case can be elusive and ambiguous.

The answer cites relevant authority to justify its claims in relation to the relevant law, and while it does not develop the law at length, time considerations preclude doing this. Its analysis is generally persuasive. Its discussion of whether the guidelines and their implications could constitute considerations which the decision-maker was bound to take into account seems correct, although it might be noted that there is one case which could be cited to support a contrary argument: *BHP Direct Reduced Iron Pty Ltd v Chief Executive Officer, Australian Customs Service* (1998) 55 ALD 665 (Carr J). However, this decision is difficult to reconcile with the cases cited in the answer, and indeed with the High Court's decision in *MIEA v Teoh* (1995) 183 CLR 273 in which the High Court had expressly rejected the ruling by Lee and Carr JJ to the effect that commitments assumed in international conventions would be relevant considerations.

 ## Common Errors to Avoid

- Assuming that the rule against the inflexible application of policy means that administrators may not attach considerable weight to policy.

- Assuming that rules against acting under dictation mean that decision-makers may not take account of the views of others (and of their hierarchical superiors in particular).
- Failing to recognise the degree to which the weight to be accorded to policy and to others' perspectives will vary according to the relevant decision-making context.

Chapter 5

The Right to Procedural Fairness

Key Issues

People directly affected by administrative decisions normally have a right to 'procedural fairness'. Procedural fairness normally entails a right to make submissions to the decision-maker in relation to one's case. It also normally entails a right to have one's submissions dealt with by a decision-maker who is — and appears to be — unbiased. There are, however, some cases where people affected by administrative decisions are not entitled to procedural fairness. There are also borderline cases where there is an entitlement to procedural fairness, but where the duty to afford procedural fairness can be satisfied by a relatively cursory hearing, conducted by a decision-maker who may not be altogether dispassionate. At the other extreme are cases where the right to procedural fairness is satisfied only by something close to a formal judicial hearing.

The right to procedural fairness arises from common law, but legislation may create additional procedural rights, and may also limit or even abolish rights to procedural fairness in particular contexts.

Traditionally, a person had a right to procedural fairness in cases where the relevant decision was one which could adversely affect their rights. Thus, a local authority with a discretionary power to order the demolition of houses built without adequate permits was required to consult the owner before demolishing the house. The conditioning of the right to procedural fairness on 'rights' which might be affected by a decision limited the range of circumstances in which people affected by administrative decisions could rely on a right to procedural fairness. It meant, for instance, that people were not entitled to procedural fairness in relation to decisions about whether they should be appointed to particular positions. People who lacked the right to stay in Australia could be deported without being given a chance to show cause why they should not be deported: see, for example, *Salemi v McKellar (No 2)* (1977) 137 CLR 396.

Over the past 30 years, Australian courts have broadened the circumstances in which people affected by administrative decisions have a right to procedural fairness. By 1985, Mason J concluded that 'there is a common law duty to act fairly, in the sense of according procedural fairness, in the making of administrative decisions which affect rights, interests and legitimate expectations, subject only to the clear manifestation of a contrary intention': *Kioa v West* (1985) 159 CLR 550 at 584. Rights continued to attract a right to procedural fairness, but the right was also attracted by 'interests' and 'legitimate expectations'. The fact that interests were protected meant that people affected by discretionary decisions had a right to procedural fairness when decisions were being made which bore on those interests. It meant that most administrative decisions now had to be made according to the procedural fairness requirements. Some ambiguity surrounded the term 'interest'. Originally, Mason J understood the term to apply to interests, such as those 'relating to personal liberty, status, preservation of livelihood and reputation': *Kioa v West* (1985) 159 CLR 550, 582. The term has subsequently been given a far more generous interpretation, and encompasses interests which Mason J appears not to have regarded as legal interests. These included the 'interest' of a licensee in having its licence renewed (which, in the circumstances, had been treated as being a 'legitimate expectation' in *FAI*).

There are, however, circumstances where an interest in a particular decision being reached will not suffice to attract a right to procedural fairness. Typically, these 'interests' are indirect interests. An interest shared by numerous others does not normally ground a right to procedural fairness. Miserly taxpayers do not have a right to be heard in relation to the granting of welfare benefits to needy applicants. Environmentalists do not have a common law right to be consulted each time a municipality considers an application for a permit to prune a tree. Nor does a decision normally attract a right to procedural fairness if it is merely a step in a process which may ultimately lead to a 'legal and operative decision'. Thus, in *Ryan v ASIC* [2007] FCA 59 at [67], the Federal Court found that there was no duty to afford procedural fairness prior to the exercise of an investigative power where the exercise was anterior to any ultimate effect its results might have on the applicant.

The phrase 'legitimate expectations' reflects awareness of circumstances where a person may not possess a relevant right or interest, but where it would nonetheless be unfair for the person to be dealt with without being given the chance to make submissions to a disinterested decision-maker. For example, in *FAI Insurances Ltd v Winneke* (1981) 151 CLR 342, the High Court considered that the insurer's interest in the renewal of its licence to offer insurance was not of itself sufficient to ground a right to procedural fairness, but that its reasonable expectation that the licence would be renewed could nonetheless ground the right. Initially, the phrase was used to describe both substantive and procedural expectations. Where people have a legitimate expectation of a particular outcome, their right to procedural fairness can now typically be treated as flowing from the fact that their *interests* may be affected by a decision. It is therefore unnecessary (and, indeed, sometimes misleading) to ask whether they have a legitimate expectation of the outcome in question. There is also something potentially tautologous about stating that people who otherwise do not have a right to procedural fairness will enjoy that right if they have a legitimate expectation that they will be afforded procedural fairness. However, there are cases where expectations of procedural fairness may ground rights to procedural fairness which would otherwise not exist. The most obvious instance includes cases where a person with an interest insufficient to ground a right to procedural fairness is assured or led to believe that they will nonetheless be afforded a hearing.

Where government practices, policies and proclamations imply that the decisions in question will be made by 'fair' procedures, governments may be held to more rigorous decision-making standards than would otherwise apply. Where governments state that 'political' decisions will nevertheless be made by an open-minded decision-maker, they will be required to act accordingly, even if otherwise they would have been permitted to base the decision on preconceived ideas about what was best in the circumstances: *Century Metals and Mining NL v Yeomans* (1989) 40 FCR 564.

Some administrative decision-making has traditionally been treated as unconstrained by a duty to afford procedural fairness. First, the duty to afford procedural fairness is much more likely to arise where the decision in question relates to the interests of a single person or a small group of people. Where people are affected by a decision only because they are members of a large class of people, it will rarely be feasible to give all those who are affected a right to be heard by the decision-maker, and it may be undesirable to condition the validity of the decision upon every person affected having been given an adequate hearing. This conclusion can be reached in a number of ways. It may be reached by differentiating between 'administrative' decisions and 'legislative' decisions, the latter being defined by their generality. It may also be derived from conceptualisations of what fairness requires. (Fairness may not always require that people be given a hearing by an unbiased decision-maker.) It may also follow from the construction placed on the legislation which confers the relevant power. If affording a right to be heard would cause decision-making to grind to a halt, it can be assumed that the relevant power was conferred on the basis that it would not be subject to a duty to afford procedural fairness to all who might be affected by the exercise of the power: *Minister for the Arts, Heritage and Environment v Peko-Wallsend Ltd* (1987) 15 FCR 274.

Second, where the decision is one which turns on political judgments rather than on the facts of the particular case, a duty to afford procedural fairness is less readily implied. This may be the case even where the decision directly impinges on the interests of a particular person or group: *Minister for Arts, Heritage and Environment v*

Peko-Wallsend (1987) 15 FCR 274; *South Australia v O'Shea* (1989) 163 CLR 378.

There is an alternative approach to this, however. According to this perspective, all executive decision-making attracts the duty to afford procedural fairness in the absence of legislation to the contrary: see, for instance *Annetts v McCann* (1990) 170 CLR 596, where Mason CJ, Deane and McHugh JJ agreed with an earlier observation by Deane J to this effect, and *Re Minister for Immigration and Multicultural Affairs; Ex parte Lam* (2003) 214 CLR 1 where McHugh and Gummow JJ at [81] and Callinan J at [150] agreed with earlier observations of McHugh J to similar effect. This analysis focuses on the duties of the government as distinct from the rights of the citizen, and is therefore not necessarily inconsistent with the argument that certain people may not be owed a duty to afford procedural fairness. For one thing, the existence of a duty to afford procedural fairness does not necessarily mean that the duty is owed to everyone who might have even the barest of subjective interests in the decision. The High Court has never said that every racist must have an opportunity to make submissions in relation to every decision to grant an entry visa. Alternatively, the duty to act in a procedurally fair manner is a duty to act fairly, and fairness must involve fairness both to those directly affected and to the public at large. On this view, there seems to have been a subtle conceptual shift, from treating the existence of a right to procedural fairness as a threshold issue to be resolved before a determination of whether there has been denial of procedural fairness, to a process which involves asking whether the treatment of a person affected by a decision has been fair. Indeed, in *Kioa*, Mason J had observed at 585 that this was 'the critical question in most cases'. Substantively little turns on this, but conceptually, it seems more elegant to focus on what (if anything) procedural fairness requires in the particular case, than on whether there is a right to procedural fairness and, if so, on what it entails.

The duty to afford procedural fairness may also be qualified by statute. Legislation may create rights which otherwise would not exist. It may create procedures which differ from those which would be required under the common law rules. Since the right to procedural fairness is a common law right, legislation is presumed not to deprive people of the rights they would otherwise enjoy. This, however, is no more than a presumption. By use of unambiguous language, a statute might deprive people of a right to procedural fairness they would otherwise enjoy.

It is not always easy to know whether a statute has unambiguously eliminated or abridged a right to procedural fairness. See, for instance, *Re Minister for Immigration and Multicultural Affairs; Ex parte Miah* (2001) 206 CLR 57, where the High Court split 3:2 when considering the implications of the detailed provisions of the Migration Act 1958 (Cth) governing the procedure to be used for determining whether visas should be issued.

Before attempting the questions, check that you are familiar with the following issues:

✓ the basis for the duty to afford procedural fairness;

✓ the concept of 'legitimate expectation';

✓ the decision-makers to whom the duty to afford procedural fairness potentially applies;

✓ the circumstances where decisions do not attract a duty to afford procedural fairness; and

✓ the circumstances where statutory schemes oust what would otherwise be an entitlement to procedural fairness.

 QUESTION 15

'The concept of "legitimate expectations" is one which has served its purpose and now serves only to confuse.' Discuss.

Time allowed: 40 mins

Answer Plan

(i)   The old law: procedural fairness only where rights are involved.

(ii) The emergence of 'legitimate expectations' as a basis for the right to procedural fairness.

(iii) With interests grounding a right to fairness, what role is left for legitimate expectations?

(iv) Can legitimate expectations give rise to substantive rights?

 Answer

In this answer, I shall argue that the quotation is largely correct, in so far as it asserts that the concept has served its purpose. Resort to the language of legitimate expectations is no longer necessary to ground a right to procedural fairness in cases where important interests are at stake, and there is authority to suggest that it is of no relevance to the existence of a duty to afford procedural fairness. There are grounds for believing that the concept may bear on the content of the duty to afford procedural fairness in cases where the duty exists, but even in these cases, it is doubtful that the concept of 'reasonable expectations' adds anything over and above what is achieved by the requirement of fairness. Finally, I shall argue, this use of the concept carries with it the potential to confuse. For if legitimate expectations of procedural fairness can ground a right to procedural fairness, it might seem to follow that legitimate expectations of a substantive outcome can ground a right to that outcome. Yet Australian courts have not been willing to accept that this is the case.

(i)   The old law: procedural fairness only where rights are involved

Historically, the right to procedural fairness was treated as limited to cases where decisions had the potential to affect a person's rights. Thus, when a person had a legal interest falling short of a right, an administrator could defeat the interest without giving the person affected a chance to be heard. In several English cases, courts held that some kinds of licence could therefore be cancelled without the licensee being given a hearing: *Nakkuda Ali v M F de Jarayatne* [1951] AC 66; *R v Metropolitan Police Commissioner; Ex parte Parker* [1953] 1 WLR 1150. Australian courts were slightly more forgiving, and in *Banks v TRB* (1968) 119 CLR 222, the High Court held that a taxi driver's licence could be cancelled only if the licensee was given a hearing. But this decision was based on licences being treated as a form of property. (They could be, and were, transferred for consideration.) If the interests of a licensee could not ground an entitlement to procedural fairness, it followed that more remote interests could certainly not do so, and even in the late 1970s, the High Court held that the exercise of the power to make a deportation order was not conditioned upon the person affected being given a prior hearing: *Salemi v McKeller (No 2)* (1977) 137 CLR 396.

(ii)   The emergence of 'legitimate expectations' as a basis for the right to procedural fairness

The concept of 'legitimate expectations' was devised with a view to expanding the range of interests which could be said to attract a right to procedural fairness. It involved recognition of the fact that, even when an interest fell short of a right, it might be not dissimilar to a right in some important respects. In practice, much administrative decision-making is so routine that, even if the power in question is nominally a discretionary power, both administrators and those affected by their decisions correctly assume that if certain facts are established the decision will flow almost as a matter of course. In such circumstances, it would not normally be fair for an administrator to defeat those expectations without at least giving the person affected a chance to comment on a proposed departure from the norm.

In the course of the 1970s, courts in the United Kingdom and Australia came to adopt the terminology of 'expectations' with a view to expanding the circumstances in which people were entitled to procedural fairness: see *Heatley v Tasmanian Racing and Gaming Commission* (1977) 137 CLR 487. The process was not a smooth one. Barwick CJ objected that the phrase was a meaningless one (*Heatley* at 491; *Salemi v McKeller (No 2)* (1977) 137 CLR 396 at 404), and several other High Court justices — notably Brennan J (and CJ) and McHugh J

— objected to the implication that the duty to afford procedural fairness could depend on the actual expectations of the person affected by the decision in question: see, for example, *Kioa v West* (1985) 159 CLR 550 at 617–24 (Brennan J); *MIEA v Teoh* (1995) 183 CLR 273 at 310–12 (McHugh J). There was some merit to these objections, but if Barwick CJ found the phrase meaningless, other justices had no trouble giving it meaning (for example, Aickin J in *Heatley*). Moreover, while the language of expectations might be taken as implying subjectivity, usage made it clear that the term was to be used objectively. Perhaps a term such as 'interest' or 'legitimate interest' could have served equally well. Indeed, by the 1980s, it is clear that some justices were content to ground a right to procedural fairness in the existence of an underlying interest: see, for example, *FAI Insurances Ltd v Winneke* (1981) 151 CLR 342, 412 (Brennan J); *Kioa v West* (1985) 159 CLR 550, 582 (Mason J, who also considered that legitimate expectations might also ground the right).

But whether it was necessary or not, use of the language of expectations helped the High Court avoid the conceptual messiness which would have been entailed by an attempt to squeeze *Heatley v Tasmanian Racing and Gaming Commission* (1977) 137 CLR 487 into a rights analysis. In *FAI Insurances Ltd v Winneke* (1981) 151 CLR 342, the terminology enabled the court to deal with the inadequacy of rights terminology to encompass a situation where the stakes involved in the case were massive, but where the interest (in a licence being renewed) could not be treated as a right.

(iii) With interests grounding a right to fairness, what role is left for legitimate expectations?

Some ambiguity surrounded the term 'interest' and while judges accepted that interests falling short of rights could ground procedural fairness, there was some uncertainty as to what kind of interest could do so, and until the 1990s, cases continued to assume that there were circumstances in which a right to procedural fairness, which could not be grounded in a right or interest, might nonetheless be capable of being grounded in a legitimate expectation. In particular, courts seem to have assumed that a right to procedural fairness which would otherwise not exist might arise when governmental conduct gave rise — or could be taken as having given rise — to procedural expectations which were subsequently defeated by government conduct. A practice of making decisions only after the hearing of submissions was held to give rise to a right to be given a chance to make submissions in relation to relevant decisions: *Council of Civil Service Unions v Minister for the Civil Service* [1985] AC 374. Undertakings that a decision would be made only after an independent, impartial and thorough assessment were held to give rise to a duty to act in an unbiased manner: *Century Metals and Mining NL v Yeoman* (1989) 40 FCR 564.

But it is doubtful whether the existence or otherwise of legitimate expectations is any longer relevant to the existence of a *right* to procedural fairness. The reason is that courts are now tending to presume a general duty to afford procedural fairness exists (subject to a contrary legislative intention as always); the critical question in most cases becomes then not whether the duty exists, but what is its content.

Legitimate expectations have, however, been treated as being relevant to the content of the duty to afford procedural fairness: *Haoucher v Minister for Immigration* (1990) 169 CLR 648; *Minister for Immigration and Ethnic Affairs v Teoh* (1995) 183 CLR 273.

Dicta in *Re Minister for Immigration and Multicultural Affairs; Ex parte Lam* (2003) 214 CLR 1 support the proposition that the existence of a legitimate expectation is irrelevant to the existence of a right to procedural fairness, and relevant only to the content of that right: see Gleeson CJ at [12]–[13]; McHugh and Gummow JJ at [82]–[83], Callinan J at [145]. Moreover, the court in *Lam* also proceeded on the basis that unless disregard of a legitimate expectation also produced unfairness, there would be no denial of procedural fairness. The court also criticised *Teoh* in so far as that case suggested otherwise. Arguably, the question of whether a relevant expectation is legitimate has been subsumed by the related question of what kind of procedure is fair in the circumstances.

(iv) Can legitimate expectations give rise to substantive rights?

Grounding a right to procedural fairness in a legitimate expectation of procedural fairness raised the question of whether a right to a substantive outcome could also be grounded in an expectation of that outcome. In *Attorney-General (NSW) v Quin* (1990) 170 CLR 1, the High Court gave an essentially negative answer to the question. Mason CJ explained that, while undertakings to behave fairly could give rise to an entitlement to procedural fairness, they did not necessarily give rise to an entitlement corresponding to the expectation in question. However, he left open the possibility that there might be some circumstances in which this could be so: at 23.

In *Lam* several members of the court revisited the issue (although it was not necessary for them to do so). McHugh and Gummow JJ at [69] and [76] reiterated the view that legitimate expectations of administrative outcomes could not give rise to substantive rights. Callinan J can probably be taken to agree since he doubted both its utility and necessity, even in the context of procedural rights. Gleeson CJ and Hayne J stated that the question did not arise for resolution, but Hayne J's judgment suggests sympathy with the McHugh–Gummow analysis.

Not since the controversial and arguably discredited decision in *Teoh* has an applicant succeeded in a High Court case on a legitimate expectations argument and only on that basis. The term served a useful function, its very open-endedness providing welcome flexibility. But its job is done and it would be as well to bury the term. It is redundant in relation to the existence of the duty to afford procedural fairness, and it is more helpful to determine the content by reference to what is fair than to whether a legitimate expectation exists, especially given that after more than 30 years, it is still unclear what the term is supposed to mean.

Examiner's Comments

This is a generally thoughtful answer which addresses the issues raised by the question. It refers to relevant case law, and demonstrates familiarity with legal developments over the last 30 years. Under examination conditions, it is not reasonable to expect the quotations and quality of documentation one would expect in, say, a term essay on this topic. Time constraints also mean that there are places where the answer is not as well developed as one might wish. The difficulties of determining the basis of the High Court's decision in *Kioa* are skated over. There is no specific reference to estoppel. While the conclusion hints at the ambiguity surrounding the term, there is little reference in the body of the answer to the debate as to whether legitimate expectations depended on the reasonable observer, or on whether they were reasonably entertained by the person asserting wrongful denial of their right to a fair hearing. The assumption that legitimate expectations should not give rise to substantive rights has much to be said for it, but could perhaps be further developed. The dismissal of *Teoh* may be controversial. Its current status may be questionable, but there are those who loved it at the time and perhaps still do.

Common Errors to Avoid

- Answers should not proceed on the basis that the quotation is either totally valid or totally misguided. It is important to recognise that, even if it is far too extreme, it may contain an element of truth.
- Answers should recognise the degree to which the law has been, and may still be, in a state of flux.
- Answers need to demonstrate the significance of the concept, and to recognise the distinction between the capacity of legitimate expectations to ground procedural rights, and their inability to ground rights to substantive outcomes. Answers should not discuss the concept at only the level of 'the right' (the implication level) since it is also used at the 'content level'.

QUESTION 16

An authorised officer refused to grant Makepeace permission to import *The Night of a Thousand Shames* (see 'The Makepeace Scenario', p xvi). Makepeace announced that it was intending to appeal to the AAT. Two days later, and before Makepeace had lodged an appeal, the Attorney-General issued a certificate stating that, in his opinion, responsibility for a permission or a refusal of a permission should lie solely with the Attorney-General and should not be reviewable by the AAT. The certificate included the following grounds:

1. Distribution of the book will severely impair the quality of our relations with Caledenia. This is likely to involve severe economic consequences for Australia and could involve hostile acts, including the shipping of boatloads of Caledenian criminals to Australia's western shores.

2. Makepeace's motive for wishing to import the book is to provoke conflict with the Caledenian authorities in the misguided hope that the subsequent turmoil will result in the overthrow of the Caledenian Government.

Makepeace, which was not warned of the Attorney-General's intentions, wants to know whether it can challenge the decision to issue the certificate on the grounds of denial of procedural fairness. It tells you that the allegations in point 2 are substantially correct, but it says that it should nonetheless have been asked whether they were true, and should also have been given the chance to argue that the overthrow of the Caledenian Government would be to Australia's benefit. The Commonwealth contends that it will argue that the Attorney-General was not obliged to afford procedural fairness to Makepeace before issuing the certificate:

(a) Is there merit in the Commonwealth's argument?

(b) Assuming the Commonwealth had been under a duty to afford procedural fairness, would Makepeace's application for judicial review be likely to succeed?

Question (b) assumes familiarity with matters covered in Chapter 6. If you have not yet read Chapter 6, defer answering (b) until you have.

Time allowed: 40 mins (Question (a) 30 mins and (b) 10 mins)

Answer Plan

(i) Does the statute evidence an intention to deprive people of a right to procedural fairness in the issuing of certificates?

(ii) Assuming there was a duty to afford procedural fairness, was there a breach of the relevant procedural fairness requirements?

(iii) Would it matter that the Attorney-General's assessment of Makepeace's motives is largely correct?

Answer

There is 'a common law duty to act fairly, in the sense of according procedural fairness, in the making of administrative decisions which affect rights, interests and legitimate expectations, subject only to the clear manifestation of a contrary [statutory] intention': *Kioa v West* (1985) 159 CLR 550 at 584 per Mason J. Alternatively, there is now considerable judicial support for the proposition that in the absence of legislation to the contrary, the government is under a duty to act with procedural fairness in making executive decisions: see, for example, *Annetts v McCann* (1990) 170 CLR 596; *RE MIMA; Ex parte Lam* (2003) 214 CLR1.

Nonetheless, in my opinion, this is a case where the Attorney-General appears not to be under a duty to give Makepeace a hearing, notwithstanding that the certificate decision clearly affects Makepeace's rights, and notwithstanding that it is a government decision. My reasons are as follows.

(i) Does the statute evidence an intention to deprive people of a right to procedural fairness in the issuing of certificates?

There is an arguable — but not conclusive — case to be made for the proposition that the legislation discloses an intention that those affected by it do not have a right to be heard prior to the making of a decision to issue the certificate. The legislation does not lay down any form of procedures governing the decision to issue a certificate and it does not purport to oust procedural fairness requirements. This would normally count strongly against the conclusion that the repository of the power must afford Makepeace a hearing. Nonetheless, there are several aspects of the legislative scheme which suggest that the Attorney-General may be entitled to issue the certificate without consulting those whose appeal rights will be adversely affected by the decision.

First, a requirement to afford procedural fairness to would-be applicants to the AAT would tend to defeat the purpose of the regulation. Under the regulation, the only effect of a certificate appears to be to preclude the making of an appeal to the AAT. It does not, on its face, seem to prevent the AAT hearing an appeal if, at the time of the application for review, no certificate had been issued, that is, if the certificate was issued after an application for review was made. Difficulties would therefore arise if an adverse permission decision was made and communicated prior to the making of a decision to issue a certificate. In this event, a person threatened with a certificate could deal with the threat by making an immediate application to the AAT. If the certificate post-dated the decision to refuse permission, the problem would arise regardless of whether the applicant was entitled to procedural fairness in relation to the certificate decision. But in cases in which the issue of a certificate following communication of the decision would otherwise prevent appeals to the AAT, the existence of a right of procedural fairness would mean that a potential appellant would almost always be able to defeat the purpose of the certificate by responding to notice of the intended certificate decision by lodging an appeal.

If it were possible to make the certificate decision *before* communicating the permission decision, there would be no danger of appeals being made before certificates were issued. This may be possible. True, subreg (6) implies that a certificate can be issued only in relation to a decision that has been made, but this does not seem to preclude commencement of the procedures for issuing a certificate prior to determining the permission application. The regulations therefore appear to be such that procedural fairness could be afforded without at the same time defeating the purposes of the regulations.

This analysis is not altogether convincing. It does not, for instance, deal with the situation where an authorised person refuses permission and communicates this to the person affected without alerting the Attorney-General to the fact that a certificate might be necessary or appropriate. But in this situation there is a danger that the regulation could be frustrated even in the absence of an entitlement to procedural fairness: the unsuccessful applicant might immediately appeal to the AAT even if blissfully unaware of an intention to issue a certificate. It could also be dealt with by administrative arrangements whereby authorised persons would be required to notify the Attorney-General of their decisions prior to communicating them to applicants.

While affording procedural fairness might potentially defeat what appears to be the purpose of the regulation, it need not have this effect, provided that the government establishes administrative procedures designed to ensure that this does not happen. I do not therefore consider that the 'danger' which I have outlined means that the regulations must be taken as evidencing an intention to oust a right to procedural fairness.

A second consideration counting against the existence of a right to procedural fairness in relation to certificate decisions is that the condition for the certificate is the Attorney-General's opinion that responsibility for issuing the certificate should lie solely with the Attorney-General: reg 4A(5). This implies that the Attorney-General possesses a broad (but not unlimited) discretion. (It should be contrasted with the much more structured process for determining whether permissions should be granted.) The considerations which influenced the full Federal Court in *Minister for Arts, Heritage and Environment v Peko-Wallsend* (1987) 15 FCR 274 seem relevant here, although this is arguably not so strong a case for the government as was the *Peko-Wallsend* case.

Third, the statutory scheme suggests an intention that the Attorney-General be politically accountable for the decision, a consideration which was treated as counting against an implication of procedural fairness in *Peko-Wallsend*. The requirement that certificates be tabled (subreg 4(9)) indicates an intention that the Attorney-General be answerable to parliament. This does not mean that the Attorney-General is not also answerable to the courts, but it does suggest that the Attorney-General's decision is to be 'political' rather than 'quasi-judicial'.

Of these arguments, each has merit, but neither individually nor collectively would they necessarily persuade a court that the Attorney-General was not under a duty to afford procedural fairness. Assuming such a duty to exist, it would, however, be an attenuated one.

In *Shergold v Tanner* the High Court observed in relation to conclusive certificates issued under the Freedom of Information Act that '[t]he content of a requirement to provide natural justice to the person aggrieved by the decision may be very limited': at [40]. This envisages both that there might well be a right to procedural fairness in relation to the decision, and that it might be a relaxed requirement. The relevant certificate regime was somewhat different to the one under consideration here, and the differences are such that, under the FOI legislation, affording a right to procedural fairness would not have the same potential to subvert the purposes of the legislation. Like the decision under consideration here, it involved political elements. Unlike the certificate under discussion here, there was no requirement that the certificate be tabled. Given these considerations, if the right to procedural fairness in relation to the conclusive certificate considered in *Shergold* was attenuated, the right in this case must be close to non-existent.

(ii) Assuming there was a duty to afford procedural fairness, was there a breach of the relevant procedural fairness requirements?

There are two bases on which Makepeace might argue that it was denied procedural fairness. The first is that it was not warned of the possibility that a certificate might be issued, and the second is that the certificate decision was based, inter alia, on matters 'personal' to the organisation, on which it was given no chance to comment.

In relation to the first argument, analogies exist with *Haoucher v Minister for Immigration* (1990) 169 CLR 648, where a decision adverse to the applicant was quashed on the grounds that the applicant had not realised that the Minister might depart from a stated policy, and had not been given an opportunity to address the question of whether the Minister should do so. A submission in relation to a permission decision would not necessarily address matters relevant to a certificate decision. As an interested party, Makepeace should perhaps have been warned that the Attorney-General was contemplating following a 'no permission' decision with a 'certificate' decision. The case is distinguishable from *South Australia v O'Shea* (1987) 163 CLR 378, where the relevant procedure involved a two-stage decision-making procedure, and where under the relevant law, O'Shea could be released only if the decision at the second stage was favourable to him.

A right to be warned and consulted might not have arisen if the 'certificate' decision were to be based solely on political criteria, although even then, a warning might have been desirable. Here, however, account has also been taken of Makepeace's collective motives. When matters personal to a person are taken into account, there is normally a duty to seek the 'person's' response.

Complicating things here is the fact that Makepeace concedes that the Attorney-General's assessment of Makepeace's motives was 'substantially correct'. In this respect, the case differs from *Kioa*. Moreover, there seems little merit to its argument that it should have been allowed to address foreign policy submissions in relation to the certificate. There is no obvious reason why it should enjoy special rights in this respect.

(iii) Would it matter that the Attorney-General's assessment of Makepeace's motives is largely correct?

If the views ascribed to Makepeace were 'substantially correct', the implication is that they were not completely correct. We are not told the respects in which they were incorrect. If they were unduly favourable to Makepeace's case, this might be one of those rare cases where relief would be refused on the grounds that the denial of procedural fairness did not produce a miscarriage of justice. But if the errors were in any way prejudicial to Makepeace's application, then I think that a court would find that there had been denial of procedural fairness, and would grant relief. Courts are reluctant to second-guess decision-makers: see *Re Minister for Immigration and Multicultural Affairs; Ex parte Miah* (2001) 206 CLR 57; 179 ALR 238; [2001] HCA 22. There is some authority for the proposition that denial of procedural fairness does not go to the validity of a decision if the decision would have been the same even had procedural fairness been afforded: *Re Refugee Review Tribunal; Ex parte Aala* (2000) 204 CLR 82, per McHugh [103]; Kirby J [130]–[131]; Callinan J [210]; cf Gaudron and Gummow JJ [59]. But in *SAAP v MIMA* [2005] HCA 24 at [81], McHugh J seems to have favoured the Gaudron–Gummow view. In any case, if there was even a possibility that the decision would have been different but for the denial of procedural fairness, jurisdictional error would be established.

Examiner's Comments

This answer recognises that it is unwise to be dogmatic about entitlements to procedural fairness. The law in this area is not always easy to apply, and those who give confident advice run the risk that a subsequent Federal Court decision will leave them with egg on their faces. This answer has concluded that there might be a duty to afford procedural fairness, but that, if so, it would be an attenuated one. Other examiners might argue that it was clear that there was no duty to afford procedural fairness, or might be a little more confident that there was indeed a duty. The answer given here is one which was clearly open to the examinee. It also demonstrates a willingness to evaluate arguments as relatively strong or relatively weak. While lack of dogmatism is usually wise in this area, recipients of advice are also entitled to more than an intellectual shrug of the shoulders, and this answer demonstrates awareness of the fact that lack of certainty in the law does not mean that the law is completely random.

The answer avoids simplistic analyses based on whether the decision is 'political' (involving questions of policy as opposed to questions of administration), or 'quasi-judicial'. These concepts can be vague, and in any case, they provide no more than guidance. For instance, while 'political' decisions are less likely to give rise to a duty to afford procedural fairness, there are cases where the duty has been held to exist, notwithstanding that the decision was clearly 'political': *Barratt v Howard* (2000) 96 FCR 428; 170 ALR 529 is a recent example. The answer recognises the importance of answering questions about entitlements to procedural fairness by reference to the relevant statutory scheme, and this is one of its strengths. It draws on analogous High Court cases and applies them well.

 ## Common Errors to Avoid

- Questions of this nature require, not an exercise in one-sided advocacy, but the making of predictions. They therefore require awareness both of arguments which could support a proposition, and arguments which undermine the proposition.
- You should not assume that simply because the decision-maker's assessment of the facts was correct, there was no entitlement to procedural fairness. For one thing, you cannot know whether the court will share your knowledge and, for another, you need to recognise that courts are concerned not with whether findings of fact were correct (which they can rarely know, anyway), but with whether they are procedurally sound.

 ## QUESTION 17

Consider 'The Makepeace Scenario', p xvi once again. Makepeace has applied for permission to import. The matter is being considered by an authorised person. Makepeace learns that the authorised person is inclined to grant permission, but has decided to ask the Australian Security Service (ASS) for information about Makepeace's bona fides. Makepeace wants to apply for a declaration that the authorised person is required to consult Makepeace before seeking information from third parties. Would it be successful? Are there circumstances in which, ➤

following the ASS report, the authorised person would be required to afford some kind of further hearing to Makepeace prior to making a final decision?

Time allowed: 15 mins

Answer Plan

(i)   Makepeace is not entitled to a declaration.

(ii) Are there any circumstances in which Makepeace would be entitled to such a declaration?

 ## Answer

(i)   *Makepeace is not entitled to a declaration*

If there is a duty to consult it might arise either from statute or common law. There is no statutory duty to consult. If there is a duty, it must be a common law duty. If there is a common law duty, it can arise only because there is a duty to afford procedural fairness to Makepeace, and if the duty requires that Makepeace be consulted about any decision which has the potential to affect it, whether directly or indirectly. In making decisions in relation to Makepeace, there are strong dicta to the effect that the executive owes a duty to make its decisions in a procedurally fair manner. In *Teoh*, McHugh J observed at 311 that:

> I think that the rational development of this branch of the law requires acceptance of the view that the rules of procedural fairness are presumptively applicable to administrative and similar decisions made by public tribunals and officials.

This observation was cited with approval by three judges in *Lam*: see McHugh and Gummow JJ at [83]; Callinan J at [150]. It follows, therefore, that in the absence of legislative provisions to the contrary the authorised person is required to act in a procedurally fair manner in making decisions. The relevant observations were, however, made in the context of what could be described as final and operative decisions. There is therefore no reason to assume that they were to be taken as suggesting that each time a step is taken in relation to the processing of an application, this attracts a duty to comply with the rules of procedural fairness.

Alternatively, if there is such a duty, its content depends on what procedural fairness actually entails and there is no authority to suggest that procedural fairness necessarily — or even usually — requires consultation in relation to the making of procedural decisions.

Nor does Makepeace's right to procedural fairness in connection with the final decision mean that it is necessarily entitled to be consulted at each step in the decision-making process. All that is necessary is that the overall process be fair: see, for example, *South Australia v O'Shea*

(1989) 163 CLR 378; *Edelsten v Health Insurance Commission* (1990) 27 FCR 56. The mere fact that the taking of a particular step may expose a person to an enhanced risk of an ultimately adverse decision is not enough to require that the step may be taken only after a potentially affected person has been given a chance to make submissions in relation to the 'decision' to take the step.

Here, there are several considerations which count against a conclusion that Makepeace is entitled to procedural fairness in relation to the 'decision' to consult ASS. The 'decision' in question is not a final and operative decision, nor a decision for which an enactment makes specific provision. It would therefore not be reviewable under the Administrative Decisions (Judicial Review) Act 1977 (Cth) (ADJR Act) as a decision, although it could be reviewable as conduct. Because it is not a decision for the purposes of the ADJR Act, it is not a 'decision' for which the 'decision-maker' must give reasons. This consideration alone counts against imputing a right to a hearing, given that the right to reasons is a consideration suggestive of a right to procedural fairness: *Kioa v West*. Further, the policy considerations which underlay the High Court's decision in *Australian Broadcasting Tribunal v Bond* point strongly against a finding that there was a duty to afford procedural fairness in relation to the 'decision' to make inquiries of the ASS. Such a requirement would be inconsistent with efficient decision-making, especially since such inquiries would constitute a waste of time and effort in cases where, despite the step in question, the decision-maker was not disposed to make a decision adverse to the person who might have been heard. If the mere fact of ASS being consulted was capable of having serious consequences for Makepeace, this might give rise to a duty to consult. But this does not seem to be the case here. The worst that seems realistically possible is that ASS's report will be adverse to Makepeace, but assuming this to be the case, Makepeace's entitlement to procedural fairness will mean that it will be entitled to be given a chance to respond to any matters prejudicial to its application prior to the making of a final decision on its permission application. That opportunity should suffice to satisfy its entitlement to procedural fairness.

Makepeace would therefore not, at this stage, be entitled to declaratory relief based on denial of procedural fairness.

(ii) Are there any circumstances in which Makepeace would be entitled to such a declaration?

Makepeace would be entitled to a 'hearing' only if, after receiving the ASS report, the authorised person decided to act on material adverse to Makepeace, and even then only in certain circumstances. The authorised person would obviously not be obliged to give Makepeace a further hearing if the authorised person had decided to grant the permission. Nor would the authorised person be obliged to give Makepeace an opportunity to make additional submissions following the ASS report if

Makepeace had already addressed those issues in earlier submissions. The position becomes more difficult if ASS draws the authorised person's attention to a consideration which Makepeace had not addressed. If the consideration amounts to an allegation adverse to Makepeace, then Makepeace must be given an opportunity to present its case: *Kioa v West* (1985) 159 CLR 550. Even if the consideration does not relate directly to Makepeace, there may be circumstances in which Makepeace should nonetheless be given a chance to present arguments in rebuttal: *Re Minister for Immigration and Multicultural Affairs; Ex parte Miah* (2001) 206 CLR 57; 179 ALR 238; [2001] HCA 22 (where the denial of procedural fairness involved an applicant for refugee status who was denied the opportunity to comment on the effects of an election which had resulted in a change of government). It is not easy to determine the limits of the decision-maker's duty to draw a person's attention to an intention to rely on 'extra-personal' considerations. An important determinant is what is fair in the circumstances (which may, however, be far from clear). Related to fairness is the question of how far it can be said that taking the new consideration into account means that the person is taken by surprise.

Arguably, Makepeace could object if it was not consulted in relation to a report which asserted that the granting of permission would certainly lead to war between Caledenia and Australia. The truth of this allegation would clearly be relevant, and it is an allegation which Makepeace would probably not anticipate, and to which it would therefore not respond unless told of it. On the other hand, I doubt that there would be any duty to consult Makepeace in relation to an assessment that national security interests should be weighted heavily, since this issue would involve a question of evaluation rather than one of fact. It would be analogous to the political considerations which were taken into account by the South Australian Government in *O'Shea's* case and which were held not to require a further hearing: *South Australia v O'Shea* (1989) 163 CLR 378. In any case, I doubt that it could be said that Makepeace had been taken by surprise were the authorised person to take account of such a consideration.

Examiner's Comments

The first part of this question involves a straightforward issue. The second part is more difficult. The first part requires that the student recognise that questions of procedural fairness relate to the fairness of the overall decision-making process. This principle is not always easy to apply, since adverse decisions at an early stage of a decision-making process may involve immediate adverse effects on a person's interests (for instance, when they expose a person to the uncertainties and expenses associated with involvement in the formal stages of the legal process). However, in this case, Makepeace's interests are not affected in this way. The only prejudice to Makepeace derives from the possibility that the ASS will report adversely. This possibility is not enough to make consulting the ASS conditional on having consulted Makepeace on whether to do so. There are, I think, various ways in which one might reach the conclusion that Makepeace was not entitled to procedural fairness in relation to the 'decision' to consult the ASS. This answer develops several cogent arguments. Another argument would be that Makepeace could not be said to be taken by surprise by the authorised person's decision to consult the ASS, and can therefore scarcely complain that this is what the authorised person did. I don't think it is necessary to consider every possible argument for a non-controversial proposition.

The second part of the question is more difficult, and it is one which could be approached in a number of ways. It requires a consideration of a variety of possibilities (and different possibilities might occur to different examinees). A good answer should identify some circumstances in which the authorised person would be obliged to give Makepeace a further hearing. An answer could formally discharge that obligation by selecting some relatively straightforward cases (for example, if the ASS stated that Makepeace was nothing but a terrorist drug cartel whose leaders all had criminal convictions in at least 10 countries). However, a good answer would also point to cases where there was no obligation to consult, and to cases which were on the borderline. This answer does so, and also refers to relevant authority.

 # Common Errors to Avoid

- Failing to discuss why there was no obligation to consult Makepeace in relation to the 'decision' to consult the ASS.
- Providing examples of situations where there would be a duty to consult Makepeace further, without suggesting why this duty would exist.

Chapter 6

The Right to be Heard

 Key Issues

Procedural fairness entails that those who might be affected by a decision be given notice of matters which are potentially prejudicial to their case, and also that they be given an opportunity to present material which might support their case. The content of these requirements can vary considerably, and it can be difficult to determine precisely what is required in particular cases. The underlying requirement is that the procedures are fair, but it is not always clear what fairness entails.

The 'notice' requirement is satisfied when a person likely to be affected by a decision is given an effective opportunity to make submissions. Difficulties arise where the decision-maker takes into account something which the person affected by the decision might not have anticipated. For instance, consider the following example. An applicant for a protection visa bases the claim on allegations of persecution by the government of Bangladesh. After the application has been made, the government is defeated in an election. The Minister's delegate, on advice from the Department of Foreign Affairs and Trade, concludes that the new government will not pursue the oppressive policies of its predecessor. Is the delegate required to advise the applicant that the change of government is a matter which will be borne in mind in assessing the application? See *Re Minister for Immigration and Multicultural Affairs; Ex parte Miah* (2001) 206 CLR 57; 179 ALR 238; [2001] HCA 22. (The ruling in that case has been reversed by legislation, but it is still of interest in so far as it bears on the content of the natural justice principles in the absence of legislation purporting to abridge those requirements.)

If the applicant recognises the materiality of the change of government and makes submissions accordingly, the issue does not arise. If, however, the applicant assumes that the change of government makes no difference, while the government assumes that it does, the test is whether it was reasonable for the government to proceed without canvassing the applicant's comments on the issue. What is reasonable will depend heavily on the facts as found by the court, and on how the court interprets those facts.

Does the decision-maker have to inform a person that they have been given information potentially prejudicial to the person's application, if the decision-maker has decided to take no notice of the information? If a favourable decision is made the question will not arise, but the issue does arise when the decision is adverse to the applicant. In these cases, it might be argued that no harm is done if the prejudicial material is treated as irrelevant, but in *Applicant VEAL of 2002 v Minister for Immigration and Multicultural Affairs* (2005) 225 CLR 88; 222 ALR 411; [2005] HCA 72 the High Court rejected this argument, finding that the decision-maker was obliged to draw the prejudicial material to the applicant's attention and to give the applicant an opportunity to respond to the allegations. The allegations were relevant in the sense that, if made out, they bore on whether the applicant was entitled to refugee status. The decision-maker was therefore obliged to consider them. And if the decision-maker was obliged to consider them, the decision-maker was also obliged to hear what the applicant had to say about them.

The requirement to afford an opportunity for the making of submissions from an applicant is usually described as involving the duty to afford a hearing. This terminology is slightly misleading, since it may be sufficient that the decision-maker provide an opportunity for the making of written submissions. Sometimes, the procedure for the making of submissions is laid down in detail by the relevant legislation. In this event, it will be enough that the decision-maker follows the statutory procedure. Otherwise, the procedure to be followed must be 'fair'; 'that is, in accordance with procedures that are fair to the individual considered in the light of the statutory requirements, the interests of the individual and the interests and purposes, whether public or private, which the statute seeks to advance or protect or permits to be taken into account as legitimate expectation': *Kioa v West* (1985) 159 CLR 550 at 585 per Mason J.

In some decision-making contexts, the content of the hearing rule may be determined in whole or in part by statute. One example is the Migration Act 1958 (Cth), which includes comprehensive provisions in relation to the processing of visa applications and appeals against primary decisions. Laws establishing administrative review tribunals normally include some procedural provisions which help define the kind of hearing to which applicants are entitled. In so far as statutes are silent on what is entailed by the hearing requirement, these must be inferred from the decision-making scheme, from principle, and from precedent. Courts have accepted that the scope of the hearing rule may be influenced by what is feasible, given the workload of a department and the budgetary constraints to which it is subject: *Zhang v Minister for Immigration, Local Government and Ethnic Affairs* (1993) 45 FCR 384 at 410 per French J. In that case, French J held that applicants for refugee status were therefore not necessarily entitled to an oral hearing by the decision-maker. Fairness does not automatically require that a person be permitted to present his or her case through a representative (*Krstic v Australian Telecommunications Commission* (1988) 20 FCR

486), and it does not require that the government provide legal assistance to those potentially affected by its decisions and activities: *New South Wales v Canellis* (1994) 181 CLR 309. (Although in criminal cases courts may achieve a similar result by staying prosecutions until defendants are provided with representation: *Dietrich v R* (1992) 177 CLR 292.) If, however, people can present a case effectively only if allowed representation, permitting representation may be a requirement of a fair hearing: see *Krstic* at 491.

People affected by a decision do not necessarily have a right to require that those giving information adverse to their case give sworn oral evidence, and do not normally have a right to cross-examine those who have supplied adverse information: *O'Rourke v Miller* (1985) 156 CLR 342. However, where questions of credibility arise, fairness may require that there be an oral hearing, along with a right to cross-examine witnesses who make adverse allegations: see *O'Rourke* at 353 per Gibbs CJ; *Chen*.

Case law must be used carefully, since decisions in this area can be closely related to the particular decision-making regime under consideration. Because they involve assessments of what is 'fair', to some extent they are likely to reflect the values of particular judges. In particular, they are likely to reflect judges' answers to such time-honoured questions as: how far are the interests of the individual to be given priority over the assessed interests of the collectivity (which include the collectivity's interest in accurate decision-making)? How far should decisions about appropriate administrative procedures be matters for judges rather than administrators? To what extent can procedures deviate from curial procedures and still yield outcomes which are similar to those which would be reached by a hypothetical 'God-administrator'?

Before attempting the questions, check that you are familiar with the following issues:

✓ the circumstances in which a person who may be affected by an administrative decision must be put on notice by the administrator of an intention to take certain matters into account in reaching the decision;

✓ the variables which determine the type of 'hearing' a person is entitled to, given an entitlement to some level of procedural fairness; and

✓ the circumstances in which the repository of a decision-making power is required to afford a hearing, and those in which it is enough that a hearing be conducted by a subordinate official who passes on details to the decision-maker.

QUESTION 18

'It is neither desirable nor practical to allow everyone affected by an administrative decision to have a full-scale, judicial-type hearing into what the decision-maker should do. Fortunately, this is recognised by the courts.' Discuss.

Time allowed: 40 mins

Answer Plan

(i)   Advantages of the right to be heard.

(ii)   Drawbacks of oral hearings.

(iii) The law tends to recognise these considerations.

- Statute law.
- Case law.

 ## Answer

I generally agree with the proposition, subject to a number of qualifications. In so far as the quotation implies that hearings as such are undesirable, I think it may under-value hearings. In so far as it claims that full-scale hearings are impractical, I think it is correct. On the whole, I agree that the law recognises administrative practicalities, but it is arguable that courts sometimes impose unduly exacting standards.

(i)   Advantages of the right to be heard

Hearings serve several important functions. First, good administration requires that decision-makers be as well informed as possible. Allowing those who are affected by decisions an opportunity to put their case will tend to mean that administrators make better-informed decisions. Without such information, administrators may fail to recognise the existence of relevant facts. They may not realise that what appear to be the facts of the case are in fact contested. Exposure to input in particular cases may also sensitise administrators to matters which they need to think about in other cases.

Administrators can often inform themselves reasonably well without the need to engage in oral hearings, but oral hearings may nonetheless be superior to hearings based solely on written submissions. They may assist those whose written skills are poor (although such people are also likely to have difficulties presenting their case orally). They provide a context in which decision-makers can seek clarifications where a person's submissions are unclear. They may also provide a forum in which those affected by administrative decisions can seek clarification from administrators when it is not clear what kind of information the administrator wants.

Allowing people a chance to be heard may also improve relations between the bureaucracy and its clientele. Even if 'hearings' prove to be unnecessary in particular cases, people affected by administrative decisions may feel happier if they have nonetheless been given an opportunity to present their case.

However, the degree to which 'judicial-type' hearings perform these functions will depend on precisely what is meant by 'judicial-type hearing'. If 'judicial-type hearing' means the kind of hearing characteristically conducted by Ch III courts, it is at least arguable that the relevant hearing rights would sometimes be less than helpful. In the absence of legal representation, people appearing before traditional courts appear to find them intimidating and, having been intimidated, may disclose considerably less information than they would disclose in the typical form which they submit to an administrative decision-maker. If, however, the phrase envisages hearings designed to ensure that people are given a real chance to present their case orally and to learn of and respond to the decision-maker's concerns, different considerations apply.

(ii)   Drawbacks of oral hearings

There are, however, limits to the degree to which hearings can be reconciled with good administration. First, hearings are likely to delay the decision-making process. While courts can handle urgent matters with admirable speed, routine cases normally take months — and sometimes years — before they are heard (in so far as they *are* heard). Moreover, whether at magistrates' court level or in the High Court, delay seems to be increasing. In the AAT and the Migration Tribunals, the median time between date of application and date of decision is now about a year. Even in the Social Security Appeals Tribunal (SSAT), the median time between application for review and a decision is four to five months.

There are several reasons for delay. One is that 'hearings' are subject to a constraint which does not apply to the same extent to traditional bureaucratic decision-making processes. A hearing is typically conducted as a one-off event. It requires the setting of a time which is acceptable to all the parties and their witnesses. A decision 'on the papers' requires no such co-ordination. A second reason is that courts and tribunals are under-resourced — which highlights the relevance of resource constraints to arguments about the appropriateness of the judicial model.

There are several reasons why oral hearings are costly. Listening to people normally takes more time than reading their submissions. The logistics of scheduling oral hearings mean that participants may have to spend a lot of time hanging around, waiting to be called on. Decisions on the papers are cheaper both to governments (which do not need to employ as many decision-makers) and — probably — to applicants, who can lodge the relevant papers without having to hang around on the day or days of the hearing waiting until they are called on to give evidence.

(iii) The law tends to recognise these considerations

Statute law

Statute law reflects the degree to which governments are aware both of the desirability of 'hearings', and of their cost. Legislation tends to structure decision-making so that 'hearings' are 'rationed'. Primary decision-making tends to be 'on the papers' and usually involves no oral input into the decision-making process. Those who receive favourable outcomes notwithstanding the lack of a comprehensive hearing are neither inclined nor able to object to the fact that their cases have been disposed of without a formal hearing. Those who receive unfavourable outcomes become entitled to appeal to a tribunal which will afford them a far more comprehensive hearing. (In the social security area, would-be appellants must have had their case internally reviewed first.) Except in the refugee area, most of those who are unsuccessful at first instance do not avail themselves of this right.

The right to a comprehensive hearing is not quite the same as a right to a 'judicial-type' hearing, but the legislation has been drafted with a view to ensuring that appellants' rights to a fair hearing are, if anything, greater than they would be if ordinary judicial procedures applied. The requirements that the tribunals be relatively informal and that they not be bound by the strict rules of evidence are designed to remove some of the obstacles which face an unrepresented person who wants to present their case before a court.

However, procedural fairness rules vary between the 'mass application' areas. The requirement that social security applicants exhaust internal review before applying to the SSAT, in so far as it produces 'appeal fatigue', may mean that social security applicants have a more attenuated right to a comprehensive hearing than do appellants in other jurisdictions. The complex rules determining when visa applicants must be put on notice about potentially adverse material do not have analogues in the other 'mass application' areas. The balance between expansive hearing rights and resource constraints appears to be drawn differently in different areas, and appears to be drawn in favour of the government where applicants are relatively powerless, and in favour of the applicant where (as in the tax and veterans' areas) the appellants are better resourced or represented by politically powerful associations.

Case law

To a considerable extent, case law recognises that a trade-off may be necessary between the desirability of comprehensive hearings on one hand, and their cost on the other. We find this in the law relating to the question of whether people are entitled to any form of procedural fairness. A right to procedural fairness is not lightly inferred when the decision is a political decision, which turns on values rather than on facts (see, for instance, *South Australia v O'Shea* (1987) 163 CLR 378; *Minister for Arts, Heritage and Environment v Peko-Wallsend* (1987) 15 FCR 274), or where it is a decision by people whose seniority is such that they could not reasonably be expected to afford a hearing: *O'Shea* and *Peko-Wallsend*; but cf *FAI Insurances v Winneke* (1981) 151 CLR 342. Such a trade-off is also grounded in authority which makes it clear that the implications of the duty to act fairly vary according to the circumstances of the case, the statutory provisions, and the public and private interests at stake: see, for example, *Kioa v West* (1985) 159 CLR 550 at 586 per Mason J. Similar calculations underlie the decision in *O'Rourke v Miller* (1985) 156 CLR 342, where the court took account of factors including the public interest in keeping people of even doubtful character out of the police force, and the unlikelihood of a rigorous hearing making any difference to the Chief Commissioner's decision. Cases which recognise that the rigour of the hearing rule can also reflect legitimate expectations relating to the nature of the hearing (see, for example, *Kioa*) are not explicable in terms of a trade-off between the desirability of information and the cost of gathering it, but they make sense when it is recognised that part of the rationale for affording a hearing is the legitimation of bureaucratic practices. Those who have been led to believe that their claims will be handled in a particular way are more likely to feel aggrieved in the event of their being deprived of the relevant hearing than those who have not been so led.

But while decisions on the scope of the hearing rule will tend to reflect trade-offs, it will sometimes be difficult to predict the outcome of such a trade-off. The criteria to be taken into account are vague; for example, what is the purpose of the statute? What are the interests involved? Moreover, the weight to be attached to different variables is not and cannot be specified with any degree of precision. According to John McMillan ('The Role of Judicial Review in Administrative Law' (2001) 30 *AIAL Forum* 47), administrators complain that case law provides them with little guidance as to how they are to behave. Exasperation with the hearing rule as applied by the courts has stimulated a variety of measures, all designed to replace the common law hearing rule with more objective (and in a sense more arbitrary) statutory rules. This is particularly so in the migration area. The existence of such legislation does not mean that the courts attach insufficient weight to administrative interests, but it does suggest that administrators think they do.

That said, it should be noted that the more controversial cases generally relate not to the issue of whether people have been wrongly denied an oral hearing, but to the question of whether they have been given an adequate chance to present their case. Even if courts are over-generous to judicial review applicants (which is probably a normative rather than an empirical question), it is hard to contend that this is reflected in decisions governing the right to oral hearings.

 ## Examiner's Comments

This essay requires a discussion of the advantages and disadvantages associated with providing a full-scale hearing to those affected by administrative decisions, and the degree to which the law relating to hearings recognises these considerations. It is a question which can be handled in a variety of ways. There are several strong arguments in favour of generous procedural fairness rules. One relates to the fact that better-informed decision-makers will normally make better decisions. Giving a hearing will normally increase the likelihood that administrators will be better informed. (Why only 'normally'? Because sometimes, people will use the chance to tell credible lies.) Another, which is less obvious, is that being heard may make people more inclined to accept the legitimacy of the decision-making system. Empirical support for this conclusion is provided by the substantial literature on the impact of perceived treatment on acceptance of outcomes and institutions. The conclusion is also implicit in respect for expectations born of administrators' behaviour.

It does not follow from this that oral hearings are necessarily superior but, if one thinks that oral hearings make it easier for people to provide relevant information, one would argue both for hearings and for oral hearings. Are oral hearings superior in this respect? Probably, but not necessarily.

This answer addresses these issues. It is healthily sceptical of the judicial model as a paradigm, but recognises that there may be alternatives which do in fact mean that allowing for oral hearings may make for better-informed decision-making.

The essay also recognises the costs associated with the use of hearings rather than reliance on the papers, and rightly notes the degree to which oral hearings tend to be associated with lengthy delay. (It does not address the question of whether routine administration is characterised by the same delays, but it is probably correct in its assumption that it is not.) It also notes some of the costs.

In discussing whether the law takes account of these considerations, the answer rightly recognises that the relevant law includes both statute law and common law. It examines the ways in which statute law seems to be designed to ensure that reasonably wide-ranging hearings are reserved for cases where they are most likely to make a difference. It also demonstrates the degree to which the common law envisages that there will be trade-offs between individual and collective interests, while highlighting the difficulty of applying general observations — such as those of Mason J in *Kioa* — to particular situations.

Examinees might choose to answer this question in a variety of ways. They might vary in the attention they give to the different components of the question. (In deciding how much weight to give different aspects of the question, it makes sense to be guided by the amount of attention each has received from the teachers of the subject.) Students might also choose different structures. An alternative approach to this might proceed, say, from Mason J's judgment in *Kioa* and discuss the criteria he outlined, relating them to the question. A good answer will demonstrate familiarity with the relevant law (since the question expressly asks about the law), but familiarity can be demonstrated in a variety of ways.

 ## Common Errors to Avoid

- Failing to address parts of the question. You should, for example, discuss both the reasons why particular kinds of hearings might or might not be desirable, and the variables which the law takes into account in determining the application of the hearing rule in particular cases.
- Failure to recognise that (as the law currently stands) the content of the hearing rule is affected both by statute and common law.
- Failing to recognise the variety of factors which determine the operation of the hearing rule in a particular situation.

 # QUESTION 19

In 2001, the Freedom Press of Loonie, Indiana, published *Transformation: How with Only a Grade School Education and a Kitchen, You Can Make a Relatively Harmless Flu Virus into a Lethal Killer.* The United States authorities immediately raided the publisher and confiscated all but a handful of the books. The author of the book died two days later after eating poisoned lasagne, and everyone associated with the production of the book suffered fatal accidents within the following six months.

Professor Listerine of the Isaacs University Institute for Epidemiological Research became aware that the book was going to be published and was anxious to read it, in order to assess whether it really was possible to do what the book claimed and, if so, whether it would be feasible to devise counter-measures which could be used to protect the population if the mutant flu were to be misused. He placed an order for it with Freedom Press which debited his credit card and dropped the book into the mail minutes before the raid. After reading news reports about the book, Professor Listerine contacted his solicitor who advised him that the book would certainly constitute a prohibited import. The solicitor suggested that he contact the Attorney-General and ask for ➤

permission under reg 4A(2) of the Customs (Prohibited Imports) Regulations. The solicitor drafted a letter for Listerine, as follows:

My client wishes to import a copy of *Transformation*. He is aware that the book may be a prohibited import under the Customs (Prohibited Imports) Regulations, but wishes to read the book in order to determine whether the processes outlined in it are indeed feasible. If they are, he will immediately embark on research oriented towards the development of counter-measures which could be used if the threat were to eventuate. My client has an international reputation for his work on modelling measles epidemics. He is aware that you may be concerned about his political past, but assures you that he joined the *Hitlerjugend* [Hitler Youth] only under duress, and resigned from it in February 1946.

In due course, a person authorised by the Attorney-General replied, refusing permission. The letter stated the following reasons:

While your client's ostensible reasons for seeking to import the book are admirable, there are several matters which concern me. First, expertise as a measles modeller does not, I am advised, mean that a person is capable of conducting the kind of research envisaged by Dr Listerine. I find it hard to believe that he could seriously contemplate conducting research of this complexity without the assistance of a team of researchers. Indeed, I regard it as a matter of notoriety that the mark of good researchers these days is the size of the grants they can amass, and the distinction of their research teams. The existence of such a team would clearly create a real risk that the contents of the work might become known to people from whom this knowledge is best kept secret.

Second, I am not persuaded that your client would be capable of maintaining the requisite levels of security. Your letter provides nothing to assure us in this respect and I can only assume that this is because there is nothing you could say which would reassure us. I would add that, in fairness to Dr Listerine, the Australian Federal Police attended at Isaacs University to ask about your client's reputation. They found his office open. His computer was on and his password (which incidentally is his old *Hitlerjugend* number) is scrawled at the bottom, left-hand corner of his monitor. His secretary describes him as 'charming but completely absent-minded'. The police report did nothing to change the opinion I had already formed.

Third, it is apparent that even if Dr Listerine joined the *Hitlerjugend* under duress, he continued as a member well after the collapse of Nazi rule. Moreover, your letter does not address the government's real concerns arising from his well-publicised activities on behalf of the White Eugenicists Alliance (WEA) in 1949–51. The WEA, as you know, conducted considerable research into the possibility of creating viruses which would impact differentially on people of particular races.

Permission is therefore denied. I am pleased to inform you that the Attorney-General has issued a certificate excluding appeal to the AAT. I should also inform you that, following my decision, the book was intercepted at the Melbourne Central Sorting Office and destroyed.

Professor Listerine's solicitor wants to know whether the decision to refuse permission was lawful, and if not, whether the professor would have an action in trespass against the Commonwealth, based on the destruction of the book. The solicitor has approached you, a junior ➤

member of the bar, for advice. Professor Listerine apparently did belong to the WEA, but says that he did not try to develop new viruses which attacked only blacks. He had, however, while still a German citizen worked on a project aimed at stopping German measles attacking German-speaking people.

Time allowed: 45 mins

Answer Plan

(i)   Did Professor Listerine have a right to procedural fairness?

(ii)   Should Professor Listerine have been warned about doubts as to his fitness to undertake the relevant research?

(iii) Should Professor Listerine have been consulted about whether he could be relied on to adhere to reasonable security requirements?

(iv)   Were Professor Listerine's political views an irrelevant consideration, and if not, should he have been given a chance to comment on adverse inferences in relation to his views?

(v)   The effects of denial of procedural fairness.

 ## Answer

In my opinion, it is likely that a court would find Professor Listerine has been denied procedural fairness. It is unlikely, however, that he would be able to sue successfully for trespass. The reasons why one action will succeed, but the other fail, and the link between the two, is set out below. It is convenient to begin with the administrative law breach.

(i)   Did Professor Listerine have a right to procedural fairness?

A person has a presumptive right to procedural fairness in relation to the making of an administrative decision if the person's rights, interests or legitimate expectations would be affected by that decision: *Kioa v West* (1985) 159 CLR 550, per Mason J at 584. The common law right is subject to there being a contrary legislative intention. Here, the decision in question bears both on the continued enjoyment of Professor Listerine's property rights in relation to the book, and in his interest in being able to use the book for his research. He clearly has a presumptive right to procedural fairness. There is no contrary legislative intention. This means that he has a right to be heard in relation to decisions affecting his book. This right entails both the right to know adverse matters which might be taken into account in evaluating his request, and the right to make relevant submissions to the decision-maker.

(ii)   Should Professor Listerine have been warned about doubts as to his fitness to undertake the relevant research?

Where a decision-maker places an interpretation, adverse to a person, on a piece of information provided by that person, the administrator may be under a duty to draw the adverse interpretation to the person's attention: *Somaghi v Minister for Immigration, Local Government and Ethnic Affairs* (1991) 31 FCR 100; *Heshmati v Minister for Immigration, Local Government and Ethnic Affairs* (1990) 31 FCR 123. Whether this is so, however, depends on the degree to which the inference is not one which the person could have anticipated. Here, the inference has been that Professor Listerine is not competent to evaluate the book or to devise precautions that could be taken against a deadly influenza virus. If the material provided by Professor Listerine could reasonably be treated as representing the best case that could be made for his being given permission to import the book, the authorised person might have been justified in proceeding to an adverse decision without having to notify the professor of her intention to draw adverse inferences from the material supplied. Relevant to the reasonableness issue is the fact that the request comes from a lawyer who might have been expected to put forward the strongest possible case for the granting of permission. However, another reading of the letter is that it was written in the expectation that the material contained in it would be sufficient to warrant the granting of permission, and that if this were not so, the professor would be given an opportunity to address the decision-maker's concerns. In my opinion, this is a reasonable reading of the letter. If so, the decision-maker erred in failing to advise the professor about her concerns about his competence to conduct the proposed research.

I would add that even if the delegate was not under a duty to advise the professor of her intention to act on the basis of his lack of competence, the decision might nonetheless be flawed. It is possible that the delegate erred in assuming that competence as a measles modeller is irrelevant to whether the professor could conduct the proposed research. I do not know whether this is so, but will give further advice once I have the necessary information.

Similar comments can be made in relation to the delegate's conclusions about the professor's apparent intention to conduct the research alone. I am not sure that the authorised person is necessarily justified in concluding that the professor would have worked with a team of researchers from the moment he received the book (in which case, the conclusion may itself be the basis for a successful application), but even if the delegate's conclusion is correct, as it probably would be if a reading of the book persuaded the professor of the need to embark on preventive research, I doubt that a court would find that the initial letter ought to have canvassed the procedures which would be used to ensure that dangerous secrets did not get out. Professor Listerine would no doubt have assumed that the proposed research would have to be approved by the Isaacs University Ethics Committee and that it would therefore proceed only if possible dangers were addressed, and he might quite reasonably have assumed either that this would be known by the delegate, or that if the delegate had concerns about it, she would ask for further details. The delegate ought not to have made the prejudicial assumption that safeguards would not be in place without inquiring further of the applicant.

(iii) Should Professor Listerine have been consulted about whether he could be relied on to adhere to reasonable security requirements?

In one sense, the professor should not have been surprised by the authorised person's finding in relation to the security issue. The regulation makes it clear that one matter which might be taken into account is the security which would accompany the use of the prohibited import. see reg 1A(3). This would have been apparent to Professor Listerine's legal adviser, and the failure to make reference to proposed security arrangements could, I think, warrant the conclusion that Professor Listerine had nothing to say in relation to them which would warrant favourable treatment of his claim. But if the letter is treated not as a definitive statement of the arguments in favour of permission, but as a statement of the stronger arguments which the solicitor considered would suffice, the position is different.

In any case, the professor ought to have been given an opportunity to comment on the police report, of which he was not made aware. It was both prejudicial and relevant. The evident lack of security displayed by Professor Listerine (assuming the police report to be accurate) could be easily explained. It might, for instance, reflect the fact that Professor Listerine was not engaged in confidential research. It might reflect an assessment on his part that the only people with access to his office were people who were to be trusted. If the apparent lack of security had been taken into account to Professor Listerine's discredit, I am confident that no court would find that he had been afforded an adequate hearing. The authorised person's letter suggests, however, that the police report was not taken into account adversely to Professor Listerine, except in a narrow sense. If the delegate is to be believed, it was commissioned on the basis that, if it showed Professor Listerine to be observant of proper security measures, it would be accepted as evidence favourable to him. Otherwise, it would simply confirm the delegate in her earlier decision. But even if that were so, and even if the provisional decision were unchallengeable, the professor should have been given a chance to reply to the potentially prejudicial allegations. The police report was relevant, and the authorised person was therefore obliged to consider it. It follows from the High Court's decision in *Applicant VEAL of 2002 v Minister for Immigration and Multicultural and Indigenous Affairs* (2005) 225 CLR 88; 222 ALR 411; [2005] HCA 72 that the decision-maker was therefore obliged to afford the professor a chance to reply to the allegations. The fact that the police report did nothing to change the decision-maker's opinion is beside the point. It is possible that the professor's reply to the report might have had that effect.

(iv) Were Professor Listerine's political views an irrelevant consideration, and if not, should he have been given a chance to comment on adverse inferences in relation to his views?

Normally, I think, a person's politics would be an irrelevant consideration in relation to a request for permission under the regulations, and a decision based thereon would be vitiated by consideration of this matter. If that were so, it would be unnecessary to consider whether there had been a denial of procedural fairness. However, if Professor Listerine's activities were as the authorised person believed, they would clearly be relevant to whether permission should be granted: they would, for instance, go to character: subreg (2AA)(c). If they were not as the decision-maker believed, this would go not to relevance but to denial of procedural fairness, or acting on the basis of a fact which did not exist.

I think, however, that the authorised person failed to give Professor Listerine adequate notice of her intention to take these activities into account. I assume that Professor Listerine hoped that the delegate would not be aware of this matter and that this was why he did not address it. In this sense, it can be said that he was taken by surprise by the delegate having taken it into account. However, it is clear that he knew that the delegate would take account of his character, and in that sense he was put on notice that he should comment on relevant aspects of his past. The 'well-publicised activities' are not particularised. In so far as they include activities in which Professor Listerine did not, in fact, engage (as well-publicised horror stories sometimes do), then there has clearly been denial of procedural fairness, since he could not reasonably be expected to rebut in advance allegations whose content he could not know. Even if the truth of the horror stories was uncontentious, I think the authorised person erred in failing to seek the professor's comments. His plight is in part a result of his lack of frankness, but this would seem to go to whether relief might be refused in the court's discretion, rather than to whether he has been denied procedural fairness.

This objection does not apply so strongly in relation to the *Hitlerjugend* matter. Your client clearly recognised that it could be relevant and chose to present information with a view to meeting such prejudicial effect as it might have. Given that he had legal advice, the authorised person was entitled to treat the information as accurate in both form and substance. Perhaps she should have raised the question of whether the reference to February 1946 was a misprint, with February 1945 intended. (I have no instructions as to whether this was indeed the case.) However, I think the delegate was entitled to rely on the assumption that lawyers do not make serious mistakes in important correspondence. But even if this is so, the authorised person has failed to make inquiries into the implications to be drawn from the delay in resignation. If the delegate was concerned about the delay (which does not seem to have been undue), especially if, as seems likely, Professor Listerine was still in his teens at the time, he could and should have been given an opportunity to provide an explanation.

(v) The effects of denial of procedural fairness

Assuming there to have been denial of procedural fairness, it is clear that the authorised person's decision has no legal force except in circumstances where the denial of procedural fairness is immaterial, in the sense that it could not have affected the decision: *Stead v State Government Insurance Commission* (1986) 161 CLR 141]. In this case, I think that further inquiries might well have affected the authorised person's decision. So long as procedural fairness could have made a difference, a decision-maker who has failed to afford procedural fairness will be treated as not having performed his or her duty, and the 'decision' will be treated as a nullity: *Re Minister for Immigration and Multicultural Affairs; Ex parte Miah* (2001) 206 CLR 57; 179 ALR 238; [2001] HCA 22.

Unfortunately for your client, the conclusion about denial of procedural fairness makes no difference to the status of his book at all material times. Even if the decision refusing importation is a nullity the book is still a prohibited import. Assuming the book to have been an illegal import, it continued to be an illegal import, and it could lose that status only if its importation had been permitted. Conversely, if the book was not an illegal import, it should never have been destroyed.

This means that it is irrelevant to the legality of the destruction of the book that Professor Listerine was or was not denied procedural fairness. He will almost certainly win his judicial review application but, because it can have no effect on a claim for trespass, it will be a pyrrhic victory.

Examiner's Comments

The purpose of this question was to examine students' capacity to recognise that the particular scenario gave rise to procedural fairness issues, and to assess whether there were any and what respects in which there had been denial of procedural fairness. The purpose of the trespass issue was to require discussion of the effects of a finding that procedural fairness had been denied, and to highlight the fact that a finding that procedural fairness has been denied does not necessarily mean a finding that an applicant for permission must be treated as having been granted that permission. The question is largely about procedural fairness, and could be disposed of on this ground alone. However, if students also discussed other grounds (including Administrative Decisions (Judicial Review) Act 1977 (Cth) (ADJR Act) 'no evidence') they would be entitled to credit for this.

This long and detailed answer generally recognises the degree to which decisions in cases like this turn on the circumstances of the particular case, and the degree to which reasoning about fairness in administrative law can be seen as a form of applied moral reasoning. I had at one stage thought that there was an argument to be made to the effect that, given that the letter had been written by a lawyer, the delegate was entitled to treat it as a comprehensive statement of the case for granting the relevant permission. If this argument were to be accepted, the applicant's argument would not be particularly strong. However, I do not think that this argument is sustainable, especially given the way in which modern courts have interpreted the procedural fairness requirements. Fairness in this case seems to me to have required dialogue, rather than treating the letter as a complete statement of the professor's case.

 ## Common Errors to Avoid

- The case turns very much on its circumstances. It is important to avoid the temptation to write a formulaic response, without regard to those circumstances.

- Recognise the limits of outcome-driven reasoning. You have accepted a brief to advise Listerine's solicitor about the professor's rights, and your job is to do so. You must, however, do your best to assess those rights as accurately as possible.

- Avoid the temptation to assume that administrative law always provides a remedy for injustice.

 ## QUESTION 20

Recalling the 'The Makepeace Scenario', p xvi, consider the following situation.

Makepeace sends a letter to the Attorney-General, asking him to consider whether to allow importation of *The Night of a Thousand Shames*. The letter states that Makepeace believes that the book is not in fact a prohibited import, but that, even assuming that it was, importation should be permitted. If the book was a prohibited import, then the same could be said of hundreds of other, far less worthy publications. The letter draws attention to Makepeace's status as a respected advocate of the rights of humans and animals, and to its commitment to human rights throughout the region. It argues that Makepeace has always believed that releasing the book would actually improve relations with Caledenia, and states that Makepeace would be happy to discuss conditions relating to the importation of the copies of the book with the Attorney-General. If the Attorney-General has any other concerns, Makepeace would also like to be given the chance to discuss these, with a view to their resolution.

The Attorney-General's delegate decides to read a copy of the book before making up her mind about Makepeace's application. She decides that it is not a prohibited import. She has before her a memorandum from the top-secret Australian Secret Service (ASS) which agrees with her assessment, but nonetheless advises against permitting the book to be imported, saying:

> One of the glories of the rule of law is that it takes so long for the law to rule. We'll lose the litigation, but we will be buying delay. It is a price worth paying.

A report by an ASS agent states that, at the last meeting of Makepeace's Inner Collective, there was much discussion of the book:

> The consensus was that the Caledenian government could not tolerate a decision by the Australian government to allow its importation. It would be likely that Caledenia would reduce the level of its diplomatic representation in Australia, and would call off the proposed visit of the Prime Minister. This, the Inner Collective concluded, would strengthen the position of the anti-Caledenian forces within the Australian government, and was therefore to be welcomed.

He comments that this demonstrates the insincerity of Makepeace's claims.

The authorised person approaches you and says:

> This is a mess. Whatever I do, I'm in trouble. If I say that Makepeace is entitled to import the book, ASS will think I'm a card-carrying terrorist. If I say they shouldn't, I'll be the person who carries the can when the case gets to the Federal Court. What I'm thinking of doing is telling ASS that I won't be able to use their agent's material unless I give Makepeace the right to cross-examine their agent before I make my decision. That should shut them up. Have I got grounds for this?

Time allowed: 45 mins

Answer Plan

(i)   The scope of the right to a hearing.

(ii) The relevance of the legislation.

(iii) The interests which must be considered.

(iv) Application of the law: the relevance of *O'Rourke*.

(v)   Other matters counting against a right to cross-examine.

- An interest which falls short of a right.
- The implications of an adverse decision.
- The effect on the decision-making process.
- An interest in security agents' identities not being disclosed.
- A lack of any case law suggesting a right to cross-examination in such cases.

(vi) Conclusions and suggestions.

Answer

(i) The scope of the right to a hearing

The considerations which determine the scope of the right to a hearing are similar to those which determine whether a right to a hearing exists in the first place; they include 'the statutory requirements, the interests of the individual and the interests, whether public or private, which the statute seeks to advance or protect or permits to be taken into account as legitimate expectations': *Kioa v West* (1985) 159 CLR 550 at 585 per Mason J.

(ii) The relevance of the legislation

The Customs (Prohibited Imports) Regulations are silent in relation to the procedure to be used by the Attorney-General or authorised person in determining whether to grant a permission under reg 4A(2). However, one effect of the silence is that authorised persons have no power to compel anyone to attend before them to give oral evidence. They therefore have no power to compel anyone to submit to cross-examination. At best, they can invite potential witnesses to give oral evidence and to subject themselves to cross-examination — lending some force to those requests by suggestions that they might attach less weight to material presented by witnesses who were not prepared to comply. The lack of provisions empowering the decision-maker to compel the giving of sworn oral evidence is, in my opinion, a matter which counts strongly against conditioning the validity of a decision upon those adversely affected by it having been given a chance to cross-examine people who have presented material adverse to their case.

(iii) The interests which must be considered

Attention to the public and private interests which the statute seeks to advance does not provide much assistance in relation to the content of the right to a hearing. The regulation recognises that there are a number of interests potentially at stake. It assumes that there is a public interest in the exclusion of objectionable literature. It also recognises that there are competing public interests, such that it may be desirable that the importation of objectionable literature should sometimes be permitted. It assumes that decisions in relation to permissions should be 'rational' in the sense of being guided by listed criteria. It should also, I think, be interpreted in the light of a common law presumption in favour of limiting statutory incursions on freedom of speech, and in the light of constitutional prohibitions on conduct which unreasonably interferes with freedom of political discourse. But the regulation also envisages that there are circumstances in which the delegate or the Minister should be the final judge of the factual and evaluative criteria which will ultimately determine how decision-makers are to exercise their legal discretion: subreg (5).

In deciding the content of the procedural fairness requirements, account may also be taken of interests other than those which arise under the directly relevant legislation. In *Minister for Immigration and Ethnic Affairs v Kurtovic* (1990) 21 FCR 193, for example, the full Federal Court accepted that it was proper that the full contents of parole officers' reports not be disclosed to a person who was subsequently threatened with deportation on the basis of the contents of those reports. It would be sufficient that the deportee be informed of the general gist of the reports. If, in cases such as these, procedural fairness does not require that a person be fully informed of the evidence against them, it would certainly not require that the person have a right to cross-examine.

(iv) Application of the law: the relevance of O'Rourke

Given that Makepeace's interests are affected by the decision, Makepeace clearly has a right to procedural fairness. This does not, however, mean that it is therefore entitled to cross-examine those who have provided information adverse to its case. The strongest argument in favour of Makepeace being entitled to cross-examine is that the credibility of a relevant part of its submission is at stake. However, while this consideration is one which points in the direction of there being a right to cross-examine, it is not conclusive: see *O'Rourke v Miller* (1985) 156 CLR 342. In that case, however, in rejecting O'Rourke's contention that he had a right to cross-examine two girls who had made adverse allegations against him, the High Court took account of two circumstances which are not necessarily applicable here. First, it took account of the public's interest in a police force whose members were beyond suspicion. It could not be said that there is an equally strong public interest in permissions being refused, except when there are very strong grounds for accepting the truth of the facts alleged by the applicant. Second, the court concluded that there was no reason for believing that the girls who had complained about O'Rourke's behaviour might have lied. Here, it is not so self-evident that the ASS agent would not have any reason for lying. A belief (whether sincere and well-founded or not) that Makepeace was a dangerous organisation might prompt slanted reports. As Murphy J's judgment in *Church of Scientology Inc v Woodward* (1982) 154 CLR 25 demonstrates, not all judges are willing to trust the bona fides of security agencies. (But then, not all judges have been associated with politically ill-conceived raids on ASIO headquarters!) Different judges would, I think, bring different perspectives to bear on this issue. All I would be prepared to advise is that one cannot be confident that a court would accord the ASS the same respect that the High Court was willing to accord to the complainants in *O'Rourke*.

(v) Other matters counting against a right to cross-examine

An interest which falls short of a right

There are other factors which suggest that Makepeace does not have a right to cross-examine the agent. First, Makepeace's 'interest' falls well short of a right. Moreover, whereas O'Rourke could be said to have a reasonable expectation that his probationary appointment would be confirmed in the absence of adverse allegations, it is not so certain that Makepeace could expect that it would receive the relevant permission.

The implications of an adverse decision

Second, the importance of Makepeace's interest seems to fall well short of interests which in other cases have proved insufficient to ground a right to cross-examine. The implications of an adverse decision for Makepeace would almost certainly be less than those of a decision adverse to *Kurtovic* and, indeed, *O'Rourke*.

The effect on the decision-making process

Third, affording a right to cross-examine would prolong the decision-making process. This, however, is not a particularly strong argument. Cases such as this are clearly rare. (It is significant that there is no directly relevant case law.) Moreover, any resulting inconvenience must be balanced against the desirability of decisions being based on tested evidence, where facts are in dispute.

An interest in security agents' identities not being disclosed

Fourth, counting against a right to cross-examination, there *may* be a countervailing interest in ensuring that security agents' identities are not disclosed. Nothing in my instructions suggests that the agent would be in danger from Makepeace, but it is arguable that disclosure of the agent's identity to Makepeace might mean that the agent's identity would eventually be disclosed to others. It is also arguable that, were the agent's identity to be disclosed, other agents might be more reluctant to incur the risk that their identities might be disclosed. At the very least, the agent would, presumably, no longer be able to provide useful information about the organisation. These arguments might not impress some judges (and they would not have impressed Murphy J). Their conclusion might be that ASS has no business infiltrating and taking part in the deliberations of a legitimate political organisation, and that if the exposure of the agent in question discourages further acts of infiltration, this would be to the public good. But a more realistic view of security would recognise that security may require surveillance of the innocent as well as the guilty, and *Church of Scientology v Woodward* is authority for the proposition that surveillance of the innocent was not, *as such*, inconsistent with the powers of ASIO.

A lack of any case law suggesting a right to cross-examination in such cases

Finally and significantly, it is rare to find cases where, in the absence of express statutory provision, the right to a hearing has been held to imply a right to cross-examine adverse witnesses. The few cases in which such a right has been found to exist (see, for example, *O'Rourke* at 352 per Gibbs CJ) have been cases where oral evidence had been delivered to the tribunal.

(vi) Conclusions and suggestions

For these reasons, I do not think that Makepeace has a right to cross-examine the maker of the report.

I would add, however, that while I doubt that you are required to give Makepeace an opportunity to cross-examine the ASS agent, you would be required to disclose to Makepeace that you had reason to doubt its claim that it was seeking to import the book in order to improve relations between Australia and Caledenia. You might even be required to disclose the report, subject to the removal from it of information which might disclose the agent's identity.

The disclosure of doubts about Makepeace's bona fides would not, I think, lead Makepeace to suspect that it had an agent in its midst. Disclosure of full details of the agent's report would suggest a traitor within the Makepeace ranks, but this would not necessarily mean the exposure of the ASS agent. Organisations on the hunt for agents not infrequently expel loyal members, while leaving spies firmly in place.

So I can't really help you. You could, perhaps, decline to act in the matter on the grounds that, as you are inclined to the view that the book is not a prohibited import, there is no power to permit its importation. Makepeace would then have to decide what to do. In the meantime, you would have satisfied those who wanted some delay. Alternatively, you could take stress leave.

Examiner's Comments

This answer canvasses the question whether 'the justice of the common law [in the form of the right to procedural fairness] will supply the omission of the legislature': *Cooper v Wandsworth Board of Works* (1863) 143 ER 414 at 420. It discusses the principles which govern the scope of the hearing rule in such cases, and attempts to apply them. It identifies most of the arguments which could be made for and against an implied right to cross-examination, and is correct in concluding that, in the circumstances of this case, a right to procedural fairness would not entail a right to cross-examine. Indeed, but for the fact that it was required to address the cross-examination issue, it could be criticised for belabouring the obvious. It probably relies too uncritically on *O'Rourke v Miller*, a case decided at a time when courts appear to have been less protective of the right to procedural fairness than is now the case. Nonetheless, given practicalities and the lack of any authority for allowing cross-examination in cases such as this, I think the reliance is acceptable.

 ## Common Errors to Avoid

- The problem is not one which can be resolved by a simple process of finding an appropriate case and applying it. Even when there are dicta which might seem applicable, they must be treated with care, and the context within which they were uttered taken into account.
- In answering the question, students should avoid the temptation to let their answers be influenced by their attitudes to ASIO, Attorneys-General, bodies like Makepeace, or the flustered delegate. Their task is to provide good advice based on the law.

Chapter 7

The Right to an Unbiased Decision-Maker

Key Issues

Procedural fairness requires not only an unbiased decision-maker, but a decision-maker who appears to be unbiased. The requirement that decision-makers be unbiased is, in a sense, redundant. A decision-maker who is in fact biased is likely either to take account of irrelevant considerations or to fail to take account of relevant ones. It is unlikely that biased decision-makers can be said to have given a hearing to the person adversely affected by their decisions. The requirement that decision-makers *appear* to be unbiased is, in part, a requirement which enables courts to deal with cases where actual bias might exist, but is difficult to prove. It is also a requirement designed to protect the integrity of the judicial and administrative systems. It recognises that the authority of adjudicative processes is enhanced if justice is, and appears to be, done.

In addition to the requirement that decision-makers be unbiased and apparently unbiased, the statutory regimes which govern some decision-making processes expressly provide that decision-makers are not to have an institutional or pecuniary interest in the outcome of an issue on which they must decide. There was some common law authority to the effect that a pecuniary interest in the outcome of a case could be sufficient to disqualify a judge from deciding it. This rule — if indeed it ever was a rule — has now been subsumed within the 'no apparent bias' rule. A large, direct pecuniary interest in the outcome of a case will be likely to give rise to a reasonable apprehension of bias. Where, however, a decision in favour of a bank might increase the value of a judge's shareholding by a dollar or so, the pecuniary interest will not give rise to apparent bias: *Ebner v Official Trustee in Bankruptcy* (2000) 205 CLR 337; 176 ALR 644; [2000] HCA 63.

Difficulties arise in relation to what is required if apparent bias is to be demonstrated. Broadly, what must be shown is a 'reasonable apprehension of bias'. It is, however, not enough to show that the decision-maker is perhaps more inclined than other decision-makers to reach a particular decision: *R v Commonwealth Conciliation and Arbitration Commission; Ex parte Angliss Group* (1969) 122 CLR 546. The bias must be such that the reasonable observer would conclude that the decision-maker was approaching the matter with an unacceptably closed mind. For a decision-maker's mind to be unacceptably closed, 'what must be firmly established is a reasonable fear that the decision-maker's mind is so prejudiced in favour of a conclusion already formed that he or she will not alter that conclusion irrespective of the evidence or arguments presented to him or her': per Gaudron and McHugh JJ, *Laws v Australian Broadcasting Tribunal* (1990) 170 CLR 70 at 100.

The second problem involves the hypothetical reasonable observer. For the purposes of the bias rule, reasonable observers are endowed with some pieces of knowledge but not others. They know that a person who issues a defence to a civil action is not to be taken as stating that anything alleged therein is true (*Laws*), but they are not taken as knowing that the judge to whose conduct someone has objected is in fact a person of the utmost integrity. In order to apply the 'bias rule' one needs to know the attributes ascribed to reasonable observers. This can come only from a knowledge of the relevant case law, combined with a feel for circumstances where courts are likely to be worried by the facts which give rise to the alleged reasonable apprehension of bias.

Third, what is the position where the decision-maker is a collective body, and one or more of whose members are biased? Is its decision biased if even one member is biased?: *IW v City of Perth* (1997) 191 CLR 1.

Fourth, distinctions are drawn between politicians, administrators and judges. As one shifts from politician to judge, behavioural expectations increase. Behaviour which would be excusable in a politician will not be excusable in a judge. Politicians can appear on talk-back radio and discuss cases which they are handling: *Minister for Immigration and Multicultural Affairs v Jia Legeng* (2001) 205 CLR 507. Judges should resist such opportunities. Politicians are therefore permitted to be somewhat more closed-minded than judges, but their minds must not be completely closed.

Fifth, problems could arise if the bias rule were applied rigorously. Suppose the Minister, and only the Minister, may issue permits. The Minister refuses a permit. The applicant argues that the Minister's decision was flawed by apparent bias, the court being critical of the Minister's description of the applicant as a person who 'has devoted his life to making a mockery of the criminal law, and whose clean record stands as a daily reproach to the inability of our criminal justice system to put people like him behind bars where they belong'. The refusal is quashed. The Minister refuses to reconsider the case, stating that she is disqualified on the grounds of apparent — and, in her case, actual —

bias. Clearly it would be absurd if the bias rules required the Minister to disqualify herself. To deal with cases where repositories of power are both under a duty to exercise it, and potentially disqualified from doing so, the law has developed the 'necessity doctrine'. This has not always proved easy to apply.

Finally, the bias rule has been qualified to deal with cases where people are aware of apparent bias, but decide to wait and see how their matter goes. If the matter goes in their favour, they accept the decision. If it goes against them, they cry foul. Courts discourage this behaviour. People may waive their right to an unbiased decision-maker, and they will be treated as having done so if they do not object, once grounds for objection have come to their notice.

Before attempting the questions, check that you are familiar with the following issues:

✓ the nature of the 'rule against bias';

✓ the knowledge that can be attributed to the 'reasonable observer';

✓ the difference between an insufficiently open mind and an inclination to decide legally ambiguous cases in particular ways;

✓ the circumstances in which the 'necessity' rule permits decision-making by a biased decision-maker; and

✓ the circumstances in which a person can be said to have waived a right to an unbiased decision-maker.

 # QUESTION 21

'Bias is inherent in administrative and judicial decision-making. The so-called rule against bias is therefore nothing but a dishonest attempt to pretend otherwise.' Discuss, making it clear what you and the law mean by 'bias'.

Time allowed: 1 hour

Answer Plan

(i)   Definitions of bias.

(ii) Bias (broadly defined) is inescapable in decision-making.

  • Law is often ambiguous.

  • Facts can be ambiguous.

  • Responses to ambiguity.

(iii) Legally unacceptable bias.

Answer

(i)   Definitions of bias

The answer to this question depends on what one means by 'bias'. Literally, bias equates with a disposition to decide particular cases in particular ways. A disposition to decide particular cases in particular ways does not mean that those cases are always decided in accordance with the disposition. The bias of a mildly biased decision-maker may be almost imperceptible. A rather more biased decision-maker's behaviour may be more readily predicted on the basis of their 'bias', but may nonetheless be even more readily predicted on the basis of legally relevant aspects of the case. Only a completely biased decision-maker would be influenced by bias and bias alone.

Legal definitions of bias tend to define the term far more narrowly: bias is usually equated with something approaching stubborn closed-mindedness. In *Livesey v New South Wales Bar Association* (1983) 151 CLR 288 at 293–4, a case involving a judge, the High Court equated bias with bringing 'other than an unprejudiced and impartial mind to the resolution of the issues'. The *Livesey* test has been reaffirmed in subsequent decisions: see, for example, *Laws v Australian Broadcasting Tribunal* (1990) 170 CLR 70. But an inclination to decide a case in a matter in a particular way is not inconsistent with impartiality and lack of prejudice at least in matters involving quasi-political issues: *R v Commonwealth Court of Conciliation and Arbitration; Ex parte Angliss Group* (1969) 122 CLR 546 (which involved a wage-fixing authority). Preconceived views about the reliability of particular expert witnesses do not constitute bias when they are based on a judge's previous curial encounters with those witnesses: *Vakauta v Kelly* (1989) 167 CLR 568. In *Minister for Immigration and Multicultural Affairs v Jia Legeng* (2001) 205 CLR 507, discussing the standard required of a Minister, Gleeson CJ and Gummow J said at [105]:

> The Minister was obliged to give genuine consideration to the issues raised … and to bring to bear on those issues a mind that was open to persuasion.

The fact that the Minister had expressed strong views about the merits of the case in question did not mean that he was not open to persuasion.

A mere disposition to decide a case in a particular way does not constitute legal bias. The legal test for bias is such that it is hard to envisage a case of actual bias which would not also amount to an improper exercise of power and denial of a hearing. The importance of the bias rule lies partly in its potential use as the basis for ordering the disqualification of a biased decision-maker, but mainly in cases where judicial review is sought on the basis of reasonable apprehension of bias — which can, of course, exist in the absence of actual bias and which can therefore logically exist in the absence of other grounds of review.

I shall argue that if 'bias' is used in its broader literal sense of a disposition to decide a particular matter in a particular way, bias is inherent in legal and judicial decision-making. If that is so, then a rule which struck down any decision which was influenced by this kind of bias would obviously be absurd. Administrative and judicial decisions could survive scrutiny only on the basis of fictitious findings to the effect that they were uninfluenced by the decision-maker's preconceptions. While the *Livesey* test, read literally, could be taken as suggesting that a mere disposition to decide a case in a particular manner could constitute bias, the application of the bias test in such cases as *Angliss* at 555 indicates that 'prejudgment' requires more than a disposition to decide a case in a particular manner, and that 'impartiality' is consistent with a disposition to exercise legal discretions in a particular way. The *Jia Legeng* test suggests that, in the case of a Minister, all that may be required is open-mindedness. The discrepancy between the apparent strictness of the *Livesey* test and the rather more tolerant way in which it has been applied suggests, on one hand, a reluctance to acknowledge the degree to which decision-making (and judicial decision-making in particular) is influenced by the decision-maker's values, but, on the other hand, awareness of the degree to which decision-making cannot but do so.

(ii) Bias (broadly defined) is inescapable in decision-making

Bias (as broadly defined) is inherent in administrative and judicial decision-making, but it is important to recognise the degree to which 'individual' bias is subordinated to what we could call 'institutional bias', and it is essential to recognise the degree to which administrative and judicial decision-making typically involves a relatively mechanical form of decision-making — partly as a result of 'institutional bias', and partly because decision-making can often involve the application of straightforward rules to uncontested facts. In both administration and adjudication, bias becomes increasingly inescapable as one moves from lower to higher positions in the relevant hierarchies. Low-level administration and adjudication tend to be relatively mechanical. Senior administrators and senior judges are far more likely to be confronted with matters which can be resolved only on the basis of personal values and assumptions.

Bias becomes inevitable once — and to the extent to which — decision-makers enjoy de facto or de jure discretion. Discretions are almost inescapable even in contexts which are ostensibly regulated by law. There are several reasons why this is so.

Law is often ambiguous

Law uses language, and therefore suffers from the ambiguities inherent in language. Moreover, laws are likely to be framed in language which builds in a degree of flexibility and therefore provides scope for a degree of discretion. Law-makers are normally mindful of the need to balance specificity, generality, flexibility, workability and acceptability. Specificity has both advantages and disadvantages. It may make for a degree of predictability, and this in turn may make for acceptability. But laws which are highly specific are likely to be unsatisfactory in situations where popular evaluations of the conduct in question require us to take into account a broad range of variables. Laws which condition an outcome on a small number of attributes of a case are likely to yield unacceptable results where most people would base their evaluation on a much larger range of considerations. Laws which seek to achieve predictability by prescribing different outcomes for a host of different situations are likely to become unwieldy, and their sheer complexity is likely to yield anomalies. They require constant updating if the law is to stay in touch with changing standards; but legislatures often lack the time, the will and the resources to devote their attention to this kind of enterprise. Not surprisingly, therefore, legal systems normally seek to achieve a balance between predictability and flexibility. But flexibility is achieved by laws which condition outcomes on relatively vague criteria:

1. dangerousness;

2. reasonableness; and

3. unconscionability.

It may be achieved by requiring that the decision-maker take account of a variety of considerations, leaving it up to him or her to decide how much weight to attach to each consideration, and what is entailed in giving a certain amount of weight to a particular consideration in a particular case.

But while it is essential that one recognise the degree to which laws often involve the creation of relatively open-ended discretions, it is also important to recognise the degree to which laws seek (with varying degrees of effectiveness) to prescribe relatively specific criteria in some areas. Social welfare, migration, taxation and drivers' behaviour are all regulated by legislation which seeks to provide for a mass of possible contingencies. Moreover, there are some legal regimes which manage to achieve a high level of predictability in relation to huge numbers of transactions without offending expectations that each case be handled on the basis of close attention to its merits. The law relating to the transfer of Torrens Title land stands as a striking example of such regimes.

Facts can be ambiguous

Uncertainty also derives from uncertainty in relation to facts. When there are disputes about facts, decisions must be made about who is to be believed. In making such decisions, decision-makers must inevitably bring to bear their assumptions about human and social behaviour. Does confidence in the witness box indicate that a person is telling the truth? Is it conceivable that a police officer could tell a lie? Is it likely that a farmer producing for the export market was unaware that the value of the Australian dollar fluctuates? Can 'no' mean 'yes'? Does 'yes' mean 'yes'? In answering these questions, decision-makers will normally have little alternative but to draw on their experience, beliefs and prejudices. In view of this, a degree of bias becomes inevitable.

Yet, while factual disputes can prove intractable, many cases do not involve factual disputes, and in some cases where these disputes do arise, they can be resolved without too much difficulty. Most administrative decision-making involves treating applications on the basis that the matters set out in the application are to be taken as true. Confidence that this is justified may sometimes be enhanced by a requirement that documentary evidence be provided, and such evidence is usually treated on the basis that unless challenged, it is an honest statement.

Responses to ambiguity

Ambiguity may mean that decisions are based on the decision-maker's values and assumptions, but it does not necessarily entail this. While one response to ambiguity may be to take full advantage of the discretion that it creates, another may be to ask how others handle similar situations. Decision-makers may also be influenced by those they work with so that they come to accept common solutions to particular problems, even when they might be personally disposed to reach different conclusions. Moreover, in hierarchical decision-making structures, decision-makers may tailor their decisions so that they are likely to be acceptable to superiors in the hierarchy. This is not always possible. It can sometimes be difficult to predict how superiors will react to particular cases, especially where their decisions involve rehearings, rather than a determination of whether the primary decision was correct on the basis of the material before the decision-maker. But, in so far as decisions by superiors provide a guide to the way in which difficult questions are likely to be resolved, those standards are likely to achieve a considerable level of compliance from subordinates.

This does not, of course, mean that their decisions can be classed as 'unbiased'. They are likely to build in such biases as characterise the relevant bureaucratic or legal culture, and they are likely to build in such biases as characterise the decisions of superordinates. But this is a particular kind of bias. While arbitrary in a sense, its role also reflects decision-makers who see their role, not as the implementation of personal values, but rather as the implementation of rules which enjoy a degree of authority by virtue of the fact that they are rules. The result may be decisions which are, in a sense, biased; but they will also be decisions which are rather more predictable than would be the case if the only bias to influence lower-level decisions was to be that of the primary decision-makers. Moreover, it will not always be appropriate to conceptualise the value-based regularities which characterise bureaucratic or judicial cultures as bias. For 'bias' carries with it the implication that biased decisions are somehow wrong. Obviously, if there is a 'correct' decision in a given context, any decision other than that decision must be incorrect. But if we assume that there is such a thing as a correct decision, it may well be that the institutional wisdom embodied in bureaucratic and judicial cultures will be more likely to be 'correct' than decisions which reflect individual values and assumptions. Indeed, this is one of the justifications for such collective decision-making institutions as three-person tribunals, juries and, of course, Cabinets and Parliaments. Moreover, from a legal standpoint, the wisdom or otherwise which is embodied in higher court decisions is, by reason of that embodiment alone, more 'correct' than the decisions of lower courts.

Bias is inherent in decision-making, but the role of bias will often be far less important than the role of authoritative standards. While the quotation rightly recognises the unavoidability of bias, it needs to be placed in perspective. The unavoidability of bias must be seen in conjunction with the importance of rules and standards as determinants of the behaviour of both administrators and judges.

(iii) *Legally unacceptable bias*

The quotation is also on questionable grounds in so far as it implies the inevitability of bias (broadly construed). True, the law may give the impression of not recognising the degree to which decisions necessarily reflect individual values and assumptions, in so far as it fails to class these values and assumptions as 'bias'. On its face, the requirement that decision-makers be 'impartial' could be taken as requiring that they have no disposition to decide, for example, in favour of employees rather than employers, on the basis of the claims of female witnesses rather than male ones, or on the basis of a preference for severe sentences over lenient ones. Yet, in practice, courts require more than evidence of general dispositions before they are willing to conclude that bias exists (see *Angliss; Vakauta v Kelly*) — realities count:

> The requirement of the reality and appearance of impartial justice in the administration of law by the courts is one which must be observed in the real world of actual litigation. That requirement will not be infringed merely because a judge carries with him or her the knowledge that some medical witnesses, who are regularly called to give evidence on behalf of particular classes of plaintiffs (for example, members of a particular trade union), are likely to be less sceptical of a plaintiff's claims and less optimistic in their prognosis of the extent of future recovery than other medical witnesses who are regularly called to give evidence on behalf of particular classes of defendants (for example, those whose liability is covered by a particular insurer). If it were so infringed the administration of justice in personal injuries cases would be all but impossible: *Vakauta* at 570–1 per Brennan, Deane and Gaudron JJ.

The law also recognises that some decision-making is likely to turn primarily on the decision-maker's personal beliefs, while other kinds of decision-making should turn primarily on relatively objective considerations: *Century Metals and Mining NL v Yeomans* (1989) 40 FCR 564.

Some formulations of the bias rule may suggest unrealistic expectations (*Livesey*; but not *Jia Legeng*), but when they are read in conjunction with decisions in which that rule is applied, it becomes clear that the bias rule is directed at egregious bias rather than the 'bias' which is inherent in decision-making. The bias rule targets 'avoidable bias' rather than the bias which is inherent in decision-making, and in relatively open-ended decision-making. The arguable contrast between the demands of the *Livesey* test for judges and tribunals and the more generous applications of that test could be taken as suggesting a degree of insincerity, but I think it can also be taken as evidence of the courts' commitment to dispassionate decision-making, coupled with their awareness that decision-making cannot be completely dispassionate especially where it is necessarily guided by subjective considerations.

Examiner's Comments

This is a challenging but not overly difficult question. It requires attention both to the nature of administrative and judicial decision-making, and to the content of the bias rule. It is a question which could be tackled in a number of ways.

This answer represents one approach. It manages to present a highly contextualised response. It is critical of the case law but not unfairly so. An alternative approach would have been to take a more legalistic approach, choosing case law to illustrate the way in which law has approached the problem of distinguishing between acceptable and unacceptable bias. This would be satisfactory, though a wider perspective is preferable.

The answer begins by discussing the different ways in which 'bias' can be defined. It examines legal definitions of bias and concludes that there may be a discrepancy between formulae and the way in which they are applied. Importantly, it recognises that law is relatively tolerant of 'dispositional' bias. The answer could usefully have done more to highlight the fact that the rigour with which the bias test is applied varies according to the decision-maker. While it notes the relatively liberal test governing Ministers, it does not note that the *Angliss* decision is partly explicable in terms of the quasi-legislative functions performed by the relevant institution, the Commonwealth Conciliation and Arbitration Commission.

The discussion of the unavoidability of bias (broadly defined) sees bias as inherent in the existence of discretions, and sees discretions as arising from the failure or inability of law to provide clear solutions to every issue. It does, however, point out that law can sometimes provide relatively clear guidelines, and it gives several examples. It also recognises the degree to which uncertainty about facts means that decision-makers will have to bring their own perspectives to bear in deciding what to treat as 'facts' in particular cases. It recognises that fact uncertainty is often not a serious problem. It concludes by acknowledging that, even when uncertainty exists, decision-makers may deal with this, not on the basis of their own dispositions, but on the basis of organisational perspectives.

There is an implicit assumption that there is such a thing as unbiased decision-making, and the answer seems to suggest that if and to the degree that decisions are guided by law they are unbiased in a legal sense. The answer might perhaps have considered whether law itself should not be regarded as reflecting particular biases (as it obviously does), and the implications of this for its analysis. However, it did not, and given the time available, this can scarcely be treated as a serious error. It also seemed to treat bias as stemming from the inability of decision-makers to do anything but base their decisions partly on extra-legal criteria, but another possibility is that it reflects the opportunities that exist for decision-makers to act in a biased manner without being held to account for this. This issue might usefully have been addressed, but I do not think that the question required this.

The answer concludes with a brief but persuasive attempt to demonstrate the degree to which the law of bias can be understood in terms of the foregoing discussion, noting that the dichotomy assumed by the question largely disappears once one recognises that law's narrow definition of 'bias' reflects, not a pretence that law is objective, but a recognition of the degree to which administrative and legal decision-making necessarily involve decision-makers' values and assumptions.

One could have approached this question in other ways. Jerome Frank's iconoclastic works are still worth reading, and anticipate much subsequent scholarship on the subject: see, for example, *Law and the Modern Mind*, Stevens, London, 1949; *Courts on Trial: Myth and Reality in American Justice*, Princeton University Press, Princeton, 1949. Self-consciously postmodern analyses develop similar themes to those developed here, while possibly under-estimating the degree to which law is not completely open-ended. Marxist, feminist and ethnic analyses all remind us of the degree to which law tends to reflect the values and assumptions of liberal, bourgeois, sons of the enlightenment, and the work of anti-elitist elitists reminds us that redneck farmers with guns are also under-represented on the courts.

Common Errors to Avoid

- This is not a question which says: 'write everything you know about the law on bias'. It requires knowledge of the law, but it also requires the capacity to identify which areas of the law on bias have implications for the question.

- When discussing a proposition an examiner has put before you, it is unwise to proceed on the basis that the proposition is either true or false (especially in this case). Rather, answers should attempt to identify those respects in which the proposition seems valid, and those where its validity is more problematic, or where it simply seems wrong.

■ It will be difficult to answer the question without discussing what you mean by 'bias'.

QUESTION 22

The decision to ban *Me and Ewe* was controversial, but the government pointed out that, even if it was a tender tale of love set in the icy mountains of central Catatonia, the fact was that it included photos which brought it within reg 4A(1A)(a). The Attorney-General told the publisher that he saw no reason why the would-be local publisher should not be allowed to import it, minus photographs: 'After the controversy which you have so carefully orchestrated, there should be a large market for it, even in its expurgated form.' After the ban, an application was made to import the book by Egon Kisch, lecturer in modern European languages and Scots Gaelic at Robert Menzies University. He wants to use the book in his forthcoming monograph, *The Love that Cannot Speak its Name*. He also intends to use it in his course, 'Homage to Catatonia: The Novels and Poetry of Arcadia'. His request having been refused by the Attorney-General, he appeals to the AAT. In view of the controversy aroused by the book, the president decides that the appeal will be heard by a three-person tribunal. The presiding member, Heffner SC, is a well-respected administrative lawyer who was regularly briefed by the Keating government to defend its interests in migration and customs cases. She was appointed to the AAT by the Howard government. The other two members are Dr David Lawrence, a part-time member who is also Professor of Animal Psychology at the University of Melbourne; and Ms Miriam de Sade, a member who normally handles taxation cases.

It soon becomes clear that the application is in trouble. Counsel for Kisch begins by arguing that the pictures were unlikely to cause offence to a reasonable adult person. Heffner SC replies:

Heffner SC: Stop. I am a reasonable adult person and the pictures certainly cause offence to me. Indeed, if they didn't, you'd face a major problem and that is that our jurisdiction is dependent on the book falling foul of the regulation.

Counsel for Kisch: If you've already made up your mind, perhaps I should simply sit down.

Heffner SC: If you'd only listen to me, you might see that what I am saying is actually assisting your case.

Counsel for Kisch: For you to assist anyone's case but the government's would be a novelty.

Heffner SC: I think it might be a good idea if we adjourned for morning tea. In the meantime, I suggest that you read subregs (2) and (4) very carefully. Your client won't be impressed if his salacious intentions are frustrated by a technicality.

After the break, the hearing resumed:

Counsel for Kisch: I am in an impossible position. I'm told that I must concede that the book falls within the regulation if the tribunal is to listen to me, so I suppose I have no alternative but to make the concession. I shall argue accordingly, but I am placing my protest at the tribunal's bias on the record.

Heffner SC (hopefully): Are you asking that we step down?

Counsel for Kisch: What's the use? I'm simply adding my ninth appeal point.

Later:

Counsel for Kisch: My client wishes to read this book in order that he might site it within the tradition of pastoral literature.

Heffner SC: Does he need the photographs to do this? The tradition doesn't extend to illustrated pornography, surely? And he wants copies for his students? How does he propose to stop them getting into general circulation? I'm told students use photocopiers.

Counsel for Kisch: I wish you'd stop using that term. Erotic, yes, but not pornographic. It's a love story.

Lawrence: But that's not so, at least from the standpoint of sheep. They like the warmth; but they don't like the sex.

Counsel for Kisch: Perhaps you'd like to swap places with counsel for the Commonwealth.

Lawrence: You should read the work of Angas and Hereford in the *ANZ Journal of Animal Psychiatry*, and that of Clydesdale in last week's *Sheep Weekly*. I think it's against you, but I'd like to hear your comments on it. If you could find work to rebut them, I'd like to know. I really would.

De Sade: And if men can't tell whether women are consenting I doubt that they are going to be any more successful when it comes to sheep. However, you might want to address this issue. Your hero seems to know his animals quite well.

Later:

Heffner SC: At this stage, we're against you, but you might like to think of an order which would accommodate our concerns and at least give your client the access he needs if he is to engage in his research. All it might take would be the removal of a couple of the more disgusting photographs.

Over dinner, counsel describes his miserable day; when he mentions de Sade, his wife says: 'Her! I remember her from St Mary's. She founded the Melbourne University Moral Minority. They burned *Portnoy's Complaint* on the Union lawns. She's still active in the cause.'

Next morning, counsel asks that de Sade disqualify herself. She refuses:

I have strong views on pornography, but you've conceded that the book is offensive for the purposes of the regulations, so we're in agreement there. The question is whether your client should be allowed to import the book for essentially academic purposes. That's quite a different question. You can disapprove of the Ebola virus and still consider it should be studied. I'm open-minded on this issue.

> Counsel then decides to seek an order restraining the tribunal from proceeding any further with the matter, and for the application to be referred to a differently constituted tribunal. Would the application succeed?
>
> **Time allowed: 30 mins**

Answer Plan

(i)   Could Heffner SC be regarded as biased?

(ii) Could Lawrence be regarded as biased?

(iii) Could de Sade be regarded as biased?

(iv) Conclusion.

 # Answer

In my opinion, the application would fail.

The only arguable ground for seeking to restrain the tribunal would be actual or apprehended bias. For the application to succeed, it would be sufficient to prove that the tribunal's conduct was such as to give rise to a reasonable apprehension of bias. This requires that its conduct be such that a fair-minded observer would conclude that it 'would bring other than an unprejudiced and impartial mind to the resolution of the issues which properly arise' in its inquiry: *Livesey v New South Wales Bar Association* (1983) 151 CLR 288; *Laws v ABT* (1990) 170 CLR 70. The fair-minded observer is assumed to be familiar with the circumstances of the case and the context in which the decision is made.

(i)   Could Heffner SC be regarded as biased?

In relation to Heffner SC, there is only one piece of evidence which might sustain a claim of apprehended bias: her reference to the client's 'salacious motives'. This assumes the answer to a question which the tribunal has not had time to consider; namely, Kisch's reasons for wanting to import the book. His interest in the book may be coldly academic, but the term 'salacious' could be taken as indicating that Heffner SC has already decided otherwise. The fact that it is used in the context of a slightly heated exchange might alter the meaning to be attached to it, but it might, I think, be open to a court to find that a fair-minded observer would conclude that Heffner SC had already formed a view about a matter still to be decided by the tribunal.

The fact that Heffner SC has concluded that the book contains offensive photographs is not evidence of bias. She has correctly drawn attention to the fact that the tribunal's jurisdiction is dependent upon the publication in question falling within subreg (1A). She could, of course, reach this conclusion on the basis that, while she did not find the book offensive, most reasonable adults would. However, this is a subtle distinction, and constitutes a tenuous basis for doubting whether she could approach the application in an open-minded way.

Nor is it evidence of bias that Heffner SC had a record of appearing on behalf of the Commonwealth in administrative law cases, prior to her appointment to the bench. It was not even evidence of bias that an industrial relations commissioner had, prior to his appointment, been active on the employer's side in a dispute similar to one which he was handling as a commissioner: *Re Polites; Ex parte The Hoyts Corporation Pty Ltd* (1991) 100 ALR 634.

In any case, counsel may be taken to have waived his right to object on these grounds. Heffner SC asked whether she was being asked to step down. Counsel's statement is ambiguous. It implies that, in counsel's opinion, Heffner SC should step down, but it also seems to envisage that the case will proceed to a decision. It is not permissible to stand by and rely on bias as an appeal point when objection could have been taken earlier: *Vakauta v Kelly* (1989) 167 CLR 568. This seems to be what counsel has tried to do.

Nor do Heffner's comments later in the case give rise to apprehended bias. True, they suggest that she has formed a view in relation to the likely outcome of the case, but she also appears open to suggestions which would give Kisch much of what he wants. The exchange can be taken as an expression of a provisional view (the advantages of which were canvassed in *Vakauta v Kelly*), and it quite helpfully suggests to counsel lines which he might fruitfully pursue. Indeed, it suggests that the reference to 'salacious intentions' did not indicate a closed mind in relation to the issues in the case.

(ii) Could Lawrence be regarded as biased?

There is nothing in Lawrence's exchange with counsel to indicate that Lawrence has formed a firm view in relation to the case. He is clearly disposed to form a particular view in relation to one issue in the case, based on his expertise, but he has indicated the basis for his views, and has asked counsel to respond to his concerns.

(iii) Could de Sade be regarded as biased?

Little weight can be placed on the initial exchange between de Sade and counsel. It is sharp, but it also, on its face, indicates that de Sade is willing to listen to argument. Nor is de Sade's commitment to the anti-pornography cause sufficient to give rise to a reasonable apprehension of bias. The position might be different if a group with which she was or had been associated was involved as a party (see *R v Bow Street Metropolitan Stipendiary Magistrate; Ex parte Pinochet Ugarte (No 2)* [2000] 1 AC 119), but there is no suggestion that this was the case here. The reference she makes to the Ebola virus suggests a continuing lack of sympathy with pornography, but it comes in the context of a discussion in which she has sought to demonstrate that she is able to separate the question of whether limited importation should be permitted from the question of whether the book is one which should be in general circulation.

(iv) Conclusion

Since none of the members of the tribunal appears to be biased (save, perhaps, Heffner SC, whose offer to step down has been declined), it is, strictly speaking, unnecessary to consider whether a finding of bias in relation to one member of the tribunal would require that the other two be disqualified from hearing the application. Some brief comments are proffered. Decisions which suggest this is the case are based on tribunals where the decision-making process is a collective one, in the sense that it is reached by vote after discussion among the members of the decision-making body. Up to a point, this is also the case for tribunal decisions. However, in contrast to the decisions in *Stollery v Greyhound Racing Control Board* (1972) 128 CLR 509 and *Re Macquarie University; Ex parte Ong* (1989) 17 NSWLR 113, this is a case where the tribunal has not yet made its decision. It is also a case where each member of the tribunal is required to give or endorse reasons for his or her decision. It is unlikely that the latter consideration would constitute a basis for distinguishing this from the earlier cases, but it is possible that the unbiased members of the tribunal might be permitted either to continue hearing the matter, or to sit on a freshly constituted tribunal.

Examiner's Comments

This is a relatively straightforward question. Bias should readily be identified as the topic for discussion. The only real difficulty is that of identifying the issues which need to be addressed.

One approach might be to conclude that some of the exchanges provide no grounds whatsoever for reasonable apprehension of bias, and that there is therefore no need to state the obvious. There are, however, hints in the exchanges that the bias issue was in the minds of both counsel and the members of the tribunal, even where counsel ought, perhaps, to have known better. This suggests the need to address possible bias even when the case for bias seems barely arguable.

The answer identifies the issues and handles them well. Where the case for bias is weak, the answer recognises this. The answer also acknowledges that there is at least one exchange which might have given rise to a reasonable apprehension of bias. The answer recognises that bias can be 'cured' by waiver, and rightly notes the slight ambiguity surrounding the waiver in this case. Arguments are supported by apposite authority. As the answer notes, the reference to collective decision-making was not necessary, given the confident and correct conclusion that none of the members could be suspected of being biased.

Common Errors to Avoid

- Do not assume that a predisposition to favour some outcomes over others is sufficient to constitute bias. To amount to a ground of review, bias requires more than this. In particular, it requires that there be reasonable grounds for fearing that the decision-maker will not bring the requisite degree of open-mindedness to the decision-making process. The requisite degree of open-mindedness varies according to the decision-maker and the decision-making process.
- Even reasonable apprehension of bias is not fatal to the decision-making process if the party which complains of it has waived his or her objection. If this issue is not addressed, students would be marked down.

QUESTION 23

> After the Tasmanian Council for Civil Liberties (TCCL) made an application to import *The Night of a Thousand Shames* (see 'The Makepeace Scenario', p xvi), the Attorney-General appeared on 7TB, Hobart Talkback Radio, where he was questioned about his attitude to the application:
>
> **Interviewer:** You won't be falling for this civil liberties rubbish, will you?
>
> **Attorney-General:** Look, I'll have to read the application. You can look a fool if you turn someone down and it turns out you didn't know what they wanted.
>
> **Interviewer:** But you'll turn them down once you've gone through the motions?
>
> **Attorney-General:** If the Minister for Immigration got a refugee application from Bin Laden he'd have to consider it. When I get an application from the TCCL, I've got to look at its details.
>
> **Interviewer:** But you're saying that you'll treat it with the contempt it deserves?
>
> **Attorney-General:** First I'll see how much contempt it deserves. Only then will I turn it down.
>
> In due course the Attorney-General turns down the application. Would the TCCL have grounds for applying to have the decision reviewed, and would it be worth challenging the decision?
>
> **Time allowed: 40 mins**

Answer Plan

(i) Was the Minister biased, or would a fair-minded observer have believed him to be biased?

(ii) If bias was found, what could the court order?

Answer

This case involves two issues. The first is whether the Minister's conduct amounts to bias or is such as to give rise to a reasonable apprehension of bias (the bias question). The second relates to the consequences of a finding of bias.

(i) Was the Minister biased, or would a fair-minded observer have believed him to be biased?

In determining the bias question, account must be taken of the fact that the standards expected of a Minister may be less exacting than those expected of a court. In *Minister for Immigration and Multicultural Affairs v Jia Legeng* (2001) 205 CLR 507; [2001] HCA 17, the High Court considered that it was enough that the Minister gave genuine consideration to the case and brought to bear a mind that was open to persuasion. It concluded that, while the Minister had made public comments indicating that he had definite opinions about the merits of a particular case, the aggrieved party had not demonstrated that he had not given the case genuine consideration, nor had he shown that the Minister had not approached the case with a mind not open to persuasion. By majority, the court also concluded that a fair minded observer would also conclude that the Minister was not biased.

There are slight differences between this case and *Jia Legeng*. In *Jia Legeng* the power was an exceptional power and one which was not subject to merits review. Here, the power is one whose exercise is presumptively subject to merits review — although it is open to the Minister, by certificate, to provide otherwise. This could be taken as suggesting that the standards expected of the Minister are more exacting than those which applied to the Minister in *Jia Legeng*. But this is not a persuasive argument. Indeed, given that the decision to deport is likely to be of more profound significance to the deportee than is a decision to refuse permission to import, it is arguable that it would attract more rigorous standards than the decision in this case. Moreover, the decision-making process under the regulation appears, if anything, to be slightly more dependent on value judgments than the decision to deport which was the basis for the *Legeng* litigation. I do not think that *Jia Legeng* can be distinguished.

Whether the Minister is, or appears to be, biased largely depends on the construction to be placed on the language he used. One construction which could be placed on the words is that he had made up his mind to turn down the application. The Bin Laden analogy suggests that he regarded the TCCL application as devoid of merit. It is unlikely that he assumed that Bin Laden would have a good case for refugee status, and — even if he did — it is hard to imagine that a reasonable observer with some knowledge of Australian politics would believe that that was what he assumed. However, there is a more benign construction; namely, that the Attorney-General is simply stating that, whatever one's beliefs about an applicant, one is obliged to give them serious attention. In any case, the remark must be taken in context. It was not a considered statement, but a statement made in a radio interview and in response to an interviewer who seemed unable to comprehend the fact that the TCCL application could even be considered. It could, I think, be taken to mean that, if Bin Laden was entitled to a hearing, then, *a fortiori*, so was the TCCL.

The final answer also suggests a mind made up. It seems to say: 'First, I'll read the application. Then I'll dismiss it.' Again, however, there is a more benign construction to be placed on the Minister's comments. 'Only then will I turn it down' might be taken to mean: 'Only if I think that it is worthy of contempt will I turn it down'. In a matter of this nature, one would expect the first law officer of the Commonwealth to choose his words carefully, but a careful choice of words may on this occasion have been reflected in a decision to use language whose meaning was deliberately blurred.

I would be better able to advise as to actual bias if I had more information about the way in which the Minister went about making this decision. Reasons under s 13 of the Administrative Decisions (Judicial Review) Act 1977 (Cth) (ADJR Act) would probably not help much, but perusal of the file might throw some light on whether serious consideration was — or was not — given to the application. If the reasons or the file indicated that serious consideration was not given, then it is almost certain that the decision could also be attacked on the grounds of failure to take account of relevant considerations, and on the grounds of the Minister's failure to afford the TCCL a hearing.

In advising on the hypothetical reaction of the fair-minded observer, I would point out that the observer would be aware of the Minister's political role and the context in which the answers were given. In my opinion, one cannot say with any confidence which construction would be attributed to the reasonable observer. It would, I think, be open to a court to find that a reasonable observer would believe that the Minister had made up his mind and could not see any circumstances in which his mind might change, but it would also be open to a court to find otherwise. In the light of *Jia Legeng*, I think the latter finding would be more likely.

(ii) If bias was found, what could the court order?

If the decision were to be quashed on the ground of apprehended bias, the TCCL would still be without its permission. It would be pointless to have the matter considered anew by the Minister, unless the TCCL could actually find some new material capable of bringing about the change of mind which the finding of bias comes close to implying could not reasonably be anticipated. There is, however, provision in the regulation for the appointment of a delegate (an 'authorised person') to make decisions under reg 4A(2). If a delegate has been appointed, an order could be made referring the matter to that person. If, in order to frustrate the court, the Attorney-General had revoked all appointments, these revocations would, I think, involve the impermissible exercise of a power for a purpose other than that for which it was conferred, and would be invalid. The court could therefore order that the matter be reconsidered by an authorised person, since the removal of their authority would have been a legal nullity.

If an authorised person had not been appointed, the only person who could consider the application would be the Attorney-General himself. On the face of the regulation, the Attorney-General is under no obligation to appoint authorised persons. (He 'may' do so.) It is possible, therefore, that the court could not, therefore, resolve the problem by ordering the appointment of an authorised person. If there was actual bias, the court could refer the matter back, with the instruction that the Attorney-General consider the matter according to law. (A finding of actual bias would involve the finding that he had hitherto not performed this duty.) If the court found that there was a reasonable apprehension of bias, the most appropriate order would be a declaration to the effect that the 'decision' to refuse permission was vitiated by apparent bias. It would then be open to the TCCL to make a second application and the Attorney-General would be obliged to consider it. The Attorney-General could, of course, reconsider the matter, arguing that the TCCL had waived its right to object to bias based on the 7TB interview. But this course of action would be one with considerable political costs. It would destroy the Attorney-General's standing with the courts and the legal profession. Faced with this possibility, I think that the Attorney-General would appoint an authorised person to reconsider the matter.

Alternatively, the court might order that the Attorney-General exercise his powers to appoint an authorised person to reconsider the case. For this to occur, it would be necessary that the court find the Attorney-General was under a duty to do so in the circumstances. There is no authority of which I am aware that a court could order the appointment simply on the basis of the achievement of 'justice'. However, I think that a prudent judge would inquire of counsel for the Commonwealth whether the Attorney-General would be prepared to appoint an authorised person for the purposes of reconsideration, should a finding of bias be made. It would be a 'courageous' Attorney-General who instructed counsel that the answer was to be 'certainly not'.

Examiner's Comments

This is a good answer which recognises the ambiguous nature of the Attorney-General's language, and the difficulties of knowing what decision a court would reach with regard to a reasonable observer's interpretation of that language. Similar difficulties underlay the disagreements within the High Court in *Jia Legeng*. The answer recognises that the bias rule operates less rigorously in relation to

Ministers' decisions, but also recognises that Ministers are nonetheless obliged to approach their decision-making with a somewhat open mind. I think the answer is correct in concluding that it is difficult to determine precisely what construction would be placed on the Minister's words.

The answer identifies the problems associated with the possibility that the Attorney-General might be the only person empowered to grant the permission in question. It suavely avoids the issue of whether the Attorney-General could come under a duty to appoint an authorised person by pointing (correctly) to the likelihood that the question would not arise in practice. Students should note that the issue of whether the Attorney-General can come under a duty to appoint an authorised person is canvassed in detail in Chapter 9, Question 29.

 ## Common Errors to Avoid

- Don't assume that only one construction could be placed on the Minister's language. Your advice must recognise that his words could be construed in a variety of ways, and that this could affect whether a court was to make a finding of actual or apprehended bias.

- Don't assume that a finding of bias is the end of the matter. Always keep in mind what the client's ultimate goals are and tailor the advice accordingly. Sometimes, as in *Laws*, a finding of bias will give the applicant what he or she wants; but sometimes, as here, the applicant wants a decision *made* because only by an administrative decision in their favour can they achieve their goal.

Chapter 8
The Availability of Judicial Review

Key Issues

A court may hear challenges to the legality of administrative actions only if it has the 'jurisdiction' to do so. In general, challenges to the legality of State or Territory administrative actions can be made in the Supreme Court of the relevant State or Territory. Challenges to the legality of Commonwealth administrative action can be brought in the Federal Magistrates Court, the Federal Court of Australia and the High Court. Conversely, State administrative decisions cannot normally be challenged in federal courts, and federal decisions should not normally be challenged in State courts. In the vast majority of cases in which someone seeks to challenge the legality of an administrative action, these principles are all that that person needs bear in mind in determining which courts may hear the matter. There are, however, some cases in which the jurisdictional issues are less straightforward.

1.   'Limited' administrative law jurisdictions

Administrative law jurisdictions are typically defined by reference to the kind of order that a person is seeking. Some orders may be made only by State supreme courts or by federal courts. These orders have traditionally been known as the 'prerogative writs', although the High Court has recently insisted that the equivalent High Court orders be called 'constitutional' writs: *Re Refugee Review Tribunal; Ex parte Aala* (2000) 204 CLR 82; [2000] HCA 57 at [20] per Gaudron and Gummow JJ and [138] per Kirby J — but compare Hayne J at [165], who is less insistent. However, administrative actions can also be attacked using other procedures.

The legality of an administrative action may be directly attacked through applications for declarations and injunctions. These are equitable orders, and can be made by any court with a general equitable jurisdiction, unless there is legislation precluding their use in public law cases. Moreover, supposing that the legality of an administrative act is relevant to the outcome in a criminal or civil action, it might be open to a party to such an action to challenge the validity of the act in the course of asserting or defending itself against the relevant claim. The party will not be seeking an order in relation to the act. It will simply be asserting the status of the act as a matter relevant to its case. In such cases, a State court may have jurisdiction to inquire into the validity of Commonwealth administrative behaviour. In the absence of legislation to the contrary, even a Magistrates' Court will have jurisdiction to decide the administrative law issue.

2.   *Statutory schemes*

In an attempt to streamline administrative law procedures, the Commonwealth, the Australian Capital Territory, Victoria, Queensland and Tasmania have established statutory regimes which enable applications to be made for orders in relation to administrative actions. One of the advantages of these procedures is that the court's jurisdiction is not limited by the particular orders sought by the applicant. (In other jurisdictions, this result has been achieved by amendments to the relevant Rules of Court.) However, if the conditions for seeking an order of review have not been established, the court cannot grant relief, and a person seeking to challenge the relevant administrative action must begin the litigation all over again, mobilising some other jurisdiction. The Commonwealth has dealt with this problem by allowing applications under the statutory scheme (the Administrative Decisions (Judicial Review) Act 1977 (Cth) (ADJR Act)) to be brought in conjunction with applications under the Judiciary Act. Queensland and Tasmania have largely dealt with the problem by establishing a very broad statutory jurisdiction, but even in those jurisdictions, cases occasionally fail at the jurisdictional hurdle. The statutory jurisdictions turn on whether the behaviour at issue is 'administrative' (as opposed to 'judicial' or 'legislative'), whether a decision is a final and operative decision, and whether a decision operates in law to affect rights.

3.   *'Ouster' and 'privative' clauses*

Legislatures sometimes seek to deprive courts of jurisdiction in relation to administrative law matters, even when courts would normally enjoy such jurisdiction. These attempts to sidestep judicial review have typically been subverted by the courts, but limited effect is sometimes given to clauses which purport to oust courts' jurisdiction. Because the High Court's jurisdiction under s 75 is constitutional, it cannot be removed by statute. However, the High Court has sometimes expressed in-principle support for the idea that what look like 'ouster clauses' may be capable of being read as clauses which confer a very broad discretion on the decision-maker, such that, while the administrator's behaviour is reviewable, applications for review will normally be doomed to fail. Such an interpretation is, however, conditional upon such an interpretation being consistent with the relevant statutory provisions.

4. 'Matters'

The Commonwealth is not empowered to confer on federal courts a jurisdiction to inquire into something which is not a 'matter'. It cannot, therefore, confer on federal courts a jurisdiction to advise on the legality of proposed administrative acts. (The giving of such advice is a matter for the Attorney-General's Department.) It could not confer a jurisdiction to inquire into purely hypothetical issues. Whether a claim does give rise to purely hypothetical issues is, however, not always clear; for a recent example of an application which was held not to constitute a 'matter', see *Re McBain; Ex parte Australian Catholic Bishops Conference* (2002) 209 CLR 372; 188 ALR 1; [2002] HCA 16. State parliaments are less constrained in this respect.

5. 'Non-justiciable' matters

Some disputes are described as 'non-justiciable'. The term implies that courts may not inquire into their legal merits. However, generally when courts use the term 'non justiciable', they mean something rather different: see Gummow J's discussion in *Re Ditfort; Ex parte Deputy Commissioner of Taxation* (1988) 19 FCR 361 at 367–73. Except for federal applications for review which do not disclose a 'matter', and applications which are precluded by a 'successful' ouster clause, there seem to be no administrative actions whose legality may not be inquired into, except for those whose legality is being challenged by a foreign power, and only by that power: *Attorney-General (UK) v Heinemann Publishers (Australia) Pty Ltd* (1988) 165 CLR 30.

Before attempting the questions, check that you are familiar with the following issues:

✓ the constitutional basis for the High Court's judicial review jurisdiction;

✓ the statutory bases for the Federal Court's jurisdiction;

✓ the requirements which must be met before the Federal Court has jurisdiction to hear an application under the ADJR Act for an order of review in relation to Commonwealth administrative behaviour;

✓ the circumstances in which the Federal Magistrates Court may review administrative behaviour;

✓ the extent and limits of the State courts' administrative law jurisdiction; and

✓ collateral review of administrative decisions.

QUESTION 24

Is there any justification for ouster clauses?

Time allowed: 30 mins

Answer Plan

(i)   Why are legislatures ambivalent towards judicial review?

- Judicial review rarely cheap and quick.
- Administrators' relative competence.
- Mistrust of courts.
- Ousting judicial review is the lesser evil.

(ii)   But even if they are desirable, are ouster clauses necessary?

 ## Answer

Ouster clauses reflect an assessment by the legislature that it is better that a repository of power be allowed to act illegally than that the activities of the repository be subject to judicial review. They are normally embodied in a statutory scheme which envisages that the repository of the relevant powers acts subject to the scheme. Yet they have the potential to insulate the repository from legal sanctions in the event of the repository disregarding his or her legislative mandate. There seem to be several reasons for legislatures' ambivalence to judicial review.

(i)   Why are legislatures ambivalent towards judicial review?

Judicial review rarely cheap and quick

The first is that judicial review is rarely cheap and rarely quick: see Kirby P in *Svecova v Industrial Commission of New South Wales* (1991) 39 IR 328 at 331. The costs associated with litigation include not only the costs of preparing legal documents and running the case in court; they also include the time devoted by administrators to providing the information which is, or might be, used in the course of litigation. Even if applications for judicial review prove unsuccessful, costs orders in the Commonwealth's favour are rarely enough to compensate it for all its legal expenses, and they provide no compensation for non-legal expenditure. In any case, if the applicant for judicial review is impecunious, a costs award is worthless.

Judicial review is also apt to take time. While courts can sometimes move with admirable speed — the *Tampa* litigation provides a recent example — most judicial review cases take months or even longer before they are finally heard and judgment given. Where it is important that decisions be finalised once and for all and as expeditiously as possible, judicial review is not a satisfactory procedure.

The importance of these considerations can vary according to the values of the particular government, and according to the relevant area. One of the reasons for attempts to restrict judicial review of the decisions of industrial tribunals seems to have been a perception that the costs of judicial review could be used as a weapon by employers to weaken their less well-endowed adversaries. Similar considerations explain attempts to limit the judicial reviewability of decisions by small claims and residential tenancy tribunals. There, the problem is that the 'villains' may be too wealthy. Concerns about judicial review in migration cases, on the other hand, are partly prompted by the fact that applicants are typically unable to meet costs orders, leaving the Commonwealth to bear all its expenses.

The importance of minimising delay has been recognised by the High Court as one reason for seeking to limit judicial review of decisions by industrial tribunals: *Houssein v Under-Secretary of Industrial Relations and Technology (NSW)* (1982) 148 CLR 88 at 95. This consideration becomes particularly important when it is desirable that a decision be reached quickly, and where there is a danger that the judicial process will be used as a means of delaying the operation of unpalatable decisions, regardless of the legality of those decisions. In some cases, delay will be of little concern to the government and to those whose interests it is seeking to support, but there are many decisions where delay can be undesirable: planning decisions, where it may be undesirable that real estate be tied up for years while argument proceeds about whether development proposals are legal; interim criminal justice decisions, where it is undesirable that the date of trial be postponed; and decisions not to award grants, where review will entail holding up payments to successful applicants. Up to a point, the legal system has developed procedures for handling these difficulties, and to the degree to which it has done so the cogency of arguments based on the need to avoid delay is diminished. That said, there may be cases where imperfect finality may be preferable to legality at the price of delay.

Administrators' relative competence

A second argument for ouster clauses is that the protected bodies may be regarded as more competent than courts: see Kirby P in *Svecova* above. This argument is not altogether convincing, since judicial review involves, not an attempt to second-guess the expert body, but rather to determine whether the body has acted legally; and when it comes to law, courts might fairly claim to be even more expert than the expert bodies they are supervising. However, the competence argument might nonetheless be sustainable. While courts possess general legal expertise, a body which is responsible for the administration of a particular area of law might come to have a better knowledge of that area of law than the courts which supervise it. Moreover, in so far as choice between alternative interpretations of law is facilitated by knowledge of the workings of the law in question, expert bodies may be in a better position to engage in law-making than are courts. While it is always open to parliament to amend the law in cases where courts develop it in an inappropriate direction, it might be more efficient that expert bodies be left to develop their own interpretations, subject to the possibility that parliament would intervene if the expert body were to develop the law in unacceptable ways.

Mistrust of courts

A third argument is based on mistrust of courts. If courts could be relied on to interpret law in the way in which the relevant parliamentary majority intended there would be limited cause for ouster clauses. But courts do not always approach legislation on this basis. The history of ouster clauses itself highlights the reluctance of courts to give full effect to legislation which they regard as offensive, and areas in which ouster clauses are enacted provide clues as to areas where parliament and the courts are in ideological conflict. The sources of such conflicts vary over time. Differences between Labor-dominated parliaments and courts whose members often had rather less sympathy for the union movement were reflected in attempts to insert effective ouster clauses to protect industrial tribunals from higher court review. Conflicts between human rights-oriented Federal Court judges and more populist governments help explain successive attempts to introduce ouster clauses into migration legislation. Whether the subordination of the judiciary to the legislature can constitute a justification for ouster clauses will depend on the degree to which one is willing to trust legislatures as opposed to courts. The legal profession tends to put its faith in judges, but in a representative democracy in which ultimate sovereignty lies with the people, there is also a case for trusting the legislature and the people who choose it.

Ousting judicial review is the lesser evil

There is a fourth argument that may be made in favour of ouster clauses, and that is that the alternative to ouster clauses may be decision-making regimes in which non-reviewability is achieved not by precluding review, but by making it pointless. This can be done in two quite different ways. The first is by establishing decision-making regimes which allow virtually no scope for administrative discretion. So long as decision-makers comply with the rules, their actions are safe. The second is by expanding discretions so that they are largely uncircumscribed by law. Each of these strategies has been used by the Commonwealth to deal with problems it has seen as arising from judicial review. The former approach is designed to limit the degree to which courts can intervene in so far as, in limiting administrators' discretion, it also limits the discretion of courts. The latter approach has the potential to create discretions so broad as to ensure that almost any exercise of them is within powers. The alternative to ouster clauses may not be an identical regime without the ouster clause; it may be a different regime which is in some ways either less flexible or less law-bound. Perhaps the alternatives are preferable. All I would argue at this stage is that one cannot be sure.

The first three arguments assume that the bodies protected by ouster clauses can be trusted with the power conferred on them. Whether this is so will, to a considerable extent, depend on the degree to which they are effectively accountable for their decisions. Where the decisions and activities of 'non-reviewable' bodies are effectively invisible, dangers of abuse are considerable and, instead of serving legitimate public interests, ouster clauses may help protect bodies from having to answer for behaviour which is self-interested and incompetent. Where bodies must give reasons for their decisions, and where their decisions are likely to be monitored by a variety of interested parties, the dangers of abuse are diminished. Moreover, while the presence of ouster clauses may reduce the degree to which bodies are accountable, protected bodies are likely to be mindful of the fact that abuse of their power may expose them to the risk of losing their protection.

(ii) But even if they are desirable, are ouster clauses necessary?

However, while ouster clauses may be justifiable, they are clearly not essential. The reality is that legislatures have found it almost impossible to devise effective ouster clauses. The Commonwealth Constitution limits the degree to which the Commonwealth parliament (and possibly the State parliaments as well) can limit access to the courts. Even where legislatures are regarded as having the power to oust jurisdiction, legislation which purports to do so is typically read as applying only to legally operative decisions, with the result that, since *Anisminic Ltd v Foreign Compensation Commission* [1969] 2 AC 147, ouster clauses can at most operate only in relation to decisions which are procedurally flawed by a failure to observe 'directory' provisions or other non-jurisdictional error. The *Hickman* compromise (*R v Hickman; Ex parte Fox & Clinton* (1945) 70 CLR 598) — whereby ouster clauses are interpreted as conferring broad powers on decision-makers — is controversial, and in any case, has never been applied so as to extend the powers of Commonwealth administrators. The Commonwealth's most recent attempt to rely on an ouster clause to limit the judicial reviewability of migration decisions resulted in a predictable High Court decision to the effect that the ouster clause neither ousted jurisdiction to review applications based on jurisdictional error (in which case, it could be adopted to this end by State legislatures) nor augmented decision-makers' powers: *Plaintiff S157/2002 v The Commonwealth* (2003) 211 CLR 476; 195 ALR 24.

Yet this does not seem to have interfered unduly with the conduct of Australian administration. For instance, had the decision in the *S157/2002* case really mattered, the Commonwealth could have legislated so as to give an almost open-ended power to the Minister to refuse residence status to whomsoever he chose, but no attempt was made to do so. This no doubt reflected political constraints, but the existence of those constraints suggests that ouster clauses were the lesser evil.

One reason may be that the advantages of ouster clauses can be exaggerated. Another may be that they are largely unnecessary, the costs and indeterminacies of judicial review applications being such as to achieve indirectly what ouster clauses attempt to achieve directly.

Examiner's Comments

This answer canvasses many of the relevant issues, and evaluates and balances arguments for and against the proposition under discussion. It draws on some illustrative material and demonstrates an understanding of the way in which ouster clauses are handled by the courts.

It might, I think, be criticised on several grounds. First, it is expressed at a relatively high level of generality. It would have been strengthened by examples of the use of clauses to achieve the various purposes attributed to ouster clauses. In a *term essay* on this subject, I would certainly have expected more detail. Second, the answer may underestimate the potential dangers posed by ouster clauses — at least at State level, where they are constitutionally feasible. The answer adverts to the fact that ouster clauses may be undesirable where decision-makers are otherwise unaccountable for the decision in question. How far are ouster clauses used in such contexts? Some of the ouster clauses enacted by the Victorian Kennett government seem to have related to relatively invisible decisions. These may reflect a relatively unusual state of affairs: a government supported by a majority in both Houses of Parliament. However, there would obviously be scope for similar measures in unicameral legislatures such as those of Queensland and the Northern Territory.

I would add that this is a question which could be handled in a variety of ways. This answer tends to take a socio-legal approach, and it tends to be sympathetic to the use of ouster clauses. A 'legalist' might prefer that the issue be evaluated from an intra-legal perspective, and might accordingly be far more critical of attempts to oust the courts' jurisdiction.

Common Errors to Avoid

■ It is not enough to describe ouster clauses and the way in which they have been interpreted by courts. While a good answer will be predicated on familiarity with these matters, the question expressly asks whether ouster clauses are justifiable.

■ Answers must be self-critical. They should not simply mobilise all the arguments that can be used for one 'side' or the other. This is particularly so in relation to this question, because ouster clauses clearly involve a conflict between competing principles: the desirability of giving effect to the intentions of the legislature, and the importance of courts as ultimate guardians of the law.

QUESTION 25

The Terrorist's Handbook was published by the Red and Black Collective, Madison, Wisconsin, in 1969. It explains how easy it would be for a group of urban guerrillas to disrupt the everyday affairs of a large city. Professor Rosa Luxembourg stumbled across the book in the course of a sabbatical at the University of California, Berkeley, where she was conducting research for her book *The Revolution Commodified*, a critical study of 1960s radicalism. On arriving at Melbourne Airport, her luggage was searched and the book confiscated. She wrote to the Attorney-General asking for permission to import the book, on the basis that it would be used solely for research purposes and subject to such security measures as the Attorney-General might wish to specify. After hearing a false report to the effect that Luxembourg was a dangerous revolutionary, the Attorney-General decided to issue a certificate excluding AAT review of any decision he might make. The certificate stated that the ground for its issue was that it was government policy to refuse permission to import books instructing in terrorism, regardless of the circumstances of the importer.

Luxembourg, who is anxious to maximise her review options, wants the Attorney-General's decision to issue the certificate to be reviewed. Advise her in relation to which courts have jurisdiction and under what legislation. Could she attack the decision collaterally?

Time allowed: 30 mins

Answer Plan

(i)   State courts.

(ii) High Court.

(iii) Federal Court.

(iv) Federal Magistrates Court.

(v)   Collateral attack.

Answer

(i)   State courts

This is a decision made under Commonwealth legislation, and would therefore not normally be entertained by a State or Territory Supreme Court. Theoretically, proceedings could be initiated in a Supreme Court, since the Jurisdiction of Courts (Cross-Vesting) Act 1987 (Cth) means that, in the event of such an application being made, it is for the Supreme Court to determine whether to hear the application. The power to hear such an application is conditional upon the court being persuaded that special circumstances exist which would warrant it doing so. If a court were wrongly to decide that these circumstances existed, it would nonetheless have jurisdiction to hear the application, but its decision would be appealable. In any case, it is hard to imagine any State court deciding to hear the case in the circumstances of this case.

(ii) High Court

The decision could be reviewed in the High Court, under ss 75(iii) and 75(v) of the Constitution. The s 75(iii) jurisdiction would be attracted by virtue of the fact that the defendant in the action would be the Attorney-General, who represents 'the Commonwealth'.

Luxembourg would also be able to make out a case for the High Court's having jurisdiction under s 75(v). The Attorney-General is an officer of the Commonwealth. She would additionally need to show that she had an arguable case for *mandamus*, prohibition or an injunction. If, on the basis of the certificate, the AAT refused jurisdiction, she could seek an order for *mandamus* (and join the Attorney-General as a defendant). This, however, would entail delay. She could also invoke the High Court's s 75(v) jurisdiction by seeking an injunction to restrain the Attorney-General from relying on the certificate. But while she could invoke the High Court's jurisdiction, it would be unwise to do so. As we shall see, the Federal Court has jurisdiction, and were the matter to be initiated in the High Court, it would almost certainly be referred to the Federal Court. All that would be achieved by going to the High Court would be delay and additional cost.

(iii) Federal Court

The Federal Court clearly has jurisdiction. Section 39B of the Judiciary Act 1903 (Cth) confers on the Federal Court a jurisdiction to hear any matter arising under a law made by the Commonwealth parliament: s 39B(1A)(c). The present dispute is a 'matter' and it arises 'under' a law made by the Commonwealth parliament.

Its jurisdiction under subs (1) would depend on whether *mandamus*, prohibition or an injunction was being sought against an officer of the Commonwealth. For the reasons I have given in relation to proceeding under s 75(v), I consider that it does have jurisdiction under the subsection; but, given subs (1A), it would not matter if it didn't.

If the matter were brought in the High Court, the High Court could — and almost certainly would — remit it for trial in the Federal Court under s 44(2A) of the Judiciary Act.

It is also likely that the Federal Court would have jurisdiction under the ADJR Act. Relevantly, an application under s 5 for an order of review under that Act may be made if the decision is a decision under an enactment and of an administrative character: s 3(1). The decision to issue the certificate is clearly one made under an enactment (namely, the Customs (Prohibited Imports) Regulations). It is clearly a final and operative decision, since it operates to affect Luxembourg's right of appeal. The only objection that could be raised would be that the decision was a decision of a legislative rather than an administrative character. In my opinion, the decision is an 'administrative' decision, at least for the purposes of the ADJR Act. It arguably possesses some legislative characteristics. In one sense the effect of a certificate is to change the law: it means that a right (to appeal to the AAT) which would otherwise exist no longer exists. Nor does it matter that the certificate operates in relation to a single individual: an instrument with legal effects may be legislative notwithstanding that it applies only to a single case: see the observations of Gummow J in *Queensland Medical Laboratory v Blewett* (1988) 84 ALR 615 at 634–5. Also suggestive is the fact that certificates must be tabled: see *SAT FM Pty Ltd v Australian Broadcasting Authority* (1997) 46 ALD 305. In *SAT FM*, Sundberg J considered that the fact that the decision in question was not reviewable by the AAT (unlike some other decisions under the relevant Act) was a matter which suggested that the decision could be classed as legislative, and this too counts in favour of certificates being classified as legislative.

But the fact that an instrument does not create a rule of general application may count against its being classified as legislative: cf *Minister for Industry and Commerce v Tooheys Ltd* (1982) 4 ALD 661; *SAT FM Pty Ltd v Australian Broadcasting Authority* (1997) 46 ALD 305. Certificates were not disallowable (although if they were of a legislative character, they would now be disallowable), nor was there any provision for gazettal or for public consultation: cf *SAT FM Pty Ltd v Australian Broadcasting Authority* (1997) 46 ALD 305.

In any case, in *Shergold v Tanner* (2002) 209 CLR 126; 188 ALR 302; [2002] HCA 19, the High Court had no doubt that the decision to issue a certificate declaring that disclosure of a document was contrary to the public interest was a decision reviewable under the ADJR Act.

The relevant provisions with respect to accountability were slightly different to those governing certificates under the regulations. They involved the giving of reasons and the tabling of the notification to parliament, but only in the event of the Minister deciding to reject a recommendation from the AAT that the certificate be withdrawn. In my opinion, this is an immaterial difference. The certificate decision would therefore be reviewable under the ADJR Act.

So long as there is any doubt about whether Luxembourg could apply for an order of review under the ADJR Act, the prudent course of action would be either to proceed under the Judiciary Act or to bring an application under both the ADJR Act and the Judiciary Act using the one application, as provided for by Order 54A of the Federal Court

Rules. I do not, however, consider that there can be any substantial doubt.

(iv) Federal Magistrates Court

It would also be possible to apply to the Federal Magistrates Court for judicial review under the ADJR Act (see s 8(2)), but not under the Judiciary Act. If there were any doubt as to whether the decision were reviewable under the ADJR Act (and I don't think there might be), it might be better to apply to the Federal Court. However, the Federal Court may refer an ADJR Act application to the Federal Magistrates Court for determination: s 32AB of the Federal Court of Australia Act 1976 (Cth). Given the seniority of the decision-maker in this case, there might be argument as to whether the Federal Court would be a more appropriate forum. To obviate the risk of such argument, it might be better to sue out of the Federal Court. However, it would probably not be necessary to do so.

(v) Collateral attack

Luxembourg could not import the book and rely on the invalidity of the certificate decision as a defence to a criminal prosecution — even if she were to be prosecuted. If the book is not a prohibited import, the validity of certificate would be irrelevant to any importation offence. If the book is a prohibited import, then this status would continue until such time as permission to import was given, and its importation would continue to be an offence. Nor, for similar reasons, could an action in trespass establish the invalidity of the refusal.

However, if the Attorney-General refused to grant permission to import, Luxembourg could challenge the validity of the certificate by attempting to appeal to the AAT against the decision to refuse permission to import. The AAT would then have to decide what to do about the certificate. If the AAT held that it was bound by the certificate, Luxembourg could appeal to the Federal Court against its decision. (She could also seek judicial review; but, when both judicial review and statutory appeals are open, courts consider that parties should proceed by appeal, rather than by application for judicial review: *Szajntop v Gerber* (1992) 28 ALD 187; *Tuite v AAT* (1993) 40 FCR 483; 29 ALD 647.) The advantage of an appeal to the AAT is that — assuming the certificate to be invalid — she has a right to have her appeal heard on the merits by the AAT. Her application having been made, it could not be defeated by a subsequent certificate, since certificates operate to prohibit application to the AAT, not the hearing of applications by the AAT: reg 4A(4) and (8).

Examiner's Comments

This is a thorough and reasonably comprehensive answer to the issues raised by the question. It rightly recognises that, while State and Territory courts have the jurisdiction to decide whether they have jurisdiction, they would almost certainly err at law if they were to hear an application for review of the Attorney-General's certificate. It was probably not necessary to discuss the issue, since there would be no question of a State court hearing the application. However, the answer has addressed the question, and handled it correctly. The discussion of the High Court's jurisdiction rightly recognises that this is one of the many cases in which applications for review could be justified either under ss 75(iii) or (v). In discussing the s 75(v) jurisdiction, it correctly distinguishes between what is required for jurisdiction, and what is required for the making of the order requested by the applicant. It also recognises that, once jurisdiction has been attracted, the High Court has the *power* to make all such supervisory orders as are necessary to do justice in the case.

The discussion of the Federal Court's jurisdiction recognises the three possible sources of jurisdiction. As a matter of practicality, it is not really necessary to consider whether the court has jurisdiction under the ADJR Act, given that it obviously has jurisdiction under the Judiciary Act. (It would, however, be relevant to the jurisdiction of the Federal Magistrates Court.) The analysis of whether a certificate decision is 'administrative' should be compared with the analysis given in Chapter 2 in relation to whether it was 'legislative' for the purposes of the Legislative Instruments Act. In view of *Shergold v Tanner,* it was probably not necessary to examine reviewability under the ADJR Act in much detail, but the answer rightly recognised the need to consider whether there were relevant differences between the certificate provisions in that case, and those which apply in relation to certificates under the regulation. The answer also recognises that the Federal Court could acquire jurisdiction by virtue of a case initiated in the High Court being referred to it for consideration.

In addition, the answer recognises the potential role of the Federal Magistrates Court.

The discussion of collateral attack demonstrates a sophisticated awareness of the different forms collateral attack could take.

Common Errors to Avoid

- Do not confuse the conditions for *jurisdiction* with the conditions for a successful *claim or outcome*. The two are obviously different, and this is evidenced by the fact that, although courts normally hear only those cases which they have the jurisdiction to hear, a considerable proportion of proceedings are brought in vain.

■ In examining the potential role of collateral attack, one must distinguish between collateral attack as a basis for challenging a decision that an import was a prohibited import, and collateral attack as a basis for challenging the decision to issue a certificate. Neither the criminal law nor tort law provide a basis for challenging the decision to issue the certificate. However, an AAT appeal against the decision to refuse permission to import would represent an attractive form of collateral attack.

QUESTION 26

Returning, once again, to the case of *The Night of a Thousand Shames* (see Question 20, p 130), suppose Makepeace asks the Attorney-General for permission to import copies of the book. After waiting a considerable time for a reply, a representative of Makepeace phones the Attorney-General and is told that the matter is being considered by an authorised person. The authorised person is out at lunch, but an assistant says:

> We're still considering your request, although we've made some progress. The good news is that we've decided that you have a good reputation and that you conduct educational activities to which the book relates. The bad news is that we suspect that you have ulterior motives for wanting to import the book. If this turns out to be potentially fatal to your application, we'll get back to you so that you can give your side of the story, but that may not be necessary.

Makepeace wants to know whether it can apply to the Federal Court or the Federal Magistrates Court for review of the decision that Makepeace may have ulterior motives for seeking to import the book.

Time allowed: 20 mins

Answer Plan

The question requires consideration of whether the 'decision' is reviewable:

(i)   Reviewability under the ADJR Act.

  • Reviewability under s 5.

  • Application under s 6.

(ii) Reviewability under s 39B of the Judiciary Act.

 ## Answer

(i)   Reviewability under the ADJR Act

Reviewability under s 5

The 'decision' is clearly not reviewable under the ADJR Act as interpreted in *Australian Broadcasting Tribunal v Bond* (1990) 170 CLR 321. This case held that, to be reviewable as an application under s 5 for review of a 'decision', it would have to be either a 'final and operative decision' or an interim decision which is expressly provided for under an enactment.

The present is clearly not such a decision. First, it is not clear that it is final in the sense that it is not going to be changed. The reference to 'suspicion' is consistent with an intention that the matter be further investigated. Indeed, this is what the informant promised. In this respect, Makepeace's case is even weaker than Bond's. Second, even if it were a final decision in relation to this particular issue, it would not be an operative decision. It does not alter Makepeace's — or anyone else's — rights. Third, it is not a decision under an enactment. The majority in *Griffith University v Tang* (2005) 213 ALR 724 held (at [89]) that for a decision to be 'under an enactment' two conditions had to be satisfied:

> First, the decision must be expressly or impliedly required or authorised by the enactment; and secondly, the decision must confer, alter or otherwise affect legal rights and obligations.

Neither of these conditions is satisfied. While the legislation clearly envisages that motives must be taken into account in determining whether to give subreg (2) permission, it does not provide that provisional suspicions must be taken into account. Nor do provisional suspicions confer, alter or affect legal rights.

The present case is similar to *Bond v Australian Broadcasting Tribunal*, in which the High Court held that there was no jurisdiction under the ADJR Act for the review of findings of fact made in the course of reaching a final and operative decision. The major difference lies in the fact that, in the present case, we do not even have a final decision in relation to a fact at issue. It would, of course, be possible to examine the legality of the finding in the context of the review of a final and operative decision, assuming that the suspicion crystallised into a finding of fact which was adverse and relevant to that decision, but this is not what Makepeace currently is seeking to do.

Application under s 6

Nor, it seems, is the finding of fact (assuming it to be a finding) reviewable as 'conduct'. *Bond* makes it clear that 'conduct' encompasses procedures, but not substantive findings along the way to the making of a final and operative decision. The present case falls into the latter category: it is neither a 'decision' nor 'conduct'.

(ii) Reviewability under s 39B of the Judiciary Act

It is unlikely that the Federal Court would have jurisdiction to hear an application under the Judiciary Act. If the question were formulated as involving the justifiability of the authorised person's suspicion, it would probably fall foul of the requirement that it amount to a 'matter'. For a dispute to constitute a matter, it must involve 'a controversy about some immediate right, duty or liability to be established by the determination of the Court': *Re McBain; Ex parte Australian Catholic Bishops*

Conference (2002) 209 CLR 372 at 459 per Hayne J. While there is a tenuous link between the suspicion and Makepeace's ultimate rights, the nexus is so weak as to suggest that it would be difficult for Makepeace to frame an application for review of the 'suspicion' in terms which would enable it to cross the constitutional threshold. To cross the threshold, Makepeace would need to formulate a claim which related more closely to its rights, duties and liabilities.

Jurisdiction under s 39B(1) also requires that the matter be one in which a writ of *mandamus*, a writ of prohibition or an injunction is sought against an officer of the Commonwealth. The authorised person is clearly an officer of the Commonwealth, but it is not clear how Makepeace could frame its complaint as an application for any of the three remedies. The application would have to specify what duty the authorised person was failing to perform, what conduct Makepeace wanted prohibited, or what the authorised person was to be restrained from doing. It is conceivable that this hurdle could be overcome, but the application would also have to assert facts which would warrant the granting of the relevant relief. The mere fact that the applicant for relief asserts that an authorised person's suspicion is groundless would not constitute sufficient grounds. The application would have to assert that the suspicion was evidence of something that could justify the issue of a writ or injunctive order. There is nothing in the facts to suggest what that 'something' might be. Thus, even if the court accepted that it had jurisdiction, it would have no alternative but to exercise that jurisdiction to strike out the claim as fruitless.

An alternative possible source of jurisdiction would be s 39B(1A). This would be applicable if the justifiability of the suspicion could be said to constitute a matter 'arising under' a law of the parliament. Officials, like everyone else, may entertain suspicions regardless of whether parliament confers on them the power to do so. The Federal Court would therefore have no power to entertain a simple application for a declaration that the suspicion was without legal foundation. It could, however, entertain an application if the suspicion was raised in the context of a challenge to the legality of an intended exercise of powers or obligations under a federal enactment. Again, there is nothing in the facts presented to suggest how the statement might be relevant to the legality of the intended exercise of power, and for that reason, even if the 'suspicion' were challenged in the context of its significance for the overall decision-making process, it is likely that the claim would be struck out.

I would add that, since Makepeace no doubt wants a substantive decision in its favour as quickly as possible, it would be foolish to embark on the proposed litigation, even if there were a possibility that the Federal Court would hear the application.

Examiner's Comments

This question is designed to test the student's understanding of the jurisdiction of the Federal Court and, in particular, his or her familiarity with the decisions in *Australian Broadcasting Tribunal v Bond* and, less centrally, *Griffith University v Tang*. The problem raises issues similar to those which arose in *Bond*, except in so far as *Bond* involved 'final' findings of fact while, in this case, the authorised person's findings are provisional.

The answer adverts to the more difficult questions which surround jurisdiction under the Judiciary Act. It recognises the need to distinguish between three related issues:

- Can the dispute be said to constitute a 'matter'?
- If so, does it fall within the jurisdiction conferred by the Judiciary Act?
- If so, would the claim nonetheless be likely to be struck out as unsustainable?

It also recognises that answers will, to a considerable extent, depend on how the relevant claim is formulated, and that the Federal Court could entertain the dispute about the 'suspicion' only if it could be subsumed within a broader dispute about the conduct of the inquiry.

Common Errors to Avoid

- Failure to recognise that it may be possible for findings of fact to be 'indirectly' reviewed in the course of an application for review of a final or operative decision.
- Failure to recognise that there are some circumstances in which, prior to the making of a final decision, the fact-finding process can be reviewed.
- Assuming that if administrative behaviour is not a 'decision' for the purposes of s 5 of the ADJR Act, it must be 'conduct' for the purposes of s 6 of that Act.
- Failure to discuss the relevance of the Judiciary Act.
- Confusion between jurisdictional questions and questions relating to the likelihood of success, assuming jurisdiction. (At a practical level, of course, this difference will often be immaterial.)

Chapter 9

Judicial Review
Remedies

Key Issues

Every branch of civil law depends on remedies. In our system 'in a real and practical sense ... where there is no accessible remedy then there is no right': A Robertson, 'Judicial Review and the Protection of Individual Rights' in J McMillan (ed), *Administrative Law: Does the Public Benefit?*, AIAL, Canberra, 1992, p 38.

Remedies remind us that law is not abstract principles; clients and their problems are the raison d'etre of legal practice: R Handley and D Considine, 'Introducing a Client-Centred Focus into the Law School Curriculum' (1996) 7(2) *Legal Education Review* 193 at 201. Court-based remedies are useful for their coercive power; it cannot be assumed that administrators will be persuaded in all cases by mere talk or negotiation. (Though negotiation and other non-legal avenues can be extremely useful; see R Douglas, *Douglas and Jones's Administrative Law*, 5th ed, Federation Press, Sydney, 2006, pp 230–3.)

The courts have, over centuries, developed a bundle of remedies to supervise the administration of government. The most common of those which have an exclusive application in questions of public law are the public law writs traditionally referred to as 'prerogative writs': *certiorari*, prohibition and *mandamus*. (Note that it is preferable to refer to the remedies of prohibition and *mandamus* as 'constitutional writs' rather than 'prerogative writs' when they issue under s 75(v) of the Constitution: *Re Refugee Review Tribunal; Ex parte Aala* (2000) 204 CLR 82 at [21], [138] and [165].)

As their definitions indicate, the functions of the public law writs differ. 'The function of certiorari is to quash the legal effect or the legal consequences of the decision or order under review': *Ainsworth v Criminal Justice Commission* (1992) 175 CLR 564 at 580. Prohibition is 'a judicial proceeding in which one party seeks to restrain another from usurping or exceeding jurisdiction': *R v Murray and Cormie; Ex parte the Commonwealth* (1916) 22 CLR 437 at 445–6, per Griffith CJ, cited in *Ex parte Aala* (2000) 204 CLR 82 at [159] per Hayne J. *Mandamus* issues 'to command the fulfilment of some duty of a public nature which remains unperformed': *R v War Pensions Entitlement Appeal Tribunal; Ex parte Bott* (1933) 50 CLR 228 at 242.

The other two common 'judicial review' remedies are the remedies of the declaration (of right) and the injunction. (They are perhaps not technically described as 'judicial review' remedies due to their origins in equity and legislation: see *Corporation of the City of Enfield v Development Assessment Commission* (2000) 199 CLR 135 at [21], but they are widely used by courts to resolve disputed questions of public law.) 'An injunction is an order or decree made by a court, in its equitable jurisdiction, requiring a party either to do a particular thing (a mandatory injunction) or to refrain from doing a particular thing (a prohibitory injunction)': R Creyke and J McMillan, *Control of Government Action: Text, Cases and Commentary,* LexisNexis Butterworths, Sydney, 2005, [16.6.1]. 'A declaration is an authoritative pronouncement by a superior court of the legal position of the plaintiff vis-à-vis the defendant in relation to the matter at issue': S Hotop, *Principles of Australian Administrative Law,* 6th ed, Law Book Co Ltd, Sydney, 1985, p 310.

In addition, in several jurisdictions there is provision for statutory remedies as part of a comprehensive regime governing judicial review. The application is for a generic order of review or a similarly named order. The remedies which may be granted are either the traditional remedies (Administrative Law Act 1978 (Vic) ss 6, 7), or remedies which parallel the traditional remedies: Administrative Decisions (Judicial Review) Act 1977 (Cth) (ADJR Act) ss 15, 16; ADJR Act 1989 (ACT) ss 16, 17; Judicial Review Act 1991 (Qld) ss 29, 30; Judicial Review Act 2000 (Tas) ss 26, 27.

Traditionally, judicial review remedies in the above expanded sense have been issued by superior courts only: the High Court, the Federal Court, and the supreme courts of each State. However, the Federal Magistrates Court, established by the Federal Magistrates Act 1999 (Cth), has been given jurisdiction to hear and determine applications under s 8(2) of the ADJR Act and to issue remedies under that Act.

The power of a court to issue remedies is conceptually distinct from a court's jurisdiction: the former is not a grant of jurisdiction; rather, it bestows a power in a matter already within the jurisdiction of the court: *Tetron International Pty Ltd v Luckman* (1985) 8 ALD 243 at 247; Creyke and McMillan, 2005, [2.2.18]. (Exceptionally, however, a jurisdiction may be defined by the availability of a writ, as in s 75(v) of the Constitution and s 39B(1) of the Judiciary Act 1903: *Ex parte Aala* at [156] per Hayne J.) Thus, once seized with jurisdiction the court may draw on all its resources to give relief: *Tetron* at 247.

The power of a court to issue remedies varies according to the court, the jurisdiction invoked, and the nature of the administrative action:

- The sources of the High Court's power to grant relief are s 75(v) of the Constitution in respect of its s 75(v) jurisdiction (writs of *mandamus*, prohibition and injunction); other remedies are available in this jurisdiction 'to ensure the effectiveness of the foregoing remedies': *Ex parte Aala* at [142] per Kirby J. The Court's remedies are also specified in s 33 of the Judiciary Act 1903: prohibition, *mandamus*, *habeas corpus* and *quo warranto*. The High Court also draws from a general bestowal in s 32 of the Judiciary Act, its establishment as a 'Federal Supreme Court' under s 71 of the Constitution (*Ex parte Aala* at [156] per Hayne J), and from its establishment as a superior court of record (High Court of Australia Act 1979 s 5): *Ainsworth v Criminal Justice Commission* (1992) 175 CLR 564 at 581 (declaration).

- The sources of the Federal Court's power to grant relief are ss 15 and 16 in respect of its ADJR Act jurisdiction; s 39B(1) (which matches s 75(v)); and ss 21 (declaration), 22 and 23 of the Federal Court of Australia Act 1976. It also draws on its establishment as a superior court of record (Federal Court of Australia Act 1976 s 5(2)): *Ainsworth* at 581.

- The Federal Magistrates Court draws on ss 15 and 16 in respect of its ADJR jurisdiction.

Grounds are 'bases upon which the applicant seeks relief': *Victorian Workcover Authority v Andrews* [2005] FCA 94 at [12]. At common law the grounds differ according to the remedy. *Mandamus* issues to command an express statutory duty to be performed, or, where a decision involving a discretionary element has been erroneously made, to compel a fresh decision or exercise of power in accordance with the law: Creyke and McMillan, 2005, p 821. *Certiorari* will issue for jurisdictional error, failure to observe procedural fairness, fraud, or error of law on the face of the record: *Craig v South Australia* (1995) 184 CLR 163 at 175–6. Prohibition will issue for want or excess of jurisdiction, including breach of procedural fairness: *Ex parte Aala* at [17], [41] per Gaudron and Gummow JJ. Declaration and injunction are general law remedies and are not restricted to jurisdictional error. For instance, in *Project Blue Sky Inc v Australian Broadcasting Authority* (1998) 194 CLR 355 at [100] the High Court opined that both remedies could go for breach of a 'directory' provision which did not result in the impugned decision being a nullity. Note that the ADJR Act does not incorporate the common law distinction between jurisdictional and non-jurisdictional error: *Jadwan Pty Ltd v Secretary, Department of Health and Aged Care* (2003) 204 ALR 55 at 74–5 per Kenny J. Remedies under the ADJR Act are conditioned, amongst other things, on the nature of the administrative action being reviewed, the Act according different remedies according to whether it is a 'decision' (s 16(1)), 'conduct' (s 16(2)) or a failure to perform a statutory duty: s 16(3). Most of the State statutory regimes are similar in this respect.

The overriding principle in judicial review is that courts exercise a 'supervisory role'; they cannot review decisions on the merits: *Minister for Aboriginal Affairs v Peko-Wallsend Ltd* (1986) 162 CLR 24 at 42. At the remedial stage, this principle means that superior courts and the Federal Magistrates Court can make orders which supervise the legal aspects of administrative decision-making, but may not go further. As Mason J explained in *Minister for Aboriginal Affairs v Peko-Wallsend Ltd* at 40, 'It is not the function of the court to substitute its own decision for that of the administrator by exercising a discretion which the legislature has vested in the administrator'. In *Minister for Immigration and Ethnic Affairs v Guo* (1997) 191 CLR 559 the High Court reaffirmed this principle, and the judgment of Kirby J emphasises that a court cannot usurp 'the ultimate functions committed by law to the decision-maker': at 599. Following review, where any residual discretion remains in the primary decision-maker, or where outstanding facts remain to be found which could affect the final decision, or where the Act makes it clear that such decision-maker, and it alone, is the recipient of the power to make the decision in question, the court is not able to give final relief, but must ordinarily if not invariably remit the matter for further consideration according to law: *Guo* at 599 per Kirby J; *Minister for Immigration and Ethnic Affairs v Conyngham* (1986) 11 FCR 528 at 541. The supervisory role does not prevent a court from giving final relief in every case. Exceptionally, courts can effectively give such relief, that is, order the thing to be done which the applicant is ultimately seeking, if, given the relevant law, the administrator may do only that thing.

The work that remedies can do follows as a consequence of unlawful decision-making. The effect of legal error is often straightforward, but it can also raise a number of issues, some of which are dealt with in other topics. A basic question is: when does the invalidity date from — the date the decision was made or the date of the court's order? The normal effect of illegality is that the decision will be void *ab initio* (from the beginning): *Wattmaster Alco Pty Ltd v Button* (1986) 13 FCR 253 at 258; Creyke and McMillan, 2005, [15.1.5]; Douglas, 2006, p 786. However, account needs to be taken of the nature of the error. If the error is jurisdictional (as most illegalities are so regarded), the decision is 'a decision that lacks legal foundation' (from the beginning): *Minister for Immigration and Multicultural Affairs v Bhardwaj* (2002) 209 CLR 597 at 614–5 per Gaudron and Gummow JJ. But if the error is not jurisdictional, as in *Project Blue Sky Inc v Australian Broadcasting Authority* (1998) 194 CLR 355, there will be no retrospectivity in the court's ruling. The issue of the date from which the court's ruling is taken to have effect can also arise in proceedings under the ADJR Act: *Jadwan Pty Ltd v Secretary, Department of Health and Aged Care* (2003) 145 FCR 1.

Other issues concerning the consequences of unlawful decision-making include:

- What is the effect of error when an official has been invalidly appointed? (see Chapter 3);
- Can a decision-maker remake an invalidly made decision? (see Chapter 3);
- What errors do ouster clauses protect against? (see Chapter 8);
- If a decision is invalid, can it be appealed to a tribunal? (see Chapter 12);
- Are errors made by decisions of inferior courts treated the same way as errors made by administrative decision-makers? (see *Craig v South Australia* (1995) 184 CLR 163).

Before attempting the questions, you need to:

✓ be able to specify the courts which have the capacity to supervise either federal or State administration;

✓ be able to set out the sources of power for those courts to issue supervisory remedies, and be able to distinguish this from the jurisdiction to review a matter where appropriate;

✓ be able to specify the remedies which may issue pursuant to each of these sources;

✓ be able to specify the traditional supervisory remedies developed at common law and in equity;

✓ understand the basic function of each of the common law and equitable remedies and the circumstances in which each may issue;

✓ understand the bases (the ground or grounds) upon which each common law or equitable remedy may be granted: see Chapters 3–7;

✓ understand the standing requirements for each common law or equitable remedy: see Chapter 11;

✓ understand the other conditions for the issue of each common law or equitable remedy;

✓ understand the conditions for the issue of remedies under the statutory regimes for judicial review (federally, the ADJR Act), including the jurisdictional requirements (Chapter 8), standing to sue (Chapter 11), and the grounds of review: Chapters 3–7;

✓ understand the limitations imposed by the supervisory nature of judicial review remedies and their equivalents, and the constitutional and public policy reasons why courts are so restricted;

✓ understand the conditions upon which statutory 'appeals on a question of law' may be made, and the remedies which may be granted as a result of such applications;

✓ be aware that the granting of relief is discretionary: see Chapter 10;

✓ understand the consequences of unlawful decision-making including the date from which a court order will be taken to have effect;

✓ understand the meaning of 'collateral attack' and the difference between this manner of review and applications for judicial review;

✓ understand why the awarding of damages is not an administrative law remedy;

✓ be aware of legal remedies besides those offered by the courts, such as that offered by merits review tribunals and the Ombudsman; and

✓ be aware of the possibility of non-legal remedies being appropriate in a particular case, such as negotiation with the original decision-maker, the intercession of a member of parliament, and discretionary compensation schemes.

 # QUESTION 27

> Set out the arguments for and against damages being recognised as a remedy which may be given in proceedings for judicial review, that is, where a court finds administrative action to be *ultra vires* or in breach of a duty to accord procedural fairness. Should the courts have the power to order that damages be granted in such proceedings?
>
> **Time allowed: 45 mins**

Answer Plan

Outline: heads of arguments for compensation and counter-arguments:

(i) Morality.

(ii) Precedent.

(iii) Tort law.

(iv) Economics.

(v) Principle.

(vi) Feasibility.

(vii) Outcomes.

(viii) Conclusion.

 Answer

The arguments in relation to recognition of a general right to compensation for unlawful administrative action may be considered under the following various headings.

(i) Morality

Arguments for compensation

Administrative action, like the action of other of my 'neighbours', can cause economic loss and inflict pain and suffering. Individuals who are harmed expect to be compensated, especially if the action is unlawful. Administrative law breaches are serious breaches of the law.

Counter-arguments

The claimed right to compensation would not be fair, as it would not necessarily be based on fault. Unlawful administrative action, such as *ultra vires* action or denial of procedural fairness, is not necessarily negligent; the decision-maker could have taken all reasonable care, such as obtaining legal advice, and yet a court could come to a different view. Though administrative action is normally intentional, it would be rare if there was an intention to harm. If there was such an intention, torts such as misfeasance in a public office are available.

Also a right to compensation would impose an additional regime on government which does not apply to private individuals. Government is already subject to actions in negligence and other causes of action which may found a right to damages. It would be discriminatory to impose on it a regime which is not imposed on the private sector.

(ii) Precedent

Arguments for compensation

There are precedents in the administrative law system. The Ombudsman can recommend compensation arising from unlawful action, and private sector Ombudsmen can award compensation up to a specified amount. There are also precedents in tort law, such as breach of statutory duty (which, if available, founds a right to damages). Above all, the Commonwealth Government has established discretionary schemes for compensation without admission of liability: see Australian Government, Department of Finance and Administration, 'Finance Circular 2006/05: Discretionary Compensation Mechanisms' (2006) at <http://www.finance.gov.au/FinFramework/fc_2006_05.html>. These schemes include the Scheme for Compensation for Detriment Caused by Defective Administration (the CDDA Scheme), and ex gratia payments. As these schemes are not premised on legal liability to compensate the person involved (Finance Circular, [12]), that is, they go beyond existing tort and other grounds of civil liability, they are a ready precedent for the legal recognition of compensation for administrative law illegalities.

Counter-arguments

The above arguments are weak. There simply is no precedent for a right to compensation in the common law of judicial review or under the ADJR Act. The High Court authority is *Park Oh Ho v Minister for Immigration and Ethnic Affairs* (1989) 167 CLR 637 at 645. The Ombudsman only has discretion to recommend compensation, and industry Ombudsmen are not comparable. The breach of statutory duty analogy is not apt: it only applies, as the name implies, to statutory duties; it does not often arise as a possible cause of action; and tort law does not offer opportunities for correcting decisions, as is the case with administrative law.

The current discretionary schemes, as the name implies, are not a legal precedent. Indeed, they purport not to create any legal obligation to pay, and are described as 'permissive': Finance Circular, [8]. The CDDA Scheme is not created under any legislation of the Commonwealth Parliament, but relies on the executive power of the Commonwealth under s 61 of the Constitution: Finance Circular, [10]; *Smith v Oakenfull* (2004) 134 FCR 413 at [19]. Payment is made on the basis 'there is a moral, rather than purely legal, obligation to the person or body concerned': Finance Circular, [6]. A recent Federal Court case, *Smith v Oakenfull*, found that an earlier version of the CDDA Scheme is no more than 'a statement of policy ... clearly revocable at any time'; seemingly it did not create legal obligations: at [20]. At best then, the CDDA Scheme, and other similar discretionary schemes, is a basis for paying compensation on a moral rather than a legal basis.

(iii) Tort law

Arguments for compensation

If compensation were available for *ultra vires* action or for denial of procedural fairness, this would overcome the need to prove that the decision-maker was personally at fault — through negligence, for example. Proving fault is a difficult hurdle at times; for instance, when the defendant's actions or omissions have the support of sections of the relevant profession.

Counter-arguments

It is a weak argument that a right to compensation should be established simply to overcome requirements worked out over hundreds of years in tort law. Also, proving fault is not impossible and, since government has a 'deep purse', it may well be easier in practice, especially if a jury is deciding the question. The trend in tort law is to require fault. The strict liability tort of *Rylands v Fletcher*, and the anomalous cause of action involving 'unlawfulness' known as the *Beaudesert* tort (see R Douglas,

Douglas and Jones's Administrative Law, 5th ed, Federation Press, Sydney, 2006, pp 753–5), have been abolished or effectively abolished: see *Burnie Port Authority v General Jones Pty Ltd* (1994) 179 CLR 520 and *Northern Territory v Mengel* (1995) 185 CLR 307 respectively.

(iv) Economics

Arguments for compensation

Liability on the part of the government would be a simple thing from an economic perspective, as the government could self-insure.

Counter-arguments

This argument is simplistic, as the government would have to budget for the payouts. This could be expensive.

(v) Principle

Arguments for compensation

Liability on government need not be seen as a radical break from administrative law principle, since the liability would still be based on administrative law grounds. Moreover, the remedy of compensation would not involve the court substituting its decision for that of the administrator. It would simply mean the award of compensation. A court could use the existing remedy of declaration and make a declaration as to entitlement to compensation.

Counter-arguments

Liability on government would be a radical break from principle. In *Guo* at 598–9, Kirby J said, 'judicial review is designed, fundamentally, to uphold the lawfulness, fairness and reasonableness (rationality) of the *process* under review' (emphasis added). This principle not only applies to the grounds of review, but also to the remedies. As Brennan J said in *Attorney-General (NSW) v Quin* (1990) 170 CLR 1 at 37:

> ... the court's jurisdiction in judicial review goes no further than declaring and enforcing the law prescribing the limits and governing the exercise of power.

In other words, the remedies which courts can issue, upon being satisfied that a ground of review is made out, are those which have been fashioned to correct an error in the process of decision-making — and no more. Thus, judicial review remedies may require decisions to be set aside, to be reconsidered, and so on. Although compensation is a benefit, it does not correct any error in the administrative process in the way of judicial review remedies. Compensation is extraneous to the decision-making process under the statute being reviewed. This is why the High Court ruled in *Park Oh Ho* at 645 that an order for damages is not an 'appropriate' remedy in judicial review of administrative decisions and actions.

(vi) Feasibility

Arguments for compensation

In many cases, such as where a person's licence is improperly cancelled, monetary losses could be calculated fairly easily. In the case of a licence refusal, a court would have the resources and experience to determine whether compensation was appropriate. Any practical problems which arose in other cases could be overcome by making the remedy discretionary. If a court was not satisfied that it was appropriate to award damages or declare an entitlement to them, the court could decline to do so.

Counter-arguments

Process errors do not lend themselves well to awards of compensation. If, upon reconsideration, the same decision was made, presumably no loss could be said to have been caused by the unlawful action. In the case of a licence refusal, monetary losses would be speculative. In the case of a licence cancellation, the existing tort law is available as a basis for compensation.

(vii) Outcomes

Arguments for compensation

Liability would increase the incentives on government to behave lawfully. There is disturbing evidence that the scale of errors in administrative decision-making is larger than previously believed, despite administrative law reforms: see the Australian National Audit Office study of Centrelink assessments discussed in Douglas, 2006, pp 10–12.

Counter-arguments

The claimed liability would create a disincentive for good decision-making, at least for decision-makers engaged in a court-ordered reconsideration, since administrators who were anxious to avoid a damages action might be disposed to affirm the primary decision to demonstrate that their initial error was immaterial. In any case, there is already a plethora of incentives on government to make it behave lawfully. They include internal constraints and a host of newer external constraints (Douglas, 2006, p 12): rights to reasons, freedom of information, Ombudsman investigations, appeals to tribunals in many cases, the possibility of court rulings, and public exposure through these mechanisms, the parliament and the media. There is some evidence that administrative unlawfulness is limited by these incentives: see Douglas, 2006, pp 8–10, 12. The Australian National Audit Office study of Centrelink, which admittedly found a high rate of administrative errors (Douglas, 2006, pp 10–12), is a study of high-volume decision-making — an area in which errors are likely to be relatively high. Moreover, even though most errors resulted in the acceptance of claims which should have been rejected, the amount of overpayments was a relatively small proportion of total payments.

(viii) Conclusion

There ought *not* be a general right to compensation for unlawful administrative action. It is opposed to fundamental principle and policy, and the arguments in favour of recognition being accorded are weak.

Examiner's Comments

The question requires a discussion of a general right to compensation being recognised. This question requires students to have a good basic knowledge of administrative law and the way the judicial review remedies work.

The question assumes an understanding of the way compensation orders work in the law. Students who have not taken torts would be at a disadvantage. However, almost all administrative law students have already studied torts.

The discussion of the discretionary schemes for compensation illustrates how non-legal remedies complement more formal (legally-based) administrative law regimes.

The strength of this answer is its clear structure. Competing arguments are grouped under headings which facilitates a lively dialectic around common themes.

The answer is superficial at times, such as where it asserts that the government is vulnerable to excessive claims because of its deep purse. If it was an assignment rather than an examination, more references would be advisable, especially to commentaries and other literature on 'damages in administrative law'. The lack of reference to such literature is not a deficiency in an examination answer, unless the prescribed readings feature such material.

Common Errors to Avoid

- Not writing in essay form; setting out a list of arguments in favour of the right to compensation, followed by a list of arguments against, without bringing them together in a discussion or in the form of a dialectic.
- Not referring to basic principles in judicial review supported by authority.

QUESTION 28

'While the declaration has proved the most flexible of the traditional remedies … declaratory relief is not always adequate': R Douglas, *Douglas and Jones's Administrative Law*, 5th ed, Federation Press, Sydney, 2006, p 766.

Discuss.

Time allowed: 1 hour

Answer Plan

(i)   Introduction.

• Definitions.

• Matters to be discussed.

(ii) 'The most flexible of the traditional remedies'.

• Appropriate to most disputes.

• Suffices in administrative law cases.

(iii) 'Not always adequate'.

• Not adequate in a relative sense, that is, relative to the strengths of other remedies.

• Not adequate in an absolute sense, that is, not satisfying all the possible demands of plaintiffs.

(iv) Conclusion.

Answer

(i)   Introduction

The declaration, also called the 'declaration of right' (*Lamb v Moss* (1983) 76 FLR 296 at 312) has been variously defined. Hotop defines it as 'an authoritative pronouncement by a superior court of the legal position of the plaintiff vis-à-vis the defendant in relation to the matter at issue': S Hotop, *Principles of Australian Administrative Law*, 6th ed, Law Book Company, Sydney, 1985, p 310. Aronson, Dyer and Groves define it as 'a court's declaration or statement resolving a dispute over the law applicable to a situation in which the applicant has a sufficient interest': M Aronson, B Dyer and M Groves, *Judicial Review of Administrative Action*, 3rd ed, Law Book Co, Sydney, 2004, p 782.

The matters raised by the statement are first, the contention that the declaration is 'the most flexible of the traditional remedies'; and second, that 'declaratory relief is not always adequate'.

(ii) 'The most flexible of the traditional remedies'

There are two main reasons for the flexibility or wide applicability of a declaration. First, most disputes about the law or the application of it can be framed in terms of a declaration. Second, a declaration will almost always suffice in administrative law disputes, even though it is a non-coercive remedy. But the declaration is not adequate for all disputes.

Appropriate to most disputes

Judicial review disputes are necessarily about questions of law. Because a declaration pronounces the law, it has a capacity to deal with most disputes. Its flexibility is particularly apparent once one compares it with the traditional judicial review remedies, traditionally referred to as the prerogative writs. A declaration is not subject to some of the key limits of the specifically public law remedies.

The classic statement on the availability of *certiorari* is that of Atkin LJ in *R v Electricity Commissioners; Ex parte London Electricity Joint Committee Co* [1924] 1 KB 171 at 205; namely, that the remedy lies:

> Wherever any body of persons having legal authority to determine questions affecting the rights of subjects, and having the duty to act judicially, act in excess of their legal authority ...

'Legal authority' means statutory authority or authority under the prerogative: *R v Criminal Injuries Compensation Board; Ex parte Lain* [1967] 2 QB 864; Creyke and McMillan, 2005, [16.2.5]. Since the source of authority for domestic tribunals lies in contract, that is, from the agreement of the parties, the prerogative writs do not apply there: *Ex parte Lain* at 882. Declarations are not so limited, having their origins in legislation and equity: *Forster v Jododex Australia Pty Ltd* (1972) 127 CLR 421 at 433–4 per Gibbs J.

The requirement of 'questions affecting the rights of subjects' means that *certiorari* will not issue unless the decision has legal effect or legal consequences. This includes a decision which 'operates as a precondition or as a bar to a course of action ... or as a step in a process capable of altering rights, interests or liabilities': *Ainsworth v Criminal Justice Commission* (1992) 175 CLR 564 at 580. That case graphically illustrated the limits of *certiorari*, which was not available to quash a report's findings because the findings did not have the requisite legal effect. However, the High Court saw no obstacle in declaring that:

> ... in reporting adversely to the appellants in its *Report on Gaming Machine Concerns and Regulations*, the respondent failed to observe the requirements of procedural fairness.

Thus, a declaration will be available where a decision or report affects interests such as reputation, but does not affect rights.

The requirement of 'duty to act judicially' is of somewhat uncertain content, if it continues to apply at all. According to Douglas it now means the duty to observe procedural fairness: R Douglas, *Douglas and Jones's Administrative Law*, 5th ed, Federation Press, Sydney, 2006, p 744. Allars is of the view that the requirement has not restricted the courts in recent cases, although it may do so in relation to the exercise of legislative or arbitral power: M Allars, *Australian Administrative Law: Cases and Commentary*, Butterworths, Sydney, 1997, [13.6.1]. Aronson, Dyer and Groves appear to agree with both views: 2004, pp 705, 707–8. By comparison, the power to make a declaration is not conditioned on a requirement that the decision-maker act judicially. It clearly is available where the impugned decision is legislative in character: see Douglas, 2006, p 730. And it does not depend on the respondent being under a duty to accord procedural fairness.

Prohibition denotes a 'judicial proceeding in which one party seeks to restrain another from usurping or exceeding jurisdiction': Griffith CJ in *R v Murray and Cormie; Ex parte The Commonwealth* (1916) 22 CLR 437 at 445–6, cited in *Re Refugee Tribunal; Ex parte Aala* (2000) 204 CLR 82 at [159] per Hayne J. It too is subject to the respondent being under a 'duty to act judicially': *R v Wright; Ex parte Waterside Workers' Federation of Australia* (1955) 93 CLR 528. And it is subject to a time limitation: in general it 'lies against relevant bodies until they have made a final decision': Douglas, 2006, p 741. A declaration is not subject to such a limitation.

Mandamus is 'issued to command the fulfilment of some duty of a public nature which remain[s] unperformed': *Aala* at [159] per Hayne J. A declaration is available whether the power concerned is a duty or a discretion: *Ainsworth* at 579–80.

A declaration may also be the basis for the provision of relief in cases where, in the exercise of their discretion, courts would refuse to make orders in the nature of constitutional or prerogative writs. For example, in cases where a third party has relied to its detriment on the validity of a decision, a court may refuse to quash the decision in question. It may, however, be able to afford recognition to the legitimacy of the applicant's claim by making a declaration to the effect that the decision-making process has been characterised by illegality. The English House of Lords did so in *Chief Constable of North Wales v Evans* [1982] 1 WLR 1155.

Suffices in administrative law cases

The declaration's main limitation is that it is non-coercive at the point of issue. However, 'The effect of declaratory relief will be to resolve finally' the disputed question of law: *Park Oh Ho v Minister for Immigration and Ethnic Affairs* (1989) 167 CLR 637 at 645. Despite being non-coercive, the declaration is an effective remedy against the government because the government can be expected to implement the law pronounced in the declaration: Douglas, 2006, p 736. It may do so because it is expected to be a model litigant, because it knows it also relies on declarations in its favour, and because of the fear of adverse publicity if it does not implement the declaration.

The statement that the declaration is the most flexible of the *traditional* remedies can therefore be supported. However, the statement has limited relevance to the ADJR Act — the leading general jurisdiction at the Commonwealth level. Under this Act, the traditional remedies were replaced by a single proceeding for an order of review, and the peculiar requirements for the traditional remedies, such as Lord Atkin's requirements for *certiorari*, were streamlined, being replaced by the jurisdictional requirements set out in ss 5, 6, 7.

(iii) 'Not always adequate'

'Adequate' might be construed here in one of two ways. The statement might be suggesting that declaratory relief is not adequate in a relative sense; that is, relative to the strengths of other remedies. Or it might be suggesting that it is not adequate in a more absolute sense of not satisfying all the possible demands of plaintiffs.

In the first sense, it is true that a declaration cannot formally quash a decision and correct a legal record of a decision as can *certiorari*. Nor is it coercive at the point of issue as are other remedies.

In the second sense it is predictably true that a declaration is not able to satisfy all the demands of plaintiffs. This occurs because it is only available to answer a question which is 'a real and not a theoretical question': per Lord Dunedin, cited by Gibbs J in *Forster v Jododex Australia Pty Ltd* (1972) 127 CLR 421 at 438. Examples of cases where plaintiffs failed for this reason include *Collins v South Australia* (1999) 74 SASR 200 (challenge to practice of doubled-up cells raised a hypothetical issue because it would have been impossible or inconvenient to give the plaintiff any relief); *Fritz v Torres Strait Regional Authority* (1999) 55 ALD 647 (no contradictor in relation to the claim by the applicant to title to certain islands in the Arafura Sea); *Young v Commissioner of Taxation* (2000) 61 ALD 173 (no administrative act to scrutinise; merely an announced policy); *Langton v ICAC* [1998] NSWSC 559 (attempted challenge to pending proceedings).

(iv) Conclusion

The statement by Douglas can be strongly supported. Compared with the traditional judicial review remedies, a declaration is a highly flexible remedy. But it is not always adequate due to inherent limitations: its non-coerciveness and the requirement that the question to be answered be real and not theoretical.

Examiner's Comments

The object of this question was to allow students to demonstrate their understanding of the principal judicial review remedies through the perspective of the declaration. As such, it is quite a straightforward question. However, students needed to read the statement carefully and note that it refers to the *traditional* remedies. Since the ADJR Act order of review is not a traditional remedy, the thrust of the question is about the remedies offered in judicial review proceedings brought outside of that Act at the Commonwealth and State levels. A good answer would have noted this fact.

The answer picked up on an ambiguity in the statement by Douglas — the meaning of 'adequate'. Students should not be afraid of noting an ambiguity in an essay question. Your answer will be stronger for addressing each possible interpretation. Indeed, examiners often pick statements for their ambiguous quality; they give students more space for discussion.

A strength of this answer is the way the analysis was sharpened by crisply defining the remedies other than the declaration, and then comparing them to the declaration. A succinct answer achieves more in a limited space and time than one which pads out the answer with general 'knowledge'.

Students need not be aware of all the particular cases mentioned. But illustrations are important, as they allow the writer to go beyond abstract principle in their response.

Common Errors to Avoid

- Describing the various remedies without comparing them to the declaration.
- Not answering both parts of the question: the twin propositions that the declaration has proved the 'most flexible' remedy but is 'not always adequate'.

QUESTION 29

Fred, Tilly, and the Computer Games Association have come to you for advice on the following issues:

29.1 The Federal Court has intimated its provisional view that, in refusing to grant Fred permission to import the work *Children and Sex: The Lies Politicians Have Told You*, the Attorney-General's decision was flawed by actual bias. In discussion of the orders which might be made, counsel for the Attorney-General reveals that the Attorney-General has not appointed any person under reg 4A(2A) of the Customs (Prohibited Imports) Regulations 1956 (Cth), and has no plans to do so, despite Fred's request that the Attorney-General do so. Fred is upset about this, as ➤

the prospect of the Attorney-General reconsidering the application is unappealing. The matter is adjourned. What orders can the Federal Court make? In particular, can it compel the Attorney-General to appoint a person under reg 4A(2A) to reconsider the matter? Would it make a difference if counsel for the Attorney-General conceded a suitable person was available to be appointed under that provision?

29.2 Tilly tells you that she has been refused permission to import the work *Marijuana: the Health Benefits*, but that the refusal was accompanied by a certificate of the Attorney-General stating that, in her opinion:

> it is in the public interest that responsibility for a permission or a refusal of a permission specified in the certificate should reside solely with the Attorney-General and should not be reviewable by the AAT.

No grounds are stated on the certificate apart from 'the national interest'. Tilly is concerned because she wishes to appeal the decision to the AAT, but the Registrar of the tribunal has intimated to her that the tribunal will not accept her application because of the certificate.

What courses of action are open to Tilly? Assume the decision to issue the certificate is plausibly beyond power.

29.3 Section 50(1) of the Customs Act 1901 (Cth) states that 'The Governor-General may, by regulation, prohibit the importation of goods into Australia.' Amendments to the Customs (Prohibited Imports) Regulations are purportedly made by the Customs (Prohibited Imports) (Amendment) Regulations 2007 (Cth). The amending regulations are signed by the Attorney-General in the absence of the Governor-General. The Computer Games Association is concerned about the amendments because they have deleted the words 'under 18' in reg 4A(1A)(c).

The association wishes to know how it may challenge the new regulations. Advise the association of the courts where the regulations may be challenged and the available remedies. Assume the amending regulations are plausibly beyond power.

Time allowed: 1 hour

Answer Plan

(i) **29.1** Fred: The Federal Court and the power to grant *mandamus* or an order directing the Attorney-General to perform a duty.

- Introduction.
- Prima facie.
- Relevant law.
- Application of the law — first set of facts (no information about whether there is a suitable person to be appointed).
- Application of the law — second set of facts (there is a concession that there is a suitable person who could be appointed).

- A duty to consider exercising the power?
- Refusal or failure to perform the duty on the facts.
- Conclusion.

(ii) **29.2** Tilly: challenging a refusal of permission to import where a reg 4A(5) certificate has been issued.

- Approaching the AAT.
- Approaching the Federal Court or Federal Magistrates Court.

(iii) **29.3** Computer Games Association: challenge to regulations.

- ADJR Act availability.
- Section 39B(1) of the Judiciary Act 1903 (Cth) and *certiorari*?
- Section 39B(1A)(c) of the Judiciary Act and a declaration under s 21 of the Federal Court of Australia Act 1976.
- Possibility of collateral attack.

Answer

(i)   29.1 Fred

Introduction

If a Judiciary Act 1903 s 39B application is made the order or remedy raised by this problem is *mandamus*. If an application under s 5 of the ADJR Act is made, the question is whether an equivalent order or remedy will be made under s 16(1)(d) of that Act. Either way the principal question is: is there a duty to be compelled? The duty might be a duty to appoint a person under reg 4A(2A) as expressly referred to in the question. Or it might be a lesser duty: a duty to *consider* exercising this power.

Prima facie

The regulations provide that the Attorney-General 'may ... appoint a person'. Prima facie, this means the Attorney-General has a discretion and cannot be compelled to exercise it. The reason why ordinarily courts cannot compel discretions to be exercised in a particular way is to avoid undermining the separation of powers, and the legitimacy and acceptability of judicial review. It is to the decision-maker that the ultimate functions are committed: *Minister for Immigration and Ethnic Affairs v Guo* (1997) 191 CLR 559 at 599 per Kirby J. Thus, 'a declaration should not be made where any residual discretion remains in the primary decision-maker': *Guo* at 599. This principle applies *a fortiori* to the grant of *mandamus* or an order requiring a duty to be performed under s 16(1)(d) of the ADJR Act.

Relevant law

However, duties are not restricted to legislation expressed in the form of 'must' or 'shall', as all members of the High Court made clear in *Samad v District Court of NSW* (2002) 209 CLR 140. In that case, Gleeson CJ and McHugh J stated (at [32]) that:

> When a statutory power is conferred by the use of words of permission, there may arise a question whether the effect is to impose an obligation, or, at least, an obligation that must be performed in certain circumstances … Issues of this kind are to be resolved as a matter of statutory interpretation, having regard to the language of the statute, the context of the relevant provision, and the general scope and objects of the legislation. [Footnote omitted.]

Gaudron, Gummow and Callinan JJ expressed a similar view at [77].

The case of *Commissioner of State Revenue (Vic) v Royal Insurance Aust Ltd* (1994) 182 CLR 51 is a good example of the principle that the circumstances of a case may call for a power expressed as 'may' to be exercised. In this case an insurer had overpaid stamp duty on workers' compensation insurance. The Stamps Act 1958 (Vic) provided that the commissioner 'may refund' an overpayment. The commissioner refused to do so, on the basis that the insurer had already recouped the overpayment from its policy holders and stood to gain a windfall if repaid the money by the commissioner (the facts are taken from Creyke and McMillan, 2005, p 824). Mason CJ held that ordinarily *mandamus* does not command a discretion to be exercised in a particular way. However, this was not the case if, as here, 'it was a discretion which, in the circumstances of this case, could be exercised only in one way': at 81. This was the case because the commissioner's purported basis was not valid and there was no permissible reason indicating why the discretion should not be exercised.

Application of the law — first set of facts

Is the present case involving Fred one where, in the circumstances, the discretion can be exercised only in one way? In other words, with the bias of the Attorney-General, is the Attorney-General under a duty to appoint a person under reg 4A(2A) to reconsider the matter in dispute?

The answer may depend on the facts. On the first set of facts we are not told that there is a suitable person to be appointed. In this situation it would be clearly improper for a court to order the appointment of an authorised person because the court ought not command something which cannot be done or ought not assume the appointment can be made when it is not so informed.

Application of the law — second set of facts

However, in the second set of facts we are asked to assume a concession by the Attorney-General that a suitable person is available to be appointed. The Attorney-General might nevertheless argue that a discretion to exercise this power (or not) exists, for the reason that biased decision-makers (here, the Minister) can still perform statutory functions: *Laws v Australian Broadcasting Tribunal* (1990) 170 CLR 70 at 88–9 per Mason CJ and Brennan J. The counter-argument is that this is in a case when there is no alternative; here (on the second set of facts) there is: a person may be appointed under reg 4A(2A). While, ordinarily, the Attorney-General has a discretion to exercise this power or to decide the matter himself or herself, it would be argued that this discretion has evaporated with the court's provisional finding that the Attorney-General is biased in this matter. The Attorney-General's defence that she would prefer to exercise the function of deciding the matter in dispute, rather than permitting an authorised person to do so pursuant to an appointment under reg 4A(2A), is no longer a valid reason, as was found to be the case in the *Royal Insurance* case.

A duty to consider exercising the power?

Notwithstanding these arguments, if a court does not find the Attorney-General to be under a compellable duty to exercise the reg 4A(2A) power, there is the alternative question of whether there is at least a duty on the Attorney-General to *consider* the appointment of an authorised person. A statutory power written in the form of 'may' normally entails a duty to consider its exercise upon the making of an appropriate request: M Aronson, B Dyer and M Groves, *Judicial Review of Administrative Action*, 3rd ed, Lawbook Co, Sydney, 2004, p 728. Exceptionally, a statute might be construed as not giving rise to such a duty (*West Australian Field and Game Association v Minister for Conservation and Land Management and the Environment* (1992) 8 WAR 64), but no reason is apparent why a duty to consider cannot arise under reg 4A(2A) in the circumstances of the Attorney-General having been found to be biased.

Refusal or failure to perform the duty on the facts

Finally, assuming there is a compellable duty, there is the question of whether there has been a refusal or failure to perform a duty to appoint, or consider appointing, an authorised person. A refusal or failure is premised on there having been a demand, actual or constructive, for the duty to be performed: R Douglas, *Douglas and Jones's Administrative Law*, 5th ed, Federation Press, Sydney, 2006, p 752. Further, a refusal must precede the initiation of proceedings: Aronson, Dyer and Groves, 2004, p 722. We have been told that Fred has made a relevant request to the Attorney-General, and this would seem to be sufficient if it was made before the initiation of proceedings.

Conclusion

If a relevant demand and refusal was made prior to the initiation of proceedings, a duty may arise — at least a duty on the Attorney-General to consider the question of appointing an authorised person to reconsider the matter. And if the Attorney-General concedes that a suitable person is available to act as an authorised person, it is strongly arguable that there is a duty to appoint such a person. But not otherwise.

(ii) 29.2 Tilly

Tilly's problem is twofold. First, she has been refused permission to import the work. Second, she has been prevented, it would seem, from appealing that decision to the AAT.

Tilly has two main options if she wishes to challenge the decision to refuse her permission. She can make an application to the AAT. Alternatively, she can approach the Federal Court or the Federal Magistrates Court and seek a clear path to the AAT.

Approaching the AAT

She can make an application to the AAT. The AAT would be unlikely to ignore the certificate in the light of the Registrar's attitude. If the tribunal had a doubt about whether its jurisdiction had been excluded by the certificate, it might refer the question of the validity of the certificate to the Federal Court under s 45 of the AAT Act. Or the tribunal might proceed to deal with the application and refuse it on jurisdictional grounds, in which case Tilly could appeal to the Federal Court on a question of law under s 44 of the AAT Act.

Approaching the Federal Court or the Federal Magistrates Court

Alternatively, she could approach the Federal Court or Federal Magistrates Court directly and seek a clear path to the AAT. Her interests would be advanced if she sought to have the certificate quashed or declared invalid because then the certificate would not be an impediment to the AAT hearing her appeal.

She could seek to have the certificate quashed or set aside under s 16(1)(a) of the ADJR Act by either court: ADJR Act s 8. Alternatively, she could seek before the Federal Court to have the certificate quashed by the writ of *certiorari* under s 39B(1A)(c) of the Judiciary Act 1903 (Cth). She could also possibly seek a writ of *certiorari* under s 39B(1), if her application was also accompanied by an application for a writ of prohibition to prevent the certificate being enforced against her in any application she might make to the AAT: *Stollery v Greyhound Racing Control Board* (1972) 128 CLR 509.

Since the jurisdictional requirements of the ADJR Act are not problematic (*Shergold v Tanner* (2002) 188 ALR 302), it would be preferable to seek the remedy under the ADJR Act, as under this Act Tilly would not have to satisfy the common law requirements of the remedy of *certiorari* (they are satisfied by the jurisdictional requirements of the Act).

Tilly could, alternatively, seek a declaration that the certificate is invalid under s 16(1)(c) of the ADJR Act. Although a declaratory order is not coercive at the point of issue, such a declaration would effectively clear the way for her to pursue an application to the AAT without the impediment of the certificate, since the effect of a declaration is to 'resolve finally' a question of law: *Park Oh Ho v Minister for Immigration and Ethnic Affairs* (1989) 167 CLR 637 at 645.

The main problem with going directly to the Federal Court is that she might be out of time for applying to the tribunal by the time the Federal Court had made a ruling in her favour. However, it would be unwise to apply to the AAT at the same time as going to the court:

1. there is a possibility of inconsistent orders by the court and the AAT;

2. it is a waste of resources;

3. courts disapprove this tactic at least when they are not informed of the other application: *R v Galvin; Ex parte Bowditch* (1979) 2 NTR 9.

In any case, it is not necessary since the tribunal would be likely to grant an extension of time (s 29(7)) on the ground that the delay is acceptable: *Hunter Valley Developments Pty Ltd v Cohen* (1984) 3 FCR 344 at 348.

(iii)   29.3 The Computer Games Association

ADJR Act availability

In this case, the association wishes to challenge the making of regulations. This cannot be done under the ADJR Act, because the regulations are of legislative character, and are not a decision 'of an administrative character', which is one of the requirements for the Federal Court or Federal Magistrates Court to have jurisdiction under that Act: see the ADJR Act s 3(1) ('decision to which this Act applies'), and *Burns v Australian National University* (1982) 40 ALR 707 at 714; *SAT FM Pty Ltd v Australian Broadcasting Authority* (1997) 75 FCR 604 at 607.

Section 39B(1) of the Judiciary Act 1903 (Cth) and certiorari?

However, the association can still seek a remedy from the Federal Court under s 39B(1) or (1A)(c) of the Judiciary Act. Under s 39B(1) one of the mentioned writs must be sought. There is some doubt about whether the regulations could be quashed by a writ of *certiorari*, in view of old authority stating that *certiorari* and prohibition do not go where the impugned decision is legislative in character: *R v Wright; Ex parte Waterside Workers' Federation of Australia* (1955) 93 CLR 528; see also Aronson, Dyer and Groves, 2004, pp 707–8.

Section 39B(1A)(c) of the Judiciary Act and a declaration under s 21 of the Federal Court of Australia Act 1976

A simpler remedy, however, is a declaration. It could be sought under s 39B(1A)(c), relying on s 21 of the Federal Court of Australia Act as a source of relief: see *Tetron International Pty Ltd v Luckman* (1985) 8 ALD 243 at 247; Creyke and McMillan, 2005, [2.2.18]. There is no problem with s 39B(1A)(c) in the case of impugned delegated legislation: Creyke and McMillan, 2005, [2.2.11]. No reason is apparent why the remedy would not be available in the present case: there is a real and not a theoretical question at issue: *Forster v Jododex Australia Pty Ltd*. The association would seek a declaration that the amending regulations are invalid *ab initio*.

Possibility of collateral attack

It would also be theoretically possible to agitate against the validity of the regulation by arranging for a member of the association to import goods prohibited under the regulation and, if that was successful (which might not be the case), then raising the invalidity of the regulation as a defence to any subsequent criminal prosecution. This course of action, known as collateral attack, is not recommended. It is risky, since the defence might fail. It would almost certainly be simpler and faster to seek a declaration in the Federal Court.

Examiner's Comments

Question 29.1 tested knowledge of the remedy of *mandamus*; specifically whether students are aware that whether a duty arises under legislation is a matter of construction and does not depend solely on the terminology employed (the use of such words as 'shall', 'must' and 'may'). In addition, the circumstances of the case need to be considered. Students should also see the discussion of a similar issue in Chapter 7, Question 23.

Question 29.2 is at one level a straightforward question on remedies under the ADJR Act. It also shows that a knowledge of remedial requirements needs to be combined with insight into how best to marshal the available law to achieve the objectives of the client. In the problem judicial review was but a means to an end; the client's objective being to pursue AAT review. As for Tilly's problem of whether to choose the court or the AAT, see the discussion of a similar issue in Chapter 16, Question 48.

The object of Question 29.3 was to ensure students practise seeking to obtain remedies under the general law (s 39B of the Judiciary Act 1903), as not all federal administrative action is subject to the ADJR Act.

The answers were brief on the availability of the various Acts affording sources of relief. A greater level of detail could have been provided.

A more complete answer to Questions 29.1 and 29.2 would have discussed whether recourse should be had to the Federal Court or the Federal Magistrates Court. To some extent this is an issue to be decided on the basis of experience as a practitioner. However, some consideration can be given at this stage of a student's education. Students ought to be aware that application fees are lower for the Federal Magistrates Court. On the other hand, applying to the Federal Court also has the advantage of combining a s 39B application in the case of doubt (Federal Court Rules, Order 54A), and the court has the power of setting binding precedents.

Another choice which could have been discussed further was the preference for the ADJR Act over the Judiciary Act as the source of remedial relief in Questions 29.1 and 29.2. The regimes are not identical in scope, grounds of review, remedies, standing, application requirements and general ease of use, and a decision to use one over the other needs careful thought and some justification. The ADJR Act is not superior on all counts or in all circumstances; see Question 29.3. However, combining the both in the one application to some extent avoids the need to choose.

Common Errors to Avoid

- Assuming that, if a section says 'may', the ordinary meaning of 'may' must be applied regardless of the circumstances, rather than considering the possibility that the decision-maker might come under a duty either to exercise the relevant power or to consider exercising the power.

- Giving detailed discussion of sources of remedy without the practical need to do so on the facts. If one source of relief is available, is suitable, and is preferable to another source of relief, that other source should receive less attention.

- Not referring to the particular provisions in s 16 of the ADJR Act when discussing the remedies which may be granted under that Act.

- Getting confused between the requirements for judicial review remedies at common law (including declaration and injunction) and the requirements for the orders which may be made under s 16 of the ADJR Act. In applying s 16 to the facts of a problem, assuming a basis for relief to be established by dint of the statutory requirements, it is not necessary to apply the common law tests for the remedies, for example, Lord Atkin's statement in *R v Electricity Commissioners; Ex parte London Electricity Joint Committee Co* in respect of *certiorari* and prohibition. The explanation is that the ADJR Act is a statutory regime intended to simplify the obtaining of relief, and in the ADJR Act the grounds and the jurisdictional requirements supply equivalent tests: Douglas, 2006, pp 743, 744, 752–3. If applying under the ADJR Act, and if a basis for relief is established, working with s 16 requires one first of all to choose the appropriate subsection ((1) for decisions; (2) for conduct; (3) for failure to perform a duty); and it next requires one to select the appropriate order or orders within that subsection.

Chapter 10

The Discretionary Nature of Judicial Remedies

Key Issues

At common law an applicant acquires a basis for relief by making an application within the jurisdiction of the relevant court, satisfying any time limit for lodging the application, proving a ground of review which is a basis for particular relief, and showing they are eligible for the grant of that relief including satisfying any standing requirements. Under the Administrative Decisions (Judicial Review) Act 1977 (Cth) (ADJR Act) proceedings, an applicant needs to satisfy the equivalent statutory preconditions for relief: *Lamb v Moss* (1983) 76 FLR 296 at 312.

The making out of a basis for relief is a strong indication that relief ought to go; otherwise the rule of law is frustrated: *Corporation of the City of Enfield v Development Assessment Commission* (2000) 199 CLR 135 at 157 per Gaudron J. However, in judicial review proceedings an applicant is not automatically entitled to relief once a basis for relief is made out. The granting of relief or the issuing of a remedy is discretionary. An applicant who has established a basis for relief is only prima facie entitled to the grant of a judicial remedy: *R v Commonwealth Court of Conciliation and Arbitration; Ex parte Ozone Theatres (Australia) Ltd* (1949) 78 CLR 389 at 400, cited in *Re Refugee Review Tribunal; Ex parte Aala* (2000) 204 CLR 82 at [56]. Refusal of relief outright is one way in which the courts may exercise discretion in relation to the granting of relief. If relief is to be granted, courts have various discretions too: as to the form of any relief; as to whether to give directions as to the constitution of a tribunal to which a matter is to be remitted for reconsideration; and as to timing (from when the court's order is to be treated as having taken effect). In addition, courts have a discretion to refuse an application.

Refusal of relief outright

The discretion to refuse to grant relief outright seemingly applies to all remedies, after the High Court in *Aala* ruled that all the s 75(v) remedies (prohibition, *mandamus* and injunction) are discretionary: at [52], [54] per Gaudron and Gummow JJ, with whom Gleeson CJ agreed at [5]. The granting of orders of review under the ADJR Act is discretionary: *Lamb v Moss* at 312.

In determining whether to refuse relief, the most basic factor is the need to do justice, having regard to all interests: *Ex parte Ozone Theatres (Australia) Ltd* at 400, cited in *Aala* at [56]; C Enright, *Federal Administrative Law*, Federation Press, Sydney, 2001, [44.100]. No exhaustive list can be given of the circumstances which may attract an exercise of discretion adverse to an applicant: *Aala* at [56]. Specific grounds which may be the basis for refusing to grant relief include:

- deception or bad faith on the part of the applicant;
- delay by the applicant in seeking or prosecuting review;
- the existence of alternative remedies;
- inconvenience to others which otherwise would be occasioned;
- futility;
- the need to avoid fragmenting, and detracting from the efficiency of, the criminal justice system;
- the remedy would be out of all proportion to the wrong;
- not coming to the court with clean hands; and
- *de minimis non curat lex* (the law is not concerned with trifles).

However, before relief is to be refused, any of these factors need to be balanced against factors which incline against such a course of action, such as justice to the applicant: Enright, 2001, [44.101] and [44.103]. This factor is clearly accorded weight in those cases in which the judge has remarked that refusal would accord the applicant a 'hollow victory' (*Styles v Secretary, Department of Foreign Affairs and Trade* (1988) 84 ALR 408 at 435) or would deny them a remedy at law of some pecuniary value: *R v Muir; Ex parte Joyce* [1980] Qd R 567 at 580. Relief will accordingly be refused where the ground is of 'sufficient order ... to make it inappropriate' to grant the remedy: *Hodgens v Gunn; Ex parte Hodgens* [1990] 1 Qd R 1 at 7.

In addition to a discretionary power under s 16 to refuse relief, the ADJR Act provides a specific basis to dismiss an application on discretionary grounds. Under s 10(2)(b)(ii) of the Act the Federal Court or Federal Magistrates Court may refuse to grant an application if adequate provision is made by another law under which the applicant is entitled to seek review by a tribunal or other authority: *Bragg v Secretary, Department of Employment, Education and Training* (1995) 59 FCR 31 at 34; R Creyke and J McMillan, *Control of Government Action: Text, Cases and Commentary*, LexisNexis Butterworths, Sydney, 2005, [16.9.3]; R Douglas, *Douglas and Jones's Administrative Law*, 5th ed, Federation Press, Sydney, 2006, p 779.

Discretion as to the form of relief

If relief is to be granted, courts have a discretion as to the form of relief: *Lamb v Moss* (1983) 76 FLR 296 at 312. This means that, if relief is not to be refused, a court will select the most appropriate remedy or remedies from those sought, or available to the court, having regard to the function and limits of each remedy and the need to do justice. This particularly applies to ADJR Act cases, where the application is for a generic order of review, but it also applies to relief granted under the general law. For example, in *Stollery v Greyhound Racing Control Board* (1972) 128 CLR 509, the applicant had been disqualified from participation in the greyhound racing industry and had sought orders for *certiorari* and prohibition. But by the time of the High Court's decision, the period of disqualification imposed by the board had expired. The court refused to reinstate prohibition, as there was now nothing to prohibit. It might also, for similar reasons, have refused to grant *certiorari*. However, having regard to the indirect consequences of the decision to disqualify, such as the effect on any subsequent application for re-registration, the court thought it appropriate to quash it.

Discretion to give directions as to the constitution of a tribunal to which a matter is to be remitted for reconsideration

As an instance of the power of courts to make supplementary orders, courts have a discretion to give directions as to the constitution of a tribunal to which a matter is to be remitted for reconsideration: Creyke and McMillan, 2005, [16.8.10]. In other words, they have a discretion as to whom should undertake any reconsideration: *Minister for Immigration and Multicultural Affairs v Wang* (2003) 215 CLR 518. The purpose of this power is to protect against the possibility or the appearance of adverse prejudgment: *Wang* at [12] per Gleeson CJ.

Discretion as to timing of relief

In exercising a discretion as to the timing of relief, courts are to consider all the circumstances, including the need to 'do justice as between the parties and any other affected persons': *Styles* at 435. At common law, quashing a decision on the ground of jurisdictional error such as failure to take into account a relevant consideration or breach of procedural fairness normally has retrospective effect, that is, the court's order has effect from the date of the administrator's decision: *Wattmaster Alco Pty Ltd v Button* (1986) 13 FCR 253 at 257–8; *Minister for Immigration and Ethnic Affairs v Taveli* (1990) 23 FCR 162 at 169 per Davies J; see also *Minister for Immigration and Multicultural Affairs v Bhardwaj* (2002) 209 CLR 597 at 614–5 per Gaudron and Gummow JJ. With the prerogative writs there is at least the capacity to suspend the operation of an order: see, for example, *Re Minister for Communications; Ex parte NBN Ltd* (1986) 12 ALD 150. And if a court were of the view that the circumstances of the case were such that the appropriate order was one which should operate prospectively, it could also achieve that result by declining to quash the earlier decision, while granting injunctive or declaratory relief. Under the ADJR Act the court has a clear discretion to give its order prospective effect: s 16(1)(a); *Styles*.

Discretion to refuse an application

In addition, courts have a discretion to refuse an application which is otherwise within its jurisdiction. If there is a time limit for making an application, coupled with a power to extend time for applying at the discretion of the court, the court has the power to refuse the application if there is delay in making the application. In the case of the ADJR Act, the power to extend time is set out in s 11(1)(c) of the ADJR Act; and see *Hunter Valley Developments Pty Ltd v Cohen* (1984) 3 FCR 344; Douglas, 2006, pp 725–6.

Before attempting the questions, check that you are familiar with the following issues:

✓ how delay in making an application under the ADJR Act may result in the Federal Court or Federal Magistrates Court refusing the application: s 11(1)(c);

✓ the legal position of an applicant once a basis for relief is established, and the rationale for judicial remedies being discretionary;

✓ the ways in which discretion in relation to the granting of relief may be exercised, including the rule in s 10(2)(b)(ii) of the ADJR Act by which the court may dismiss an application under that Act on the basis that adequate provision is made by another law for review by a tribunal or other authority;

✓ the circumstances which may attract an exercise of discretion adverse to an applicant; and

✓ the considerations which are to be weighed against any circumstances attracting an adverse exercise of discretion.

QUESTION 30

What are the purposes of the law according the courts a discretion to refuse to grant relief or to refuse to grant the relief asked for?

Time allowed: 45 mins

Answer Plan

(i)   Introduction and overview.

(ii) To effect justice.

(iii) To maintain the authoritative position of the court.

(iv) To promote efficiency in government.

(v)   Conclusion.

 Answer

(i)   Introduction and overview

Three basic purposes underlie the discretion to refuse relief or to refuse the relief asked for:

1. to effect justice;

2. to maintain the authoritative position of the court; and

3. to promote efficiency in government.

(ii)   To effect justice

In *R v Commonwealth Court of Conciliation and Arbitration; Ex parte Ozone Theatres (Australia) Ltd* (1949) 78 CLR 389 at 400 (cited in *Re Refugee Review Tribunal; Ex parte Aala* (2000) 204 CLR 82 at [56]), the High Court said:

> The court's discretion is judicial and if the refusal of a definite public duty is established, the writ issues unless circumstances appear making it *just* that the remedy should be withheld. (emphasis added)

What is meant by 'just' in this context? The content of justice is flexible. The discretion is 'judicial', which suggests that the discretion is to be exercised in a reasoned way and with regard to basic values in the law, as well as to past cases.

In all cases proof by the plaintiff of a basis for relief must be accorded weight: *Ex parte Ozone Theatres (Australia) Ltd* at 400. In *Styles v Secretary, Department of Foreign Affairs and Trade* (1988) 84 ALR 408 at 435 the court was concerned that it should not make a decision which 'leaves [the applicant's] grievance unanswered' because 'to deny her any relief upon discretionary grounds, would be to accord to her a hollow victory'. In *R v Muir; Ex parte Joyce* [1980] Qd R 567, the court accorded weight to the claim of the applicant to a remedy at law against his former employer, which would only be possible if *certiorari* issued.

The courts will give weight to a morally upright course of conduct by the plaintiff. In *R v Muir* the delay in seeking the assistance of the court did not act as a bar to relief because the solicitors reasonably sought counsel's advice and found it necessary to seek legal aid. This contrasts on the facts with *Hodgens v Gunn; Ex parte Hodgens* [1990] 1 Qd R 1 at 6, where the delay was unexplained, and *Whittaker v Child Support Registrar* (2000) 106 FCR 105, where the long delay was accompanied by a weak excuse.

Conversely, the courts make it clear that, given the opportunity, they would not reward poor behaviour. In *R v Galvin; Ex parte Bowditch* (1979) 2 NTR 9 at 19–20 the court was highly critical of the failure of counsel for the applicant to inform the court about a parallel application in the court.

The courts will also recognise and take account of any difficult circumstances to which an applicant may be subject. Examples are *Mishra v University of Technology, Sydney* [1999] NSWSC 1324, where the unrepresented applicant was inadvertently misled by an officer of the Supreme Court of New South Wales about the appropriate avenue of appeal, and *South-West Forests Defence Foundation Inc v Lands and Forest Commission* (1995) 86 LGERA 365, a case of delay in which the court intimated (at 380) that it would have been prepared to take account of the fact that the 'public interest litigant' had very limited resources and was seeking to agitate matters in the public interest.

A concern to protect innocent third parties is apparent in *Styles*, and in *R v Liquor Commission of the Northern Territory; Ex parte Pitjantjatjara Council Inc* (1984) 31 NTR 13, where the court was willing to hear argument as to whether to post-date the judgment. See also *R v Muir*, where, by the time of the court's hearing, the probation period had lapsed and the position had been filled.

The courts attempt to do justice to animals as well! This was the case in *Hodgens*, where the court declined to order the removal of seized dogs, now domestically assimilated.

However, courts give little or no weight to a preference of an applicant to pursue court action rather than an alternative avenue which the court thinks is preferable or which parliament has indicated is to be the prime route, particularly where the court senses that the application is being pursued for 'tactical forensic reasons'. Examples are *Whittaker* (from which, at [39], that phrase is taken) and *McBeatty v Gorman* [1975] 2 NSWLR 262. *Meagher v Stephenson* (1993) 30 NSWLR 736 is similar — there the attempt to circumvent a leave requirement in the statutory appeal procedure was frowned upon.

In general, when courts refuse to grant relief on the grounds of justice, they do so in cases where there would be a general consensus in the community as to where justice lay in the particular case. However, not all cases are uncontroversial, particularly where enforcement of the criminal law is concerned. An example is *Attorney-General for the State of Queensland (Ex rel Kerr) v T* (1983) 57 ALJR 285, where Gibbs J refused an injunction sought to restrain a breach of the criminal law. The injunction had been sought by the former partner of a pregnant woman to restrain her from having an abortion. Gibbs J observed that 'There are limits to the extent to which the law should intrude upon the personal liberty and personal privacy in the pursuit of moral and religious aims': at 287.

(iii) To maintain the authoritative position of the court

When courts refuse relief because it would be unjust to grant it, this is an act also calculated to maintain the authoritative position of the court, since the legitimacy of the court depends on it being seen to do justice.

The need to maintain the authoritative position of the court is particularly evident in those cases in which the courts avoided making futile rulings which would unnecessarily have exposed the court as weak and ineffective. Thus, clear cases of futility require the refusal of relief because public confidence in the authority of the court might suffer if court orders could have no practical effect. Examples are: *Midland Metals Overseas Ltd v Comptroller-General of Customs* (1989) 85 ALR 302, where the inquiry objected to would go ahead in any case; *Church of Scientology v Woodward* (1982) 154 CLR 25, where, according to Mason J at 62, a claim for relief in respect of past acts long since completed was 'academic'; and *Doyle v Chief of General Staff (No 2)* (1982) 70 FLR 94, where a procedural irregularity was not responsible for the applicant not being promoted. Similarly, if a court has serious doubts about the consequences of a ruling it has been asked to make, this may also be a reason for declining relief asked for. In *Chief Constable of North Wales Police v Evans* [1982] 1 WLR 1155, four years had passed by since the impugned decision requiring the respondent to resign. The House of Lords declined to rule that the decision was void because, in the circumstances, there was doubt over the consequences of such a ruling.

But in several cases the court clearly put off possible concerns about the limited effects of its rulings in favour of achieving a level of justice for the applicant. Examples include *Stollery v Greyhound Racing Control Board* (1972) 128 CLR 509, where the High Court took a broad view of the indirect effects of the impugned decision and granted a writ of *certiorari*; and *FAI Insurances Ltd v Winneke* (1982) 151 CLR 342, where the court recognised that a declaration could have sufficient indirect effects not to be hypothetical — particularly since it would allow the applicants to make a fresh application for approval to carry on a business in the area of workers' compensation.

(iv) To promote efficiency in government

Some cases show the courts recognising the importance of saving the resources of the state — including the courts' limited resources. An example is *Sankey v Whitlam* (1978) 142 CLR 1, where the concern was the efficiency of the criminal justice process and the damage which can be caused (deliberately or otherwise) by the attempt to fragment proceedings. This consideration also underlay the decision in *Attorney-General for the State of Queensland (Ex rel Kerr) v T*, referred to above. In *Du Pont (Australia) v Comptroller-General of Customs* (1993)

30 ALD 829, the court had regard to the fact that the relevant legislation recognised the need for a prompt decision-making process. And in *Mishra*, the court took account of the delay and expense which would result if the applicant was forced to seek alternative relief.

(v) Conclusion

Cases such as *Whittaker* and *McBeatty*, where the applicants avoided an alternative avenue for forensic reasons, and those concerning futility, show that the courts do not exist simply to advance an applicant's interests and desires. In *Lamb v Moss* (1983) 76 FLR 296 at 312 the Federal Court pointed out that one of the reasons for there being discretion under s 16 of the ADJR Act was the 'nature of the rights given by the Act'. The discretion which courts on occasion exercise at the remedial stage of judicial review reflects the important public purposes which are served by judicial review.

Examiner's Comments

It was not the aim of this essay question to see if students could recite the principal grounds for the exercise of discretion. Rather, the object of this question was to test students' deeper understanding of this topic. By focusing on purposes, students were required to think about the more fundamental motivations in this area.

The answer discusses the main purposes; it does not stray from the question and discuss judicial discretion generally.

Another strength of the answer is the conclusion. A more ordinary response might not have bothered with a conclusion, and this would be understandable given the nature of the question, which did not use open-ended words such as 'discuss' or 'to what extent' which call for a resolution. However, the writer of the above answer has managed to make a point which is not trite and which draws from the preceding discussion. While, contrary to popular mythology, conclusions are *not* the most important part of essays (see G Taylor, *The Student's Writing Guide For the Arts and Social Sciences*, Cambridge University Press, Cambridge, 1989, Ch 6), a well-resolved ending nevertheless tends to leave the examiner in a positive mood.

Common Errors to Avoid

- Not stating at all, or not stating clearly, the purposes to be served by judicial discretion.
- Not giving examples or sufficient examples.
- Not including headings when, if included, the structure of an essay would have been clearer.

QUESTION 31

Madeleine has been refused permission to import the unpublished drafts of *Loliter*. These drafts had been given by Bobakov, the author of *Loliter*, to a friend of the author; on the friend's recent death, they were found in his New York attic. *Loliter* is a famous work involving a man who has a relationship with a 14-year-old girl. It was banned when it was first written.

Madeleine has sought an order of review from the Federal Court to overturn the decision of an authorised person refusing her permission to import the drafts.

Madeleine accepts that the goods are prohibited imports. She says the drafts are truly shocking. However, as she is writing a biography of Bobakov, she says she wants to examine the drafts to find out more about what makes the man 'tick'.

In her case assume that the Commonwealth has not contended, and will not contend, that instead of approaching the court she should have appealed the decision to the AAT.

A policy is before the court which reads:

> In deciding cases under reg 4A(2A) of the Customs (Prohibited Imports) Regulations, the government's view is that if a good is a prohibited import it is only Cabinet which can allow importation.

In evidence before the court, it came out that the primary decision-maker, Ms Linda Wong, had taken the view that, as Cabinet had not yet decided on whether the goods ought to be released, she would refuse permission.

Consider the following:

- Certain portions of *Loliter* are available on the Internet. (The most titillating bits are included in that version.)
- Madeleine's biography of Bobakov is unauthorised, and Bobakov is personally opposed to her examining the drafts for what they might reveal about him or his work. Evidence of this is before the court.

Now answer the following question: Assuming Madeleine can establish a basis for relief, is there any bar or bars to Madeleine obtaining relief?

Time allowed: 35 mins

Answer Plan

(i)   Introduction.

(ii) Futility.

(iii) Inconvenience to others.

(iv) Justice to the applicant.

(v)   Conclusion.

Answer

(i)   Introduction

Having regard to the assumption in the question regarding alternative avenues, two possible bars will be considered: futility and inconvenience to others.

(ii)   Futility

An applicant may be refused relief on the basis of 'futility': *Hodgens v Gunn; Ex parte Hodgens* [1990] 1 Qd R 1 at 6. Other expressions of the same concept are that the court may withhold relief 'if no useful result could ensue' (*R v Commonwealth Court of Conciliation and Arbitration; Ex parte Ozone Theatres (Australia) Ltd* (1949) 78 CLR 389 at 400, cited in *Re Refugee Review Tribunal; Ex parte Aala* (2000) 204 CLR 82 at [56]), and where granting a remedy would be of 'manifest inutility': *Church of Scientology v Woodward* (1982) 154 CLR 25 at 62.

The first issue, therefore, is whether an order by the court ordering reconsideration would be futile because of the publication on the Internet of parts of the work Madeleine is seeking.

On the one hand, it could be argued that, as Madeleine already has access to this version through her own computer or her local library, the court's order would be futile. And it is possible that the rest of the drafts could be so released. A court ought not to make an order where it would have no practical effect: *Church of Scientology*; *Midland Metals Overseas Ltd v Comptroller-General of Customs* (1989) 55 ALR 302. Arguably, the order would have little practical effect if the most salacious portions are already available, as they might be more interesting to the author.

On the other hand, the matter is not entirely academic, since only part of the unpublished material is publicly available at present. As the applicant is writing a biography she would be expected to benefit from having a full version of the drafts. An edited version could be misleading. Courts do not refuse to grant relief when an order merely has a reduced effect in the circumstances: see, for example, *FAI Insurances Ltd v Winneke* (1982) 151 CLR 342 and *Stollery v Greyhound Racing Control Board* (1972) 128 CLR 509.

In the present case the court could, on the assumption that some relevant material is not currently available, be persuaded that an order for reconsideration would not be futile.

(iii)   Inconvenience to others

In exercising their discretion courts have regard to the effects their orders may have on third parties: see, for example, *Styles v Secretary, Department of Foreign Affairs and Trade* (1988) 84 ALR 408 (first instance), where the court considered the effect on the successful appointee of a successful challenge by a disappointed applicant; *Hodgens*, where the court considered the effect on the assimilated dogs and their new owners; and *R v Liquor Commission of the Northern Territory; Ex parte Pitjantjatjara Council Inc* (1984) 31 NTR 13, where the court took account of the money and effort expended by the licensee. In *Styles* (at 435), the court noted that it had a duty to 'do justice as between the parties and any other affected persons'. In *Hodgens* (at 7), the court noted that 'the inherent change of situation [was] of sufficient order ... to make it inappropriate to grant the prerogative remedy'. However, the weight to be given to the interests of third parties varies according to the circumstances, and they may be accorded only limited weight: R Douglas, *Douglas and Jones's Administrative Law*, 5th ed, Federation Press, Sydney, 2006, p 768. See, for example, *R v Liquor Commission of the Northern Territory*, where the court ultimately exercised its discretion in favour of the applicant council.

The present question therefore is — whether granting relief to the applicant would be sufficiently inconvenient to the author of the drafts as to warrant the court exercising its discretion to refuse relief. On the one hand, it is clearly inconvenient to Bobakov, since he opposes the writing of the biography. Presumably the drafts can reveal something of the author's thinking by a process of analysis, and will therefore aid the completion of the unauthorised biography.

On the other hand, having freely given the drafts away, the case for inconvenience and harm to his reputation is significantly weakened. Madeleine is in a stronger position than the applicants in both *Styles* and *Hodgens*. In these cases, the relevant inconvenience arose from the fact that the third party had relied on the correctness of the primary decision. In *Styles*, the third party had moved to London to take up the appointment. In *Hodgens* the dogs had been given new homes; the court noted that the dogs had been 'domestically assimilated to the extent that removal would produce loud cries of anguish': at 7. In contrast, there is no reason to believe that Bobakov relied on the decision to refuse importation.

(iv) Justice to the applicant

A positive factor in the applicant's favour is that she has a strong case on the merits; that is, the case for legal error seems clear and warrants correction. The court will wish to avoid substantial injustice being done by the withholding of a remedy: *Styles* at 435; C Enright, *Federal Administrative Law*, Federation Press, Sydney, 2001, [44.103].

(v) Conclusion

Neither futility nor inconvenience to others are of sufficient order in the present case to act as a bar to relief. Hence, the discretion to refuse relief would not be exercised adversely to Madeleine, and it is likely that she would be granted relief, assuming other requirements are met.

Examiner's Comments

In this problem students are required to recognise applicable heads by which discretion *could be* exercised adverse to the applicant, and to make analogies with existing cases to the extent possible.

The question makes the assumption that the Commonwealth has not contended, or will not contend, that Madeleine should have appealed to the AAT instead of the court. For convenience, the issue of dismissing an application or refusing to grant relief on the basis that there is a satisfactory alternative avenue is pursued in the next problem.

Discretion is an area for judgment. It can be a 'difficult area': *Styles* at 435. The court may be faced with a lack of evidence and the need to make assumptions, as was the case in *Styles*: at 435. In making these judgments courts seek to act on credible evidence, community values and common sense. The above answer, supported by cases, seems sound in this respect.

Common Errors to Avoid

- Not recognising the issue of judicial discretion — assuming that applicants have a right to a remedy once a ground of review and a basis for relief is made out.
- Not giving reasons — assuming that in a 'straightforward' case reasons are not necessary as the answer is 'obvious'.

QUESTION 32

> Harry has been refused permission to import a videotape of cock fighting. A document setting out the decision has been furnished to him. He has sought an order of review from the Federal Court under s 16 of the ADJR Act. Pursuant to Order 54A(3) of the Federal Court Rules, he has also sought, in the same application, *certiorari* and *mandamus* from the Federal Court under s 39B(1) and (1A)(c) of the Judiciary Act 1903 (Cth).
>
> He does not dispute that the tape is a prohibited import.
>
> Harry says he is an RSPCA investigative officer. He investigates and prosecutes cruelty to animals. He says the tape, which he purchased with his own money, is for his personal video library, so he knows what the 'enemy' is like. He intends to claim the purchase of the tape as a tax deduction on the grounds it is a work-related expense.
>
> A policy is before the court which reads:
>
>> In deciding cases under reg 4A(2A) of the Customs (Prohibited Imports) Regulations, the government's view is that if a good is a prohibited import it is only Cabinet which can allow importation.

In evidence before the court, it came out that the primary decision-maker, Ms Linda Wong, had taken the view that, as Cabinet had not yet decided on whether the goods ought to be released, she would refuse permission.

Assume a basis for relief can be made out.

Consider the following additional information:

- Harry did not commence proceedings until six months after becoming aware that the tape had been seized. He says that he had just been too busy in the office to get around to it for three months. And then he went on three months' long service leave. During that latter period he had to fly overseas for personal reasons: he had to attend a funeral in Rome for a much-loved great aunt, and while overseas he conducted negotiations for the purchase of valuable Italian antiques. He says that if he does not use his frequent flier points in any year he risks losing them.

- The respondent has argued (promptly; see Order 54, r 7 of the Federal Court Rules) that the court ought to refuse to grant the application, for the reason that adequate provision is made by another law, namely the AAT Act, under which the applicant is entitled to seek a review of the impugned decision: s 10(2)(b)(ii) of the ADJR Act. Harry says he did not seek that avenue because, first, court review was simpler and more direct, since the government had simply not had its 'eye on the ball'; second, he was out of time with respect to the AAT; and third, he had heard of recent empirical evidence that successful court review led to favourable outcomes for applicants in most cases.

Now answer the following question: Is the court likely, on discretionary grounds, to refuse or dismiss either or both of Harry's applications, or to refuse him relief? Give advice in relation to both his ADJR Act application and his application under s 39B of the Judiciary Act.

Time allowed: 45 mins

Answer Plan

(i)   Introduction.

(ii) Undue delay.
- Relevant legal principles.
- Application of the law.

(iii) Adequate alternative avenue not taken.
- Relevant legal principles.
- Application of the law.

(iv) Justice to the applicant.

(v)   Conclusion.

Answer

(i)   Introduction

On the basis of undue delay, Harry's ADJR Act application might be refused or he might be refused relief in respect of his application under s 39B of the Judiciary Act 1903. And on the basis that there is an adequate alternative avenue (the AAT), his ADJR Act application might be dismissed or he might be refused relief in respect of his s 39B application.

(ii)   Undue delay

Relevant legal principles

Under the general law, if a party is guilty of 'unwarrantable delay' (*R v Commonwealth Court of Conciliation and Arbitration; Ex parte Ozone Theatres (Australia) Ltd* (1949) 78 CLR 389 at 400, cited in *Re Refugee Review Tribunal; Ex parte Aala* (2000) 204 CLR 82 at [56]) or 'undue delay' (*Hodgens v Gunn; Ex parte Hodgens* [1990] 1 Qd R 1 at 6) a court may withhold a remedy. The general law applies to the application under s 39B of the Judiciary Act.

In relation to an ADJR Act application, there is a time limit for making applications under the Act: s 11. The time limit for making an application is coupled with a judicial power to extend time for applying at the discretion of the court: s 11(1)(c). Undue delay in making the application may therefore result in the court refusing the application.

The consideration of undue delay is similar with respect to both applications. One difference is that, in the case of the ADJR Act application, delay is assumed if an application is made after the prescribed period for lodging an application. Where a written decision has been furnished to the applicant, the prescribed period is 28 days from the time the written decision was furnished to the applicant: s 11(3)(b)(iii).

The leading case on the consequences of delay in relation to the ADJR Act applications is *Hunter Valley Developments Pty Ltd v Cohen* (1984) 3 FCR 344. The court held that, in deciding whether to extend time to allow a late application, factors considered include whether there is 'an acceptable explanation for the delay'; what is 'fair and equitable in the circumstances'; whether the applicant has 'rested on his rights'; 'the need for finality in disputes'; any 'prejudice to the respondent'; whether the application, if successful, would lead to 'the unsettling of other people ... or of established practices'; any 'prejudice which may be caused to an applicant by the refusal of an application'; and 'generally, what the justice of the case requires': at 348.

Application of the law

Is there a case for refusing Harry's application or refusing to grant him relief on account of undue delay? If he can provide solid evidence that he was completely occupied at work during that first three months, the court might be sympathetic as far as this period goes. However, his problems lie more in the latter three-month period as, except for the time spent going to the funeral overseas, he is struggling to demonstrate an acceptable explanation. We do not know of any prejudice to the respondent, but even so, the need for finality in disputes may go against him. There is authority that the absence of any prejudice to the respondent is *not* necessarily enough to save a late applicant: *Hunter Valley Developments* at 348. The absence of prejudice, if that is the case, will nevertheless lend some support to Harry.

(iii) Adequate alternative avenue not taken

Relevant legal principles

Under the general law, a court may decide not to grant a remedy if 'a more convenient and satisfactory remedy exists': *Ex parte Ozone Theatres (Australia) Ltd* at 400, cited in *Aala* at [56]. In this case, Harry could have sought review by the AAT under reg 4A(4) of the Customs (Prohibited Imports) Regulations.

The ADJR Act clarifies that this consideration may be considered at the commencement of a proceeding under the Act. Section 10(2)(b) states that:

> ... the Federal Court ... may, in its discretion, refuse to grant an application ... for the reason ...
>
> ...
>
> (ii) that adequate provision is made by any law other than this Act under which the applicant is entitled to seek a review by ... another tribunal, authority or person ...

'When assessing whether an alternative remedy is adequate, many factors are relevant, but the scope of the remedy is fundamental': *Garde-Wilson v Legal Services Board* [2007] VSC 225; see also *Kwan v Victoria Legal Aid* [2007] VSC 122 at [19]–[20]. Although there is no hard and fast rule, ordinarily judicial review jurisdiction will not be exercised where there is an alternative remedy by way of appeal and the appellate body 'has full capacity to make a fresh decision about what is "correct or preferable" in a given case': *Kwan* at [21]; *NSW Breeding and Racing Stables Pty Ltd v Administrative Decisions Tribunal of New South Wales* (2001) 53 NSWLR 559 at 564 [16].

Apart from regard to the scope of the appeal, a court will be inclined to dismiss an application or to refuse to grant relief where:

- a decision of the court would not be conclusive of the matter because it involves mixed questions of fact and law: *Du Pont (Australia) v Comptroller-General of Customs* (1993) 30 ALD 829;

- the court is being asked to grant relief before a complex decision-making process is completed: *Du Pont*;

- there were relevant indications from the statute: *Du Pont*;
- the applicant has sought judicial review rather than pursuing an alternative avenue for personal 'tactical forensic' reasons: *Whittaker v Child Support Registrar* (2000) 106 FCR 105 at [39].

However, a court may decide not to refuse to dismiss the application or refuse to grant relief:

- where the law does not make adequate alternative provision for review, such as where the scope of the appeal is limited or where the tribunal's decision is recommendatory only and can have no binding force upon the initial decision-maker: *Bragg v Department of Employment, Education & Training* (1995) 59 FCR 31 at 34.
- where the dispute involves a dispute of law which can be expeditiously handled by the court, and where the alternative would involve unnecessary delay and increased expense: *Mercantile Credits Ltd v Commissioner of Taxation No 1* (1985) 8 FCR 510 at 517;
- where hardship would be occasioned to the applicant by refusing relief: *Du Pont*;
- having regard to the circumstances of the applicant: *Mishra v University of Technology, Sydney* [1999] NSWSC 1324; and
- having regard to the volume of work already done by the court: *Mishra.*

Application of the law

Having had regard to the above factors, it would appear that the court would be likely to exercise its discretion in a manner adverse to Harry. For the application under the ADJR Act it would be likely to dismiss the application under s 10(2)(b)(ii). For the application under s 39B of the Judiciary Act it would be likely to refuse relief. Three factors are particularly relevant.

First, the right to seek review by the AAT constitutes adequate provision for review. The appeal is not limited in scope and it is determinative. The appeal is at least as adequate as the Disciplinary Appeal Committee in *Bragg*.

Second, the issues in dispute (between him and the government) are not pure questions of law. They involve mixed questions of fact and law: *Du Pont*. To succeed in his ultimate claim, Harry would wish to argue that the purposes for which the goods are to be imported are work-related (reg 4A(2AA)(a)); that his endeavour is an activity of an 'educational' nature (reg 4A(2AA)(b)); and that his reputation is sound as he works for a reputable organisation: reg 4A(2AA)(c). But these are mixed questions of fact and law. It is true that questions of law are involved, such as the meaning of 'educational'; for instance, does this term extend to self-education? Harry might wish to argue that, if his argument for the tape being work-related is *not* accepted, self-education is still within the term 'educational' in reg 4A(2AA)(b). But the case does not turn on this question of law alone, since, assuming 'educational' means educational for others, he has available to him the alternative argument that it *is* a work-related expenditure and that his activity is educational in terms of benefiting the community through his work at the RSPCA, a well-known community organisation. This is not to suggest his arguments will necessarily succeed; the point is that whether the tape is 'educational' in this sense is a mixed question of fact and law. In judicial review proceedings, the Federal Court is not generally able to tackle such questions (with some exceptions which are not relevant).

Third, the nature of Harry's reasons for his decision not to seek review by the AAT does not assist him. Harry's personal 'tactical forensic' reasons (*Whittaker* at [39]) for preferring the court to the tribunal would carry little weight, based on past cases such as *Whittaker* and *McBeatty v Gorman* [1975] 2 NSWLR 262.

(iv) Justice to the applicant

Prima facie, Harry stands to lose on discretionary grounds on account of undue delay or there being an adequate alternative avenue.

What about the considerations which incline against the court exercising its discretion adversely? In Harry's favour, there is the strength of his case as to the legal error. The merits of a case are relevant to allowing a late ADJR Act application (*Hunter Valley Developments* at 348), and they are relevant to the refusal of relief generally, because, if a case is made out, the court will wish to avoid substantial injustice being done by the withholding of a remedy: see C Enright, *Federal Administrative Law*, Federation Press, Sydney, 2001, [44.103]; *Styles v Secretary, Department of Foreign Affairs and Trade* (1988) 84 ALR 408.

(v) Conclusion

There is a discretionary ground for refusing Harry's ADJR application or refusing him relief under s 39B of the Judiciary Act (undue delay). There is also a discretionary ground for dismissing the ADJR application or refusing him relief in respect of the s 39B application (adequate alternative avenue). The question whether judicial discretion ought to be exercised against an applicant involves a balancing exercise, for the one fundamental consideration is 'on balance whether justice is best achieved by issuing or not issuing the remedy': Enright, 2001, [44.101].

Harry's overall position is weak. It is true that Harry has a plausible legal case. But unfortunately for Harry the merits of the substantial application are not determinative in the area of discretion. Moreover, in his case there is not one, but two, possible bases upon which the court might exercise its discretion adversely to him, and both are reasonably strong on the facts.

Examiner's Comments

Although judicial discretion may appear, at first sight, to be an area of judicial review less fettered than other areas by legal principles, the law can be applied in much the same manner as for any area of law:

1. identify the general category or categories of law which are relevant, and any relevant statutory provisions;

2. identify the elements or make-up of this law;

3. raise issues after considering whether any element or part of the law is in doubt when applied to the facts;

4. in respect of each issue, consider the various arguments which may be made; and

5. weigh the contending arguments and conclude the discussion.

Compare this method to the structure of the analysis above.

A complication in the problem, with respect to which advice is to be given, is the joint applications under the ADJR Act and s 39B of the Judiciary Act. Both undue delay and adequate alternative avenue attract special provisions of the ADJR Act. These provisions have different legal consequences to the effects those discretionary grounds may have in respect of the s 39B application. A good answer would follow this distinction through, referring to the relevant provisions of the ADJR Act and using the correct terminology. An ordinary answer would more or less ignore the ADJR Act provisions and simply discuss, under the general law, undue delay and alternative avenue not taken.

Another distinguishing feature between a good and an ordinary answer would be in the referencing to relevant cases. Students who refer to authorities to support each legal proposition would be well rewarded.

Common Errors to Avoid

- Approaching the question of judicial discretion as if it were an unregulated area: deciding the problem on emotional grounds and not by reference to relevant statute and case law.
- Not referring to and applying the relevant provisions of the ADJR Act: s 10(2)(b)(ii) (adequate alternative avenue); and s 11 (late applications giving rise to undue delay argument).
- Not addressing both grounds upon which the court may exercise its discretion adversely.

Chapter 11

Standing to Seek Judicial Review

 Key Issues

Introduction

The High Court has said of standing, or locus standi, that it is 'a metaphor to describe the interest required, apart from a cause of action as understood at common law, to obtain various common law, equitable and constitutional remedies': *Allan v Transurban City Link Ltd* (2001) 208 CLR 167 at [15].

With some exceptions, standing is generally required in public law proceedings, including judicial review of administrative action, in the sense that, if a court finds a plaintiff does not have standing, the application must be dismissed. Compare private law: the issue of standing to sue does not there arise: M Allars, *Administrative Law: Cases and Commentary*, Butterworths, Sydney, 1997, [13.1.2]. In private law areas such as tort law the requisite interest is bound up in the elements of the relevant cause of action (as intimated in the above definition): R Creyke and J McMillan, *Control of Government Action: Text, Cases and Commentary*, LexisNexis Butterworths, Sydney, 2005, [17.1.1].

There is no single standing rule across all judicial review proceedings. The tests vary from remedy to remedy and even from statute to statute. Nevertheless, 'there is a measure of broad agreement as to locus standi both for legal and equitable remedies in public law': *Australian Institute of Marine and Power Engineers v Secretary, Department of Transport* (1986) 13 FCR 124 at 132 per Gummow J.

The case law and legal principle are of limited assistance in this area. 'The cases are infinitely various' said Mason J in *ACF* at 547; in other words, cases turn largely on their facts or, more precisely, the nature and subject matter of the litigation: *Shop Distributive and Allied Employees Association v Minister for Industrial Affairs (SA)* (1995) 183 CLR 552 at 558.

The main issues concerning standing are briefly introduced below.

In what circumstances is standing an issue?

Standing becomes an issue if, under the relevant court rules, the defendant makes it an issue. The general principles were stated by Aickin J in *Onus v Alcoa of Australia Ltd* (1981) 149 CLR 27 at 57:

> On an application to strike out a statement of claim and dismiss an action on the basis of want of locus standi the defendant bears the onus of showing that the facts as alleged or proved in evidence are incapable of sustaining a cause of action.

The question of standing does not have to be dealt with as a preliminary issue. Indeed, the courts are reluctant to dismiss proceedings summarily: *Access for All Alliance (Hervey Bay) Inc v Hervey Bay City Council* [2007] FCA 615 at [14], [66]–[67]. A court may postpone dealing with the issue until after the merits of the case have been examined: *Australian Conservation Foundation Inc v Commonwealth* (1980) 146 CLR 493 (*ACF*) at 532.

Who has standing to seek judicial review?

The Attorney-General of the relevant government has the right to initiate or authorise court proceedings, both for declaration and injunction (*ACF* at 526), and for the prerogative writs: *Inland Revenue Commissioners v National Federation of Self-Employed and Small Businesses Ltd* [1982] AC 617 at 644 per Lord Diplock.

For the right of other persons to commence a proceeding, it is salient to examine each of the remedies, for traditionally '[t]he principles relating to standing to seek judicial review have differed according to the remedy sought': Allars, 1997, [13.2.1]. This remains true to some extent.

Declaration and injunction

For declaration and injunction the leading case has been *ACF* (although arguably it has been modified in practice by a line of cases concerning public interest groups: see Creyke and McMillan, 2005, [17.2.4]).

The *ACF* case set out the classic rule from *Boyce v Paddington Borough Council* [1903] 1 Ch 109 at 114:

> A plaintiff can sue without joining the Attorney-General in two cases: first, where the interference with the public right is such as that some private right of his is at the same time interfered with ...; and, secondly, where no private right is interfered with, but the plaintiff, in respect of his public right, suffers special damage peculiar to himself from the interference with the public right.

This statement was approved by Gibbs J (whose judgment is regarded as authoritative) with certain qualifications: 'peculiar to himself' did not mean that the plaintiff, and no one else, must have suffered damage; and the expression, 'special damage peculiar to himself', said his Honour, 'should be regarded as equivalent in meaning to "having a special interest in the subject matter of the action"': at 527.

The 'special interest in the subject matter of the action' test involves three interrelated elements. First, there is the question of what is an interest. Mason J in the same case helpfully referred to 'property or proprietary rights, business or economic interests and perhaps to social or political interests': at 547. It is clear that an interest does not have to be material; a cultural interest sufficed in *Onus* at 77 per Brennan J.

However, not every 'interest' is a 'special' interest: the second element. The cases need to be read as a guide. What is not sufficient is 'a mere intellectual or emotional concern', since any plaintiff who felt strongly enough to bring an action would thereby be able to maintain it: *ACF* at 530 per Gibbs J.

The third element is 'the subject matter of the action'. This has been interpreted to mean 'the acts or omissions which the applicant seeks to remedy and ... the relief or remedies which the applicant seeks': *OneSteel Manufacturing Pty Ltd v Whyalla Red Dust Action Group Inc* (2006) 94 SASR 357 at 366.

The law on declarations and injunctions is of wider importance because the *Boyce* principle, as reformulated by Gibbs J in *ACF*, is 'the general rule of the common law': *Truth About Motorways Pty Ltd v Macquarie Infrastructure Investment Management Ltd* (2000) 200 CLR 591 at [131] per Kirby J. The special interest component has added significance in administrative law because it is also, in essence, the test for who may apply to the Administrative Appeals Tribunal under s 27(1) of the AAT Act: see below.

Mandamus

Recent cases are sparse with respect to this remedy. Commentators suggest aligning the special interest test with *mandamus* (R Douglas, *Douglas and Jones's Administrative Law*, 5th ed, Federation Press, Sydney, 2006, p 802), and this seems broadly correct. In *West Australian Field and Game Association Inc v Pearce* (1992) 27 ALD 38, the full court of the Supreme Court of Western Australia adopted a test of 'sufficient interest in the matter to which the application relates', but made it clear that it was applying *ACF*: at 44. But the court also adopted the test of whether the complainant was within the scope or ambit of the duty: at 44. This latter test was applied by the full court of the Supreme Court of Victoria in *Federal Commissioner of Taxation v Biga Nominees Pty Ltd* [1988] VR 1066.

Prohibition, certiorari, habeas corpus

These remedies have a more liberal test of standing. A 'stranger', or a person without a special interest, may obtain prohibition, *certiorari*, *habeas corpus* or *quo warranto*: see *Truth About Motorways* at [2], [94], [95], [162] and [211]; *Re McBain; Ex parte Australian Catholic Bishops Conference* (2002) 209 CLR 372 at 413 [89] per McHugh J, with whom Callinan J agreed at 475 [293]. But 'a stranger's lack of standing will frequently result in the court refusing to issue [*certiorari* or prohibition] on discretionary grounds': *Re McBain* per McHugh J at 422 [109], with whom Callinan J agreed at 475 [293]. The origins of the rule appear to lie in the history of the prerogative writs; they were the means by which superior courts supervised the operation of tribunals inferior to them in the judicial hierarchy: *John Fairfax and Sons Ltd v Police Tribunal of New South Wales* (1986) 5 NSWLR 465 at 468; *Master Retailers' Association of NSW v Shop Assistants Union of NSW* (1904) 2 CLR 94 at 98.

Administrative Decisions (Judicial Review) Act 1977 (Cth) (ADJR Act)

In form, the ADJR Act dispensed with applications for the common law and equitable remedies and opted for applications for an order of review: ss 11, 16. The Act has a uniform standing test of 'a person who is aggrieved': ss 5, 6, 7. This in turn is defined as a person whose 'interests are adversely affected': s 3(4). Courts have noted that:

> ... formulae for determining standing to sue should not be given a rigid or inflexible meaning. They are flexible words which derive their meaning and take their colour from the context in which they appear and the nature of the particular statute concerned: *Ogle v Strickland* (1987) 13 FCR 306 at 309–10.

However, the ADJR Act cases are heavily influenced by the special interest cases (Creyke and McMillan, 2005, [17.4.9]), and the Federal Court has observed that 'it has never been held that the principles governing the award of declarations and injunctions under the general law [including the special interest test] have been superseded by different and broader conceptions under the ADJR Act': *North Coast Environment Council v Minister for Resources* (1994) 55 FCR 492 at 511–12. See also *Right to Life Association (NSW) Inc v Secretary, Department of Human Services and Health* (1995) 56 FCR 50 at 63.

Particular legislation

An Act may impose its own standing rules for challenging decisions under it: *Bateman's Bay Local Aboriginal Land Council v Aboriginal Community Benefit Fund Pty Ltd* (1998) 194 CLR 247 at [48]; *Allan* at [16]. The Act may impose a regime more restrictive than the special interest test: *Allan* (AAT review). On the other hand, it may impose a more liberal test, for example, s 475 of the Environment Protection and Biodiversity Conservation Act 1999 (Cth), or even an open test for judicial enforcement: see s 80(1) of the Trade Practices Act 1974 and the examples in *Truth About Motorways* per Kirby J at [133].

If an Act imposes its own standing rule, a court will see the question of the scope of the rule as an issue to be determined on the proper construction of the Act rather than an issue to be determined solely by reference to principles of general law: *Access for All Alliance* at [33].

Hot spots

Except in an area with an open standing rule, a line has to be drawn somewhere. As Brennan J put it with typical eloquence:

> ... a decision which affects interests of one person directly may affect the interests of others indirectly. Across the pool of sundry interest, the ripples of affection may widely extend. The problem ... is the determination of the point beyond which the affection of interests by a decision should be regarded as too remote: *Re McHattan and Collector of Customs (NSW)* (1977) 1 ALD 67 at 70 (AAT).

Creyke and McMillan point out (2005, [17.1.2.]) that there have been four main hot spots in standing litigation. These, together with the relevant cases featured in the major casebooks are:

- public interest groups: *ACF*; *North Coast*; *Right to Life Association*; *United States Tobacco Co v Minister for Consumer Affairs* (1988) 20 FCR 520;
- trade unions and trade associations: *Shop Distributive and Allied Employees*; *Australian Institute of Marine and Power Engineers*;
- trade rivals: *Bateman's Bay*; and
- 'the concerned citizen': *Re McBain*.

If a problem falls in these areas, the relevant cases should be addressed.

What evidence is needed?

It is a trite observation that the resolution of legal issues depends on the evidence adduced. Thus, if standing becomes an issue, a plaintiff's application can be dismissed if no relevant evidence, or insufficient evidence, is adduced. In *Right to Life* the appellant did not adduce evidence of the type relied on in *North Coast*: at 82 per Beaumont J. In *Access for All Alliance* the applicant, an incorporated community organisation, had contended in written submissions that 'the majority of its members' were affected by unlawful discrimination: at [56]. But the court, in giving reasons for dismissing the application, observed that '[t]he evidence here does not disclose how many of the members of the applicant are people with disabilities or who live in the Hervey Bay region, or both': at [60]. Compare *Bateman's Bay*, where the primary judge held that it was highly probable that, if not restrained, the appellants would cause severe detriment to the business of the respondents. This inference was made because the parties would be operating in substantially the same limited market: at [52].

What is the rationale of standing?

A number of justifications have been advanced. One flows from the traditional role of the courts. It is said that the civil courts exist to protect rights and legally recognised interests and legitimate expectations. They are not established 'to ensure that individuals or public officials obey the law': *Bateman's Bay* per McHugh J at 275. A second justification is that '[g]reat evils would arise if every member of the Commonwealth could attack the validity of the acts of the Commonwealth whenever he thought fit': *Anderson v Commonwealth* (1932) 47 CLR 50, cited in *ACF* at 528. In *Onus*, Gibbs CJ referred to the possibility that, without standing rules, the processes of the law could be abused by busybodies and cranks and persons actuated by malice, and he referred to the possibility that defendants might be subject to great cost and inconvenience in defending the legality of their actions: at 35. A third justification is that standing promotes effective litigation: 'it is desirable, in an adversary system, that the courts should decide only a real controversy between parties each of whom has a direct stake in the outcome of the proceedings': *Onus* at 35. A fourth justification is that a standing rule avoids a multiplicity of actions: *Onus* at 75 per Brennan J.

The arguments against standing, in brief, are, that 'in a community which professes to live by the rule of law the court should be open to anyone who genuinely seeks to prevent the law from being ignored or violated' (*Onus* at 35); the floodgates fear has no basis; persons without a direct personal stake are not necessarily incapable of running litigation; and it is a heavy-handed response.

What should be the test for standing? — the debate about the current law

The rationale and functions of standing is discussed in the cases. As well as Gibbs CJ's and Brennan J's judgments in *Onus*, there are more critical discussions in the judgment of Wilcox J in *Right to Life* and in the joint judgment in *Bateman's Bay* at [39]–[41]. Two reports of the Australian Law Reform Commission proposing alternative liberal formulations have fuelled the controversy: see Creyke and McMillan, 2005, [17.2.4]; Allars, 1997, [13.5].

In what circumstances, apart from seeking judicial review, is there a standing or a standing-like requirement?

Joinder

When a third party applies to be made a party to a proceeding that has already commenced, a standing test often applies. For example, the ADJR Act provides that 'a person interested in' a decision, conduct or a failure to perform a statutory duty, to which an application has been made to the court, may apply to the court to be made a party to the application: s 12(1). The court has a discretion to allow the application: s 12(2).

Statutory appeals on a question of law

Statutory appeals on a question of law, such as the right to appeal to the Federal Court under s 44(1) of the Administrative Appeals Act 1975, provide that appeals may be made by 'a party to a proceeding before the Tribunal'.

AAT

Section 27(1) of the AAT Act provides that 'an application may be made by or on behalf of any person or person ... whose interests are affected by the decision'. It has been observed that there is 'very little if any practical difference' to the common law special interest test: *Re Fearnley and Australian Fisheries Management Authority* (2005) 87 ALD 159 at [49]; see also *Re Control Investments Pty Ltd and Australian Broadcasting Tribunal (No 1)* (1980) 3 ALD 74 at 79. In addition, though, the AAT Act provides a separate and more liberal entitlement for an organisation to apply to the tribunal: s 27(2), (3).

Before attempting the questions, check that you are familiar with the following issues:

✓	in what circumstances does standing become an issue in judicial review?
✓	who has standing generally to seek judicial review?
✓	the rights and role of the Attorney-General as a plaintiff in civil cases with a public element;
✓	the role which legislation may play in a particular area of decision-making to determine or influence the standing rules;
✓	the main requirements and criteria of the 'special interest in the subject matter of the action' test, and the remedies to which it applies;
✓	whether public interest groups may have standing to sue;
✓	who may bring proceedings for *certiorari* and prohibition;
✓	what evidence is needed?
✓	what is the rationale of standing?
✓	what should be the test for standing? — the debate about the current law;
✓	in what circumstances, apart from seeking judicial review, is there a standing or a standing-like requirement?

QUESTION 33

Cannibalism! is a film which is proposed for screening in Australia. It purportedly shows graphic footage of starving sailors, well south of the Cape of Good Hope, eating one of their fellows in order to survive. Some people are of the view that portions of the film are loosely based on an infamous 19th century occurrence which culminated in a criminal ➤

trial (*R v Dudley and Stephens* (1884) 14 QBD 273), but the film does not include a court case. The film is scheduled for screening at the West Brighton Film Festival, Melbourne. The Attorney-General has given permission for the film to be imported under reg 4A(2) of the Customs (Prohibited Imports) Regulations 1956 (Cth), on the basis that it is relevant to the education of law students and gourmets. (She later said that the reference to gourmets was tongue-in-cheek.) The Attorney-General is also a devotee and the patron of the festival. Assume the Censorship Board has classified the film for an adult audience.

The decision of the Attorney-General is opposed by three individuals: Polly, Jill and Jack.

Polly, who is a vegetarian, objects because, from what she has read about it, she fears the film is in extremely bad taste. She also thinks it unacceptable that the film-makers have not acknowledged the English case as a source of their creative ideas.

Jill runs the South Melbourne Film Festival. Her festival runs at the same time as the West Brighton Film Festival. She opposes the importation because she believes the film's notoriety will unfairly take audiences away from her festival.

Jack is the President of a group known as Australians for Moral Decency. He has a letter addressed to him by the previous Attorney-General, promising to give his group a hearing before a decision is made about whether *Cannibalism!* should be allowed into Australia. (Assume an election has occurred since the letter was written.) Jack's group was not given such a hearing and Jack is furious.

Advise Polly, Jill and Jack whether each would have standing to sue for a declaration or an equivalent order under the ADJR Act, to the effect that the Attorney-General unlawfully exercised her discretion under reg 4A(2). Assume each has a reasonable case on the merits; that is, that the film is a prohibited import and that arguably the Attorney-General has made an error in exercising her discretion or the decision is legally flawed.

Time allowed: 45 mins

Answer Plan

(i)   General principles.

  • Main requirements of a 'special interest in the subject matter of the action'/a 'person who is aggrieved'.

  • Criteria for determining whether an interest is a 'special interest'.

(ii) Polly.

(iii) Jill.

(iv) Jack.

Answer

(i)   General principles

Main requirements of a 'special interest in the subject matter of the action'/a 'person who is aggrieved'

In the leading case of *Australian Conservation Foundation Inc v Commonwealth (ACF 1)* (1980) 146 CLR 493 the law of standing was reformulated. A person could sue for a declaration or injunction without joining the Attorney-General where either some private right of the plaintiff is interfered with or the plaintiff has a 'special interest in the subject matter of the action'. In outline, the main requirements flowing from such a special interest are:

- the plaintiff must have an 'interest';
- the plaintiff's interest must be a 'special' interest;
- the plaintiff's special interest must be 'in the subject matter of the application'.

Criteria for determining whether an interest is a 'special interest'

The courts have elaborated some broad criteria for determining what amounts to a 'special' interest at common law. (Note that the standing test for the ADJR Act is essentially the same as the test at common law for injunctions and declarations: *North Coast Environment Council Inc v Minister for Resources* (1994) 55 FCR 492 at 511–12; see also *Right to Life Association (NSW) Inc v Secretary, Department of Human Services and Health* (1995) 56 FCR 50 at 63.) The criteria include:

- 'The nature and subject matter of the litigation': *Shop Distributive and Allied Employees Association v Minister for Industrial Affairs (SA)* (1995) 183 CLR 552 at 558.

- 'The necessary interest need not be a legal, proprietary, financial or other tangible interest': *United States Tobacco Co v Minister for Consumer Affairs* (1988) 20 FCR 520 at 527 (ADJR Act). But the interest must be more than a 'mere intellectual or emotional concern': *ACF 1* at 530. A belief that a particular law should be observed is not sufficient: *ACF 1* at 530.

- The plaintiff must be interested in the sense of having 'a special interest in the outcome of proceedings': *Re McBain; Ex parte Australian Catholic Bishops Conference* (2002) 209 CLR 372 at 423). In the words of Gibbs J in *ACF 1*:

  A person is not interested within the meaning of the rule, unless he is likely to gain some advantage, other than the satisfaction of righting a wrong, upholding a principle or winning a contest, if his action succeeds or to suffer some disadvantage, other than a sense of grievance or a debt for costs, if his action fails: at 530.

- 'The importance of the concern which a plaintiff has with particular subject matter': *Onus v Alcoa of Australia Ltd* (1981) 149 CLR 27 at 42 per Stephen J.

- 'The closeness of that plaintiff's relationship to that subject matter': *Onus* at 42 per Stephen J.

- Whether the plaintiff 'in comparison with the public at large ... has been affected to a substantially greater degree or in a significantly different manner': *Onus* at 74 per Brennan J. The ADJR Act equivalent is that the applicant must show 'a grievance which will be suffered as a result of the decision complained of beyond that which he or she has as an ordinary member of the public': *Tooheys Ltd v Minister for Business and Consumer Affairs* (1981) 36 ALR 64 at 79.

- 'The nature, scope and purpose of the particular enactment under which the decision has been made', and whether the applicant is concerned and seeking to advance, by the processes of judicial review, the purposes or ends which the parliament sought to advance: *Right to Life Association* at 84–5 per Gummow J; see also at 68–9 per Lockhart J (ADJR Act).

- Community values and beliefs: *Onus* at 42 per Stephen J.

- Whether the applicant is a body corporate or an unincorporated association (the former, but not the latter, needs to establish that it is a person aggrieved in its own right: *Access for All Alliance (Hervey Bay) Inc v Hervey Bay City Council* [2007] FCA 615 at [58]).

These general principles will guide the application of the law to the cases of Polly, Jill and Jack.

(ii) Polly

Polly has a negligible chance of succeeding in her claim to standing. Apart from her concern for good taste and intellectual honesty in film production, she can point to no other interest in the subject matter of the possible action or in the relief she would be seeking. In other words, she is objecting only as a matter of principle to the film. In *Ogle v Strickland* (1987) 13 FCR 306, the priests who objected to the importation of a particular film at least had a vocation to which the subject matter of the action (repelling blasphemy) was a 'necessary incident': at 318 per Lockhart J. Polly's case is analogous to the ideological objection by the Roman Catholic bishops in *Re McBain* and by the applicant in *Cameron v Human Rights and Equal Opportunity Commission* (1993) 46 FCR 509. In the language of *ACF 1*, Polly would be regarded by a court as having a mere intellectual or emotional concern in the subject matter of the action. As such, it is not necessary to consider the other criteria for a special interest or as a person aggrieved.

Thus, Polly would not be accorded standing to sue if objection was taken to her making an application for a declaration, or an order under the ADJR Act.

(iii) Jill

Jill is in a somewhat different position because, unlike Polly, she can at least argue that she has more than a mere intellectual or emotional concern, and is interested in that she stands to gain 'some advantage, other than the satisfaction of righting a wrong': *ACF 1* at 530. Jill would argue that she has a financial interest to protect from unfair competition. A business or economic interest can be a recognised interest: *ACF 1* per Mason J at 547; an example is *Bateman's Bay Local Aboriginal Land Council v Aboriginal Community Benefit Fund Pty Ltd* (1998) 194 CLR 247.

Jill's interest is quite important to her (*Onus* at 42) in that her business depends on revenues and the market for cinema-goers is limited.

However, Jill does not enjoy a close relationship with the subject matter: *Onus* at 42. She is only indirectly affected by the decision: her *potential* customers will choose to go to see the film in question.

For similar reasons, it is doubtful whether Jill is *sufficiently* affected to be accorded standing. She needs to be affected to a substantially greater degree or in a significantly different manner: *Onus* at 74. The plaintiffs in *Central Queensland Speleological Society Inc v Central Queensland Cement Pty Ltd* [1989] 2 Qd R 512 failed for lack of sufficient material interest. Closer to home, in *Australian Foreman Stevedores Association v Crone* (1989) 20 FCR 377, unions and a number of their members failed to be accorded standing in relation to a challenge to the importation of vessels by a rival company which did not employ union labour. Their interest was regarded as too tenuous. Jill is not in the same limited market as the plaintiff was in *Batemans's Bay*, where it was held that their interest in the observance of the statutory limitations on the defendant's activities was 'immediate, significant and peculiar' to them: at [52]. While Jill's interest need not be unique (*ACF 1* per Gibbs J at 527), it is doubtful whether Jill can show a sufficient interest in the observance by the Attorney-General in the limitations on her powers under the Customs (Prohibited Imports) Regulations 1956 (Cth). Jill is just one of many cinema proprietors (not to mention proprietors of other leisure businesses) who stand to suffer by cinema lovers attending the West Brighton Film Festival to watch *Cannibalism!*

Further, Jill's financial interest is not within the range of interests the concern of the Customs (Prohibited Imports) Regulations: *Right to Life*.

In conclusion, it is most unlikely that Jill would be accorded standing to sue should objection be taken.

(iv) Jack

Of the three, Jack is in the strongest position, notwithstanding that his interest is unusual.

It is possible Jack personally has standing to sue for a declaration on two bases:

1. he has a 'private right' which has been interfered with: the first limb of the *Boyce* principle approved in *ACF 1* at 526–7;

2. he has a 'special interest in the subject matter of the action' at common law: the second limb of the *Boyce* principle as reformulated in *ACF 1*.

Similarly, he could argue that he is 'a person who is aggrieved' for the purposes of an application under the ADJR Act because his rights are at stake, or because his interests are adversely affected to a sufficient extent.

Alternatively, Jack's group, Australians for Moral Decency, could possibly argue that it has standing to sue under the principles applicable to public interest groups developed in *Australian Conservation Foundation v Minister for Resources* (1989) 19 ALD 70 (*ACF 2*) and *North Coast* (the *North Coast* basis).

The *North Coast* basis will not be discussed, however, because there are insufficient facts given concerning the organisation. We would need to know whether it can adduce evidence of the matters set out in *North Coast* at 512–3. Going by the name of the group and the breadth of its possible concerns, its case does not look at all promising.

Whether Jack has a 'private right' for the purposes of a declaration will also not be discussed. The concept is unclear (*Access for All Alliance* at [24]), and the special interest test (as the interests test clearly does in s 3(4) of the ADJR Act) in any event encapsulates rights and other legal interests: *ACF 1* at 547; *Onus* at 71, 73.

Whether Jack has a special interest in the subject matter of the application or is a person aggrieved turns on the nature of Jack's interest. If he has a legal right or a legal interest he would be accorded standing. If he does not he would appear to have a 'mere intellectual or emotional concern' (*ACF 1*) and therefore lack a basis to be accorded standing. The question then is whether he has that right or interest.

For Jack it could be argued that he has a legal right or at least a legal interest arising from the promise to consult his organisation. It could be argued that there is case law that an undertaking, including an undertaking to give a hearing, can be a source of a legitimate expectation to be afforded procedural fairness in the making of a decision. This in turn can ground a right to be afforded procedural fairness: *Kioa v West* (1985) 159 CLR 550 at 583 per Mason J; *Attorney-General (Hong Kong) v Ng Yuen Shiu* [1983] 2 AC 629; *Cole v Cunningham* (1983) 81 FLR 158. An undertaking can raise the content of a duty which a decision-maker would otherwise be obliged to afford: *Century Metals and Mining NL v Yeomans* (1989) 40 FCR 564. Further, it could be argued there is practical injustice by the failure to honour the undertaking (distinguishing *Re Minister for Immigration and Multicultural and Indigenous Affairs v Lam* (2003) 214 CLR 1).

However, there are a number of difficulties with the above submissions.

First, the undertaking is quite possibly given in 'the political field': *South Australia v O'Shea* (1987) 163 CLR 378 at 411 per Brennan J. That arena is understood as 'the area of ministerial policy giving effect to the general public interest'. Administrative action in that arena does not give rise to a duty to afford procedural fairness and hence to a correlative right. In the present case the undertaking is alleged to have been given by a Minister. The Customs (Prohibited Imports) Regulations seem designed to allow the government, in the public interest, to allow the importation of designated goods which would otherwise be prohibited imports: reg 4A(2AA).

Second, there are suggestions in *Re Minister for Immigration and Multicultural and Indigenous Affairs v Lam* (2003) 214 CLR 1 that legitimate expectation is now relevant only to the content stage of procedural fairness: see Gleeson CJ at [12]–[13]; McHugh and Gummow JJ at [82]–[83]; Callinan J at [145]. If so, this means that breach of an undertaking does not, if it ever formerly could, automatically give rise to a breach of procedural fairness. The undertaking is just one of the factors to be taken into account in determining whether there has been a breach of procedural fairness.

Third, the circumstances of the undertaking, including its political character and the fact that it has been given by a previous government need to be taken into account in determining any duty. It is possible that the undertaking has been withdrawn by the new government.

In conclusion, Jack has an arguable case that he has a legal right or a legal interest (a right to a hearing) based on the undertaking set out in the letter he holds. As such he has an arguable case for standing at common law and under the ADJR Act. An arguable legal right is probably sufficient to ensure any application by him for judicial review would at least not be summarily dismissed: *Access for All Alliance* at [14].

Examiner's Comments

This problem illustrates how the law of standing is a 'question of degree', to quote Brennan J in *Onus v Alcoa of Australia Ltd* (1981) 149 CLR 27 at 75. To say that is not meant to imply that standing is forever contentious; rather, interests assessed by the law of standing span a spectrum, as vividly described in Brennan J's 'pool' metaphor, quoted above. In our problem there is, first of all, Polly, whose 'interest' is a mere intellectual or emotional concern; one which is clearly not capable of recognition for present purposes. Next, there is Jill, whose interest is slightly arguable, but is probably too tenuous, or not sufficiently substantial, for her to be accorded standing either at common law or under the ADJR Act. Jack has an arguable right on which to base his claim to standing.

None of the hypothetical plaintiffs has perfectly clear cases and two have very weak cases (Polly and Jill). This is not unusual in law exams. Examiners often design problems to test those students who are inclined to want to 'help' their clients, especially the disadvantaged or the relatively powerless, on moral rather than legal grounds.

Jack's position required an analysis of the right to procedural fairness, another topic of administrative law: see Chapters 5 and 6. As this question shows, problem solving in administrative law may require combining two or more relevant areas of law.

The answer glosses the authority of some of the statements made in the 'leading' case: *Australian Conservation Foundation Inc v Commonwealth (ACF 1)* (1980) 146 CLR 493. For instance, it refers to statements of Gibbs J in that case as if they have the authority of a majority of the High Court. As it happens, they have: see, for instance, the approval his reasons, or portions of it, received in *Onus* at 36–7, 41, 62 and 74, and in *Shop Distributive and Allied Employees Association v Minister for Industrial Affairs (SA)* (1995) 183 CLR 552 at 558. Students need to remember that, just because a statement is made by one member of an appellate court, that does not necessarily mean the statement is authoritative in the sense of standing for the court, even if the member is in the majority on the ultimate decision.

The answer does not discuss whether Jack's group might have standing to sue on the basis of any activities as a public interest group. This issue is discussed in Question 34.

 ## Common Errors to Avoid

- Referring simply to the need for some 'special interest', rather than setting out the applicable law, at least at some length.
- Only referring to *ACF*, as if it were the only standing case of importance. Analogous cases on the facts should also figure in the answer wherever possible.
- Assuming that the facts which are supplied are necessarily complete — in other words, failing to consider possible 'missing' facts.
- Not making connections with other parts of administrative law, on the mistaken assumption that only one law is ever applicable to a problem.

QUESTION 34

Consider 'The Makepeace Scenario', p xvi, once again. Assume that Makepeace requested permission to import a copy of *The Night of a Thousand Shames* and that the Attorney-General refused the application. Makepeace applied to the AAT for review of the Attorney-General's decision. The AAT is now ready to proceed with that review. The Presiding Member of the tribunal is John Spofforth QC. Before his appointment to the tribunal he had been an outspoken and well-known critic of Caledenia's human rights record and was refused a visa to visit Caledenia in 2005.

Now consider the following facts.

A group known as Friends of Caledenia (FOC) wishes to join the Australian Government in seeking to have Spofforth disqualified from hearing the Makepeace application. FOC is an incorporated association whose objectives include 'the protection of Caledenia's reputation in Australia'. It has a contract with the Victorian Government to teach Linguaji Caledenia in 20 Victorian secondary colleges. The Australian Government has made an application for an order of review under the ADJR Act to have Spofforth disqualified. Advise whether FOC can be made a party to that application.

Time allowed: 45 mins

Answer Plan

(i) The main conditions for a person being made a party to an ADJR Act application, under s 12 of the Act, in respect of the review of conduct.

(ii) Law of standing regarding public interest groups.
  - *ACF 1* and *Onus*.
  - Alternative reading.
  - What is the current law? Determining the weight to be given to a non-binding precedent.

(iii) Application of law of standing to the facts.
  - Do either of these readings matter in the present case?
  - Assuming the alternative view is arguable.

(iv) Requirement of exercise of discretion by court.

Answer

(i) Main conditions for being made a party to an ADJR application, under s 12 of the Act, in respect of the review of conduct

A person who wishes to be made a party to an ADJR proceeding must satisfy s 12 of the ADJR Act. The following conditions apply in the case of the review of conduct:

1. the person must be 'interested' in the conduct; and

2. the court must agree to exercise its discretion to grant the application.

In *United States Tobacco Co v Minister for Consumer Affairs* (1988) 20 FCR 520 at 527, the full Federal Court held that 'interested' and 'person aggrieved' in ss 5 and 6 of the ADJR Act were 'concomitant and a similar approach is to be adopted in construing them, subject to the qualification that membership of the class defined in subs 12(1) confers no right to joinder in a proceeding for an order of review'. 'Person aggrieved' has in turn been understood as concomitant with the common law of standing to seek injunctive or declaratory relief: *North Coast Environment Council Inc v Minister for Resources* (1994) 55 FCR 492 at 511–12; *Right to Life Association (NSW) Inc v Secretary, Department of Human Services and Health* (1995) 56 FCR 50 at 63 per Lockhart J. Hence, the relevant law on the content of 'interested' includes decisions on 'person aggrieved' under the ADJR Act as well as the common law of standing to seek injunctive or declaratory relief.

Is FOC interested in the light of the relevant law? FOC's objectives refer to 'the protection of Caledenia's reputation in Australia'. Before considering that interest, we might first ask whether FOC has any special interest in the subject matter of the action other than being a public interest group. On the facts there is no other possible basis for its special interest. Although it has a material interest in contracts with the State government, this does not amount to a relevant special interest.

(ii) Law of standing regarding public interest groups

In order to determine whether FOC can have standing as a public interest group we need to work out the relevant law. Can a public interest group have a special interest for the purposes of the law of standing? There are two opposing readings of the current law in relation to 'public interest groups'.

ACF 1 and Onus

The first reading, under the leading case of *Australian Conservation Foundation Inc v Commonwealth of Australia* (1980) 146 CLR 493 (*ACF 1*), is that a public interest group such as FOC does not in general qualify for standing: M Allars, *Administrative Law, Cases and*

Commentary, Butterworths, Sydney, 1997, [13.4.12]. This rule does not apply if the group participated in proceedings below as of right: *United States Tobacco* at 531.

In *ACF 1* the Foundation's objects, its 6,500 strong membership, the fact that it was well known for its involvement in the public discussion of issues affecting the environment in Australia, the funds it regularly received from government, and its endeavours to influence national policy were merely noted in passing: at 518–19. In the judgment of Gibbs J, it was famously held that a 'mere intellectual or emotional concern' does not suffice (at 530), and 'The fact that the Foundation is incorporated with particular objects does not strengthen its claim to standing': at 531. Its environmental activities were not seen as relevant.

Furthermore, in *Onus v Alcoa of Australia Ltd* (1981) 149 CLR 27 (the Aboriginal relics case), a majority of the High Court went out of their way to emphasise that an environmental lobby group does not normally have standing. For instance, Gibbs CJ said at 37, in an apparent reference to *ACF 1*:

> The position of a small community of Aboriginal people of a particular group living in a particular area which that group has traditionally occupied, and which claims an interest in relics of their ancestors found in that area, is very different indeed from that of a diverse group of white Australians associated by some common opinion on a matter of social policy which might equally concern any other Australian.

Stephen J at 42, Mason J at 43, and Wilson J at 62, expressed agreement or similar views in that case.

ACF 1 has been followed in a recent South Australian case, *OneSteel Manufacturing Pty Ltd v Whyalla Red Dust Action Group Inc* (2006) 94 SASR 357. A public interest group attempting to restrain a manufacturer of steel products failed to satisfy a statutory test that its 'interests are affected by the subject matter of the application'. The court held that an order restraining OneSteel from causing manufacturing harm by its emissions or an order that OneSteel record and monitor emissions would not:

> ... in any way affect the interests of [the public interest group], except perhaps to satisfy its intellectual or emotional concern for the environment. The interests of [the public interest group] after the application is heard will be no different from its interests before the application is heard: at [26].

Alternative reading

The other reading of the law of standing as it pertains to public interest groups takes into account the activities of a public interest group in deciding whether such a group can have a special interest in its area of interest, though it does not mean that all public interest groups will necessarily be accorded the right to seek relief in the courts.

Lobby groups which 'act in the public interest' (*Australian Conservation Foundation v Minister for Resources* (1989) 19 ALD 70 (*ACF 2*) at 73) and whose 'activities illustrates a strong commitment to the values it regards ... as under threat' (*North Coast* at 514) have been accorded standing in several Federal Court cases including *ACF 2, North Coast*, and *Alliance to Save Hinchinbrook v Environmental Protection Agency* (2006) 145 LGERA 32. See also *Right to Life* at 82 per Beaumont J. *North Coast* was approved by the full Federal Court in *Transurban City Link Ltd v Allan* (1999) 95 FCR 553 at [44].

In *North Coast*, the most cited of the cases, Sackville J took account of such facts as North Coast's standing as a peak environmental organisation, its recognition by the Commonwealth and New South Wales governments as a significant and responsible environmental organisation, its participation in official decision-making processes, its submissions to government bodies, and its funding of research work.

In the above cases the Federal Court has found that public interest groups, such as the applicants in *ACF 2* and *North Coast*, can have a special interest if their activities demonstrate 'the importance of its concern with the subject matter of the decision and the closeness of its relationship to that subject matter': *North Coast* per Sackville J at 512, drawing on the reasoning of Stephen J in *Onus v Alcoa*.

What is the current law? Determining the weight to be given to a non-binding precedent

At first instance in the Federal Court or Federal Magistrates Court judicial comity supports the single instance decisions of the Federal Court (*ACF 2; North Coast; Hinchinbrook*) being ordinarily followed: A MacAdam and J Pyke, *Judicial Reasoning and the Doctrine of Precedent in Australia*, Butterworths, Sydney, 1998, [8.56].

If the precedents are considered by an appellate court, wider considerations would be brought to bear. According to Zander, there are various considerations which assist in determining the weight which should be given to a non-binding precedent: M Zander, *The Law-Making Process*, 6th ed, Cambridge University Press, Cambridge, 2004, pp 278–80.

Applying Zander, factors giving weight to *ACF 2* and *North Coast* as non-binding precedents include:

- When were the cases decided?
  - The cases are reasonably well established. They date back to the 1980s.
- How does the precedent fit in with the surrounding law?
  - *ACF 1* was distinguished in *ACF 2*.
  - The judgments in both cases derive support from a passage in the judgment of Stephen J in a High Court case which was decided after *ACF 1*: *Onus*.

- — *Onus* recognised that a special interest can be non-material.
- The cogency of the reasoning:
  - — The judgments in those cases are detailed and well reasoned on the whole. In *North Coast*, it is demonstrated how the group's concern is not 'a mere intellectual or emotional concern': at 513–4.
  - — The cases are apt for modern conditions.
- How the cases have been dealt with in later cases:
  - — *North Coast* was approved by the full Federal Court in *Transurban City Link Ltd v Allan* (1999) 95 FCR 553 at [44].
- The reputation the precedents enjoy generally:
  - — The cases are extracted in scholarly texts presenting the current law: R Creyke and J McMillan, *Control of Government Action: Text, Cases and Commentary*, LexisNexis Butterworths, Sydney, 2005 (*North Coast*); R Douglas, *Douglas and Jones's Administrative Law*, 5th ed, Federation Press, Sydney, 2006 (*North Coast*);
  - — The cases are cited without being criticised in M Aronson, B Dyer and M Groves, *Judicial Review of Administrative Action*, 3rd ed, Lawbook, Sydney, 2004, pp 658–9;
  - — The Commonwealth Parliament has legislated in the environmental area to create liberal standing rights for public interest groups: Environment Protection and Biodiversity Conservation Act 1999 (Cth) s 475, which suggests community support for public interest groups having standing to sue in the courts at least in the environmental area.

Factors going against giving much weight to *ACF 2* and *North Coast* as precedents include:

- Which court decided the case:
  - — The precedents are decisions of single judges.
- How does the precedent fit in with the surrounding law:
  - — In *Onus*, the High Court made it clear that a public interest group such as a white conservation group does not have standing: see above.
  - — A South Australian court (Debelle J) has followed *ACF 1*, and not applied *North Coast*, in holding that having an intellectual or emotional concern for the environment is not sufficient: *OneSteel* at [26].
- The cogency of the reasoning of *ACF 2* and *North Coast*:

— An aspect of the reasoning of *ACF 2* was questioned by Lockhart J in *Right to Life* at 67.

— *ACF 2* distinguished *ACF 1* as turning on a local environmental issue, but this is an interpretation of *ACF 1*, not an express holding in that case.

— The cases suggest that a threat to the group's values is sufficient (*North Coast* at 514), but this seems indistinguishable from the ruling in *ACF 1* that beliefs that the law should be observed do not suffice to give its possessor locus standi: at 530. In other words, it is not clear how these cases show the applicant is 'likely to gain some advantage, other than the satisfaction of righting a wrong, upholding a principle or winning a contest': *ACF 1* at 530.

• The reputation the cases enjoy generally:

— The literature has pointed out that the cases cannot all be reconciled: M Aronson, B Dyer and M Groves, *Judicial Review of Administrative Action*, 3rd ed, Lawbook, Sydney, 2004, p 658; J Barnes, 'Standing: Environmental Groups Get the Green Light' (1990) 18 *Australian Business Law Review* 338.

In conclusion, neither point of view on the status of public interest groups appears certain to be upheld by an appellate court. Each has its strengths and weaknesses. There is a further 'spanner in the works': if the issue reached the High Court, it could liberalise the law further, if the dicta by Gaudron, Gummow and Toohey JJ in *Bateman's Bay* at [39] is a guide.

(iii) Application of law of standing to the facts

Do either of these readings matter in the present case?

On the surface, they appear to. If *ACF 1*, as interpreted in *Onus* and *OneSteel*, is the law on the standing of public interest groups, then FOC cannot be 'interested' (entitled to standing) because it cannot show how its interest is beyond that of an ordinary member of the public. Its lobby group activities and its government recognition, as evidenced by the teaching contract, do not assist it as these will continue after the decision. Its interests would be seen as unaffected by the conduct, as in *OneSteel* at [26]. If, on the other hand, *ACF 2* and *North Coast* are accepted as making a modification to the law, a public interest group can put forward its activities to show that it has more than a mere intellectual or emotional concern. In the latter scenario then FOC may have standing, if it can make out such a case.

Assuming the alternative view is arguable

Are the activities of FOC of which we are aware sufficient to bring it within the line of decisions created by *ACF 2* and *North Coast*? The mere fact that its objectives would be promoted by the court action are not enough: *North Coast* at 512. The grants it receives for language teaching are not, however, irrelevant. In *North Coast*, Sackville J noted that the applicant group had engaged in activities which, though they were not specifically concerned with the precise subject matter of the action (wood chipping), nevertheless reflected the group's standing as a 'respected and responsible environmental body'. It may be that FOC could lead evidence to show that it was the peak group concerned with relations with Caledenia in the same way that North Coast was found to be the peak interest group in that case: at 514.

There is also the question of 'current community perceptions and values', consideration of which in *ACF 2* was said to be 'necessary': at 74. In *Onus*, Stephen J relied on 'community values and beliefs' to distinguish the interest of the applicants from the concern of (white) conservationists: at 42. Several years later, in *ACF 2*, Davies J discerned what 'the community at the present time expect' from groups such as the Australian Conservation Foundation: at 74. While it is understandable how environmental concerns and large, respectable environmental groups can be said to have community support, it is not as clear that relations with Caledenia and the work of groups such as FOC would be recognised in the same way.

I would conclude that, if the line of authority established by *ACF 2* and *North Coast* is recognised to be the law, then FOC can *possibly* demonstrate it has standing, but only if it can adduce evidence of its standing as the leading respectable commentator on Caledenian affairs and a key participant in the maintenance and development of Australian–Caledenian relations.

(iv)   Requirement of exercise of discretion by court

Assuming FOC is 'interested' within s 12(1) of the ADJR Act, the second and final question is whether a court would be likely to exercise its discretion in FOC's favour: s 12(2) of the ADJR Act. There is no suggestion that the court will be inundated with parties if FOC is admitted as a party. Nor is there any suggestion that FOC might act inappropriately if allowed to join. The argument before the court might benefit from a non-governmental advocate, especially as the tribunal is not to act as a protagonist: *R v Australian Broadcasting Tribunal; Ex parte Hardiman* (1980) 144 CLR 13. On the assumption the *North Coast* doctrine is good law and FOC can adduce evidence that it is a leading commentator and participant in the development of Australian–Caledenian relations, a court would be likely to find that it is appropriate to be admitted as a party.

Examiner's Comments

Although this question deals with rights to joinder under s 12 of the ADJR Act, it mainly involves the issue of whether a public interest group has interests affected by administrative conduct, equivalent to those required for standing to seek review under the ADJR Act.

At the time of writing the law is unsettled at the appellate level. Examiners latch onto uncertainty in the law like bears go for honey. They do so because, when there is uncertainty as to the principles of the law, students are required to undertake a higher-level intellectual task in the law: determining what law would be applied having regard to the doctrine of precedent and other predictive factors.

The question is also uncertain at the factual level. The facts are thin on the activities of FOC. Students need to remember that not all the material facts are necessarily given in problems. Frequently they are not, to see how students manage factual uncertainty: J Barnes, 'Teacher v Student: The Role of Fundamental "Conceptions of Reality" in the Preparation of a Legal Opinion', in K Chanock (ed), *Sources of Confusion*, La Trobe University, Melbourne, 2001, pp 19–36 at <http://www.latrobe.edu.au/lasu/conference.html>. On handling missing and other facts see H Gensler, 'Law School Examinations and Factual Analysis' (1997) 31(2) *The Law Teacher* 198.

Despite its basic predictability, the question is a challenging one, as students must weigh the apparently conflicting authorities and predict what principles would be applied if the matter got to court.

A strength of the answer is the detailed evaluation of the weight of the Federal Court precedents on the standing of public interest groups. An ordinary pass or low C answer would assume one or other of the lines of authority applied without canvassing the issue. Even so, the answer is not complete. It does not refer to how the decisions have been dealt with in later cases in State courts: see M Aronson, B Dyer and M Groves, *Judicial Review of Administrative Action*, 3rd ed, Lawbook, Sydney, 2004, p 659.

 ## Common Errors to Avoid

- Assuming that the applicable principles of law are clear. Refraining from discussing both *ACF 1* and the line of authority established by *ACF 2* and *North Coast*. Not seeing a possible conflict between the authorities. Not discussing which line of authority better represents the law.

- Assuming that the facts are clear. Not thinking of missing facts — facts which might improve the position of FOC, assuming such facts can be found.

QUESTION 35

'There can be little doubt that the present law of standing is far from coherent': McHugh J in *Bateman's Bay Local Aboriginal Land Council v Aboriginal Community Benefit Fund Pty Ltd* (1998) 194 CLR 247 at [91].

Discuss.

Time allowed: 50 mins

Answer Plan

(i)   Introduction.

(ii)   Inconsistency across the board.

(iii) Fundamental assumptions of the law of standing.

(iv)   Incoherencies in the special interest test.

* Particularly problematic areas.

* Rambling case law; cases turning on their facts?

* Non-principled decision-making? bases which lack logical force.

* Inconsistencies: public interest groups.

* Source of incoherencies.

(v)   Clear-cut applications of the law.

* Persons directly and adversely affected.

* Individuals with a mere intellectual or emotional concern.

(vi)   Conclusion.

 Answer

(i)   Introduction

'Standing' refers to the entitlement of an applicant to bring proceedings before a court or tribunal and to obtain relief from such a body: *Right to Life Association (NSW) Inc v Secretary, Department of Human Services and Health* (1995) 56 FCR 50 at 63 and 66 per Lockhart J.

To assess the coherence of the law of standing, it will help if we clarify what 'coherent' can mean. It has two main meanings. One is 'not rambling or inconsequent': *Pocket Oxford Dictionary*. Its stricter meaning is 'well knit or consistent' (*Pocket Oxford Dictionary*) or 'logical' (*Macquarie Dictionary*).

Whether the law of standing is coherent can be seen to depend partly on what meaning of 'coherent' we are assuming, but also on what aspect of the law of standing one is referring to — for instance, is it standing law across the board, or just individual remedies? The fundamentals? The special interest test? The directly affected? Or individuals with a mere intellectual or emotional concern? Each is now examined in turn.

(ii)   Inconsistency across the board

If we are talking about standing across the board, the test for standing varies enormously. In a few statutes there is an open test, for example, the right may apply to 'any person': see *Allan v Transurban City Link Ltd* (2001) 208 CLR 167 at [56]. *Certiorari* and prohibition also have an open test: *Re McBain; Ex parte Australian Catholic Bishops Conference* (2002) 209 CLR 372 at 413 [89] per McHugh J, with whom Callinan J agreed at 475 [293]. (But 'a stranger's lack of standing will frequently result in the court refusing to issue [*certiorari* or prohibition] on discretionary grounds': *Re McBain* per McHugh J at 422 [109], with whom Callinan J agreed at 475 [293].)

Legislation may confer generous rights on certain public interest groups: for example, s 475 of the Environment Protection and Biodiversity Conservation Act 1999 (Cth). At the same time, legislation may greatly restrict rights of standing — to those who are directly and adversely affected by the decision: *Allan* (HC) at [29].

Despite all these variations there is some consistency at the level of principle: the common law rule for declarations, injunctions and (possibly) *mandamus* is that an applicant, who lacks a private right to enforce and who cannot join the Attorney-General, requires a special interest in the subject matter of the action: *Australian Conservation Foundation Inc v Commonwealth* (1980) 146 CLR 493 (*ACF 1*). The ADJR Act's test of 'person who is aggrieved' is essentially the same as the test for declarations and injunctions: *North Coast Environment Council Inc v Minister for Resources* (1994) 55 FCR 492 at 511–12.

If there were space it might be possible to examine all these different tests to see if they may be rationally and logically justified. For example, the prerogative writs, which apply in public law only, might be expected to have different standing rules to remedies which apply in public and private law (declarations and injunctions). There might be a stronger case for environmental interest groups to be afforded standing than other groups, and so on. But on the surface at least it cannot be denied that standing is a ragbag of disparate rules lacking coherency in the sense of being well knit or consistent.

(iii)   Fundamental assumptions of the law of standing

Some of the fundamentals seem to lack coherence, in the sense of a logical basis. In *Bateman's Bay Local Aboriginal Land Council v Aboriginal Community Benefit Fund Pty Ltd* (1998) 194 CLR 247 at [34] the joint judgment referred to one supposed fundamental:

> The evolution of the Boyce doctrine of "sufficient special interest" represents an attempt to alleviate that state of affairs whilst keeping at bay "the phantom busybody or ghostly intermeddler".

There is an admission then that the law of standing is partly built on a fiction. Fictions lack a logical or rational basis.

Underlying legal policies are conflicting to some extent. In *Bateman's Bay* the joint judgment referred to the 'equity' or 'public interest' in due administration: see *Bateman's Bay* at [25]–[26]; *Allan* (HC) at [71] per Kirby J. This equity would suggest a prima facie open test of standing: [39]. But in *Bateman's Bay* the members conceded that, under the current law, even where there is an abuse or threatened abuse of public administration, the plaintiff must, in an application for a declaration or injunction, still show some special interest in the subject matter of the action: [34]. In other words, the rationales commonly advanced for standing (see *Onus v Alcoa of Australia Ltd* (1981) 149 CLR 27 at 35, 75) conflict with the equity or public interest in due administration.

A counter-argument to the above is that conflicting policies *underlie* much, if not all, law; it is the job of legal principle to affect a compromise. This is suggested by Gibbs CJ in *Onus* where, after referring to 'conflicting considerations' underlying the law of standing, he says 'The principle which has been settled by the courts does attempt a reconciliation between these considerations': at 35.

(iv) Incoherencies in the special interest test

Particularly problematic areas

The special interest test is a 'difficult field', said Mason J in *ACF 1* at 548. It is particularly difficult to apply with confidence and in a consistent fashion where the applicant claims to be affected but it is apparent that any effect is indirectly suffered. This especially applies in the case of third parties who object to a decision that is favourable to the person immediately affected. A large number of the disputes about standing, certainly most of the leading cases, fit into this category: see *Allan* (HC) at [35]–[36] and [70]; *ACF 1*; *Ogle*; *Australian Conservation Foundation v Minister for Resources* (1989) 19 ALD 70 (*ACF 2*); *North Coast*; *Right to Life*; *Australian Foreman Stevedores Association v Crone* (1989) 20 FCR 377; *Alphapharm Pty Ltd v SmithKline Beecham (Australia) Pty Ltd* (1994) 49 FCR 250; and *Alliance to Save Hinchinbrook v Environmental Protection Agency* (2006) 145 LGERA 32. The test can also be problematic where the applicant seeks to enforce the law against others: see *Central Queensland Speleological Society Inc v Central Queensland Cement Pty Ltd (No 1)* [1989] 2 Qd R 512; *Onus*; *OneSteel Manufacturing Pty Ltd v Whyalla Red Dust Action Group Inc* (2006) 94 SASR 357; *Access for All Alliance (Hervey Bay) Inc v Hervey Bay City Council* [2007] FCA 615.

Rambling case law; cases turning on their facts?

'The cases are infinitely various' said Mason J in *ACF 1* at 547. Several examples may be given of its rambling, fact-driven nature. Despite considerable case law, there is no general rule that commercial competitors either have standing or lack standing: see *Bateman's Bay* at [48]. And, while the possession of a non-material interest does not necessarily preclude recognition (*Onus*), a 'mere intellectual or emotional concern' does *not* suffice: *ACF 1* at 530. But which non-material interests are special, and which are mere intellectual or emotional concerns? Can the distinctions be justified on the basis of principle, or merely differing judicial perceptions? In *Onus*, the Aboriginal plaintiffs were guardians of relics according to their laws and customs. This was sufficient to give them standing. But in *Western Australia v Bropho* (1991) 5 WAR 75 at 90 a majority of the Supreme Court of Western Australia was not inclined to grant standing on analogous facts. In *Bropho* the claim to standing (which was conceded by the appellants) was based on the respondent's interest in the contested land as a person of Aboriginal descent and a 'custodian' of the relevant site in accordance with the customs of his people. Is there a justifiable difference in the direct physical association with the subject site in *Onus* and the lack of it in *Bropho*? Even if there is, how can the interest in *Bropho* be distinguished from the spiritual interest of a priest which was upheld in *Ogle v Strickland* (1987) 13 FCR 306? Because the Aboriginal custodian has no such 'vocation'?

Non-principled decision-making? Bases which lack logical force

It can also be asked whether the emphasis laid on judicial perception of community values makes the law incoherent. Stephen J's judgment in *Onus* at 42 is often referred to, his Honour stating that 'Courts necessarily reflect community values and beliefs, according greater weight to, and perceiving a closer proximity to, a plaintiff in the case of some subject-matters than others'. This observation led Davies J to comment in *ACF 2* at 74 that the community now expects there to be a body such as the Australian Conservation Foundation (ACF) to put forward a conservation viewpoint: cited in *Right to Life* at 82. Compare *Right to Life*, where the viewpoint of that organisation was seen as merely an expression of free speech: at 67 per Lockhart J. The courts may be reading community values and beliefs well, but is this principled?

Inconsistencies: public interest groups

There is a seeming inconsistency between the decisions of the High Court and decisions of the Federal Court (and other courts) over whether interest groups such as the Australian Conservation Foundation can have a special interest in particular environmental issues. The problem is *not* that the ACF is not credited with standing in one case (*ACF 1*) but is credited in another (*ACF 2*). This could be explained by the facts of the cases (and was attempted so in *ACF 2*). It is that part of the reasoning appears to be at loggerheads.

In *ACF 1*, more than a mere intellectual concern was required. *In addition*, a person must be 'interested' in the following sense:

A person is not interested within the meaning of the rule, unless he is likely to gain some advantage, other than the satisfaction of righting a wrong, upholding a principle or winning a contest, if his action succeeds or to suffer some disadvantage, other than a sense of grievance or a debt for costs, if his action fails: at 530.

This principle was followed by McHugh J in *Re McBain* at 423. He described it as requiring 'a special interest in the outcome of proceedings'.

In *Onus*, the High Court took the opportunity to make it clear that a public interest environment group could not be interested:

The position of a small community of Aboriginal people of a particular group living in a particular area which that group has traditionally occupied, and which claims an interest in relics of their ancestors found in that area, is very different indeed from that of a diverse group of white Australians associated by some common opinion on a matter of social policy which might equally concern any other Australian: per Gibbs CJ at 37.

Stephen J at 42, Mason J at 43, and Wilson J at 62, expressed agreement with, or similar views to, Gibbs CJ in that case.

But in *ACF 2* and in *North Coast*, the 'interested' principle was either overlooked or read down as requiring something more than a mere intellectual or emotional concern. In *North Coast* Sackville J seemed to concede that it was sufficient that values were threatened:

While its expressed opposition to Sawmillers' operations does not suffice of itself to confer standing on North Coast, its opposition over a long period, in combination with its other activities, illustrates a strong commitment to the *values* it regards (whether rightly or wrongly) as under threat by the licence granted to Sawmillers: at 514. (emphasis added)

The tension between the *ACF 1* and *ACF 2/North Coast* continues. *North Coast* was approved, in dicta, by the full court in *Transurban City Link Ltd v Allan* (1999) 95 FCR 553 at [44]. A similar approach was taken by the Federal Court in *Alliance to Save Hinchinbrook*. However, the *North Coast* doctrine was not applied in *Onesteel*, *ACF 1* being applied to a statutory test for standing.

A further logical problem in some of the cases concerning interest groups occurs at the evidentiary level. In *Access for All Alliance* the court refused to say that, overall, the members of the interest group were affected (at [60]), even though it accepted that some, perhaps a majority, *were* affected: at [55].

Source of incoherencies

The formulation of the special interest test makes it difficult for the courts to reach consistent and principled decisions across the board. The courts admit that the law supplies no precise formula to apply (*Bateman's Bay* at [46]) and that it is 'the nature and subject-matter of the litigation [which] will dictate what amounts to a special interest':

Shop Distributive and Allied Employees Association v Minister for Industrial Affairs (SA) (1995) 183 CLR 552 at 558.

But the special interest test is not always a source of incoherency. Its application is often clear and straightforward.

(v) Clear-cut applications of the law

Persons directly and adversely affected

Even though the law of standing seems to lack coherence in a number of respects, it is notable that in the *Bateman's Bay* case all members of the High Court found no difficulty in applying the relevant law and coming to the same decision. Further, if we consider administrative law cases as a whole, it is evident that the law of standing is overwhelmingly 'plain' on the facts. And the number of clear-cut instances balloons when one has regard to applications of the law which never become disputes or court cases.

These observations have important implications for the present discussion. If the law can be readily and consistently 'applied', or is assumed to be clear-cut, we can deduce that it is coherent in these categories of case.

Why is there no dispute about standing in many instances then? Two reasons may be proffered. The first is that the general rules of standing are 'wide and liberal': *Right to Life* at 254. It is not necessary that a person's rights be interfered with: *ACF 1* at 527. It is not necessary that the special interest be proprietary, or even legal or equitable: *Alphapharm* at 272. It is not necessary that the interests be affected directly: *Bateman's Bay*. And it is not necessary that the plaintiff be the only one affected: *ACF 1* at 527. Standing is ordinarily accorded to persons who are 'directly and adversely affected in a singular and distinctive way by an administrative decision': *Bropho* at 87; see also *Re McHattan and Collector of Customs*, cited in *Allan* (HC) at [62] per Kirby J. Thus, in the ordinary case where a decision adversely affects a particular person (such as the denial of an unemployment benefit or the revocation of an occupational licence), standing is not an issue.

The second reason why there is usually no argument about standing flows from the fact that most disputes, naturally enough, arise in relation to decisions which are unfavourable to those who are directly affected. Because these persons have the most to lose, they are more likely to wish to mount a challenge. It is these challengers who are normally not troubled by the law of standing — in contrast to those who are indirectly affected or who are third parties.

Individuals with a mere intellectual or emotional concern

There is another 'clear-cut' category. In a number of cases the courts have had no difficulty in deciding that the individual does *not* meet the special interest test or its statutory equivalent. This is where the case is brought by an individual, not a public interest organisation, and where the person is only emotionally or intellectually concerned with the subject matter of the case. See, for example, *Cameron v Human Rights and Equal Opportunity Commission* (1993) 46 FCR 509; *Everyone v State of Tasmania* (1983) 49 ALR 381.

(vi) Conclusion

McHugh J's claim that the present law of standing is far from coherent can be supported to an extent, for it is inconsistent across the board, and there are aspects of the law of standing which are not consistent or logical, or which suggest a lack of rigorous content.

And McHugh J's claim has considerable force from the standpoint of an applicant (often an interest group) who is indirectly affected and who objects to a decision which is favourable to the person or group immediately affected. The same applies to an applicant or interest group which seeks to enforce the law against private individuals or corporations.

While these matters are significant, the basic point is that whether the law of standing is coherent depends on one's standpoint. This can be illustrated with the clear-cut cases. From the point of view of the person directly and adversely affected in a distinct or singular way, standing will be clear; any lack of coherency in the law of standing is theoretical or at the level of fundamental theory. At the other end of the spectrum, in the *Cameron*-type case involving an ideological objector, the law can also be applied without difficulty.

Examiner's Comments

This answer is a detailed response to a complex issue. This level of detail would be way beyond the capacity of students in the time frame imposed by an examination, though a student writing an assignment would be expected to write a detailed response.

What grade a student answer would receive would depend on how closely it addresses the question and what level of skill is demonstrated. As a crude guide, a 'D' or pass answer might discuss only problems; at the lower end briefly. A middle 'C' or upper-pass paper would mention inconsistencies to show that the student understands the notion of incoherence. A 'B' or credit paper would go into more detail and contain the sketch of a narrative structure. A good 'B' or a distinction paper would contain strong arguments put for the law being both incoherent and coherent. A clear 'A' paper, or high distinction, would contain a solid narrative structure and would have defined what coherent meant.

A strength of this answer is the way it clarifies, at the outset, the evaluative criterion, namely 'coherent'. The humble dictionary is often useful in this task. Without a definition, the discussion might have proceeded with a woolly idea of 'coherent'; for example, equating 'incoherent' with any problem.

Second, the answer clearly identified incoherencies.

Third, the answer was not one-sided. It was critical of the statement to a degree. Students need to develop the facility (and, if necessary, the necessary attitude of mind) to critically analyse all important statements about the law. As Dworkin once said, 'the more we learn about law, the more we grow convinced that nothing important about it is wholly uncontroversial': R Dworkin, *Law's Empire*, Fontana Press, London, 1986, p 10. The model answer did not pull back from criticism just because the author of the statement under discussion is a judge. In the present case, the judge has made an evaluation of the law. There is no reason why this statement ought not to be subject to critical scrutiny. Of course, the tone of the criticism should be measured and the arguments balanced (not one-sided).

The answer could have restricted the discussion to the kind of remedy at issue in *Bateman's Bay* (an injunction) or to the test at issue in that case: the special interest test.

Common Errors to Avoid

- Describing the law of standing rather than addressing the particular issues raised by the question.
- Not addressing the question well: equating 'incoherent' with any problem.
- Failing to consider the possibility of criticism or qualification simply because the author of the statement is a judge.
- Giving a black or white response to the statement (agreeing or disagreeing) instead of making a less one-sided response.
- Writing imprecisely; for example, arguing that the courts have made conflicting decisions without stating and demonstrating what quality of the law of standing has led to that inconsistency.

PART 4

Other Avenues of Accountability

Chapter 12

Merits Review

Key Issues

Judicial review is concerned with whether administrative behaviour is lawful. It is not usually concerned with whether an administrative decision is factually correct. Less still is it concerned with whether it is the 'best' decision in the circumstances. Courts should inquire into findings of fact only in the limited circumstances discussed in Chapter 4. They should inquire into the quality of the decision only in so far as it bears on reasonableness (in the *Wednesbury* sense) or suggests unlawfulness. Sometimes courts seem unable to resist the temptation to engage in de facto merits review, but it is a temptation which courts are expected to resist. It is, however, inevitable that primary decision-makers will make mistakes, and good government requires that there be procedures for correcting them.

Typically, administrative or merits review has been entrusted to 'tribunals', bodies which resemble courts, but which differ in that they tend to lack some of the legal trappings of courts, and they tend to be more informal. Like courts, tribunals vary. In some, the decision-making process closely resembles administrative decision-making. Other tribunals bear a distinct resemblance to magistrates' courts. Some bear a close resemblance to higher courts. Because of the Commonwealth Constitution, however, it is necessary — at least at the Commonwealth level — to distinguish between tribunals and courts. 'Administrative' functions may be conferred on tribunals, but they may not be conferred on courts, except in so far as this is incidental to the courts' exercise of the judicial power of the Commonwealth. Members of tribunals may, because they are performing executive or advisory functions, be appointed for fixed terms. Judges must be appointed to courts for terms which expire when they turn 70. Tribunals are not empowered to enforce their decisions. Courts may order that action be taken against those who are unwilling to act in accordance with their orders.

The position at the State level is less straightforward and is complicated by cases in which the High Court has held that, as repositories of a federal jurisdiction, State courts may not be structured or empowered in a manner which would undermine the exercise of the federal judicial power: see *Kable v DPP (NSW) (1996) 189 CLR 151*. But some State tribunals, such as the New South Wales Administrative

Decisions Tribunal, the Victorian Civil and Administrative Tribunal (VCAT) and the Western Australian State Administrative Tribunal, exercise powers which could not be conferred on a Commonwealth tribunal, and there are no constitutional problems with this since the tribunals do not exercise any federal judicial powers. Conversely, in South Australia and Tasmania, extensive merits review powers have been conferred on State courts. It is unlikely that the conferral of this jurisdiction offends the *Kable* principle.

Tribunals may be established to exercise a variety of powers. Here, our concern is with administrative tribunals, but tribunals have also been established to inquire into 'private law' matters and some are established by private bodies rather than by the state. Some of these latter tribunals are very important. In Melbourne, at least, the national broadcaster devotes a far greater proportion of its evening news to the fate of Australian Rules footballers charged before the AFL Tribunal, than it does to the activities of lesser tribunals such as the VCAT (or the High Court, for that matter). And anyone familiar with administrative law will be aware of the activities of racing tribunals, and the high stakes in the cases they handle.

It is not possible to discuss Australia's chaotic tribunal system in much detail. Broadly, however, the salient features of Commonwealth merits review are as follows:

- Specialist merits review tribunals are responsible for the review of social security, migration, and veterans' decisions. Each of these tribunals has its own culture and procedure. People practising in these areas need to know the relevant legislation. They also need to be aware of practice directions, and, of course, of the tribunal's culture.

- The AAT handles appeals from a large variety of other administrative decisions, as well as appeals from the specialist social security and veterans' tribunals.

Before attempting the questions, check that you are familiar with the following issues concerning the AAT, together with the legislation and case law which establish these propositions:

✓ The AAT has only such jurisdiction as is conferred upon it: s 25 of the AAT Act. To know whether a decision under a particular enactment is reviewable by the AAT, one should examine the legislation to see whether it (or any other legislation) makes specific provision for AAT review. In this respect, AAT jurisdiction contrasts with jurisdiction under the Administrative Decisions (Judicial Review) Act 1977 (Cth) (ADJR Act).

✔ The AAT is not bound by the strict rules of evidence which normally govern judicial proceedings and it is expected to conduct itself less formally than courts. It may conduct its own inquiries: s 33(1). It is, however, subject to the rules of natural justice: s 39. Moreover, while it may admit evidence which would not be admissible in a court, it should not give weight to such evidence unless the evidence is probative. Critics of the AAT argue that it is far too formal.

✔ The tribunal is not obliged to act in accordance with government policy (*Drake v Minister for Immigration and Ethnic Affairs* (1979) 24 ALR 577) and, in the absence of legislation to the contrary, is not even obliged to give it weight. However, good decision-making may require that policy — and especially ministerial policy for which the government is politically responsible — should be given considerable weight. In so far as consistency among decisions is an administrative virtue, departmental policy should also be given some weight: *Re Drake and Minister for Immigration and Ethnic Affairs (No 2)* (1979) 2 ALD 634.

✔ The tribunal may be constituted to include more than one (but not more than three) members (s 21), and it may be constituted by people who are not legally qualified. Multi-member tribunals have, however, become the exception.

✔ The tribunal's task is not to decide whether the primary decision was properly made. It is to decide what is the 'correct or preferable' decision on the material before it: *Drake v Minister for Immigration and Ethnic Affairs* (1979) 24 ALR 577 at 589. The phrase recognises that sometimes there is a unique 'correct' decision. Sometimes, however, there may be several decisions, each of which is open to the tribunal. In that case, the tribunal must decide which of these is the 'best' one. In reaching its decision, the tribunal acts on the evidence before it, regardless of whether the evidence was presented to the primary decision-maker. The tribunal is said to possess all the powers of the primary decision-maker. What this means is that the tribunal possesses all the powers which were possessed by a person empowered to make the original decision and who acts according to law.

✔ The tribunal normally acts on the basis of the facts and the law as they stand at the time that it makes its decision. For instance, a decision refusing a benefit involves a question of a continuing entitlement. The tribunal will, however, apply an earlier law in the case of accrued rights (*Esber v Commonwealth* (1992) 174 CLR 430; s 8 of the Acts Interpretation Act (1901) (Cth)), and ➤

it will consider the facts at the date of the primary decision where a decision concerns a cancellation of a benefit: *Freeman v Secretary, Department of Social Security* (1988) 19 FCR 342.

✓ Appeal lies from the AAT to the Federal Court on a question of law: s 44. The AAT is also subject to judicial review, but an application for judicial review should not be made unless it relates to the *conduct* of the tribunal prior to a final decision, or its failure to act.

QUESTION 36

The Last Days of Emilio Firunze is a film made by the well-known German producer Franz Eisenstein. Eisenstein followed Emilio Firunze, a drug addict, for a week, filming him constantly. (On the whole, there is no evidence that Emilio noticed.) It ends with Emilio lying on a lavatory floor, slowly choking on his vomit, after an overdose. It was designed to confront, and it did. Eisenstein was subsequently charged in Germany with failure to render assistance to a dying person and imprisoned, and the film was banned in a number of countries. The Australian Minister for Culture and Customs described it as nothing but a 'snuff movie masquerading as a social message'.

Shock Treatment, as its name implies, is an organisation which believes that drug users must be shocked into realising the possible consequences of their behaviour. It asked that it be permitted to import a copy of *Last Days* to show to people attending its programs. The request was considered by Justina Darling, an official in the Attorney-General's Department. On 1 April, Justina retired to take up a position with a large law firm. However, she decided it would be unfair to her colleagues to leave them to sort out a few unfinished tasks, so she took a number of outstanding files home with her. On 4 April, she read the Shock Treatment file, decided that permission should not be granted, and sent off a letter to this effect, with reasons. She left a copy in the file, which she then returned to the department. Shock Treatment appealed to the AAT, which upheld its appeal, subject to a number of conditions. Its reasons were, broadly, as follows:

1. Ms Darling's reasons for her decision proved extremely helpful. Her decision was clearly correct, given the material before her.

2. Ms Darling regretted that there was no evidence before her as to the effects of Shock Treatment's programs. The tribunal asked Shock Treatment for evidence, but it had not been able to provide any. This was obviously a relevant issue, so one of the members of the tribunal rang up a person she knew in the Department of Politics at La Trobe University. He [name stated] said that programs like that offered by Shock Treatment sometimes worked. He had been able to provide a number of helpful references. They suggested that there were ➤

circumstances in which programs like Shock Treatment's could work. This material strengthened Shock Treatment's case.

3. It was government policy that permissions in cases such as this should be given only in exceptional circumstances. The tribunal noted that this was the case, but its view was that no weight should be given to this policy in this case or any other case, for that matter.

4. This was an issue over which people could reasonably disagree. It all boiled down to one's values. The tribunal thought that permission should be granted, but it recognised that a different tribunal might well decide differently.

The department decided to appeal against this decision, arguing that:

1. The tribunal had no jurisdiction to hear the application.

2. Having acknowledged the correctness of the primary decision, the tribunal acted perversely in departing from it.

3. In soliciting the advice of a non-expert, the AAT had exceeded its powers.

4. While the tribunal was not required to act in accordance with government policy, it was obliged to give it some weight.

5. If the tribunal had doubts about its decision it should have deferred to the government, which had no doubts whatsoever as to what was right.

Would its appeal be likely to succeed?

Time allowed: 30 mins

Answer Plan

(i)   Did the AAT have jurisdiction?

(ii) Did the tribunal err in departing from the original decision?

(iii) Did the tribunal err in seeking additional information?

(iv) Was the tribunal obliged to give weight to government policy?

(v)   Should the tribunal have deferred to the government given its doubts?

(vi) Conclusion.

 ## Answer

(i)   Did the AAT have jurisdiction?

The jurisdictional question is a difficult one. The issues are:

1. Is it only decisions of the Attorney-General which are reviewable?

2. If not, is there jurisdiction to review a decision of a person who has left employment of the tribunal?

The tribunal has a power to review decisions of the Attorney-General under reg 4A(2) of the Customs (Prohibited Imports) Regulations, in the absence of a certificate issued under subreg (5): subregs (4) and (8). There is no mention of a certificate, and we should assume that one has not been issued. However, subreg (4) only mentions the Attorney-General. Does this matter? Ms Darling is clearly not the Attorney-General. This, however, is not fatal to her purported exercise of power, notwithstanding the wording of subreg (4). The exercise of a power by a delegate is deemed to be an exercise of power by the repository: Acts Interpretation Act 1903 (Cth) s 34AB(c). But was Ms Darling at any time an authorised person under reg 4A(2), which we can assume is the same as a 'delegate' for the purposes of s 34AB? We are not told whether Ms Darling had ever been authorised in writing to make the decision in question. It is likely that she had been authorised.

Assuming she was an authorised person, there is the problem created by her exercise of power after she left the employment of the tribunal. It is unlikely that the authorisation would have been such that she was empowered to exercise public power after having left public employment. Of course, if the authorisation *was* of this nature, no jurisdictional problems would arise. The appeal would be from a decision made by a person authorised to make such decisions. If, however, her authorisation had expired on her retirement, then the decision was not made by a person authorised by the Attorney-General. Subregulation (4) would appear not to be satisfied unless it could be read broadly to include decisions *apparently made* by persons authorised by the Attorney-General.

There are, however, several cases where the tribunal has been found to have had jurisdiction, notwithstanding that the primary decision was a legal nullity, and notwithstanding that the person who purported to make the primary decision was not authorised to do so. In *Collector of Customs (NSW) v Brian Lawlor Automotive Pty Ltd* (1979) 41 FLR 338, the full Federal Court ruled that the tribunal had jurisdiction to hear an appeal from a 'decision' which was a nullity, flawed by an error of law made by the primary 'decision'-maker. Its reasoning was that 'decision' was to be read to include 'purported' decisions. To interpret it otherwise would be to defeat the purpose of the Act.

This is not the problem here, however. The decision was not flawed by virtue of any error of law. It was flawed because the decision-maker had no power to consider the application at all. This, however, may not matter. In *Re Baran and Secretary, Department of Primary Industries and Energy* (1988) 9 AAR 458, a 'decision' was made by a particular decision-maker who lacked the power to make such decisions. On the orthodox view the AAT lacked the power to act for the reason that the primary decision-maker lacked the power to act. However, the AAT held that it had jurisdiction. It was enough that the 'decision' was one which *could have* been made by an authorised officer. In the present case, the fact that Ms Darling was not an officer of the Commonwealth might be a basis for distinguishing *Re Baran*, but, given that she arguably could have been authorised, notwithstanding her non-official status, *Baran* suggests that this may not be a relevant difference. In any case, another person could have been authorised to make the decision. *Baran* is not a Federal Court authority so it should not be presumed to have the status of a judicial precedent. Nevertheless, I think this ground of objection would probably fail.

(ii) Did the tribunal err in departing from the original decision?

The issue here is whether, given that the tribunal regarded Ms Darling's decision as correct on the basis of the material before the primary decision-maker, did the tribunal err in departing from it?

The fact that the AAT considers that Ms Darling's decision was correct when made, on the basis of the material before her, is immaterial. The tribunal's task is *not* to decide whether the primary decision was correct, but to determine what was the correct or preferable decision, given the material before the tribunal: *Drake v Minister for Immigration and Ethnic Affairs* (1979) 24 ALR 577. Moreover, the tribunal acted on different material to that before Ms Darling. (Whether it handled this material correctly is quite another matter.) There is therefore no inconsistency between its conclusion that Ms Darling was correct and its conclusion that permission should nonetheless be granted. This ground of appeal would fail.

(iii) Did the tribunal err in seeking additional information?

The tribunal did not err in seeking additional information. It is entitled to do so under the AAT Act (s 33(1)(c)), providing it affords the parties procedural fairness: s 39. Nor did it err in placing weight on that material. It is not clear from the facts whether or not the lecturer was an 'expert'; a lecturer in politics is not self-evidently an expert on drug programs, but the contrary cannot be assumed either. But even if the lecturer was not an expert, information about his beliefs would nonetheless be admissible. The tribunal is not bound by the strict rules of evidence: s 33(1)(c). If the lecturer was not an expert, the tribunal would have to be careful not to place undue reliance on his views, but it might be entitled to place some weight on them if they had some rational basis. It would also be entitled to take account of the published material which had been drawn to its attention.

But while the tribunal is not bound by technical rules of evidence, it is bound by the rules of natural justice: s 39 and see, for example, *Australian Postal Commission v Hayes* (1989) 23 FCR 320. Having decided to take account of the lecturer's evidence and the suggested references, the tribunal was at the very least obliged to give the parties a chance to comment on that material. It does not appear to have done so. The Attorney-General has been denied procedural fairness, and for this reason, the appeal would be allowed.

(iv) Was the tribunal obliged to give weight to government policy?

The tribunal did not err in failing to take account of the government's policy. The tribunal is not bound to apply government policy: *Drake v Minister for Immigration and Ethnic Affairs* (1979) 24 ALR 577. Brennan J's decision in *Re Drake and Minister for Immigration and Ethnic Affairs (No 2)* (1979) 2 ALD 634 assumes that government policy should — if lawful — be considered, but this is as a matter of good administration rather than legal obligation. But here, the policy appears to be unlawful. There is nothing in the regulations to suggest that permissions are to be granted only in exceptional circumstances. The policy is therefore a policy which requires under-utilisation of the power conferred by the legislation. It is unlawful. Not only may the tribunal disregard it. It is obliged to do so.

(v) Should the tribunal have deferred to the government given its doubts?

The fact that the tribunal recognised that other tribunals might disagree with it does not vitiate its decision. Where there is not a unique 'correct' decision, the tribunal's duty is to reach what *it* regards as the preferable decision (*Drake*), not what someone else might (reasonably or otherwise) consider the preferable decision.

(vi) Conclusion

Because of the denial of procedural fairness, the tribunal's decision would be set aside. The court might order that the appeal be reheard by a differently constituted tribunal.

Examiner's Comments

The list of grounds of appeal is an invitation to students to use the grounds as issues which they must address. This answer has done so and has handled the issues well. Its conclusions have been stated with confidence, and while it is not always wise to be dogmatic in relation to legal questions, most of the issues discussed here are such that the outcome of the appeal can (and therefore should) be predicted with considerable confidence.

Section (i) of the answer did not address the question of whether Ms Darling could be treated as a de facto officer, but I doubt that anything would have been gained by consideration of this question. It seems clear that the jurisdictional issue could not be disposed of on the basis of the de facto officer doctrine, whereas it could be disposed of on the basis of the authority cited in the answer. That said, if the de facto officer issue was handled well, I would make some allowance for this in my mark.

In discussing the third issue, the answer avoids the trap laid by the examiner. A poor answer would have focused on the admissibility issue, and neglected the fact that, in relying on the 'expert' evidence, the AAT was acting in breach of its duty to afford procedural fairness to the Commonwealth.

The discussion of the fourth ground did not consider whether the AAT would have been obliged to consider a legal policy had one been formulated, but it was not necessary to consider the issue, given that the relevant policy was clearly not a lawful one. Discussion of whether there was a duty to consider policy would have involved wasted effort.

Common Errors to Avoid

- Failing to address the issue of Ms Darling's resignation. While it is unlikely that an instrument of delegation would continue after the resignation of the person to whom the power was delegated, students should at least make it clear that they are proceeding on the basis of this assumption.

- Assuming that, if the primary decision-maker's decision is a nullity, the AAT necessarily lacks the power to review the decision and exercise the power available to the primary decision-maker.

- Failing to recognise and discuss the procedural fairness issue arising from the AAT's apparent failure to give the Commonwealth a chance to comment on the 'expert' advice.

- Assuming that *Drake (No 2)* requires that tribunals take account of government policy.

- Failing to recognise that the policy in this case is an unlawful one.

QUESTION 37

Makepeace is appealing to the AAT against a decision by the Attorney-General refusing it permission to import *The Night of a Thousand Shames* (see 'The Makepeace Scenario', p xvi). Makepeace has learned that the government has been illegally taping its meetings. The government has learned that Makepeace's campaign to import the book has been heavily financed by the Diuris Liberation Front, a secessionist group dominated by Animist fundamentalists with a record of terrorist attacks on people and governments associated with Caledenian development projects. One member of the Makepeace governing collective is recorded as having said:

> I think they'll find that this is money well spent. The Catholics are already angry. The opposition's asking why human rights abuses in Caledenia are a taboo topic. Our campaign's making Caledenia hostile to Australia, and it's also making Australia less inclined to appease Caledenia.

The Attorney-General apparently intends to rely on this evidence, along with lawfully obtained banking records which confirm a number of very large transfers of money from the DLF to Makepeace.

Makepeace wants to argue that *The Night of a Thousand Shames* is not a prohibited import and that, even if it is, Makepeace should be permitted to import it. Advise Makepeace about its prospects before the AAT.

Time allowed: 45 mins

Answer Plan

(i)   Can Makepeace argue that the book is not a prohibited import?

(ii) Assuming the book to be a prohibited import, would permission to import be granted?

(iii) Conclusions.

 Answer

(i)   Can Makepeace argue that the book is not a prohibited import?

The AAT's jurisdiction under the Customs (Prohibited Imports) Regulations (Cth) is limited to the review of decisions by the Attorney-General under reg 4A(2) which involve the refusal of permission or the granting of conditional permission: subreg (4). This does not extend to review of the Attorney-General's implicit decision that the book is a prohibited import. The reason for this is that the book's status as a prohibited import or otherwise is not the result of a decision by the Attorney-General. It is a status which the book enjoys by virtue of its attributes and the operation of subreg (1A), and one which it enjoys independently of any belief the Attorney-General might have as to its nature. The only legally operative decision that the Attorney-General has made has been the decision to refuse to grant permission to import the book, assuming it to be a prohibited import. That is the only decision that Makepeace can take on appeal to the AAT.

This does not mean that the nature of the book is necessarily irrelevant to the question of whether the AAT can grant permission to import the book. The wording of subreg (2) implies that permissions under the subregulation are permitted only when they relate to goods to which the regulation applies. It provides for permissions for the purposes of the subregulation, and this purpose appears to be permitting the importation of goods whose importation would otherwise be prohibited, not permitting the importation of goods whose importation might otherwise be prohibited. If the AAT were to conclude that the book in question was not a prohibited import, it would, on this reading of the legislation, be required to refuse to grant permission to import it, on the grounds that the condition precedent to granting the permission would not exist.

In one sense this would be a victory for Makepeace, but since the status of the book depends not on any decision that the AAT might make, but on the operation of law, a decision by the AAT that the book did not fall within the regulation would not preclude a subsequent prosecution and conviction in the event that the trial court formed a different view about the book. If Makepeace is clearly correct in its assumption that the book is not a prohibited import, there is little point appealing to the AAT. An appeal to the AAT makes sense only if the book is or might be regarded by Customs officials, police and the courts as a prohibited import so that it would be to Makepeace's advantage that it be given permission to import it.

It would therefore be pointless and self-defeating for Makepeace to try to convince the AAT that the book was not a prohibited import. If it wants an authoritative decision on this issue, it should either seek a declaration to this effect in the Federal Court, or canvass the issue as a defence to a charge of importing a prohibited import.

Regardless of whether Makepeace raises the issue, it is possible that the AAT could independently conclude that the book was not a prohibited import. It could, moreover, reach this conclusion even if both Makepeace and the Commonwealth were to agree that, for the purposes of the appeal, the book should be treated as a prohibited publication. Legislation is the tribunal's sole source of powers; agreements by the parties cannot fill a statutory gap. Regardless of what Makepeace and the Commonwealth may say, it is therefore possible that the AAT could decide that the book is not a prohibited import and that Makepeace's appeal should be dismissed on the ground that it is not convinced of the satisfaction of a condition precedent for the granting of a certificate. But so long as it was not clear that the book was not a prohibited import, it is likely that the tribunal would make a decision based on the assumption that the book was indeed a prohibited import. There are precedents for this course of action: see, for example, *Re Reserve Bank of Australia and Comcare* (1989) 17 ALD 682 (where the tribunal doubted the constitutionality of the legislation on which its jurisdiction was purportedly grounded, but where it nonetheless delivered a decision predicated on the legislation's validity, this being what both parties wanted).

(ii) Assuming the book to be a prohibited import, would permission to import be granted?

If the tribunal were to assume that the book was a prohibited import, it would have to decide whether permission should be granted to import the book, and on what conditions, if any. This would depend on the law, on the facts as found by the tribunal, and on the tribunal's values. The major problem that would face Makepeace in this case is that it might fall foul of reg 4A(2AA). The phone intercepts suggest that the purpose of importing the book is to promote ill-will between Australia and Caledenia. In so far as the evidence suggests that Makepeace has been working with a terrorist organisation, this might be treated as another 'relevant matter'. (It would not go to reputation, unless these dealings were more widely known.) It would, in my opinion, be difficult to persuade the tribunal not to admit the relevant evidence, even if the evidence would not be admissible in judicial proceedings. The tribunal is not bound by the rules of evidence (AAT Act s 33(1)(c)), and the policy arguments in relation to the protection of the integrity of the courts — which underlie the exclusion of some illegally obtained evidence — are, I think, less pressing in relation to tribunals.

That said, Makepeace might nonetheless succeed. What matters is not what the government thinks, but what the tribunal thinks. If the tribunal were to share Makepeace's attitudes to the Caledenian Government, it might regard the purpose of importation as a legitimate one, and, to employ a tired old cliché, it might even prefer to describe the DLF as freedom fighters rather than terrorists. It might, however, agree with the government or, alternatively, consider that it should be guided by the government's foreign policy. If so, its decision would be likely to be adverse to Makepeace unless Makepeace could point to countervailing considerations. Makepeace might be able to point to educational and cultural activities which bring it within subreg (2AA)(b). It might also argue that there is another relevant matter: cf subreg (2AA)(e). If the book in question is a prohibited import, it arguably ranks among the least objectionable of prohibited imports. The former argument might carry some weight, but the latter argument would, I think, carry very little, given that Makepeace seems to want to import the book in order to ensure the widest possible audience for its contents. Even if the book is 'only just' a prohibited import, the tribunal would be likely to conclude that its importation for diffusion to a large audience would be inconsistent with the purposes of the regulation, given that this is a matter for which the government bears obvious political responsibility. One solution which might commend itself to the tribunal would be to permit importation on condition that the two offending photographs were removed as soon as possible after importation and prior to distribution of copies of the book to the broader public.

(iii) Conclusions

Makepeace is not entitled to a legally operative decision to the effect that the book is not a prohibited import. If it wants an authoritative decision to the effect that the book is not a prohibited import, it must choose another forum. If it raises this issue in the AAT, any success it might have in persuading the tribunal that the book is probably not a prohibited import will mean that its application must fail. So it must argue its case on the assumption that the book is a prohibited import.

In my opinion there is a real likelihood that the AAT will find that it lacks jurisdiction, in which case, Makepeace will have a win with considerable symbolic importance, but one which would leave it legally vulnerable if it were to decide to start importing copies of the book. If it wants the issue resolved, it could appeal against the AAT's refusal to hear the appeal. It is, however, more likely that the tribunal would not address the issue, or that, if it did, it would decide to proceed on the assumption that the book was a prohibited import. If so, the most I would be prepared to advise would be that Makepeace might well succeed. However, while the tribunal might well not grant permission to import the book in its existing form, I think it is likely to allow importation on the basis of minor excisions.

Examiner's Comments

This is a difficult question and raises a number of issues which students must address. These include the jurisdiction of the AAT to decide on whether something is a prohibited import; the problems that arise from the fact that it can allow an appeal against refusal of permission to import only if the item in question is a prohibited import; and the question of how the AAT would handle the appeal. This answer handles these issues reasonably well and its analysis is, I think, correct. In relation to the question of whether the AAT may make findings in relation to whether the book is a prohibited import, the answer might usefully have referred to relevant AAT decisions, including *Re Huseyin and Director of Classification Board* (2003) 76 ALD 163. But this would not be necessary, and, depending on pre-exam instructions, might well be an unrealistic expectation.

One strategy it does not discuss is the possibility of seeking to have the jurisdictional issue referred to the Federal Court under s 45 of the AAT Act. The fact that the answer does not address the procedures which might be used to achieve an authoritative resolution of whether the book is a prohibited import is not a defect. The question does not require this.

Needless to say, this turns the problem into a rather artificial one. A lawyer who treated a request for advice in a similarly narrow way might be in trouble; at the very least, the lawyer would be advised to include a statement putting the requester of advice on notice that it might be wise to consider alternatives to the AAT. A student who chose to do likewise would, I think, be entitled to receive some credit if the additional advice was good advice.

In discussing the likely substantive issue, the answer correctly recognises that the tribunal is engaged in a decision-making process which involves it doing more than simply interpreting law. It also recognises that even if Makepeace did not get the outcome it wanted, it might receive a conditional permission which would give it much of what it wanted.

Common Errors to Avoid

■ Failure to recognise that the right to appeal relates to applications for permission to import prohibited imports, and not to whether an import is prohibited.

■ Failure to recognise that it would be open to the AAT to dismiss Makepeace's appeal on the very ground which Makepeace wants canvassed before the tribunal.

■ Assuming merits review is only ever about jurisdictional issues, and consequent failure to consider the merits of Makepeace's case.

QUESTION 38

Since Makepeace's application to the AAT (see Question 37, p 257), there have been a number of developments:

1. The book has been seized by Customs officials as a prohibited import.

2. The Caledenian Government has been overthrown and replaced by a new government representing all major ethnic groups, including the Diurans.

3. There has also been an amendment to the Customs (Prohibited Imports) Regulations, whereby reg 4A(2AA) has been amended by the addition of these paragraphs:

(ab) the extent to which the proposed importation would increase the number of people who would see, read, hear or feel the prohibited import; and

(ac) any relevant government policy; and ...

Advise Makepeace as to whether these developments will have any impact on the likely success of its application for review of the decision to refuse importation.

Time allowed: 15 mins

Answer Plan

(i) What is the effect of the proposed amendments?

(ii) What is the effect of the changed situation in Caledenia?

(iii) Conclusions.

Answer

(i) What is the effect of the proposed amendments?

In general, the law which the AAT must apply is the law in force at the time that the AAT makes its decision, and not the law in force at the time the decision under review was made. This seems to arise from its power to review de novo the primary decision: s 43(1). However, in identifying the law that is to be applied, the law must be interpreted in the light of common law and statutory presumptions against retrospectivity. If the effect of a law would be to derogate from accrued rights, the relevant law is the earlier law unless there is a contrary legislative intention: *Esber v Commonwealth* (1992) 174 CLR 430; s 8 of the Acts Interpretation Act 1901 (Cth). Accrued rights include rights which are conditional upon a person proving certain facts: *Esber.*

The present case is, however, distinguishable from *Esber* in a number of ways. First, Makepeace never had a right to require that it be given permission to import the goods in question conditional upon the proof of any specified facts. At best it had a right to demand that the Attorney-General exercise a discretion taking account of a number of considerations and not taking account of others. Second, it did not even have a right to insist that only these considerations be taken into account. While prior to the amendment, the Attorney-General was not required to take government policy into account, government policy was nonetheless something which he or she was entitled to take into account: see *Drake (No 2)*. Nor does it seem likely that the consideration set out in para (ab) was one which the decision-maker was not entitled to take into account. Indeed, it is arguably one which would otherwise have fallen within subreg (2AA)(e). The only basis for arguing that the amendment has altered rights would be on the basis that prior to the amendment Makepeace had a right to have its application determined on the basis that while policy could be taken into account, it was not mandatory for the decision-maker to do so.

Even assuming an accrued right, it seems to me that the legislation can be taken as demonstrating an intention to operate so as to defeat that right. The regulation is not one which on its face, necessarily weakens the position of people applying for permission to import. It would no doubt assist some while disadvantaging others. Indeed, in some respects, it may work in Makepeace's favour. The rights conferred by the original legislation were procedural rather than substantive and this also counts against a presumption that they became accrued rights. Procedural legislation is generally treated as having immediate application from the date it comes into operation. The legislation is, I think, best seen as intended to apply to all cases falling within its ambit, regardless of when the decision or the application to the tribunal was made.

If I am wrong, almost nothing turns on it, except in so far as under the old law, the tribunal is not *required* to take government policy into account. Given that the relevant policy (if any) would be policy for which the government would be politically accountable, it is inconceivable, in the light of *Drake (No 2)* that the tribunal would not take the policy into account even were it able to. If I am right, the tribunal must consider policy as well as 'size of audience'.

(ii) What is the effect of the changed situation in Caledenia?

The present case deals with a continuing entitlement: the entitlement to be granted a permission. The tribunal must accordingly act on the basis of the facts as they appear to exist at the time it makes its decision: *Freeman v Secretary, Department of Social Security* (1988) 19 FCR 342. This will clearly be to Makepeace's advantage. The publication in Australia of a book which discredits the old Caledenian Government is likely to win the approval of the new one. Links with the formerly discredited Diurans are likely to enhance Makepeace's reputation rather than detracting from it. The government's policy of appeasing Caledenia, in so far as it continues, is likely to count as a plus for a body which wants to do things which will probably make the new Caledenian Government happy.

(iii) Conclusions

In view of the changed circumstances, I consider that the AAT application has an increased likelihood of success. While the 'size of audience' consideration will weaken Makepeace's claim, it would have been relevant anyway, and the new implications of government policy (assuming the government's commitment to appeasement continues) is likely to strengthen Makepeace's case. The new developments mean that Makepeace's purposes acquire a different significance and that Makepeace's reputation is likely to be enhanced. Makepeace should, however, recognise that the tribunal's decision will in part be influenced by the values brought to bear by the member or members who consider its application.

Examiner's Comments

This question highlights some of the difficulties involved in determining the law and the facts to be applied by the tribunal when these have changed between the date of the application and the date when the tribunal decides the appeal. The most difficult issue involves the question of the law which is to be applied by the tribunal when there has been a change of law between the time of the application and the time of the tribunal's decision. This answer recognises that the issue ultimately boils down to one of statutory interpretation and develops a reasonably cogent argument to the effect that the change to the regulation was intended to apply to the handling of all subsequently considered applications for permission to import. It also recognises that little turns on this. It further recognises that as the present case is one of continuing entitlement, the facts that count are those which the tribunal has found to exist, regardless of whether they were known or existed at the time of the earlier primary decision.

Common Errors to Avoid

- Failing to recognise that government policy is not a matter which can be the subject of an accrued right.
- Failing to recognise that the presumption against retrospective operation of the law applies to proceedings before the AAT, subject to any contrary legislative intention.
- Failure, in a question about merits review, to attempt an analysis of the merits.

Chapter 13
The Ombudsman

Key Issues

The Ombudsman is an independent statutory office holder with a distinctive role in the administrative law system. There is a Commonwealth Ombudsman, whose position was established under the Ombudsman Act 1976 (Cth), and State Ombudsmen established under equivalent State and Territory legislation.

The office was adopted in several Western countries in the light of particular assumptions about post–World War II government and a perceived need for an investigative outfit with a broad remit. It has been said that 'It is quite possible nowadays for a citizen's right to be accidentally crushed by the vast juggernaut of the government's administrative machine': Rowat, cited in *Re British Columbia Development Corp and Friedmann* (1984) 14 DLR (4th) 129 at 139 (Supreme Court of Canada). As Dickson J, for the court, said in that case (at 138):

> The traditional controls over the implementation and administration of governmental policies and programs — namely, the legislature, the executive and the courts — are neither completely suited nor entirely capable of providing the supervision a burgeoning bureaucracy demands.

That court (at 139) approved the observation of the doyen of English administrative lawyers, Professor H W R Wade, that:

> The vital necessity is the impartial investigation of complaints ... What every form of government needs is some regular and smooth-running mechanism for feeding back the reactions of its disgruntled customers, after impartial assessment, and for correcting whatever may have gone wrong.

The Ombudsman is 'neither legal nor political in a strict sense' (*Re British Columbia Development Corp* at 137), but has been commonly said to be concerned with facilitating 'administrative justice': E Biganovsky, 'The Australian Ombudsman — Another Guardian of the Public Interest' in M Harris and V Waye (eds), *Administrative Law*, Federation Press, Sydney, 1991, p 163.

From an aggrieved individual's point of view, the particular functions which the Ombudsman performs include:

- the investigation of complaints;
- the provision of an avenue for redressing a grievance, especially where there are no adequate alternatives; and
- 'holding agencies within his jurisdiction fully accountable for their administrative actions': Biganovsky, 1991, p 163.

Other aspects of the Ombudsman's role include:

- investigation of systemic problems in administration;
- the provision of administrative justice by the employment of an 'essentially ... rational process of inquiry that resorts to objective standards of evaluation and assessment': Biganovsky, 1991, p 151;
- 'facilitating, through his recommendations [and public disclosure], such emendation of administrative action, and the relevant law and practice, as will lead to improving public administration': Biganovsky, 1991, p 163;
- exhorting agencies to improve their performance through educational initiatives; and
- giving further protection of the rule of law: see D Pearce, 'The Ombudsman and the Rule of Law', *AIAL Forum*, vol 1, 1994, p 1.

Students must understand the legal framework governing investigations by the Ombudsman: the Ombudsman Act 1976 (Cth) and State and Territory equivalents, and accompanying case law. The main topics and the principal sections of the federal Act are:

- the jurisdiction of the Ombudsman: s 5, read with definitions in ss 3, 3BA;
- the requirements which complainants must observe in making a complaint: s 7;
- the power to decide not to investigate action the subject of a complaint: s 6;
- the investigative discretions and duties of the Ombudsman: ss 7A, 8, 9, 12, 13, 14, 36, 37;
- the statutory grounds upon which an Ombudsman may report adversely: s 15(1); and
- the remedial action which it is open to the Ombudsman to recommend: ss 15, 16, 17.

The grounds upon which the Ombudsman may make an adverse report are wide and include the ground that 'in all the circumstances [the action was] wrong': s 15(1)(a)(v). It is noteworthy that many of the grounds upon which the Ombudsman may form an opinion that remedial action is warranted replicate the grounds upon which courts may find administrative action invalid: see s 15(1). However, even if the Ombudsman is of the opinion that an illegality has occurred, the

Ombudsman may only make a report, initially to the department or prescribed authority concerned: s 15(2). Other important legal matters dealt with in the Ombudsman Act include the method of appointment (s 21) and tenure of the Ombudsman (s 22), and the requirement for annual reporting of the operations of the office: s 19.

Equally, students should be aware of how the Ombudsman's powers are exercised (or not exercised) in practice; for instance:

- how and why most complaints are not investigated: R Douglas, *Douglas and Jones's Administrative Law*, 5th ed, Federation Press, Sydney, 2006, p 210; R Creyke and J McMillan, *Control of Government Action: Text, Cases and Commentary*, LexisNexis Butterworths, Sydney, 2005, p 191;

- how the Ombudsman 'does not usually proceed to a formal investigation under s 8 of the Act when a complaint is first lodged': in D Pearce (ed), *Australian Administrative Law Service*, LexisNexis Butterworths, Sydney, looseleaf, [534];

- how the Ombudsman 'seldom proceeds to make a formal report' under s 15(2) of the Act: *Australian Administrative Law Service*, [555].

Before attempting the questions, check that you are familiar with the following issues:

✓	the rationale for the office of the Ombudsman;
✓	the jurisdiction of the Ombudsman under the Ombudsman Act 1976;
✓	the general legal framework governing the Ombudsman under the Ombudsman Act;
✓	how the powers of the Ombudsman are typically exercised in practice; and
✓	the operation of the office in practice and its impact on Commonwealth administration.

 # QUESTION 39

Read the 'The Makepeace Scenario', p xvi. Suppose that, in the case of *The Night of a Thousand Shames*, Makepeace had asked the Attorney-General to grant permission to import the book, but the Attorney-General had taken no action for several months, hoping the matter would go away.

Now suppose that Makepeace has subsequently gone to the Ombudsman seeking his or her intervention:

(i) Is the Ombudsman able to help?

(ii) What if, instead of the Attorney-General, the person handling the matter was:

    (a) the secretary of the Attorney-General's Department, authorised pursuant to reg 4A(2A) of the Customs (Prohibited Imports) Regulations; or

    (b) the parliamentary secretary to the Attorney-General (a senator).

Would the Ombudsman be able to help in either case?

Time allowed: 15 mins

Answer Plan

(i)   Jurisdiction of the Ombudsman to investigate delay by the Minister.

(ii) Jurisdiction of the Ombudsman to investigate the delay if certain other persons are responsible.

- A person authorised by the Attorney-General for the purposes of reg 4A(2); or

- The parliamentary secretary to the Attorney-General.

 ## Answer

(i) *Jurisdiction of the Ombudsman to investigate delay by the Minister*

From a complainant's point of view, the Ombudsman has jurisdiction to investigate 'action' 'that relates to a matter of administration'. Relevantly for present purposes, it must be 'by a Department, or by a prescribed authority': Ombudsman Act 1976 s 5(1). The Ombudsman cannot investigate 'action taken by a Minister': s 5(2)(a). Section 3(7) provides that 'a reference to the taking of action includes a reference to … failure or refusal to take any action, to make a decision'. This means that the Ombudsman would not be able to investigate the *Minister's* personal failure to make the decision, whether pursuant to a Cabinet decision or otherwise.

However, s 5(3A) of the Ombudsman Act states that:

> … action taken by a Department or by a prescribed authority shall not be regarded as having been taken by a Minister by reason only that the action was taken by the Department or authority in relation to action that has been, is proposed to be, or may be, taken by a Minister personally.

This means that the Ombudsman would be able to investigate any departmental action or inaction. It is not clear whether the department has been involved. Information regarding its involvement needs to be sought (for example, by means of a freedom of information application).

(ii)   Jurisdiction of the Ombudsman to investigate the delay if certain other persons are responsible

A person authorised by the Attorney-General for the purposes of reg 4A(2)

If the power to permit the importation of prohibited goods is in the hands of a person authorised by the Attorney-General under reg 4A(2A) — here the secretary of the department — then it is clear that the Ombudsman retains jurisdiction: Ombudsman Act 1976 s 5(1). The secretary is a secretary of a 'Department' as defined in s 3(1). There is also no difficulty with the other elements of the jurisdiction. Delay comes within the definition of 'taking of action' in s 3(7)(c). Failure to make a decision in a particular case clearly relates to 'a matter of administration'.

The parliamentary secretary to the Attorney-General

If, however, the matter is being handled by the parliamentary secretary, it is necessary to return to the exclusion of 'a Minister' in s 5(2)(a) of the Ombudsman Act. The questions are: first, is a parliamentary secretary a Minister of State within the ordinary meaning of that term? The answer to this question is not decisive, but it is weighty. And second, is a parliamentary secretary a 'Minister' within s 5(2)(a) of the Act?

It is common knowledge that a parliamentary secretary functions like a Minister in that, when on duty, he or she is responsible for actions of the government in the parliament and elsewhere. Further, there is legal authority which supports this contention. Section 4 of the Ministers of State Act 1952 (Cth) states:

> The number of the Ministers of State must not exceed:
>
> (a) in the case of those designated, when appointed by the Governor-General, as Parliamentary Secretary —12;

This provision indicates a parliamentary view that parliamentary secretaries are Ministers. More definitively, the High Court has determined that parliamentary secretaries are appointed as Ministers, and validly so, under ss 64 and 65 of the Constitution: *Re Patterson; Ex parte Taylor* (2001) 207 CLR 391. In that case it was held that the Parliamentary Secretary to the Minister for Immigration and Multicultural Affairs was a 'Minister' within the meaning of the phrase 'the Minister, personally' in s 501(4) of the Migration Act 1958 (Cth).

Since a parliamentary secretary falls within the ordinary meaning of a Minister of State, the remaining question is whether a parliamentary secretary falls within the term 'a Minister' in s 5(2)(a) of the Ombudsman Act. The ordinary meaning of Minister, the reference to parliamentary secretaries in the Ministers of State Act, and the holding in *Re Patterson* strongly suggest that a parliamentary secretary would be caught by the provision. Is there any reason to read the Ombudsman Act in a special way so as to exclude assistant Ministers, that is, parliamentary secretaries? It is submitted that there is not. The High

Court has observed in *Re Patterson* that Ministers and parliamentary secretaries are responsible to the parliament for the administration of their departments: at [214]–[215] per Gummow and Hayne JJ, with whom Gleeson CJ at [1] and Kirby J at [323] agreed. It can be inferred that the personal action of Ministers was excluded in s 5(2)(a) because, under the inherited but developing system of responsible government, a Minister is responsible in parliament for everything done under his or her direction. If this is correct, then the rationale extends equally to parliamentary secretaries who share that function with 'senior' Ministers of State.

Examiner's Comments

This question is primarily designed to test students' knowledge of the legislative provisions covering the Ombudsman's jurisdiction. Students need to appreciate that the Ombudsman has a wide but not all-encompassing jurisdiction.

The answer is quite comprehensive, but it did not supply an authority for the view that Ministers were excluded from the Ombudsman's jurisdiction on account of responsible government. One learned text referring to this point is G Flick, *Federal Administrative Law*, Law Book Co, Sydney, 1983, p 128.

Some aspects of the question were quite straightforward. The reviewability of the actions of parliamentary secretaries is more difficult. Unless the matter had been discussed in administrative law, an examiner would not be looking for a knowledgeable answer on this point except at the A or upper Distinction level. This does not mean a complete answer would be expected at this level either; merely some discussion which is correct and in the right direction.

The issue concerning the parliamentary secretary underlines the fact that the study of administrative law is carried out against the backdrop of constitutional law and general legal knowledge. If students wish to do well in administrative law, they need an up-to-date and detailed knowledge of the composition of the executive when they come to administrative law, or to have acquired it by the time they are assessed in that unit.

If you needed to find out whether a parliamentary secretary was a Minister for the purposes of a take-home examination or a research assignment, how would you do it? Would you make a search using Google? Comlaw or AustLII legislation database? A constitutional law text? A legal encyclopaedia? What are the advantages and disadvantages of each?

Common Errors to Avoid

- Taking a mere glance at the Ombudsman Act. It is not enough to take a glance at the Act because this technique may only bring to light some, but not all, of the relevant provisions. There is no substitute for reading legislative provisions closely.

- Taking a purely literal approach to the question whether a parliamentary secretary is a 'Minister' within the meaning of s 5(2)(a) of the Act.

 # QUESTION 40

You are in legal practice as a solicitor. Anderson Jones comes to you for advice. He tells you that he has been refused permission to import a collection of photos called *Children at Play*. The photos are all of young children and practically all are without clothing. They were all taken at overseas beaches.

Mr Jones tells you that he is a freelance, professional photographer with previous collections called *People at Work*, *Sportsmen on the Field* and *Horses on the Track*.

He shows you the letter from the decision-maker, which reads in toto:

Dear Mr Jones,

I refer to previous correspondence relating to the seizure of a collection of photos belonging to you called *Children at Play*.

I am writing to inform you that permission has been refused by the undersigned to import the collection of photos known as *Children at Play*.

Yours faithfully,

Betty Bright
A person authorised by the Attorney-General

The letter is dated three months ago.

Mr Jones tells you that he did not apply for a review by the AAT as he was not aware that he could do so.

Mr Jones tells you that he subsequently complained to the Ombudsman by letter. An investigations officer replied by telephone, advising him of the office's 'preliminary view':

1. Because ministerial policy is involved, the Ombudsman cannot do anything. The ministerial policy states that material which could be used by paedophiles is not to be allowed into Australia unless there are bona fide and lawful reasons for the importation.

2. Even if the Ombudsman could act, the Ombudsman is not inclined to investigate the action further because it was the AAT to which Mr Jones should have turned; it has or had jurisdiction to review the decision complained of.

3. The office cannot substantiate the complaint of maladministration by Mr Jones because the decision-maker has not returned numerous phone calls.

4. In any event, the office would also not likely find in Mr Jones' favour in the light of his prior conviction for child sex and the lack of evidence that the photographs are to be used for a bona fide exhibition or for lawful purposes.

Mr Jones tells you that the reference to the conviction is correct, but it was 10 years ago.

Assist Mr Jones as follows:

1. Assume your interview with Mr Jones is not over:

   (a) Write out questions you would ask Mr Jones in the interview to clarify any matters you think are in doubt.

   (b) Make up answers not inconsistent with the above facts.

   Record both in the form of a file note.

2. On the basis of the given facts, and the facts added under point1(b), advise Mr Jones whether a lawyer can help him in dealing with the Ombudsman, or whether Mr Jones should write a letter himself.

   Record your advice in the form of a file note.

3. Assuming you are of the opinion that you can help in dealing with the Ombudsman, write an authority for the client to sign, authorising your firm to receive the response to the submission to the Ombudsman's office and any further communications on this complaint from that office.

4. Write a letter to the Ombudsman on Mr Jones' behalf, based upon the given facts and the facts added under point 1(b), for the purpose of:

   (a) responding to the four points in the 'preliminary view' above;

   (b) adding any further submissions you think are necessary having regard to s 15(1) of the Ombudsman Act; and

   (c) adding submissions on the action which ought to be taken having regard to s 15(2) of the Act.

5. Write a short letter to Mr Jones advising him what you have done.

Time allowed: 1 hour 30 mins

Answer Plan

(i) File note of interview with Mr A Jones.

(ii) File note of advice re possible complaint to Ombudsman.

(iii) Drafting — authority to act on behalf of client.

(iv) Drafting — letter to Ombudsman.

(v) Drafting — letter to Mr A Jones.

Answer

(i)   *File note of interview with Mr A Jones*

[date]

At interview today I asked client the following questions and received answers as set out below:

1. *Apart from the seizure itself, have you been upset at the way Customs made their decision to refuse permission to import the collection of photos?*

    A: I have not been given any reasons. And I was not told I had a right to appeal to the AAT.

2. *What were the purposes of the collection being brought into Australia?*

    A: To exhibit at the Green Doors Gallery.

3. *Do you have a contract to display the photographs?*

    A: Yes.

4. *With whom? and Where? and When?*

    A: With Green Doors Pty Ltd. I will send you a copy of the agreement.

5. *How many of the photographs are to be displayed?*

    A: All of them.

6. *After the exhibition what will you do with the photographs?*

    A: See if makers of greeting cards are interested. Otherwise keep in private collection.

7. *Would you be agreeable to conditions on their use if their importation is allowed?*

    A: Yes, if the conditions allow the exhibition to go ahead as planned.

(ii)   *File note of advice re possible complaint to Ombudsman*

[date]

Advised client today of the advantages and costs of having a lawyer involved in dealing with the Ombudsman. On the advantages, I told him that:

1. The letter could make submissions based upon a knowledge of the Ombudsman Act.

2. The investigive officer had made some legal errors which, once pointed out, could lead to a favourable reconsideration.

3. There were advantages in leaving the submission to a professional to avoid the problem of a writer being 'too close' to the problem.

4. I was experienced in writing to the Ombudsman.

5. If the request for reconsideration was written under the letterhead of a solicitor's office it might lead to the submission receiving more weight than if it were written by the client himself.

On costs, I told the client that the submission would be around [$].

JB

(iii)   Drafting — authority to act on behalf of client

I, Anderson Paris JONES, of 10 Blue Street, Brownsville, authorise Jerome Broadbent of Sly and Broadbent Solicitors, 901 Collins Street, Melbourne, Victoria to:

1. receive all communications from the Ombudsman's office in this matter; and

2. generally, act on my behalf in my complaint to the Commonwealth Ombudsman regarding the proposed importation of the collection of photos known as *Children at Play*.

Signed

Anderson Jones

[date]

(iv)   Drafting — letter to Ombudsman

The Commonwealth Ombudsman
GPO Box 1234
Canberra, ACT

Your ref: XYZ123

Anderson Jones: Refusal to grant permission to import prohibited goods

Request for reconsideration of preliminary view in relation to his complaint

Dear Sir,

I act on behalf of Mr Jones who complained to your office by letter [date] about the decision by B Bright, a person authorised by the Attorney-General, to refuse to grant permission to import a collection of photos known as *Children at Play*. See the attached authority from my client.

Mr Jones informs me that on [date] he received a reply by voice mail, indicating a preliminary view about the administrative action and the Ombudsman's role.

Your preliminary view

I submit that you ought to reconsider your preliminary view. Each of the points made by your investigative officer is now addressed:

1. While the Ombudsman Act precludes the Ombudsman from investigating the action of a Minister (s 5(2)(a)), it does not preclude your office from investigating departmental action based upon ministerial policy. The Ombudsman can investigate the authorised person's action. In this case, it is the application of the ministerial policy which can be investigated.

2. The Ombudsman ought not decline to investigate in this case because the AAT has or had jurisdiction to review the decision complained of. It is appreciated that the AAT has or had jurisdiction to review the decision and that, in an appropriate case, the Ombudsman may decline to act on this ground: Ombudsman Act s 6(3). However, in this case our client did not realise he had a right of review or a case to make. He had not been given any reasons, nor had he been advised (as he should have been) of the right to obtain review of the decision (as provided under cl 4(1)(a) of the Code of Practice for Notification of Reviewable Decisions and Rights of Review made under s 27B of the AAT Act).

3. The apparent difficulty your office is having with obtaining reasons and information from the decision-maker seems to stem, with respect, from a misconception of the powers of your office. Your office need not conduct inquiries solely on a 'voluntary' basis, that is, accept non-cooperation as the right of an official. Your office is equipped with powers compulsorily to require persons to attend your office and to furnish information as well as producing documents: s 9. A refusal or failure to attend before the Ombudsman, to furnish information or to answer a question is an offence: s 36. I submit that in the present circumstances consideration ought to be given to using these powers.

4. In the message it is asserted that the importation of the photos is not bona fide and is without lawful excuse. I am advised that this is not the case and, further, that my client can support his claim that the photos are part of a legitimate artistic display. I attach documentation evidencing an agreement between my client and Green Doors Gallery. I acknowledge that my client does have a past criminal conviction relating to a child. However, this was a long time ago and, as this attached documentation shows, the purposes of the importation are lawful and for artistic purposes only. He has a right to have his application for permission to import the photos assessed on the merits.

The complaint against Betty Bright, the person authorised by the Attorney-General

Since your office ought to investigate the matter further, I will take this opportunity to add the following submissions regarding the core of my client's complaint. If it turns out that the action by the person authorised by the Attorney-General was based wholly or substantially on my client's criminal record, it is:

- Contrary to law (Ombudsman Act s 15(1)(a)(i)), because it is mere suspicion. There is no evidence to show that the importation is for any unlawful purpose.
- Unreasonable and unjust (s 15(1)(a)(ii)), because my client is being prevented from pursuing his lawful occupation of a freelance photographer.
- Based wholly or partly on a mistake of fact (s 15(1)(a)(iv)), because the facts are that the importation is being made for artistic purposes only.
- Wrong (s 15(1)(a)(v)), because my client is being hounded for his past misconduct — conduct which occurred a long time ago.

Possible remedial action

1. At the least, you should recommend that reasons ought to be provided: s 15(2)(e).

2. Should you, upon further consideration, come to the view that defective administration has occurred — namely, that the decision was flawed by the baseless suspicion that the photos were to be used as child pornography — then I submit that the proper action to take is to recommend to the decision-maker that the goods ought to be allowed in. I am advised that my client will abide by any conditions which may be put on the use of the photos once importation is allowed.

I thank you for your patience in giving further consideration in this matter. Please do not hesitate to contact me should you have any query about this letter.

I look forward to your reply at your earliest convenience.

Yours faithfully,

J Broadbent

Sly and Broadbent Solicitors

(v) Drafting — letter to Mr A Jones

Mr A Jones
The White House
10 Blue Street, Brownsville

Our ref: JB/9658

Your complaint to the Ombudsman

Dear Mr Jones,

I am writing to you about your complaint to the Commonwealth Ombudsman concerning the government's refusal to allow you to import the collection of photos called *Children at Play*.

Under an authority signed [date], you agreed that I would act on your behalf in relation to your complaint. I am writing to you to confirm certain understandings and to bring you up to date with developments in this matter.

You will recall that at our meeting in my office on [date], we discussed various options, including:

- whether a written submission ought to be made to the Commonwealth Ombudsman disputing the 'preliminary view' of his office; and

- whether such a submission ought to be written by you, or by this office on your behalf.

As agreed, I have written a submission to the Ombudsman on your behalf. A copy of the submission, which has been forwarded to the Ombudsman, is attached. The document responds to the office's preliminary view, and makes submissions on your complaint and on how it ought to be resolved.

I have since rung the Ombudsman's office (this morning) and they confirmed that they have received the submission and that it is currently receiving high-level consideration in that office.

I will continue to monitor this situation and will contact you as soon as I am aware of further developments.

If you have any queries, do not hesitate to contact me on 9123 4567.

Yours sincerely,

J Broadbent

Sly and Broadbent Solicitors

Examiner's Comments

This question tests essential knowledge of the Ombudsman scheme: the Ombudsman's jurisdiction; discretion not to investigate action; procedures; grounds for forming an opinion specified in a report to the department or authority concerned; and remedial action which can be recommended.

The question tests these issues in a different format to that which normally applies in administrative law units. The usual question format in administrative law is a legal opinion as to someone's rights to take legal action. In this question students are asked to undertake a number of 'clinical' or practitioner-oriented tasks, including preparing of interview questions, writing up file notes, drawing up an authority to act, preparing a 'submission' to the Ombudsman, and drafting a letter to a client.

There are a number of reasons behind this format. The first is variety — to engender added interest! The second is better comprehension of the substantive law. As has been noted, 'the comprehension and retention of legal concepts is far better when the teaching/learning method is set in a social and practical context': R Hyams, S Campbell and A Evans, *Practical Legal Skills*, OUP, Melbourne, 1998, p 3. The third is realism. It is rare for the Ombudsman to be subject to legal action. It is much more common for the Ombudsman to be on the receiving end of legal submissions, particularly from corporate clients. Hence, it is appropriate, in the case of the Ombudsman, to ask students to write a submission.

If you wish to know how the topic of the Ombudsman might be examined in a more traditional format, consider the following question:

> Advise Mr Jones whether the 'preliminary view' of the Ombudsman's office involves any legal errors or misconceptions, and (if so) advise him on his options (if any) for taking the matter further.

The submission above is dependent, to a large extent, on the answers to the additional questions put and drafted as part of the interview. At the interview we were informed of the contract with the Green Doors Gallery. What if the Green Doors Gallery specialised in pornographic art? What if our 'client' could not vouch for any bona fide and lawful use of the photos? If we entertained serious doubts about our client's bona fides would we have been required to continue to act on his behalf? Not necessarily. There is no duty to act for clients whose 'instructions' we believe to be unreasonable: Hyams, Campbell and Evans, 1998, p 42. If you suspected Mr Jones was telling lies or deliberately not revealing information so as to hide the real facts, you may need to confront him (tactfully), for you owe a duty to the court to which you have been admitted to behave ethically: Hyams, Campbell and Evans, 1998, pp 41–2. If by acting for a client you would feel compromised in this way it would be wise to decline to act for them.

Common Errors to Avoid

- Not citing relevant provisions of the Ombudsman Act 1976, including the provisions of the Act regarding what can amount to defective administration.
- Not completing the practical tasks in a professional manner, for example:
  - not giving the date of the file note;
  - using inappropriately informal language;
  - writing in legalese;
  - not enclosing an authority;
  - not attaching the submission in the letter to the client; and
  - not confirming, in writing, what has been agreed with the client.

QUESTION 41

'[T]he functions of the Ombudsman appear to many to represent not only a more accessible but also a less certain kind of justice [than that provided by the courts]': E Biganovsky, 'The Australian Ombudsman — Another Guardian of the Public Interest' in M Harris and V Waye (eds), *Administrative Law*, Federation Press, Sydney, 1991, p 153.

Discuss.

Time allowed: 1 hour

Answer Plan

(i)   Introduction.

(ii) 'More accessible'.

  • Barriers to reaching.

  • Barriers to entry.

  • Barriers to use.

  • Summary.

(iii) 'Less certain'.

(iv) 'Kind of justice'.

(v)   Conclusion.

Answer

(i)   Introduction

The statement by the South Australian Ombudsman raises three main issues for discussion:

1. Does the Ombudsman provide a 'more accessible' kind of justice than that provided by the courts, and if so how?

2. Does the Ombudsman provide a 'less certain' kind of justice in that regard?

3. How, generally, does the Ombudsman provide a 'kind of justice'?

(ii) 'More accessible'

'Accessible' means 'that can readily be reached, entered, or used' (*Australian Concise Oxford Dictionary*). It is therefore necessary to look at the barriers to reaching, entering, and using courts and the Ombudsman.

Barriers to reaching

Applicants for judicial review must approach the right court: one with jurisdiction. They normally ought not approach a State court concerning a federal matter; less still a federal court concerning a State matter. Applicants in a State matter cannot approach a State inferior court for judicial review. Applicants in a federal matter are likely to incur added costs if they approach the High Court in the first instance: see the court's power to remit to the Federal Court: Judiciary Act 1903 s 44(2A).

The choice with Ombudsmen is simpler. A complainant must approach the relevant State and federal Ombudsman, each having a separate jurisdiction. Importantly, applications to the federal Ombudsman may be made orally (s 7(1)) and the vast bulk of complaints and inquiries are by telephone: Creyke and McMillan, 2005, [4.2.19]. State Ombudsmen also receive numerous oral communications: R Douglas, *Douglas and Jones's Administrative Law*, 5th ed, Federation Press, Sydney, 2006, p 208. Ombudsmen receive a large number of inquiries and complaints each year (Creyke and McMillan, 2005, [4.2.19]); the number is far more than the number of applications made to courts (see Douglas, 2006, pp 653–4), which indicates that Ombudsmen are highly accessible in this regard. However, Ombudsmen are not necessarily well known by all sectors of the community, particularly people from minority and disadvantaged groups: Douglas, 2006, p 217.

Barriers to entry

To enter the judicial review system, that is, for an application to be heard, an applicant must make a written application (for example, Administrative Decisions (Judicial Review) Act 1977 (Cth) (ADJR Act) s 11(1)). The application will need to address a number of technicalities: the appropriate jurisdiction; a recognised ground of review; standing; and available relief: see, for example, Federal Court Rules 1979 O 54, Form 56 for applications under the ADJR Act. And the application must be made within time deadlines or without undue delay. Legal assistance is strongly advisable in making an application.

Compare the federal Ombudsman and the Ombudsman Act 1976: the jurisdiction is broadly framed in s 5 of the federal Act and is not limited to investigating 'maladministration': *Anti-Discrimination Commissioner v Acting Ombudsman* (2003) 11 Tas R 343; [2003] TASSC 34 at [37]; a complainant does not need to base their complaint on a claim of illegality (s 15); does not have to conform to standing rules (cf s 6(1)(b)(ii)); does not have to nominate relief; and is subject to more generous and less formal time limits for approaching the Ombudsman: s 6(1)(a). And complaints to the Ombudsman are free and do not have to be made in writing, though a complaint may be required to be reduced to writing: s 7.

However, the Ombudsman is in some jurisdictional respects less accessible than the courts, in that he or she cannot examine the conduct of Ministers: s 5(2)(a). In addition, there are some State precedents which put a narrow interpretation on the jurisdictional limitation of 'matter of administration'. Some state that 'policy' decisions are not within the Ombudsman's jurisdiction — even, it seems, if they are also administrative acts: *Booth v Dillon (No 2)* [1976] VR 434; *City of Salisbury v Biganovsky* (1990) 54 SASR 117. And actions by 'the courts' (generally accepted as excluded from the Ombudsman's jurisdiction) have been held to extend to the actions of government solicitors in failing to brief counsel and in delaying a matter coming on for hearing: *Glenister v Dillon* [1976] VR 550; *Glenister v Dillon (No 2)* [1977] VR 151. But the Commonwealth Ombudsman has not accepted these precedents as binding or authoritative interpretations of the Commonwealth Act: Creyke and McMillan, 2005, [4.3.24].

Further, the federal Ombudsman frequently exercises a discretion not to investigate a complaint pursuant to s 6 of the Ombudsman Act. Indeed, the greater majority of complaints (70%) 'are handled initially by advising the complainant how to raise the issue with the agency': Creyke and McMillan, 2005, [4.2.19]; Douglas, 2006, p 210, fn 2.

But for the discretion to refuse to investigate, the Ombudsman would be clearly more accessible to entry. Nevertheless, there are more complaints which are investigated by Ombudsmen than there are applications which are made to the courts.

Barriers to use

The Ombudsman is more accessible with respect to barriers to use in the sense that less is required of the complainant. Whereas courts conduct hearings and in practice require an expert lawyer to manage the process for an aggrieved citizen, the Ombudsman carries out the investigation with much less input from the complainant being necessary. There is no general obligation to afford the complainant a hearing: s 8(4). Quite obviously, the Ombudsman is considerably cheaper.

Summary

The courts and the Ombudsman both impose obstacles on their accessibility. The Ombudsman is more accessible in terms of being reached and in terms of use.

(iii) 'Less certain'

The claim that the Ombudsman delivers 'less certain' justice is intriguing — but what does it mean? In one sense it is clearly true. Whereas courts issue binding or enforceable orders in disposing of a matter, this power is not available to the Ombudsman due to the administrative nature of the office. In the final result, the Ombudsman can only come to 'opinions' about defective administration and make recommendations as to appropriate corrective action: s 15. Justice is, as a result, less certain with the Ombudsman, because it is not certain whether the department or authority will agree with the Ombudsman's recommendation. However, given that in the majority of cases investigated there is a substantial or partial remedy for the complainant

(Douglas, 2006, p 214), this limitation should not be over-emphasised. Also, in practice, lower court orders in civil matters are often disobeyed, so not too much should be made of the formal difference between the Ombudsman and courts in this regard.

A second related way in which the Ombudsman delivers less certain justice than the courts is that, at the end of an investigation, the Ombudsman cannot make determinations on the issues identified, or purport to make findings in any final sense: *Chairperson, Aboriginal and Torres Strait Islander Commission v Commonwealth Ombudsman* (1995) 39 ALD 570 at 580 and 581. In that case, the Ombudsman made a report on the conduct of the Aboriginal and Torres Strait Islander Commission (ATSIC) and two members of its senior management. The Federal Court found that the Ombudsman's report made findings of individual culpability by the use of language such as 'untrue', 'misled', 'departures from the standard of impartiality required', and 'knowingly provided a misleading briefing'. The court found such statements to be *ultra vires* with regard to the powers granted by the Ombudsman Act, because that Act did not permit *findings* of individual guilt, although the Ombudsman could report *opinions* regarding an individual's guilt: at 581–2. Further, use of qualifiers such as 'in my view' would only be satisfactory if the Ombudsman is 'in truth reporting her opinions': at 581. In coming to this view, the court took account of the 'administrative nature' of the office of the Ombudsman and the statutory prescription of his or her duties, along with a consideration of the intention of parliament.

Even though the South Australian Ombudsman has properly identified a degree of uncertainty as a broad limitation of the Ombudsman, this concession does not mean that in every respect the Ombudsman delivers less certain justice than the courts. The Ombudsman has the power to scrutinise administrative actions from a considerably wider perspective than the courts, and this allows a wider category of 'injustice' to be addressed. Human rights, justice and community morality may be considered, rather than just black-letter law. Under the Ombudsman Act the Ombudsman may come to an adverse opinion based on mistake of fact as well as law (s 15(1)(a)(iv)), and where action is merely 'wrong': s 15(1)(a)(v). The Ombudsman even has the capacity to come to an adverse opinion where the relevant rule of law is or may be 'unreasonable, unjust, oppressive or improperly discriminatory': s 15(1)(a)(iii).

(iv) 'Kind of justice'

If justice is to be measured strictly by the judicial standard, the Ombudsman would not measure up for at least four reasons. First, the Ombudsman need not be a judge or judicial officer, and in any case does not enjoy judicial tenure until 70 years of age. Second, the Ombudsman's processes are private rather than open or public (s 8(2)) and there is no general obligation to afford a hearing: s 8(4). Third, the

Ombudsman is not, in effect, constrained to form opinions based on existing law (particular legislation or common law), since he or she may form an adverse opinion where the action is 'in all the circumstances, wrong': s 15(1)(a)(v). Fourth, the Ombudsman's recommendations are not strictly binding: s 15.

However, the question is not whether the Ombudsman delivers formal, curial justice. The question is whether he or she delivers a '*kind* of justice'. This suggests that we ought to consider whether the Ombudsman functions in such a way that a number of features of curial justice are met, even though some are not. The exercise is reminiscent of the analysis of the AAT by Sir Anthony Mason, who reasoned that the tribunal delivered 'administrative justice': A Mason, 'Administrative Review: The Experience of the First Twelve Years', *Federal Law Review*, vol 18, 1989, p 130.

Upon analysis, there are several features of the Ombudsman's office which suggest that it provides a kind of justice:

- *Establishment and position in the legal system* The Ombudsman is established by the Ombudsman Act 1976. The Ombudsman is linked to, and can draw upon, other features of the legal system, such as the AAT (s 10A), the Federal Court (s 11A) and the parliament: s 17.

- *Independence* The Ombudsman is independent of both the citizenry and the government. Although the Ombudsman is appointed by the government (s 21(1)), the Ombudsman has a fixed tenure of up to seven years (s 22(1)), and the procedure for removal is similar to that applying to Federal Court and High Court judges: s 28(1).

- *Binding powers* The Ombudsman has compulsory powers to order information to be furnished and documents to be produced (s 9), and to enter government premises: s 14.

- *Procedural fairness* The Ombudsman must afford a hearing in certain cases in the course of his or her formal investigations: s 8.

- *Truth-getting facility* The Ombudsman has ample powers to get to the truth. These powers include powers of examination: s 13.

- *Reasoned decisions* The Ombudsman must give reasons where a complaint is not investigated (s 12(1)) or where a complaint is formally upheld: s 15(3)(a).

However, just because the Ombudsman is armed with certain powers, that does not mean that those powers are often used, nor does it mean that, if used, they are ultimately persuasive (that is, successful). Examples of the first proviso are the compulsory powers and formal s 15 reports. An example of the second is the power to report to parliament.

(v) Conclusion

The South Australian Ombudsman, Mr Biganovsky, has pointed to key features of the Ombudsman. The statement on the whole is a fair and balanced view of the Ombudsman's role when it is compared with the courts' supervisory role over the administration. The statement is fair because it is a generally accurate one: the Ombudsman is more accessible than the courts. It is balanced because it makes significant concessions. In the words 'less certain', it is conceded that the Ombudsman is less effective than the courts in a certain respect, while in the reference to a '*kind of* justice', it demonstrates an awareness that the Ombudsman's function in the legal system requires some qualification. Ultimately, these features demonstrate how the Ombudsman, while not superior to the courts on every count, is nevertheless a distinctive and important mechanism.

Examiner's Comments

The statement of Biganovksy which students are called upon to discuss was chosen because it requires students to engage with the strengths and limitations of the office. As James Boyd White has said, eloquently, 'The comprising of contrary tendencies, the facing of unresolved tensions, is an essential part of life, as our artists repeatedly teach us': J Boyd White, 'Thinking About Our Language' in T Morawetz (ed), *Law and Language*, Ashgate, Aldershot, 2000, p 15.

The answer is well thought out and structured. The dictionary is used to tease out issues. Issues are clearly identified at the outset and the main body of the essay elaborates on each in turn, with competing arguments being presented. The conclusion sums up the discussion.

An alternative way to answer the question would be to use a case study, drawing upon a report of the Ombudsman. This method would be acceptable (and may indeed be very fruitful), provided that the student discusses its limitations as a methodology.

Common Errors to Avoid

- Giving a one-sided discussion. A 'discuss' question requires students to discuss points of view — not just advance arguments which support their overall view.
- Failure to supply legal support. Good answers will, wherever possible, supply references to relevant legislative provisions and case law.
- Regurgitating your notes on the Ombudsman rather than addressing the particular issues raised by the question.
- Not addressing the question well. Students should not attempt to rework the question, but should constantly refer explicitly to the

key claims that the Ombudsman provides an 'accessible' but 'less certain' 'kind of justice'.

■ Not addressing the question fully. A good answer would not overlook the concluding comment that the Ombudsman delivers a 'kind of justice'.

■ Cobbling together various sources rather than adopting an overall stance of your own.

■ Considering that Ombudsmen provide a less certain kind of justice because their recommendations are not binding in law, without considering how effective they are in practice.

■ Writing on the accessibility and the relative certainty of the Ombudsman, without comparing the office to courts in the specified respects.

PART 5

Access to Information

Chapter 14
The Right to Reasons

 ## Key Issues

1. Rationale

The statutory right to obtain reasons for a decision has been hailed as 'Perhaps the single most important reform contained in the Commonwealth review package': D O'Brien, 'The Impact of Administrative Review on Commonwealth Public Administration' in M Harris and V Waye (eds), *Administrative Law*, Federation Press, Sydney, 1991, p 108. According to Kirby J, the rationale for this great advance is five-fold:

1. to act as a 'salutary discipline' for decision-makers and encourage good administration through a proper consideration of decision-making powers;

2. to 'promote acceptance of decisions once made';

3. to facilitate individuals obtaining redress through the courts;

4. to 'provide guidance for future like decisions'; and

5. to increase 'public confidence in, and the legitimacy of, the administrative process': *Re Minister for Immigration and Multicultural and Indigenous Affairs; Ex parte Palme* (2003) 216 CLR 212 at [105].

2. Sources of the obligation to give reasons

To date, the advance has been largely achieved through express statutory duties, but the courts are increasingly recognising implied statutory obligations to give reasons.

There is no general common law obligation upon administrative officers or administrative tribunals to give reasons for a decision: *Osmond v Public Service Board of NSW* (1986) 159 CLR 656; *Campbelltown City Council v Vegan* [2006] NSWCA 284 at [106] per Basten JA with whom Handley and McColl JJA generally agreed.

There are three main circumstances in which decision-makers can come under such an obligation. First, some officials and tribunals must give reasons as a consequence of making a decision, that is, the decision-maker must include reasons in their decision or their decision must be accompanied by a statement of reasons. The duty may be expressly stated. The relevant laws are ad hoc. They include s 43(2) of the AAT Act, s 26 of the Freedom of Information Act 1982 (Cth), and, for adverse decisions, s 47(3) of the Australian Citizenship Act 2007 (Cth). A court may also find the decision-maker to be under an implied statutory duty to give reasons: *Osmond v Public Service Board of NSW* (1986) 159 CLR 656 at 676 per Deane J; *Campbelltown City Council v Vegan*. Statute law, as interpreted by the courts, thus qualifies the *Osmond* decision: *Vegan* at [110] per Basten JA. This latter area of law is developing; a recent instance is *Campbelltown City Council v Vegan*, in which an appeal panel hearing workers compensation disputes was held to be under an implied statutory obligation to give reasons for its decisions. Since not all States and Territories have request schemes comparable to the totality of the federal regimes (see R Creyke and J McMillan, *Control of Government Action: Text, Cases and Commentary*, LexisNexis Butterworths, Sydney, 2005, [18.2.12]) it is an area of law to watch.

A second circumstance in which a decision-maker comes under an obligation to give reasons is a consequence of a request being made by a person affected by an administrative decision. At the Commonwealth level, there are two chief laws in this category: s 13 of the Administrative Decisions (Judicial Review) Act 1977 (Cth) (ADJR Act) and s 28 of the AAT Act. While both are 'general' in the sense they apply to classes of decisions, the AAT Act is more limited, since it applies only to decisions which are subject to review by the AAT. The ADJR Act provision is tied to the entitlement to make an application for an order of review under s 5 of that Act. Other jurisdictions have similar laws: Creyke and McMillan, 2005, [18.2.12]; R Douglas, *Douglas and Jones's Administrative Law*, 5th ed, Federation Press, Sydney, 2006, pp 141–3.

Third, some decision-makers must give reasons as a consequence of an *application being made to certain review tribunals*. For instance, where an application is made to the AAT for the review of a decision which is reviewable by the tribunal, the decision-maker must lodge a statement of reasons with the tribunal: AAT Act s 37.

In addition, in the special circumstances of the case, the duty to accord natural justice or procedural fairness may require reasons to be given: *Osmond v Public Service Board of NSW* (1986) 159 CLR 656 at 670 per Gibbs CJ (with whom Wilson, Brennan and Dawson JJ agreed), and at 676 per Deane J; *Campbelltown City Council v Vegan* at [118] per Basten JA.

3. Content of the obligation

Where a statement of reasons must be given under Commonwealth law, there is a fairly uniform Commonwealth requirement in respect of *what* the statement generally must contain. Under s 13 of the ADJR Act and ss 28 and 43(2B) of the AAT Act the decision-maker is required to set out the findings on material questions of fact and refer to the evidence or other material on which those findings were based, as well as giving the reasons for the decision. By force of s 25D of the Acts Interpretation Act 1901 (Cth), the same requirement applies to any reference to a duty to give written reasons under particular federal laws. (Some other jurisdictions have similar laws: Douglas, 2006, p 144.) These requirements also apply to decision-makers subject to an implied statutory obligation to give reasons: *Campbelltown City Council v Vegan* at [121] per Basten JA.

There is no necessary failure to comply with the obligation to give reasons where the decision-maker gives reasons which are wrong in substance. The obligation is one which demands merely adequate 'expression of reasons': *O'Brien v Repatriation Commission* (1984) 1 FCR 472 at 486 per Keely and Fitzgerald JJ. The requirement to set out the findings on material questions of fact thus focuses upon the subjective thought processes of the decision-maker rather than on an objective or external standard of materiality: *Minister for Immigration and Multicultural Affairs v Yusuf* (2001) 206 CLR 323 at 346. If bad reasons are given, then *ultra vires*, denial of procedural fairness, or error of law must be shown to ground relief. However, if any relevant matter is not mentioned in a statement of reasons, a court may infer it was not considered by the decision-maker to be material. This too may reveal some basis for judicial review: *Yusuf* at [69].

4. Consequences of breaching obligation

Where the decision-maker is required to give reasons accompanying the making of a decision a failure to give adequate reasons is an error of law vitiating the decision: *Dornan v Riordan* (1990) 21 ALD 255 at 259; *Campbelltown City Council v Vegan* at [130] per Basten JA. It would appear that the error is not jurisdictional and hence the decision is not void *ab initio*: *Ex parte Palme* at [44]–[45]; cf *Dornan* at 261. Note that a court has a discretion regarding the relief to be afforded: to quash the decision, or simply order adequate reasons to be given: *Dornan*.

The statutory request regimes also provide remedies in this regard: ADJR Act s 13(7); AAT Act s 28(5); Douglas, 2006, p 143. Finally, it may be noted that the Ombudsman frequently investigates a complaint that a decision-maker has failed to give reasons or adequate reasons: Creyke and McMillan, 2005, [4.2.20].

5. Evidentiary value of statement of reasons

A statement of reasons is admissible if part of the *res gestae* (decision-making process) or if verified by affidavit: *Minister for Immigration and Ethnic Affairs v Taveli* (1990) 23 FCR 162 per Davies and Hill J. It is evidence of the reasoning process, such as the holding of an opinion, but is not evidence of the facts which lie behind a decision: *Minister for Immigration and Ethnic Affairs v Arslan* (1984) 4 FCR 73 at 75. On its own it is not conclusive of correct or incorrect decision-making: *Taveli* per French J at 179; *Vanstone v Clark* (2005) 147 FCR 299 at [233].

The inference which may be drawn from it is subject to a contrary inference being drawn from other evidence: *Taveli* at 179. But if a statement of reasons omits to state a relevant consideration, it is a 'starting point along a path to that conclusion': *Vanstone* at [233]. And a decision-maker does not escape a finding of legal error merely because the reasons on the face of it are free from error: see *Kioa v West* (1985) 159 CLR 550 at 588.

Before attempting the questions, check that you are familiar with the following issues:

✓ the rationale for imposing obligations on administrative decision-makers to give statements of reasons;

✓ the sources of the obligation to give reasons on request;

✓ some of the more important examples of when decision-makers come under an obligation to give reasons at the time of making a decision;

✓ the conditions for becoming entitled to be furnished with a statement of reasons under s 13 of the ADJR Act, together with the accompanying case law;

✓ the conditions for becoming entitled to be given a statement of reasons under s 28 of the AAT Act, together with the accompanying case law;

✓ the statutory functions and statutory contexts in which the courts may imply a statutory duty upon a decision-maker to give reasons;

✓ the content of the obligation to supply reasons under s 13 of the ADJR Act, s 28 of the AAT Act, s 43(2) of the AAT Act, and the various federal legislative provisions governed by s 25D of the Acts Interpretation Act;

✓ the legal consequences of a failure to give adequate reasons as required by law; the remedies available under the general law and under the statutory request regimes; and the discretion of a court as to the orders it may make;

✓ the evidentiary value of a statement of reasons;

✓ something of the impact of these requirements — for example, some evidence of the success or otherwise of the key legislative provisions, including evidence of how the requirements have generally been received by the legal, political and administrative cultures.

QUESTION 42

Two weeks ago, after a seizure by Customs officials, Mary Leong, a bookseller, was refused permission to import the book *Euthanasia: a Guide for Sufferers*. She wished to import the book so that she could sell it. The decision was made by an authorised person, the parliamentary secretary to the Attorney-General. The parliamentary secretary is a well-known opponent of euthanasia, who had been appointed by the Attorney-General under reg 4A(2A) to make decisions about importation of 'prohibited goods'. Mary wishes to be given:

(i)   reasons for the decision to refuse permission to import the book; and

(ii) reasons for the decision of the Attorney-General to give the parliamentary secretary the power to make the decision.

Advise Mary whether she is currently entitled to be given the reasons referred to, and (if not) whether there are any steps she may presently take to become so entitled.

Time allowed: 30 mins

Answer Plan

(i)   Entitlement to reasons for the decision to refuse permission to import the book.

• Outline of relevant law.

• Application of the law.

• Conclusion.

(ii) Entitlement to reasons for the decision of the Attorney-General to give the parliamentary secretary the power to make the decision.

• Overview of relevant law.

• Application of the law.

• Conclusion.

 Answer

(i)   Entitlement to reasons for the decision to refuse permission to import the book

Outline of relevant law

The law governing the right to reasons for a decision has a number of sources:

1.   express statutory obligations in particular statutes;

2.   implied statutory obligations in particular statutory contexts;

3. common law obligations arising in the special circumstances of the case; and

4. obligations arising from the federal statutory 'request' schemes:

(a) s 28 of the Administrative Appeals Tribunal Act 1975; and

(b) s 13 of the Administrative Decisions (Judicial Review) Act 1977.

Each is now examined.

Application of the law

First, there is no express legislative obligation upon the Attorney-General or an authorised person to give reasons at the time of the decision to refuse permission to import a prohibited good.

Second, is there an implied statutory obligation to give reasons at the time of making the decision? The indicia of such an obligation include:

* right of appeal to a court: *Attorney-General of NSW v Kennedy Miller Television Pty Ltd* (1998) 43 NSWLR 729 at 734–5; *Yung v Adams* (1997) 80 FCR 453 at 481–2; upheld *Adams v Yung* (1998) 83 FCR 248;

* substantial sums at stake: *Kennedy Miller Television Pty Ltd* at 737;

* workability of any duty: *Kennedy Miller Television Pty Ltd* at 737;

* consideration of written documents: *Yung* at 482;

* decision-making body is chaired by present or former judge: *Yung* at 481;

* livelihood is in jeopardy: *Coope v Iuliano* (1996) 65 SASR 405 at 408 (dicta);

* the duty of the decision-maker, being an appellate body, to correct error: *Campbelltown City Council v Vegan* [2006] NSWCA 284 at [26];

* the decision-maker's function is judicial in the sense that it involves the application of a statutory test by which legal rights are determined: *Vegan* at [109].

But the difficulty of pursuing judicial review in the absence of a statement of reasons is not sufficient justification: *Vegan* at [106].

In Mary's case there is no legislative right of appeal to a court; substantial sums are not at stake; the decision is not preceded by written documents and decisions; the decision-maker is not a judge or former judge; her livelihood is not in jeopardy; the decision-maker is not an appellate body bound to correct error; and the function is not judicial. A consideration of the indicative factors therefore suggests that a court would not imply a duty to give reasons at the time of making the decision.

Third, the decision-maker is not obliged, pursuant to a duty to accord Mary procedural fairness, to give reasons. There are no special circumstances which might require reasons to be given.

Mary does not therefore have a present entitlement to be given reasons for the decision.

Fourth, I next consider her entitlement under the request schemes. As the AAT Act scheme takes priority over the ADJR Act scheme (ADJR Act s 13(11)(a)), it is sensible to examine first Mary's entitlement under the AAT Act scheme. If there is an entitlement under this regime, there is no need to examine any entitlement under the ADJR Act scheme. If there is no entitlement under the AAT Act scheme, the ADJR Act scheme will be examined.

The right of a person to be given, under s 28 of the AAT Act, a statement of reasons for a decision is subject to five main conditions:

1. the decision is reviewable by the AAT: s 28(1);

2. the person requesting the statement is a person who is entitled to apply to the tribunal for a review of the decision: s 28(1);

3. the person requests the decision-maker to give him or her a statement of reasons: s 28(1);

4. the request is made within the time limits set out in s 28(1A); and

5. the applicant is not precluded from making the request by s 28(4), by reason that she has already been furnished with a statement.

In addition, rights may be limited under s 28(2), (3), (3A).

Each of the above conditions is now examined.

The first condition is satisfied because the decision of the parliamentary secretary is reviewable by the tribunal under reg 4A(4)(a) of the Customs (Prohibited Imports) Regulations.

The second condition is satisfied because Mary is entitled to apply to the tribunal for a review of the decision. She is so entitled because she is a bookseller and her financial interests are directly affected by the refusal.

The third condition will be satisfied if she takes the step of making a request.

The fourth condition will be satisfied if Mary complies with the time limit. (If Mary does not comply there is no obligation to comply with the request.) We are not told if the decision was furnished in writing to Mary. If it was (as is likely), the request must be made within two weeks from today, as the time limit is 28 days from the day on which the document setting out the terms of the decision is furnished to the applicant. If the decision was not furnished in writing to Mary, the time limit is simply a 'reasonable time after the decision was made'.

The fifth condition appears to be satisfied as there is no information to hand which suggests that she is precluded by s 28(4).

Conclusion

Mary is entitled to be given a statement of reasons under s 28 of the AAT Act, provided she makes a request and complies with the applicable time limit for doing so.

(ii) Entitlement to reasons for the decision of the Attorney-General to give the parliamentary secretary the power to make the decision

Overview of relevant law

For the reasons given in answer (i) above, it is necessary to examine the request regimes. On this occasion, the right to be given reasons set out in s 28 of the AAT Act 1975 is not applicable, since the decision of the Attorney-General to give the parliamentary secretary the power to make the decision is not reviewable by the AAT. It is not reviewable as no provision is made in legislation for such review as required by s 25 of the AAT Act.

The question then is: does Mary have a right to be given reasons under s 13 of the ADJR Act? The main conditions by which a person becomes entitled to be given a statement of reasons under s 13 are:

1. the decision is a 'decision to which this section applies': s 13(1) (elaborated below);

2. the person requests the decision-maker to furnish him or her with a statement of reasons;

3. the request is made by a person who is entitled to make an application for an order of review under s 5 in relation to the decision: s 13(1); and

4. the request is made within the time limit set out in s 13(5).

The first condition, that the relevant decision is a 'decision to which this section applies' is elaborated on in s 13 (8), (11). Section 13(8) provides that regulations under the Act may provide that a decision is *not* a decision to which the section applies; see ADJR Regulations 1985 reg 2A (only one class of decisions to date).

Section 13(11) is more detailed. It defines a 'decision to which this section applies', prima facie, to mean 'a decision to which this Act applies'. That phrase, in turn, is defined in s 3(1) as, in summary, requiring the decision to be:

• a 'decision' as defined;

• of an administrative character; and

• made under an enactment.

Further, decisions of the Governor-General or a decision falling within Sch 1 are excluded under s 3(1).

But, even if a decision is a 'decision to which this Act applies', s 13(11) excludes from the ambit of a 'decision to which this section applies' the following:

- a decision in relation to which s 28 of the AAT Act applies: s 13(11)(a);
- a decision that includes, or is accompanied by, a statement of reasons: s 13(11)(b);
- a decision included in any of the classes of decision set out in Sch 2: s 13(11)(c).

Application of the law

If one of the essential conditions in the scheme is clearly not satisfied, Mary will not be entitled. After browsing the relevant legal framework, in Mary's case it is simpler and more convenient to consider whether the decision is caught by the exclusion in Sch 2, para (t). (If the decision is excluded it is irrelevant whether it would otherwise have fallen within the s 13 regime.)

Paragraph (t) relevantly refers to:

decisions relating to:

...

> (iii) the making of appointments under an enactment or to an office established by, or under, an enactment.

This exclusion comprises three main elements:

1. 'decisions';
2. 'relating to the making of appointments';
3. 'under an enactment' or 'to an office established by, or under, an enactment'.

We shall assume the first element is satisfied. (If that element is *not* satisfied, that is, the decision to appoint the parliamentary secretary is not a relevant 'decision', the decision under consideration would fall outside the s 13 regime altogether.)

The second element is satisfied. The authorisation of the parliamentary secretary in this case comes about because of an appointment, as explicitly made clear in the Customs (Prohibited Imports) Regulations:

> (2A)The Attorney-General may, by instrument in writing, *appoint* a person to be an authorized person for the purposes of subregulation (2). (emphasis added)

The singular appointment of the parliamentary secretary is a decision 'relating to the making of appointments' under para (t)(iii). It would be wrong to argue that the plural ('appointments') in para (t)(iii) does not include the singular ('appointment') in this case. Section 13(11)(c) provides for the singular decision; it refers to '*a decision* included in any of the classes of decision set out in Schedule 2' (emphasis added). There is therefore no need to resort to the presumption in s 23(b) of the Acts Interpretation Act 1901 (Cth) that, unless the contrary intention appears, words in the plural number include the singular.

The third element in the exclusion in para (t)(iii) of Sch 2 is also satisfied. The appointment is made under an enactment because the definition of 'enactment' in s 3(1) of the ADJR Act includes 'regulations' and the appointment in this case is under the Customs (Prohibited Imports) Regulations.

Conclusion

It is clear that the decision to appoint the parliamentary secretary is excluded from the right to reasons scheme under the ADJR Act. Mary is therefore not entitled to be given reasons for this decision.

 # Examiner's Comments

The answer to the first part of the problem focuses on the request regime under s 28 of the AAT Act. This scheme was crucial on the facts. To give a comprehensive consideration of her present entitlements the answer also briefly discussed the implied statutory obligation to give reasons. It would not have been necessary to discuss the implied obligation to obtain a good mark. But students who did would be rewarded.

The second part of the problem involves students applying Sch 2 to the ADJR Act. Students need to appreciate that the scheme for reasons under the ADJR Act is a complex one. As Gibbs CJ explained in the *Osmond* case (*Osmond v Public Service Board of NSW* (1986) 159 CLR 656 at 670), approving a comment by Glass JA, the legislation is a 'finely tuned system'. Not only does it include the broad principles of reviewability under s 5, and standing to sue under the ADJR Act; an additional, essential part of the scheme is the scope of the scheme fleshed out by the *detail* of Sch 2 of that Act. (Note: because the right to reasons involves a number of key administrative law concepts, it is an area of law that appeals to examiners.)

In both parts of the question the complex legislative framework needed to be 'navigated'. It is always easier to apply the law if it is first set out clearly and logically. Examiners will always reward a student who outlines the law. A student will not pass a law problem merely by setting out the relevant legal framework, but will gain marks for doing so even if there are errors in applying the law.

However, having navigated one's way to the relevant law, both parts of the problem, but especially the second part, lacked any real doubt about the legal position on the facts. What does this tell us about the nature of administrative law — that on occasion it is plain and beyond dispute? It is worth recalling Question 5 in Chapter 1 and the discussion of legalism and other theories of the judicial role in administrative law. The question answered above would appear to be, in the language of the Chief Justice, an instance of 'the ordinary day-by-day application of statutory rules and settled legal principles'. It is important to appreciate such ordinary applications so that the contested applications of administrative law can be put in perspective.

Common Errors To Avoid

- Not setting out a clear summary of the statutory scheme which clarifies the decision-making path a student adviser needs to take.

- In respect of s 13 of the ADJR Act, interpreting the requirement that the applicant is 'a person who is entitled to make an application under s 5' to mean a person who is entitled to relief under s 16. A person who is entitled to make an application under s 5 is 'a person who is aggrieved' by the decision: s 5(1). Thus, an applicant under s 13 must have interests which are adversely affected by the decision: s 3(1) (a special interest). Such an applicant does not have to make out a case for challenging the decision, that is, make out a ground of review or a basis for relief.

- Not examining the detailed, 'boring' parts of the ADJR Act reasons scheme: Sch 2.

QUESTION 43

Mary Leong (whom we met in Question 42, p 293) decides to appeal, to the AAT, the decision by the parliamentary secretary to the Attorney-General refusing permission to import the book *Euthanasia: A Guide for Sufferers*. The appeal is heard by a John W Smith, a new member of the tribunal.

John W Smith's reasons for decision are as follows:

1. Mary Leong has appealed the refusal by the parliamentary secretary to the Attorney-General to grant permission to import the book *Euthanasia: a Guide for Sufferers* by Dr Harold Donaldson. I am informed that the first draft of this book was titled *Euthanasia: a User's Guide*.

2. I have read this book. The book contains the following chapters:

   Foreword by Dr Erika Stunna

   1. Do You Want to Die?
   2. The Dutch Experience of Euthanasia
   3. The Criminal Law in Australia Relating to Euthanasia and How to Get Around It
   4. How to Find a Sympathetic Doctor
   5. What Methods are Most Efficacious?

6.   Remedies in Case It Doesn't Work

7.   Cold Feet? Alternatives to Euthanasia

3.   The relevant legislation is the Customs (Prohibited Imports) Regulations 1956 (Cth) reg 4A, the relevant extracts of which are as follows:

(1)   In this regulation, unless the contrary intention appears:

... *publication* means any book, paper, magazine, film, computer game or other written or pictorial matter.

(1A)   This regulation applies to publications and any other goods, that:

...

(d)   promote, incite or instruct in matters of crime or violence; or

(2)   The importation of goods to which this regulation applies is prohibited unless a permission, in writing, to import the goods has been granted by the Attorney-General or a person authorized by the Attorney-General for the purposes of this subregulation.

(2AA)   In considering whether to grant a permission under subregulation (2), the Attorney-General or the person authorised by the Attorney-General is to have regard to:

(a)   the purposes for which the goods are to be imported; and

(b)   the extent to which the person to whom any permission to import the goods would be granted conducts activities of an artistic or educational, or of a cultural or scientific, nature to which the goods relate; and

(c)   the reputation of the person referred to in paragraph (b), both generally and in relation to an activity referred to in that paragraph; and

(d)   the ability of that person to meet conditions that may be imposed under subregulation (3) in relation to the goods; and

(e)   any other relevant matters.

(2A)   The Attorney-General may, by instrument in writing, appoint a person to be an authorized person for the purposes of subregulation (2).

...

(4)   Application may be made to the Administrative Appeals Tribunal for review of a decision of the Attorney-General under subregulation (2):

(a)   refusing to grant a permission; or

(b)   granting a permission subject to conditions by the person to whom the permission was granted subject to conditions.

4.   The issue for determination in this case is 'whether the decision was the correct or preferable one on the material before the tribunal': *Drake v Minister for Immigration and Ethnic Affairs* (1979) 24 ALR 577 at 589 per Bowen CJ and Deane J.

5. I have given serious consideration to this matter including the considerations set out in reg 4A(2AA) of the Customs (Prohibited Imports) Regulations.

6. But in the end I agree with the submissions of counsel for the parliamentary secretary that permission ought not be granted.

7. This is principally because, having regard to reg 4A(2AA)(a), the purposes for which the goods are to be imported are to assist criminal elements in the medical profession. This is apparent from Chapter 3. The following is an illustrative and typical passage from Chapter 3:

> You need to know that the criminal law does not support euthanasia advocates. The criminal law is wrong, wrong, wrong in my view. The criminal law constitutes an obstacle for those who wish to engage in euthanasia, but not for the sufferers. Despite the criminal law, there is something you can do about it: you can see a sympathetic doctor.

The bookseller argued that I ought to regard the 'purposes for which the goods were imported' as financial in her case, but this is facile. The nature of the work must also be considered.

8. In relation to reg 4A(2AA)(b), the bookseller also argued that she conducted activities of an 'educational ... nature' and pointed to Chapter 7 of the work as evidence that the work was intended to be broadly educational. I reject this.

9. Regulation 4A(2AA)(c) was only faintly raised in argument, if at all, by the bookseller (the tribunal was told that she was a successful bookseller), and accordingly it carries negligible weight in this case.

10. I apologise for the brevity of these reasons, but I have many cases currently before me which are urgent and expedition is a statutory objective of the tribunal. The decision is all-important.

11. I must confess that when I began to write these reasons I did not know how to decide this case.

12. I hope these reasons are of benefit to the parties and are appeal-proof.

13. I thank my associate for writing a draft of these reasons.

Answer the following questions:

(i) What are the general principles for assessing whether there has been a breach of s 43(2) of the AAT Act? State the principles in terms of: (a) the obligations upon tribunal members; and (b) the obligations upon courts scrutinising a statement of reasons.

(ii) Would points 5 and 6 be adequate in themselves?

(iii) In points 7–10, has there been a breach of s 43(2)?

(iv) Do you agree with the approach to the preparation of reasons described in points 10–13?

Time allowed: 1 hour

Answer Plan

(i) Relevant general principles.

- Obligations upon decision-makers.
- Obligations on courts reviewing a statement of reasons.

(ii) Whether points 5 and 6 would be adequate in themselves.

(iii) Whether, in points 7–10, there has been a breach of s 43(2) of the AAT Act.

- Point 7.
- Point 8.
- Point 9.
- Point 10.

(iv) Whether one agrees with the approach to the preparation of reasons described in points 10–13.

- Point 10.
- Point 11.
- Point 12.
- Point 13.

 Answer

(i)   Relevant general principles

Obligations upon decision-makers

The obligations upon decision-makers are stated in two different ways. There are, on the one hand, positive requirements: obligations which must be fulfilled. On the other hand, there are pronouncements as to what is not required or what does not amount to a breach.

Positively speaking, the decision-maker must:

- state the basis of the decision: *Soulemezis v Dudley (Holdings) Pty Ltd* (1987) 10 NSWLR 247 at 279 per McHugh JA, cited in *Cypressvale Pty Ltd v Retail Shop Leases Tribunal* [1996] 2 Qd R 462 at 476–7;
- 'deal with the substantial points that have been raised': *Re Poyser & Mills' Arbitration* [1964] 2 QB 467 at 478 per Megaw J, cited in *Re Palmer and Minister for the Capital Territory* (1978) 1 ALD 183 at 193;
- give at least the fundamental reasons: *Cypressvale* at 477;
- give an explanation of the reasoning process which goes further than vague general statements and unexplained conclusions: *Cypressvale* at 477. The duty 'cannot be discharged by the use of vague general words which are not sufficient to bring to the mind

of the recipient a clear understanding of why his or her request is being refused': *Elliott v London Borough of Southwark* [1976] 2 All ER 781 at 791 per James LJ, cited in *Re Palmer* at 193–4. The decision-maker must explain why one conclusion is preferred to another: *Campbelltown City Council v Vegan* [2006] NSWCA 284 at [121] per Basten JA with whom Handley and McColl JJA generally agreed;

- express the reasons in 'plain language intelligible to a layman': *Re Palmer* at 196;

- give the actual reasons for the decision: *Re Palmer* at 196;

- include the 'findings on material questions of fact and a reference to the evidence or other material on which those findings were based': AAT Act s 43(2B); *Campbelltown City Council v Vegan* at [121];

- give reasons such as to 'enable a person aggrieved to say, in effect: "Even though I may not agree with it, I now understand why the decision went against me"': *Ansett Transport Industries (Operations) Pty Ltd v Wraith* (1983) 48 ALR 500 at 507.

These positive requirements are tempered by general pronouncements in which the courts attempt to formulate a duty which is realistic — that is, achievable. This has resulted in statements of what is not required or what does not amount to a breach of the obligation:

- 'A line by line refutation of every submission of a party' is not required: *Minister for Immigration and Multicultural Affairs v Yusuf* (2001) 206 CLR 323 at [117] per Kirby J. Nor is a detailed exposition of every aspect of the evidence and the arguments, or an intellectual dissertation upon the chain of reasoning required: *Cypressvale* at 477.

- A tribunal is not bound to set out findings that it did not make, by reference to some objective or external standard of 'materiality'. As McHugh, Gummow and Hayne JJ put it in *Yusuf* at [68] (with whom Gleeson CJ agreed at [1]):

    A requirement to set out findings and reasons focuses upon the subjective thought processes of the decision-maker ... [In that context, the decision-maker is only obliged to] set out its findings on those questions of fact which *it* considered to be material to the decision which it made and to the reasons *it* had for reaching that decision. (emphasis in original)

- There is no failure where the tribunal 'omits to make an express finding about a material fact which was not in issue because it was conceded, expressly or impliedly, by the way in which the case was conducted' or where the tribunal 'omits to discuss a contention of a party which has no relevance to the process of reasoning leading to its decision': *Commonwealth v (K C) Smith* (1989) 18 ALD 224 at 225.

- In matters which involve an expert decision-maker making a professional evaluation and judgment a duty to give precise explanations may not arise as it may not be possible for the decision-maker to give such explanations: *Campbelltown City Council v Vegan* at [122], [128] per Basten JA.

- The obligation to give reasons is not breached because of a mere 'looseness in the language, nor ... unhappy phrasing': *Collector of Customs v Pozzolanic Enterprises Pty Ltd* (1993) 43 FCR 280 at 287, approved in *Minister for Immigration and Ethnic Affairs v Wu Shan Liang* (1996) 185 CLR 259 at 272.

- 'Wrong' reasoning must not be treated as a failure to give reasons, for 'a court ... must beware of turning a review of the reasons of the decision-maker upon proper principles into a reconsideration of the merits of the decision': *Wu Shan Liang* at 272.

Obligations on courts reviewing a statement of reasons

The obligations *on courts* reviewing a statement of reasons are two-fold:

1. Courts must avoid using the obligation to set out the findings on any material questions of fact as a basis for exposing 'all findings of fact, or the generality of them, to judicial review [for that would] bring about a radical change in the relationship between the executive and judicial branches of government': *Australian Broadcasting Tribunal v Bond* (1990) 170 CLR 321 at 341, approved in *Yusuf* at [63].

2. More generally, the courts must not engage in over-zealous judicial review: 'the reasons for the decision ... are not to be construed minutely and finely with an eye keenly attuned to the perception of error': *Pozzolanic* at 287, approved in *Wu Shan Liang* at 272.

(ii)   *Whether points 5 and 6 would be adequate in themselves*

While the law is imprecise on how far a decision-maker must go — statements above such as 'the basis of the decision' (*Soulemezis*), 'at least the fundamental reasons' (*Cypressvale*), 'to understand why the decision went against me' (*Ansett Transport Industries*) are common — it is at least clear that it is *not* sufficient that the decision-maker pay lip service to the statutory criteria mentioned in point 5. The decision-maker must explain *why* the statute supports the ultimate holding.

The decision-maker must seek to make the party 'understand why the decision went against me' (*Ansett*), must 'deal with the substantial points that have been raised' (*Re Poyser*), and must explain why one conclusion is preferred to another: *Vegan*. It is therefore not sufficient, in point 6, simply to state agreement with one side or another. If Ms Leong is to understand the reasoning process, she needs to be told *why* the decision-maker agrees with one side rather than the other.

(iii) Whether there has been a breach of s 43(2) (points 7–10)

Point 7

Point 7 of the reasons, which deals with reg 4A(2AA)(a), seems to be more a case of bad reasons rather than an inadequacy in the expression of reasons. The reasons are not unintelligible. The decision-maker has plainly paraphrased the statute ('assist criminal elements'), whereas the statute is clearly more precise about the connection between the crime or violence and the likely effects of the work. It refers to 'promote, incite or instruct', which is qualitatively different to 'assist'. This is more than a case of loose language or unhappy phrasing (*Pozzolanic*), because there is no evidence elsewhere of the statutory prescriptions being followed. The passage as a whole does not show that the decision-maker was thinking about the statutory prescriptions regarding crime or violence. Indeed, they are not necessarily supportive of any 'promotion, incitement or instruction', since moral opposition to the criminal law is not the same as promotion of euthanasia, and the conclusion that you should see a sympathetic doctor is ambiguous.

If there are substantive errors, as there seem to be, then the relevant ground is not a breach of s 43(2), but a claim that the decision was *ultra vires*, for this avoids intruding on the merits of the decision.

Point 8

With respect to reg 4A(2AA)(b), the decision-maker has not adequately presented the reasoning process, because his reasons do not allow the aggrieved person to say 'I now understand why the decision went against me': *Ansett* at 507. The decision-maker has referred only to the case which was presented (but rejected). The reasoning is effectively in the form of 'unexplained conclusions': *Cypressvale* at 477.

Point 9

While there is a passing reference to the evidence, there are no *findings* on essential matters set out in reg 4A(2AA)(c). Is the omission telling here? On the one hand, the legislature has taken the trouble to identify reputation as a mandatory consideration in reg 4A(2AA)(c). Accordingly, the 'reasoning process' ought normally to be evident. On the other hand, the decision indicates that the matter was in this respect faintly raised (at best). This suggests the matter was not truly in issue and the principle in *Smith's* case would excuse the tribunal: that there is no failure where the decision-maker omits to make an express finding about a material fact which was not in issue because, by the way the case was conducted, it was conceded, expressly or impliedly.

Point 10

The tribunal has stated that the decision of the tribunal is 'all-important' in the context of a perceived need for brevity. If one were reading these reasons 'minutely and finely with an eye keenly attuned to the perception of error' (*Wu Shan Liang* at 272), one might argue that this statement wholly misunderstands the requirement to give reasons, which is an account of 'the reasoning process', and not just the decision. However, since the decision-maker does give some reasons, it is likely that this would be treated as mere 'looseness in the language' (*Pozzolanic*) arrived at by too much emphasis on the attainment of brevity.

(iv) Whether one agrees with the approach to the preparation of reasons in points 10–13

Point 10

The decision-maker exaggerates the duty to be expeditious. While expedition is a statutory duty, so too is the preparation of proper reasons — which must go beyond revealing the final conclusions.

Point 11

This is not a helpful way to write, because the author cannot indicate the overall structure of the reasons from the outset. The reader is left in the dark unnecessarily for too long.

More seriously, the statement is ambiguous, and could imply that some of the initial reasons given might not be the ultimate reasons for the decision: see point 12 below.

Point 12

A decision-maker ought not write reasons to make them appeal-proof because, as far as possible, they must be the actual reasons for the decision (*Re Palmer*) — not an artificial construct influenced by purposes which border on the improper. However, it is not clear whether the need to make the reasons appeal-proof has been an objective or is just a naive hope the decision-maker has referred to in passing at the last moment.

Point 13

It ought not be the role of an associate to write a draft of the reasons, since this takes too much away from the tribunal, in whom the statute has reposed the function of reason writing.

Examiner's Comments

The preparation of reasons is an important issue for administrative law students to grasp. While the focus in administrative law is on executive decision-making, the same general principles apply to the giving of reasons by courts and legal advisers. This topic is thus an opportunity to further basic legal skills, the foundations of which are laid in introductory skills subjects.

The first part of the question asked students to set out relevant principles of law. This is a basic but underrated intellectual task. Of course, students will receive guidance from various quarters including lectures and secondary sources, but it is nevertheless a skill that students need to acquire. Setting out the law involves far more than note taking and more than summarising. It involves careful reading, analysis and synthesis. The statement of the obligations upon decision-makers in the model answer is a fine example. The reference to the case law shows a close and attentive reading of the primary sources. The arrangement of the obligations upon decision-makers into two contrasting sets of principles, 'positive' requirements and principles by which the courts temper those requirements, is illuminating and persuasive. The resulting synthesis clarifies that there are actually two *general* principles at work in this area: the principle that administrators have positive obligations which cannot be avoided by a pretence of giving 'reasons'; and the principle that some allowance must be made for the fact that it is an administrator's reasons which are the subject of the present obligation.

The remainder of the question tests students' ability to apply the law applying to decision-makers. The question involves one of the basic differences between judicial review for breach of the obligation to give reasons, and merits review. If a court could engage in merits review of a statement of reasons, the reviewer would effectively be entitled to substitute their judgment for that of the original decision-maker. However, with judicial review, the function remains supervisory, and hence review of the duty to 'give reasons ... for its decision' is not a free-for-all. The Federal Court has pointed to this by stating that review of the failure to give reasons is for 'inadequacy in the expression of reasons'.

The discussion of the judge's associate's role in Question 43, question (iv) is sound: the associate's role ought not involve reason writing. But it should be noted that the role is not insignificant in the process of judicial decision-making as a whole. An associate's main tasks in relation to the preparation of reasons are:

1. research — discovering or obtaining relevant law for study by the decision-maker;

2. preparing a draft of non-contentious aspects such as agreed facts and relevant legislation; and

3. checking the draft thoroughly for any factual or legal inaccuracies or slips, as well as for clarity of expression and structure.

Common Errors to Avoid

- Not being aware of the relevant legal principles.
- Assuming that an obligation to give reasons requires the decision-maker to do more than record what was found; for instance, to *make* findings it did not in fact make. In other words, confusing the obligation to give a satisfactory *expression* of reasons with the obligation to avoid making substantive legal errors.

■ Not understanding that the way in which a case is presented affects what the decision-maker has to say in his or her reasons.

 QUESTION 44

In *Minister for Immigration and Ethnic Affairs v Pochi* (1980) 4 ALD 139 at 156, Deane J said that:

> The Administrative Appeals Tribunal Act 1975 ... did ... effect a quiet revolution in regard to [decisions subject to review]. The Act lowered a narrow bridge over the moat of executive silence in that, subject to limited exceptions, it conferred upon a person entitled to apply to the tribunal for a review of a decision, the right to be supplied with a statement ... giving the reasons for the decision (s 28).

Discuss. In your answer refer to one or more cases concerning the right to be given reasons under the AAT Act or other legislation.

Time allowed: 1 hour

Answer Plan

(i) Introduction.

(ii) What was 'the moat of executive silence'?

(iii) How s 28 of the AAT Act 'lowered a narrow bridge'.

(iv) Whether, and if so, s 28 effected 'a quiet revolution'.

- Extending the right of an aggrieved person to obtain a statement of reasons.
- Revolutionising judicial and merits review.
- Counter-arguments.

(v) Case study: *Soldatow v Australia Council.*

(vi) Conclusion.

 Answer

(i)   Introduction

The statement by Deane J raises three matters for discussion relating to the right to be given reasons for a decision:

1. what is meant by 'the moat of executive silence';

2. how s 28 of the Administrative Appeals Tribunal Act 'lowered a narrow bridge'; and

3. whether, and if so, s 28 effected a 'quiet revolution'.

(ii)   What was 'the moat of executive silence'?

Deane J assumed, aptly, that before the Commonwealth administrative law reforms of the 1970s and early 1980s 'executive silence' was largely the rule. There was an administrative and legal tradition of secrecy. At an administrative level there was 'an almost obsessive concern with official secrecy': I Thynne and J Goldring, *Accountability and Control*, Law Book Company, Sydney, 1987, p 120. Common law and statute law were weak in that, outside of litigation, they gave no right of access to personal files or to government policy, and no general right to be given reasons for administrative decisions.

Indeed, both the law and administrative conventions were strongly opposed to the giving out of information which was not otherwise required to be released. The government's information was regarded as the government's property: Australian Law Reform Commission and Administrative Review Council, *Freedom of Information*, AGPS, Canberra, 1995, [2.6], in R Douglas, *Douglas and Jones's Administrative Law*, 4th ed, Federation Press, Sydney, 2002, p 91. The convention of Cabinet solidarity and collective ministerial responsibility for Cabinet decisions meant that Ministers were forbidden to reveal Cabinet discussions. The public service operated according to conventions of anonymity, was tenured and not party-political; it was the Minister who was politically responsible. Many statutory provisions forbade disclosure, and officers releasing information without clear legislative authority additionally might be liable for breach of confidence or for defamation: R Douglas, *Administrative Law*, 2nd ed, LexisNexis Butterworths, Sydney, 2004, [14.1.3].

(iii)   How s 28 of the AAT Act 'lowered a narrow bridge'

The right set out in s 28 is limited. The right only extends to decisions which are subject to review by the AAT: s 28(1). Since many Commonwealth decisions are not subject to review, the AAT right is far from being universal. However, his Honour did qualify the claim of a quiet revolution by saying that it was in respect of the decisions subject to review. One may also note that most of the residual decisions not caught by the AAT scheme were subsequently caught by the scheme in s 13 of the ADJR Act.

Flowing from the requirement that the applicant be a person entitled to apply for a review of the decision concerned, is a second important limitation of the AAT right: the person seeking the statement must have standing to apply for a review of the decision. Since the purpose of the right to reasons is to satisfy the grievance of knowing why the decision went against me (*Ansett Transport Industries (Operations) Pty Ltd v Wraith* (1983) 48 ALR 500 at 507), the standing requirement does not count terribly against Deane J's claim.

Under the AAT Act there are, additionally, public interest grounds for limiting the right. These relate to security appeals (s 28(1AAA)), prejudice to the security, defence or international relations of Australia (s 28(2)(a)), the disclosure of the deliberations of Cabinet (s 28(2)(b)), and grounds which come within public interest immunity: s 28(2)(c). Such cases can be expected to be rare.

There are two further limitations of a practical nature. A person must request a statement of reasons: s 28(1). And the time for applying for a statement is short if the applicant has been given the decision in writing: only 28 days from the day the decision was given to the applicant: s 28(1A).

(iv) Whether, and if so, s 28 of the AAT Act effected 'a quiet revolution'

The statutory duty was revolutionary in two main respects:

1. It greatly extended the right of an aggrieved person to obtain a statement of reasons.

2. It greatly facilitated judicial and merits review.

Extending the right of an aggrieved person to obtain a statement of reasons

At common law there was (and is) no general duty on administrative decision-makers to give reasons: *Public Service Board of New South Wales v Osmond* (1986) 159 CLR 656. The granting of rights to request reasons under the AAT Act effected a near reversal of that common law position, at least where a request for reasons is made.

Though not a universal duty, the statutory duty created by the AAT Act impacts widely on federal administration. The right is tied to the decisions which are reviewable: s 28(1). From modest beginnings in a Schedule to the AAT Act, the AAT's jurisdiction has grown steadily. It currently has jurisdiction to review administrative decisions under approximately 400 different Commonwealth enactments: Creyke and McMillan, 2005, [3.2.13]. The right to reasons has grown likewise.

The obligation in the AAT Act was facilitated by the ease with which a statement could be applied for. A notice in writing must be sent to the decision-maker: s 28(1). The decision and the decision-maker must be specified. There is no fee.

The drafter of the AAT Act spelt out with some care and in some detail what the statement of reasons must contain. Not only must the decision and the reasons be set out; the decision-maker must also set out the findings on material questions of fact, and refer to the evidence or other material on which those findings were based: s 28(1). The statement is therefore far from being a short form requirement to give the principal grounds or chief conclusions.

The Act provides means of enforcement to ensure that the 'revolution' was not a mere paper right. 'Rights' without means of enforcement are not worthy of that name. Where a dispute has arisen, the tribunal may decide, under s 28(1AC), whether a person is entitled to a statement of reasons. Further, if the aggrieved person thinks a statement is inadequate, the tribunal may be asked to make an appropriate declaration: s 28(5). And if a decision-maker refuses to give a statement or limits a statement on public interest grounds under s 28(2), this decision would be judicially reviewable.

Revolutionising judicial and merits review

The statutory duty also revolutionised the ability of courts and tribunals to correct administrative error. Before the advent of statement of reasons courts were often unable to correct error because they were unable to assume from the absence of reasons that the decision was affected by legal error. It is true that in a famous case, *Padfield v Minister of Agriculture, Fisheries and Food* [1968] AC 997, the House of Lords had not ruled out the possibility. Lord Pearce held at 1053–4 that:

> If all the prima facie reasons seem to point in favour of [the decision-maker] taking a certain course to carry out the intentions of Parliament in respect of a power which it has given him in that regard, and he gives no reason whatever for taking a contrary course, the court may infer that he has no good reason and that he is not using the power given by Parliament to carry out its intentions.

A statutory obligation supplied a more informed basis for inferring whether a decision was affected by legal error.

Counter-arguments

Some qualifications should be made to the above arguments. The statement by Deane J refers only to s 28 of the AAT Act, but this Act was quickly followed by the general duty to give reasons upon request in s 13 of the ADJR Act. Although the ADJR Act operates only where the s 28 AAT Act right is not available (s 13(11)(a)) it operates generally in respect of final administrative decisions made under an enactment, whereas the AAT Act applies only to AAT-reviewable decisions. Other laws have also played a fundamental role in requiring administrators to give reasons. They include the ad hoc requirements on administrators to give reasons at the time of every decision or every adverse decision, for example, s 43(2) of the AAT Act, s 26 of the Freedom of Information Act 1982 (Cth) and s 47(3) of the Australian Citizenship Act 2007 (Cth).

A more fundamental qualification is that because the right is *upon request*, this must raise suspicions that the decision-maker might seek to 'doctor' the statement by *ex-post facto* justifications.

(v)   Case study: Soldatow v Australia Council

Soldatow v Australia Council (1991) 22 ALD 750 is a good illustration of the claims made by Deane J. In this case a writer was not awarded a writer's fellowship by a committee of the Australia Council. The writer sought and received a statement of reasons. The reasons stated that 'Mr Soldatow's application was considered not to have sufficient merit to be rewarded a grant', and stated that the deliberations took into account budgetary limitations, the genre of the works, the subject of the applications, the desirability of achieving a geographically equitable distribution of grants, and the desirability of achieving an equal distribution of grants between male and female applicants. The writer was dissatisfied with the statement, and subsequently sought the intervention of the Federal Court under s 13(7) of the ADJR Act.

The Federal Court (Davies J) found the statement was not adequate and ordered that a statement of reasons complying with s 13(1) be delivered. The court examined who authorised the statement. It was critical of the fact that the statement was signed by members of the council who were not members of the committee to whom power of decision-making had been delegated. The court held that '[the] statement should express the reasons of the decision-maker, that is to say, of the committee which actually considered the matter and made the decision': at 753. Next, the court examined the substance of the statement. It held that the legislation required 'proper and adequate reasons which are intelligible, which deal with the substantial issues raised for determination and which expose the reasoning process adopted': at 750. It found that the statement did not do this because it was almost exclusively concerned with 'matters of a procedural nature': at 751. What the committee did was essentially to refer to considerations so general there was a 'dearth of explanation about the reasoning process ... [regarding] Mr Soldatow's application and why it was refused': at 753.

The case illustrates vividly how an executive body attempted to maintain a silence over its decision-making process in relation to individual applications for grants. The case demonstrates the teeth in the federal request-based reasons regimes. The Federal Court imposed quite rigorous (but fair) requirements upon the council, rejecting as adequate a simple allusion to the general considerations which applied equally to all applicants. However, the revolution obviously had not reached the Australia Council!

(vi) Conclusion

The sentiments of Deane J regarding the right to request reasons in s 28 of the AAT Act are worthy of general support. They colourfully and accurately express the background, nature and effect of the reasons law.

Examiner's Comments

In form, this question is a classic examination essay question. From the examiner's perspective the metaphor in the statement of Deane J creates a nice ambiguity or 'space' for discussion.

The ability to discuss, in a scholarly way, matters arising in a discipline is a generic skill which needs to be mastered by all university graduates. Some students misunderstand what scholarly discussion involves. An essay question which requires a student to 'Discuss' a statement is not an opportunity to engage in a frolic of one's own: rewriting the statement or talking only about the general topic raised by the statement. Below are four tips for answering these kinds of questions and an indication of how the model answer benefited from this approach.

First, the student should identify *what matters* are to be discussed. Breaking the general task down into particular tasks makes the task manageable and ensures attention to detail. In the model answer, a close reading of the statement by Deane J revealed three matters for discussion.

Second, the student needs to *pose questions* about the identified matters. 'Discuss' is open-ended. Not all questions can be asked. What questions are put is to a large extent up to the student. But this does not mean that the examiner does not take account of the kind of questions asked. The questions asked will themselves reveal a student's awareness of the topic. The student should raise questions which will enable him or her to demonstrate a mastery over the identified matters. In the model answer the questions are posed in the headings.

Third, in the course of addressing the questions posed (the discussion), the student should explore the possibility of being *critical* of the statement. This does not mean that a student must disagree with the statement. For one thing, to be 'critical' does not require a purely negative stance. Put simply, it means being open to evaluating the strengths and weaknesses of the statement. In the model answer the statement of Deane J that the AAT Act had effected a 'quiet revolution' is qualified.

Fourth, an answer to a 'Discuss' question needs to *conclude* the discussion by answering the questions posed and discussed. As a piece of writing an essay has a particular form; it is not a list of points. In the model answer the essay concludes by stating in what sense the statement of Deane J can be broadly supported.

If this structure is followed an answer to a 'Discuss' question will begin crisply and proceed logically. There will be no unnecessary, waffly background. The body of the answer will be well addressed to the statement to be discussed. The answers to the questions posed by the student (the conclusion) will leave the reader persuaded or at least satisfied by the response.

Finally, the model answer opted for a separate 'case study', but it would have been acceptable to have referred to the case in the course of the discussion.

Common Errors to Avoid

- Not distilling the matters to be discussed.
- Not posing questions in relation to the matters raised by the statement.
- Not directly referring to the statement's metaphors in the answer.
- Not commenting on all the crucial parts of the statement.
- Not exploring the possibility of being critical of the statement by Deane J.
- Writing an essay about right to reasons generally instead of addressing the precise terms of the statement.
- Summarising the illustrative case rather than relating the case to the statement by Deane J, that is, integrating it into the discussion.
- Not concluding the answer.

Chapter 15
Freedom of Information

Key Issues

Freedom of information, or 'FOI' as it is commonly called, has been described as an indispensable element in representative government: *Re Eccleston and Department of Family Services and Aboriginal and Islander Affairs* (1993) 1 QAR 60 at 86. FOI was established by the Freedom of Information Act 1982 (Cth) and equivalent State and Territory legislation. The two basic democratic justifications for the enactment of FOI legislation are the promotion of government accountability and the fostering of informed public participation in government: *Re Eccleston* at 83.

FOI is not a single right, but concerning access to, and amendment of, information in the hands of government. The principal rights conferred by the federal Act are:

* A general right of access to a document of an agency or an official document of a Minister: s 11. The right is subject to a number of exceptions.

* The obligation of the responsible Minister to publish certain information: a statement setting out the organisation and functions of the agency (s 8(1)(a)(i)); a statement of the categories of the documents that are maintained in the possession of the agency (s 8(1)(a)(iii)); and a statement of any information that needs to be available to the public concerning particular procedures of the agency in relation to obtaining access to documents: s 8(1)(a)(v).

* The obligation of the principal officer of an agency to make available, for inspection and purchase, documents that are used by the agency in making decisions, such as manuals containing guidelines and practices: s 9.

* The right to apply for an amendment or annotation to the record of personal information: Pt V.

Review arrangements, including complaints to the Ombudsman and independent merits review, are dealt with in Pt VI.

In the study of administrative law, emphasis is usually placed on the right of access to documents. A useful starting point is the statement of the conditions of entitlement set out in s 18 and related provisions. As a rough guide, the main conditions of entitlement (other than for personnel records, see s 15A) are that:

- a request is made: s 15(1);
- the request is in writing: s 15(2)(a);
- the request is for a 'document of an agency' or an 'official document of a Minister' (see s 4(1)), with the exception of:
  — certain documents of a court (s 5), a tribunal, authority or other body (s 6), the official secretary to the Governor-General (s 6A), or an eligible case manager: s 6B;
  — documents of agencies that are wholly or partly exempt: s 7 and Sch 2;
  — a document which is an exempt document (s 11(1) and Pt IV), although access to an exempt document is not prohibited: see s 14;
  — a document which is publicly available: s 12(1);
  — a document falling within s 13; and
  — a document upon which access is refused on other grounds: see, for example, ss 24 and 24A;
- the request provides such information concerning the document as is reasonably necessary to enable a responsible officer of the agency or the Minister to identify it: s 15(2)(b); and
- the request is accompanied by any fee payable under the regulations: s 15(2)(e).

In situations other than where access to personal records is sought, disputes often concern the issue of whether access to a document has been rightfully refused on workload grounds (s 24) or on a ground of exemption in Pt IV. Hence, students particularly need to be aware of the grounds for exemption. This includes the particular requirements and any exceptions specified in the Act.

A brief note about the depth of treatment of FOI is in order. With a substantial Act devoted to it, augmented by a considerable amount of case law, this topic is a potential unit of study on its own. Because of a crowded curriculum in administrative law units taught over one semester, the study of FOI in these units is usually severely reduced to allow time for other administrative law topics to be studied. It is customary to study the federal or State Act, together with a sample of the case law to illustrate general concerns of the Acts. This approach is reflected in the scope and treatment FOI receives in casebooks such as R Douglas, *Douglas and Jones's Administrative Law*, 5th ed, Federation Press, Sydney, 2006, ch 3, and R Creyke and J McMillan, *Control of Government Action: Text, Cases and Commentary*, LexisNexis Butterworths, Sydney, 2005, ch 18. The summary of key issues below, and the questions that follow, are accordingly drawn up on the assumption that administrative law students are expected to have studied the Act closely and a sample of the case law, but not the case law on all the exemptions and other provisions; and certainly not to the extent which would be expected if FOI were a unit of study in its own right. This essentially means that problems may call for a close examination of only relevant provisions of the Act together with a knowledge of statute law. If writing an essay, you should be able to show a good understanding of the structure of the FOI Act, be able to draw on illustrative cases where possible, and be able to relate the Act conceptually to other administrative law topics.

Before attempting the questions, check that you are familiar with the following issues:

✓   the democratic justifications for FOI legislation;

✓   the basic rights and obligations laid down in FOI legislation;

✓   how to make an FOI request;

✓   the main conditions of entitlement for access to documents;

✓   the legislative regime concerning 'exempt documents';

✓   one or more illustrative cases on provision(s) of the Act;

✓   rights to challenge decisions made under FOI legislation.

QUESTION 45

Consider again the 'The Makepeace Scenario', p xvi. Assume that the Attorney-General has now refused Makepeace permission to import the book, *The Night of a Thousand Shames*. Makepeace tells you that it has learned that, at the Cabinet meeting which decided that the book was to be treated by Customs as a prohibited import and that the Attorney-General was to be asked to refuse any request that it be allowed to import the book, the Minister for Agriculture and Telecommunications suggested that the appropriate course of action would be for the Attorney-General to refuse permission to import the book.

Makepeace tells you it has also learned of earlier events involving the Australian Government. Last May the newly elected Australian Prime Minister visited Caledenia and was told by the Caledenian Minister for Culture and Aircraft Production that the Caledenian Government regarded Makepeace's proposal to distribute the book as nothing less than an act of war against the Caledenian Government. The Minister for Culture warned the Prime Minister that Caledenia would not hesitate to take whatever action it regarded as appropriate against any organisation which distributed the book, and warned that, in the event of the book being distributed in Australia, his government might not be able to contain the anger of Mindu militants who might conduct a ➤

demonstration involving as many as 200,000 people outside the Australian embassy. He explained that he hoped that this was all 'off the record', and that the matter could be handled without hotheads on either side becoming involved. He also said that he hoped that Telstra was still intending to tender for the contract for the reorganisation of the Caledenian telephone system.

Makepeace suspects that the Attorney-General's decision to refuse permission was prompted in part by a desire to help Telstra win the Caledenia contract. Makepeace asks you for advice as to whether it may obtain relevant information under the Commonwealth and State FOI Acts and, if so, how to go about it.

Time allowed: 45 mins

Answer Plan

(i)   Which Act may be of assistance?

(ii) A preliminary question: do the documents exist?

(iii) The request to be made.

(iv) Whose documents? (To whom is the request to be made?)

(v)   What exemptions might be claimed?

   •   International relations.

   •   Cabinet documents.

   •   Internal working (deliberative) documents.

(vi) Conclusion.

 Answer

(i)   Which Act may be of assistance?

The State FOI Act is of no assistance to Makepeace. It only applies to information possessed by the State government. The Freedom of Information Act 1982 (Cth) is the relevant FOI Act.

(ii)   A preliminary question: do the documents exist?

It is no surprise that the FOI Act empowers an agency or a Minister to refuse a request for access to a document if the document does not exist: s 24A. In our case, we do not know whether any relevant documents do exist. The Cabinet leak states that the Minister for Agriculture and Telecommunications suggested that the appropriate course of action would be for the Attorney-General to refuse permission to import the book. But assuming this occurred, this is not direct evidence for Makepeace's suspicion that the Attorney-General's decision was prompted in part by a desire to help Telstra win the Caledenia contract. In other words, there may be no documents answering the description sought by Makepeace. (Indeed, there may even have been no illicit verbal consideration of the Caledenian tender.) Either way, there may be no relevant documents in the possession of the government. While this means that the request may not reach first base, this is not a reason in itself for deciding not to make a request.

(iii) The request to be made

I am asked to advise on how to go about obtaining the information Makepeace is seeking. The request might take one of two forms. It could be broad:

> All documents concerning the decision of the Attorney-General to refuse permission to import the book *The Night of a Thousand Shames*.

Or it could be more specific (and optimistic):

> All documents concerning the consideration, by the government, of the Telstra Caledenian tender in the refusal by the Attorney-General to give permission to import the book, *The Night of a Thousand Shames*.

There are advantages in narrowing requests, because requests can be refused on workload grounds: s 24. However, in our case, the broader request is simpler from an administrative point of view — it does not result in a hunt for the consideration referred to. Also, there may not be any documents answering the more specific request and, while the broader request in this case may be equally unsuccessful, it may be more satisfying to be given the file to check personally. But if the broader request is pursued, the photocopying charges could mount up if access in the form of copies of the files is requested: s 20(1)(b). Also, copies could be wasted if no documents of the kind sought come to light. Hence, if the broader request is made, it might be wise to request access by way of *inspection* rather than by way of copies: s 20(1)(a).

It should also be noted that the FOI officer in the relevant department or authority can be very helpful in giving advice about how to frame a request.

(iv) Whose documents? (To whom is the request to be made?)

Although the FOI Act makes provision for the transfer of requests if the original application is not properly made (s 16), it is desirable that the request be sent in the first instance to the appropriate official. The records sought might be in the possession of the Attorney-General; alternatively, they may also be in the possession of Telstra. But Telstra Corporation Ltd is no longer subject to the FOI Act: Telstra (Transition to Full Private Ownership) Act 2005 (Cth) s 5, Sch 1 Pt 2. Hence, the documents should be sought from the Attorney-General.

(v) What exemptions might be claimed?

Several exemptions might be claimed by the government. If they are rightfully claimed, the government is entitled to refuse access to the documents: s 11(1).

International relations

Under s 33, a document is an exempt document if disclosure of the document would, or could reasonably be expected to, cause damage to 'the international relations of the Commonwealth'. Arising from the leak of the meeting between the Caledenian Minister for Culture and the Australian Prime Minister, the possibility is raised of international relations allegedly being affected *if the book is imported*. (The Minister for Culture is alleged to have told the Australian Prime Minister that importation of the book would result in 'nothing less than an act of war'). While the statements of the Minister for Culture seem far-fetched — the book was written by a Caledenian, and the Australian Government's role is minimal, restricted as it is to deciding whether to grant permission for its importation — it can be accepted that granting permission to import a book which is critical of a foreign power could cause some temporary damage to international relations with that country. However, the present issue is not whether the *decision* would affect international relations — this may be conceded — but whether the *disclosure* of the documents Makepeace is seeking would, or could reasonably be expected to, cause damage to Australia's international relations.

If Makepeace made a broad request as outlined above *and* the meeting between the Minister for Culture and the Australian Prime Minister was recorded, then the sensational claims of the Minister for Culture may themselves affect our international relations. This might be so even if the claims were seen by many to be far-fetched. On the other hand, if the meeting between the Minister for Culture and the Australian Prime Minister was not recorded, the possible effect on Australia's international relations of the disclosure of the documents that Makepeace are seeking might be much more muted.

Assuming information could be found linking Telstra's Caledenia tender and the importation of the book, the question would then be: could such a disclosure reasonably be expected to cause damage to the international relations of the Commonwealth? At first sight, the answer might depend on how one characterises 'international relations'. If a purely self-interested perspective is taken, such revelations would no doubt be embarrassing to both sides if the issue of the book's suitability for importation appears to have been affected by what appears to be an extraneous consideration — revenue raising. In this scenario of mutual embarrassment, international relations could reasonably be expected to be damaged, as nobody likes their dirty linen aired in public, especially nations which seek to protect their good reputations. However, can international relations be damaged if what is aired discloses an improper dealing (morally improper, if not legally so) by the Australian government? Is there not a public interest in such dealings being known by the Australian public? The difficulty with this argument is that there is no 'public interest' test as such in s 33, so it would seem that the self-interested perspective is the better view on the current law. My tentative view, then, is that *if* there are documents which do provide evidence that the Telstra Caledenian tender was mixed up with the discussion of the book, then such documents would be exempt under s 33.

Cabinet documents

A second exemption to consider is under s 34, the Cabinet exemption. This exemption is more straightforward. There is an exemption both for records of Cabinet deliberations (s 34(1)(b)) and for documents submitted to Cabinet: s 34(1)(a). 'Purely factual material' is not covered by the exemption: s 34(1A). But even if the Telstra tender appeared as a 'fact' on a Cabinet submission relating to the importation of the book, it is still exempted under s 34(1A) if the disclosure would involve any deliberation or decision of the Cabinet: s 34(1A)(a).

Internal working (deliberative) documents

A third possible exemption is s 36 (internal working documents). Given that deliberative documents which are submitted to Cabinet are exempted under s 34(1)(a), s 36 will only be relevant to those documents which are deliberative in nature and which did not go to Cabinet.

Section 36 has two main requirements. First, the document must be deliberative in nature: s 36(1)(a). It is possible in the present case that deliberative documents of the kind sought by Makepeace exist, but little more can be said because we do not know even if there are any such documents.

Second, the disclosure must also be 'contrary to the public interest': s 36(1)(b). There is authority that:

> In evaluating where the public interest ultimately lies ... it is necessary to weigh the public interest in citizens being informed of the processes of their government and its agencies on the one hand against the public interest in the proper working of government and its agencies on the other: *Harris v Australian Broadcasting Corporation* (1983) 78 FLR 236 at 245 per Beaumont J.

If there has been an improper consideration of the importation of the book, the public interest in citizens being informed is heightened. But we need to consider the Act to see if it would, in fact, be improper to link the issue of the importation of the book with the Telstra tender. Some relevant considerations with respect to the discretion to grant permission to import goods falling within reg 4A(1A) of the Customs (Prohibited Imports) Regulations are set out in reg 4A(2AA). None of the specific considerations sanction the taking into account of financial considerations such as furthering the Telstra tender. It is difficult to say what 'any other relevant matters' includes (reg 4A(2AA)(e)), but the self-interest of the government seems a long way from the specified considerations. Hence, it is difficult to see how the consideration of the Caledenian tender (if it occurred) was anything other than the taking into account of a legally irrelevant consideration. The government might argue that linking the Caledenian tender to the issue of importation was not improper, since the Telstra contract, should it eventuate, would be 'good for Australia'. Presumably, this view emphasises the economic return to Telstra and, through it, to the Australian people and Australian shareholders. The answer to this assertion is that what is good politics or even good economics is not necessarily good in law. Whether a consideration is legally improper turns on what *the Act* permits, and not on the imperatives of politics. Even if one puts aside the legality issue, there is a public interest in the citizens knowing about the politics.

However, s 36 requires a 'balancing of the different facets of the public interest': *Re James and Australian National University* (1984) 2 AAR 327 at 343. It has been suggested that various factors, if present, suggest that disclosure will be contrary to the public interest. They are the so-called '*Howard* factors', derived from *Re Howard and Treasurer of Commonwealth of Australia* (1985) 7 ALD 626 at 634–5. The *Howard* factors were trenchantly criticised in *Re Eccleston and Department of Family Services and Aboriginal and Islander Affairs* (1993) 1 QAR 60. However, accepting the *Howard* decision as having greater legal authority than the decision of the Queensland Information Commissioner, do they suggest that any documents discussing the Telstra Caledenia tender ought not be disclosed? Since we do not know what documents are involved, it would be speculative to consider these factors in detail. However, even assuming that any documents raise the *Howard* factors to a strong degree, they must be balanced against the public interest in their disclosure. It is suggested that the possible involvement of the Australian Government in clearly unlawful action ought to outweigh the *Howard* factors. But this is a most tentative finding, given that, in the absence of the documents, we do not know what weight to give to the *Howard* factors.

(vi) Conclusion

There are many obstacles facing Makepeace if it attempts to obtain the documents sought. The documents may not exist. Even if they do, there are a number of exemptions which may be claimed, although they may only pertain to some of the documents sought. The Cabinet exemption (s 34) seems strong if the documents concerned fall within the range of documents covered by the exemption. Because we can be confident that the Telstra tender was mentioned in the relevant Cabinet meeting, there is a strong likelihood that the Cabinet exemption will hold good. Even if the documents do not wholly fall within s 34, the s 33 (international relations) exemption could be claimed by the government with some confidence.

However, Makepeace may fare better in relation to claims for exemption which squarely raise the public interest. In the space available, attention was given to the s 36 (internal working documents) exemption. (Others of relevance are ss 39 and 43.) It was seen that a good *argument* can be made against a claim for exemption under s 36. But a detailed consideration of the opposing case was stymied by the lack of knowledge of the nature of the documents sought. Hence, no conclusion could be made on the public interest question.

Despite these possible obstacles, it is not suggested that a request of the kind contemplated ought not be made.

Examiner's Comments

How well students can be expected to answer a problem in this area depends on the depth of treatment in the particular unit. This particularly applies to case law. Court and tribunal cases bearing upon relevant provisions may not have been studied, in which case an examiner is mainly looking for a close study of the relevant provisions of the Act read against the background of statute law. However, this task should not be underrated. Students need to be aware that, unless otherwise advised, they are examined on all the provisions of the Act.

The problem illustrates the practical issue of how to frame an FOI request. FOI can involve requests which are quite vague. This is not always the case. In *Harris v Australian Broadcasting Corporation* (1983) 78 FLR 236 and *Commissioner of Police v District Court of NSW* (1993) 31 NSWLR 606, for instance, a citizen sought a clearly identified document. On the other hand, in *Re Eccleston and Department of Family Services and Aboriginal and Islander Affairs* (1993) 1 QAR 60, a citizen sought a wide class of information. In the latter type of case, where the client may not be able to identify the particular documents, the request is necessarily a hazy one. The problem for the adviser in the latter situation is that, without knowing the nature of the documents, the advice is to some extent speculative and not all the legal issues may be anticipated. This is what has occurred in the present problem. The difficulty is accentuated in the present case because the adviser does not even know whether any documents match the request.

To some extent, some of the challenges in this question are a result of the deliberate way in which the question was asked. The question did not break down into several parts by asking, for example:

1. Which FOI Act is relevant?

2. What request should be made?

3. To whom should the request be made?

4. If a request is made, what exemptions might legitimately be claimed?

While the examiner might take this course to assist students and to reduce the discretion in the marking process, it must be remembered that, in practice, the client cannot be expected to raise these questions, and requiring students to raise issues themselves tests their capacity to do so. Having said this, the main issue the examiner would normally be looking for in the short time frame of an examination would be a discussion of the exemptions under the federal Act.

Students will also have noticed the red herring in the question in the reference to the State FOI Act. It is not unfair for the examiner to employ the odd red herring in an examination. It is not in students' interests for the facts of legal problems to be completely sanitised — that is, uniformly correct and comprehensive (on which, see the classic essay, R E Megarry, 'Law as Taught and Law as Practised', *Society of Public Teachers of Law Journal*, vol 9, 1967, p 176).

 ## Common Errors to Avoid

- Falling for the red herring — the reference to the State FOI Act. Because administrative law — including FOI — is federalised (that is, subject to national and State laws applying to the respective governments), students constantly need to make choices about whether the remedy lies in the federal or State arena.

- Not being aware of the details of the FOI Act.

- Discussing only one relevant exemption, rather than trying to canvass as many as possible.

- Failing to give reasons why an exemption might apply on the facts of the case.

 ## QUESTION 46

> Information is the lynch-pin of the political process. Knowledge is, quite literally, power: Fitzgerald Report, cited in *Re Eccleston and Department of Family Services and Aboriginal and Islander Affairs* (1993) 1 QAR 60 at [82] per The Information Commissioner.
>
> Compare the contribution which FOI, statutory rights to be given a statement of reasons, and civil procedure mechanisms (discovery and interrogatories) make to increasing knowledge of the political and governmental process from the standpoints of:
>
> - a litigant or potential litigant;
> - an investigative journalist or opposition member of parliament; and
> - a member of the general public with a request for personal information.
>
> **Time allowed: 1 hour**

Answer Plan

(i)   A litigant or potential litigant.

(ii) An investigative journalist or opposition member of parliament.

(iii) A member of the general public with a personal query.

(iv) Conclusion.

 Answer

(i)   A litigant or potential litigant

Discovery and interrogatories are complementary mechanisms, in that discovery makes possible the production of documents, whereas interrogatories constitute written questions to be asked of the other party.

Ostensibly, a litigant or potential litigant should benefit from either mechanism because they have been specially designed to assist parties to litigation. Because these procedures are part of the court process, in theory they must be taken very seriously, or a party may be guilty of perjury. While class claims used to be able to be made for 'Crown privilege', there is now no class of government documents (even Cabinet documents) which is absolutely immune: *Sankey v Whitlam* (1978) 142 CLR 1; *Commonwealth v Northern Land Council* (1993) 176 CLR 604. It has been held that these general civil procedure mechanisms continue to be available in litigation against the government after the advent of the 'information mechanisms' (FOI and rights to be given a statement of reasons): *ASC v Somerville* (1994) 51 FCR 38. This has the consequence that, where a party is not entitled to apply for a statement of reasons because the decision is exempted from the relevant statutory scheme, that party can resort to the general civil law: *ASC v Somerville*. In the case of interrogatories, the question format may be a more penetrating method of inquiry than a general request for reasons. And objections based on workload grounds, which may be raised to block FOI requests, may receive less sympathy in the context of a civil action before a judge.

However, these court-based mechanisms have significant limitations when compared with the information mechanisms which accompanied the 1970s and 1980s revolution in administrative law. The first concerns timing. Generally speaking, an action must have commenced before discovery and interrogatories may be brought into play: Douglas, 2006, p 150. By comparison, the information mechanisms do not depend on an action having being brought or being brought. In the case of the right to reasons, an applicant must be merely *entitled* to apply to the AAT for a review of the decision (AAT Act s 28(1)) or *entitled* to make an application to the Federal Court or Federal Magistrates Court under s 5 of the Administrative Decisions (Judicial Review) Act 1977 (Cth) (ADJR Act), as the case may be.

Second, flowing from this timing requirement is the financial outlay involved in the court-based mechanisms: Douglas, 2006, pp 150–1. While some financial outlay may be involved in making a FOI request (see s 15(2)(e) of the FOI Act, and the Freedom of Information (Fees and

Charges) Regulations), an applicant can mitigate the cost by tailoring his or her request as specifically as possible. And with requests for statements of reasons, there is no fee involved.

Third, a related point is that the court-based mechanisms are not available for 'mere fishing': *WA Pines Pty Ltd v Bannerman* (1980) 41 FLR 175 at 182, per Brennan J. This means that a party cannot use them to determine whether they have a case or not — at least in circumstances where they otherwise have no reason to believe that they might have a case. Again, the information mechanisms are not so limited. Indeed, they were designed to encourage fishing expeditions in the cause of open government.

Fourth, the documents which may be sought under the general civil procedure laws must pass a 'relevance' test. As stated by the High Court in the *Northern Land Council* case, the documents must 'relate to matters in issue in the action in the sense they would, or would lead to a chain of inquiry which would, either advance [the party's] case or damage that of the [other party]': at 613–14. No such relevance test applies to the information mechanisms, except that a person is not entitled to be furnished with a statement of reasons if they are not specially affected by the decision: AAT Act ss 27 and 28(1); ADJR Act ss 3(4) and 13(1).

Fifth, the procedures of discovery and interrogatories are not necessarily available as of right. Depending on the relevant rules of court, they may be available at the discretion of the court: see Douglas, 2006, p 149. By comparison, the information mechanisms set out clear rights (see, for example, the FOI Act s 11; the AAT Act s 28; and the ADJR Act s 13), notwithstanding that — as is the case with the civil procedure mechanisms — exemptions or privileges may be claimed in relation to certain kinds of documents in particular circumstances (for example, under Pt IV of the FOI Act).

There are some partial exceptions to the above limitations. In most jurisdictions, 'preliminary discovery' is available; that is, discovery can be sought before a case has formally commenced. But the right of preliminary discovery is greatly restricted when compared with FOI and rights to reasons. For instance, in Victoria, under r 32.05 of the Supreme Court (General Civil Procedure) Rules 1996, the applicant must still satisfy the court that 'there is reasonable cause to believe the applicant has or may have the right to obtain relief from an ascertained person'; 'reasonable inquiries' must have been (unsuccessfully) made; and the documents must be ones 'relating to the question whether the applicant has the right to obtain the relief'. These requirements do not apply to the information mechanisms.

So far I have discussed the limitations of the court-based mechanisms. It remains to say something about the comparative advantages of the information mechanisms from the standpoint of the litigant. Both FOI and rights to reasons have their own advantages. The principal advantage of rights to reasons over FOI was evident in *Soldatow v Australia Council* (1991) 22 ALD 750. In that case, the applicant wanted to know why he had been refused a writer's fellowship by the Australia Council. The applicant had previously made a FOI application which had turned up the assessment sheets. But these sheets merely had the result of putting the applicant onto a short-list. It appears that there were no documents on file to explain why the decision-maker refused the applicant a fellowship, other than a copy of the letter of rejection which merely referred to some general considerations that pertained to all grant applicants. Thus, as a source of information, FOI is highly dependent on the record-keeping practices of the relevant authority. If, as seems was the case in *Soldatow*, no records of the final decision-making process which specifically pertained to the applicant were kept, then FOI is of no use (other than perhaps revealing sloppy procedures), because the request aspect of the scheme only applies to existing information: see the definition of 'document of an agency' and 'official document of a Minister' in the FOI Act s 4(1). However, rights to reasons legislation requires a statement of reasons to be *given or furnished* (AAT Act s 28(1); ADJR Act s 13(1)), and if reasons are not on file, then, as in *Soldatow,* once a valid request is received, they must be prepared and communicated to the applicant.

An advantage of FOI over rights to reasons was evident in *Kioa v Minister for Immigration and Ethnic Affairs* (1985) 159 CLR 550. The High Court found that a breach of the rules of natural justice had occurred because a damaging allegation had not been put to the applicant for his reply. The allegation was not on the statement of reasons. But it was on a submission to the delegate of the Minister (the decision-maker). The court noted that the statement of reasons did not disavow the allegation, and accordingly attributed the allegation to the decision-maker's processes. From this case study we may note that in some circumstances statements of reasons may not be as revealing as the file. Statements of reasons are written for the applicant and with an eye to avoiding legal error. But documents on file, such as the submission to the delegate in the *Kioa* case, are a written record of the processes of the organisation as they happen (to the extent they are committed to paper), and hence they are less prone, it may be thought, to being 'tailored' as a result of a request for access to information.

(ii)   An investigative journalist or opposition member of parliament

A public-spirited person seeking access to important government information, such as an investigative journalist or opposition member of parliament, relies to some extent on 'leaks' of Cabinet decisions: see *Sankey v Whitlam* at 41 per Gibbs ACJ. Such a person has few rights to access government information other than through FOI. Their right to use FOI arises because the Act has no standing requirements: s 11 ('every person').

Rights to reasons are not available to people in this group, since, as mentioned above, the schemes are only available to those who are *entitled* to make the relevant application to the AAT or one of the federal courts. A public-spirited person will not have the necessary standing because the fact of being public-spirited, without some additional interest, equates to a mere intellectual or emotional concern, and this is not enough to qualify for a special interest: *Australian Conservation Foundation Inc v Commonwealth* (1980) 146 CLR 493 at 530. For similar reasons, it is unlikely that a public-spirited person would be able to bring a court action based on administrative law grounds, and therefore bring into play the civil procedure mechanisms.

Because of these limitations, FOI is of enormous importance from the standpoint of the public-spirited individual or organisation. This is notwithstanding obstacles: the numerous grounds for exemption contained in Pt IV of the federal Act; other grounds for refusing a request elsewhere specified; restrictions on AAT review as evident in *McKinnon v Secretary, Department of Treasury* (2006) 229 ALR 187; and an unsupportive administrative culture in some agencies which has been documented by various independent investigators: the Australian Law Reform Commission and Administrative Review Council, the Commonwealth Ombudsman, and the Australian National Audit Office: see Douglas, 2006, pp 124–8. These obstacles are manifested in the rate of refusals for non-personal information, which sees less than half of applications accepted in full: Douglas, 2006, p 102, citing a report by the Australian National Audit Office.

(iii) A member of the general public with a personal query

Members of the general public who want to check their personal files would not wish to initiate legal proceedings (even if they could), so again they must rely on the information mechanisms as a matter of law. The Australian Law Reform Commission and Administrative Review Council found that this aspect of the Act appeared satisfactory: see *Freedom of Information*, Discussion Paper No 59, [2.14], in Douglas, 2002, p 98. Rights to reasons legislation can also be used for personal information requests, but a decision must have been made (AAT Act s 28(1); ADJR Act s 13(1)), and a statement of reasons will not necessarily reveal what documents are held on the file.

(iv) Conclusion

From the standpoints of the litigant, the public-spirited individual, and the member of the general public with a personal request, FOI is a hugely significant information mechanism for disclosing the political and governmental process. It plays or ought to play a crucial role in each category of case. The right to reasons is extremely valuable for the litigant (and surpasses FOI in key respects), but is not available for the other players mentioned. Court-based procedures have certain procedural advantages for litigants and are particularly valuable where a statement of reasons is not available — but at a significant cost.

Examiner's Comments

Examination questions are designed with a great deal of thought. Two assumptions underpin the decision to ask the present question. The first is that it is not enough to know 'the rules' concerning the information mechanisms. Students need to have a contextual understanding of the rules — which includes an understanding of how the rules operate. Particular standpoints were identified to test such a functional understanding. Second, students need to be knowledgeable about alternative mechanisms. In this respect, administrative law is not like, say, the law of torts, where students can advise on causes of action without considering any different procedural mechanisms to enforce substantive rights. In administrative law, common law and statute law frequently present the aggrieved citizen with a banquet of different remedial *mechanisms*, even when the problem is a lack of information. Although this question is not in the 'problem' format, such a question does assist students making informed choices down the track because it requires students to compare, at a conceptual level, various schemes for the provision of information.

As for the particular wording of a question, examiners take care in the amount of information that is supplied in the question. In the present question, the examiner has identified particular standpoints to allow students to demonstrate what they know about the topic rather than requiring students to demonstrate how they can interpret, and elaborate for themselves, a more broadly worded question. But this does not mean the examiner had no alternative. The examiner could have asked the question in this way:

> Assess the contribution which freedom of information, statutory rights to be given a statement of reasons, and civil procedure mechanisms (discovery and interrogatories) make to increasing knowledge of the political and governmental process.

If the question were framed in this broader way, students would, as a preliminary matter, have had to work out a *methodology* or *approach* for addressing the question; that is, for assessing the contribution referred to.

The question which was settled upon tests students' conceptual understanding of the principal information mechanisms usually studied in administrative law: (FOI and rights to reasons), together with an understanding of information mechanisms usually studied in depth in civil procedure law (discovery and interrogatories). However, the civil procedure mechanisms may not be included in a particular administrative law unit; if that is the case, an examination question would not require students to discuss those mechanisms.

The answer refers to the relevant legislation as much as possible. In this way the conceptual understanding which lies at the heart of the question is fully demonstrated — by matching it up with the relevant legislation.

 Common Errors to Avoid

- Failing to refer, wherever possible, to the relevant legislation — the FOI Act and the rights to reasons legislation.
- Assuming that discovery and interrogatories are not part of the practice of administrative law.
- Drawing on a casebook or textbook for points concerning the law of civil procedure, without citing or properly citing that work. (This does not mean that references in examination answers must follow to the letter a particular citation style. It means that, if you are relying on a source verbatim, this fact must be acknowledged.)

 QUESTION 47

> Compare the obligation to disclose information pursuant to a duty to accord procedural fairness with the obligation to grant access to documents under FOI legislation. To what extent are they complementary mechanisms in so far as the disclosure of government information is concerned?
>
> **Time allowed: 45 mins**

Answer Plan

(i)   Freedom of information and the duty to accord procedural fairness — overlapping obligations.

(ii) Comparative strengths of FOI.

(iii) Comparative strengths of the duty to accord procedural fairness.

(iv) How complementary?

 Answer

(i)   Freedom of information and the duty to accord procedural fairness — overlapping obligations

The obligation to accord procedural fairness has more in common with FOI than just 'disclosure of information'. Both accord legal rights to the disclosure of information in the possession of government. Both have the rationale of furthering participation in administrative decision-making.

Their scope is similar. Both apply to government broadly. In the case of procedural fairness, the courts are close to recognising a general obligation on government: *Haoucher v Minister for Immigration and Ethnic Affairs* (1990) 169 ALR 648 at 653 per Deane J, approved by Mason CJ, Deane and McHugh JJ in *Annetts v McCann* (1990) 170 CLR 596 at 598; *Minister of State for Immigration and Ethnic Affairs v Teoh* (1995) 183 CLR 273 at 311 per McHugh J, approved of in *Re Minister for Immigration and Multicultural Affairs; Ex parte Lam* (2003) 214 CLR 1 at [81] per McHugh and Gummow JJ and at [150] per Callinan J. Federal FOI legislation applies to 'information in the possession of the Government of the Commonwealth': s 3(1). State FOI laws are similar.

Litigation is not necessary for either obligation to arise. Procedural fairness is a common law right which is required to be observed in administrative decision-making, unless statute or common law provides otherwise. Access to documents under FOI requires an application; it does not require court proceedings to have commenced. Compare discovery and interrogatories which, with limited exceptions, are rights which apply only once civil proceedings have commenced.

Procedural fairness and FOI are also subject to similar exceptions. A document is an exempt document under the federal FOI Act 'if its disclosure ... would found an action, by a person (other than an agency or the Commonwealth), for breach of confidence': s 45(1). The obligation to accord procedural fairness is also subject to claims to confidentiality if the effective operation of an Act requires that confidentiality be respected: *Ansett Transport Industries Ltd v Minister for Aviation* (1987) 72 ALR 469. More recently the High Court has affirmed this principle in *Applicant VEAL of 2002 v Minister for Immigration and Multicultural and Indigenous Affairs* (2005) 225 CLR 88 at [22]–[29].

However, reflecting their different underlying policies, there are important differences in the two obligations.

(ii) Comparative strengths of FOI

Freedom of information is fundamentally concerned with promoting open government; at least with 'the assumption that information held by Government is available unless there are reasons to the contrary': Attorney-General (Qld), as cited in *Re Eccleston and Department of Family Services and Aboriginal and Islander Affairs* (1993) 1 QAR 60 at [73]. There is no restriction to personal files or to particular decisions. Thus, FOI goes way beyond the disclosure of personal information. Indeed, FOI legislation *requires* manuals or other documents containing interpretations, rules, guidelines, practices or precedents to be made available for inspection and purchase by members of the public: s 9. Compare procedural fairness: information in the nature of 'policy, comment and undisputed statements of fact' is not caught by the obligation because they are not considerations personal to the applicant or cannot be considered to be a critical issue or factor in the decision-making process: *Kioa v West* (1985) 159 CLR 550 at 588 per Mason J. Illustrative is *Peninsular Anglican Boys' School v Ryan* (1985) 7 FCR 415, where the Federal Court (Wilcox J) rejected the suggestion that a decision-maker was bound to give the school notice of a change in policy with respect to the funding of private schools.

The object of open government is supported by the lack of any standing requirement in FOI legislation. Section 3(1) of the federal Act states that 'The object of this Act is to extend as far as possible the right of the Australian community to access to information in the possession of the Government of the Commonwealth'. In contrast, proceedings seeking the enforcement of a duty to accord procedural fairness can only be maintained by a person with standing to sue, and, indeed, a duty to afford procedural fairness does not normally arise unless the person is affected by a relevant decision to the point where they have standing to challenge it. While rules of standing vary, 'the general rule of the common law' is 'the special interest' test: *Truth About Motorways Pty Ltd v Macquarie Infrastructure Investment Management Ltd* (2000) 200 CLR 591 at [131] per Kirby J. The test for standing under the ADJR Act is similar: *North Coast Environment Council Inc v Minister for Resources* (1994) 55 FCR 492 at 511–12 per Sackville J.

Similarly, FOI does not require a person's rights, interests or legitimate expectations to be affected before a person becomes entitled to be granted access to documents. Whereas, with procedural fairness, the basic orthodox position is that such a requirement applies: *Kioa* at 582, 584 per Mason J.

But compare the duty to accord procedural fairness: the High Court has laid down that material which, objectively speaking, is evidently 'not credible, not relevant or of little or no significance to the decision that is to be made' need not be disclosed: *Applicant VEAL* at [17].

And the success of a FOI application does not depend on the effect that disclosure would have on the applicant. Compare the rule applying to procedural fairness, which leaves open that possibility:

> ... an appellate court will not order a new trial if it would inevitably result in the making of the same order as that made by the primary judge at the first trial. An order for a new trial in such a case would be a futility. For this reason not every departure from the rules of natural justice at a trial will entitle the aggrieved party to a new trial: *Stead v State Government Insurance Commission* (1986) 161 CLR 141 at 145.

Finally, FOI provides for disclosure of documents in full (subject to a claim that a document is an exempt document in whole or in part). By comparison, the duty to disclose the critical issue or factor pursuant to the duty to accord procedural fairness does not necessarily extend to the actual documents on which a body will rely; a summary may be sufficient: Creyke and McMillan, 2005, [10.4.13].

(iii) Comparative strengths of the duty to accord procedural fairness

While FOI has its comparative strengths in providing for the disclosure of government information, so does the duty to accord procedural fairness. The latter is essentially concerned with the adoption of 'fair procedures which are appropriate and adapted to the circumstances of the particular case': Mason J in *Kioa* at 585. No application is required to bring the duty into play as is the case with FOI. Breach of the duty to disclose information pursuant to a duty to accord procedural fairness also has consequences which do not apply to breach of FOI legislation. Denial of procedural fairness amounts to a ground of review of an administrative decision. By comparison, FOI is a self-contained regime giving enforceable rights of access; but breach does not afford a right to have a related decision set aside.

The duty to accord procedural fairness is a substantially broader obligation in important respects. It is concerned not just with the disclosure of *documents* but more broadly with:

> ... the need to bring to a person's attention the critical issue or factor on which the administrative decision is likely to turn so that he may have an opportunity of dealing with it. F.A.I. is one illustration. *Cole v Cunningham* is another: per Mason J in *Kioa* at 587.

Illustrative is the rule that an expert tribunal is required to give notice that it proposes to drawn on its own expertise where it is not reasonable to assume a party is on notice that the members of the tribunal are likely to make use of their own expertise and experience: *Minister for Health v Thomson* (1985) 8 FCR 213.

Further, the obligation to disclose the critical issue or factor may even extend to an evaluation of material emanating from the applicant. Now, the ordinary rule is that 'a decision-maker is not obliged to expose his or her mental processes or provisional views to comment before making the decision in question': *Commissioner for Australian Capital Territory Revenue v Alphaone Pty Ltd* (1994) 49 FCR 576 at 592. However, a decision-maker has been found to be obliged to disclose an 'unfavourable animadversion ... if the animadversion is not an obviously natural response to the circumstances which have evoked it': *Somaghi v Minister for Immigration, Local Government and Ethnic Affairs* (1991) 31 FCR 100 at 108 per Jenkinson J. In *York v General Medical Assessment Tribunal* [2003] 2 Qd R 104 the Queensland Court of Appeal found that the tribunal had denied the applicant procedural fairness in failing to warn him that it was contemplating rejecting uncontested medical evidence. In short, while FOI does not provide for disclosure of thought processes which have not been reduced to writing, procedural fairness may do so.

(iv) How complementary?

Freedom of information legislation and disclosure obligations pursuant to the duty to accord procedural fairness are complementary in the sense that each has comparative strengths and a certain scope of operation which is not open to the other.

Their complementarity is illustrated by the well-known *Kioa* case, in which the appellant challenged a decision of the Minister to deport him, his temporary visa having expired. The appellant succeeded in making out he had been denied procedural fairness on the basis that he had not been given an opportunity of replying to a departmental report which included the following prejudicial material:

> 22 Mr *Kioa*'s alleged concern for other Tongan illegal immigrants in Australia and his active involvement with other persons who are seeking to circumvent Australia's immigration laws must be a source of concern.

How did the departmental report come to light? The case extracts do not tell us. It is quite possible that it came to light through a successful FOI application. Let us assume for illustrative purposes that that occurred. If so, it illustrates the close, working complementarity of FOI and procedural fairness. FOI can lead to the discovery of key information, information which ought to have been disclosed pursuant to the duty to accord procedural fairness but was not (understandably in *Kioa* given the prior case law). However, Mr Kioa was not seeking access to information as a general inquiry of the federal government. He was seeking to overturn a decision to deport him and his family. It is here that the duty to accord procedural fairness was vital from the appellant's point of view, for the breach of duty paved the way for the setting aside of the decision to deport him and his family.

Even though FOI and the duty to accord procedural fairness are highly complementary, they both leave large gaps in the disclosure of government information. Neither supplies a formal statement of reasons for the making of decisions. Now, other statute law gives rights to a person, who is specially affected by a decision, to require the decision-maker to give them a statement of reasons for the decision. But if a person is not specially affected and wishes to know *why* governmental action was taken or not taken by government, there may be no document which answers that question; in which case neither records-based FOI nor standing-based procedural fairness is of help. Some have suggested an expanded statement of reasons requirement to fill the gap: P Shoyer, 'FOI or FO Why?', Australian Institute of Administrative Law, 2006 National Administrative Law Forum, 'Administrative Law: Protection of Individual and Community Interests' (2006) at <http://law.anu.edu.au/aial/Publications/2006conferencepapers/index.htm>. In the meantime, interested individuals must fall back on the resources of the media and the political processes.

Examiner's Comments

This question requires students to compare two bodies of knowledge: the obligation to disclose documents under FOI, and the obligation to disclose information pursuant to the duty to accord procedural fairness. From an examiner's perspective this is a highly useful and appropriate question. It is useful because the examiner can test a student's knowledge in a way which calls for original analysis. A student cannot pass the question merely by going to their notes and regurgitating them. It is appropriate because, while it tests a student's general understanding of FOI, it does not call for a detailed knowledge of the case law on the FOI exemptions. Commonly, one-semester administrative law units do not examine FOI at that level of detail.

The answer is strong in several departments. It is clearly structured. It answers both parts of the question in depth. A comprehensive comparison between the two regimes is entered into: the answer examines aspects in common as well as differences. It is well argued, with good use made of case illustrations. The overall response is well-rounded, alluding to the overall gaps in both regimes as well as their relative strengths.

Common Errors to Avoid

- Summarising each topic, with no attempt made to compare the two regimes.
- Not addressing each question asked.
- Not describing the extent to which the regimes overlap.

PART 6

Evaluating Review Mechanisms

Chapter 16
Choice of Avenue of Redress

 ## Key Issues

People aggrieved by administrative decisions have a sometimes bewildering variety of possible avenues of redress. They may ask administrators to reconsider their decisions. They may seek political redress. They may complain to the Ombudsman. They may be able to seek merits review from a formally constituted tribunal, and they may be able to seek judicial review.

Choosing between alternatives involves taking account both of legal and non-legal considerations.

It is essential to consider which options are legally open to people aggrieved by administrative behaviour. AAT review is available only for review of decisions, and only if there is statutory provision for it: AAT Act s 25. Some decisions cannot be investigated by the Ombudsman (for example, decisions of a Minister: Ombudsman Act (Cth) s 5(2)(a)). In a federal system, it is important to recognise that federal decisions are almost never reviewable by State bodies (and vice versa).

Even when review bodies possess the power to review administrative behaviour, they may not be obliged to exercise the relevant power. If an application for judicial review is made to a court, it must exercise its jurisdiction, but in certain circumstances, it may, in the exercise of its jurisdiction, dismiss the application without inquiring into whether the administrator has committed legal error. Review bodies rarely exercise their right to decline to act, but this is partly because aggrieved individuals normally bring their complaints before the 'right' body. But there will be cases which the Ombudsman considers will be better handled by the AAT or even the courts: Ombudsman Act s 6(2), (3). There will be cases where courts will dismiss an application on the grounds that the issue should have been pursued in another forum: see, for example, Administrative Decisions (Judicial Review) Act 1977 (Cth) (ADJR Act) s 10(2)(b)(ii).

In choosing between avenues of redress, it is essential that one take account of the likely success of different courses of action. Because different institutions deal with different issues, what might be a strong case in one context may be a hopeless one in another. If, following legally impeccable procedures, an administrator nonetheless makes what is regarded as the 'wrong' decision, AAT review may prove successful. Judicial review would obviously be pointless, and a complaint to the Ombudsman is likely to be to no avail. Conversely, if the decision is or is likely to be in fact the correct or preferable one on the merits, notwithstanding that it is legally flawed, a person who would like the decision set aside in the hope this might lead to a reconsideration in their favour would be advised to seek judicial review, rather than merits review.

Moreover, 'success' in one context may have different implications to 'success' in another. A successful application for judicial review will not necessarily mean an end to the aggrieved individual's conflict with the bureaucracy. If the person or corporation needs a positive bureaucratic decision to be made in his, her or its favour, final success will require reconsideration of the original application. Even if the person simply wants an adverse decision set aside, there is no guarantee that the administrator will not reconsider the matter and make the same decision. (Usually, however, success in the courts means that reconsideration yields an improved outcome.)

Account must also be taken of considerations such as the cost and the expeditiousness of different procedures. Normally people will want to minimise cost and often they will want a quick decision. If so, the Ombudsman and the first-tier tribunals will normally be the preferable review options. Occasionally, however, a well-endowed person or organisation may prefer costly procedures, hoping that the government will compromise, rather than incur the expenditure necessary to defend its actions. If so, judicial review will tend to be the most attractive option. There is, apparently, a saying among American criminal lawyers that 'justice on time is justice denied'. The seamy side of administrative law is reflected in applications whose sole point seems to be taking advantage of the review system to delay adverse decisions.

Before attempting the questions, check that you are familiar with the following issues:

✓ the range of bodies capable of reviewing administrative decisions;

✓ the jurisdiction of the major administrative review bodies, and the circumstances under which review bodies may decline to exercise their jurisdiction or decline to act;

✓ the remedies which can be provided by different review bodies; and

✓ the relative expeditiousness and cost of different review bodies.

QUESTION 48

> *In a Monastery Bedroom* was written by a French pornographer in 1753, and is generally acknowledged to be totally devoid of literary merit. It is basically a plotless list of sexual acts involving monks, nuns, babies, adolescents, dogs, crucifixes and (at p 109) porridge. Praise the Lord Knox is Secretary of Protestants against Catholic Sexual Abuse (PACSA) and wants to import a copy of the book so that he can add its revelations to a book he is writing on Romish evils. He states in a radio interview that he doubts that the Attorney-General, Sean O'Reilly, will give him permission to import: 'The Antichrist at St Peters will forbid him, and being the child of Satan that he is, he will comply'. O'Reilly is interviewed on talk-back radio the following day and says:
>
>> Knox is wrong. Even if his Holiness the Pope were to beg me to allow Knox to import this filth, I would refuse, for I know that Knox is a despicable traducer of our faith. He is a dangerous bigot who has been or should have been refused entry to several European countries. He is an evil man (if I might loosely use that word to describe him). There is no way known that I will permit him to advance his vicious and seditious cause.
>
> Knox has not been refused entry to any European country, but he was imprisoned in Austria for incitement to religious hatred, and he has been denied entry to Israel and Iran on the basis of his writings. Knox's application for permission to import the book is indeed refused, and the Attorney-General issues a certificate precluding AAT review. Knox claims that the Attorney-General was overheard saying:
>
>> That'll teach the bastard. I've loathed him ever since he kneed me in the balls in the Newman-Ormond grand final 20 years ago.
>
> Some weeks earlier, reg 4A had been amended so that only the Attorney-General had the power to make permission decisions.
>
> At the last elections, PACSA negotiated a preference exchange deal with the Green Democrats, the Two Nations Party, and the Red Alliance, and thanks to the vagaries of the Hare-Clark system, managed to win two Senate seats. The government needs the support of three non-government senators if it is to pass its controversial Bank Nationalisation Bill.
>
> PACSA wants your advice in relation to what Knox should do. It asks: is there any point in complaining to the Ombudsman? Is there any point in seeking judicial review? Isn't there some way to get review on the merits, since it is clear where the merits lie?
>
> **Time allowed: 1 hour**

Answer Plan

(i)   The Ombudsman.

(ii) Judicial review.

  • The decision to refuse permission to import.

  • The decision to issue a certificate precluding AAT review.

(iii) The AAT.

(iv) Politics.

(v) Conclusions.

 Answer

(i) The Ombudsman

The Ombudsman is not empowered to investigate a complaint about an action taken by a Commonwealth Minister: Ombudsman Act 1976 (Cth) s 5(2). There is therefore no point in complaining to the Ombudsman.

(ii) Judicial review

The Attorney-General has made two judicially reviewable decisions: the decision to refuse permission to import (the refusal decision), and the decision to issue a certificate precluding AAT review (the certificate decision).

The decision to refuse permission to import

The Attorney-General's radio broadcast suggests that the decision to refuse is flawed by the Attorney-General's failure to handle the matter in a procedurally fair manner. It seems clear that the decision is one which attracts a duty to afford procedural fairness. The Attorney-General is obliged to take account of a number of considerations, including considerations personal to the applicant. While the Attorney-General might be entitled to take account of political considerations, the decision is not 'political' in the same senses as the decisions which gave rise to *Minister for the Arts, Heritage and Environment v Peko-Wallsend Ltd* (1987) 15 FCR 274, and *Peninsula Anglican Boys' School v Ryan* (1985) 7 FCR 415. In any case, he has apparently chosen to base his decision on matters personal to Mr Knox, and that alone would be capable of giving rise to a right to procedural fairness, even when no such right might otherwise exist: see, for instance, *Kioa v West* (1985) 159 CLR 550.

It also seems clear that the Attorney-General's conduct is such as to give rise to a reasonable apprehension of bias. It seems clear from his radio interview that he has made up his mind and that he would not approach Mr Knox's application with an open mind. His case can be distinguished from *Minister for Immigration and Multicultural Affairs v Jia Legeng* (2001) 178 ALR 421; [2001] HCA 17, where the Minister's comments indicated a definite disposition to make a particular decision, while not, however, disclosing a totally closed mind.

However, since the Attorney-General is the only person empowered to make decisions in relation to applications for permission to import, it is arguable that the bias rule is trumped by the necessity principle: *Laws v Australian Broadcasting Tribunal* (1990) 170 CLR 70. The alternative to applications for permission not being considered by a biased decision-maker is that they not be considered at all. The legislative purpose would, I think, be better achieved by allowing a hearing by a biased decision-maker (if this was the only course available) than by not allowing the application for permission to import being considered at all in the circumstances. I therefore think that this is a case where the legislative scheme must be taken to override the normal right to an unbiased decision-maker.

However, the Attorney-General did err in failing to afford Mr Knox an adequate hearing in relation to several of the matters he appears to have taken into account. These include the purposes and reputation ascribed to Mr Knox. This amounts to a breach of the procedural fairness principles.

I think, too, that the Attorney-General's behaviour could also be said to involve a breach of his duty to take account of relevant considerations and not to take account of irrelevant ones. A totally closed mind (such as that evidenced by the radio interview) strongly suggests that the Attorney-General did not base his decision on the matters set out in reg 4A(2AA) of the Customs (Prohibited Imports) Regulations. Even if his statement of reasons were to suggest otherwise, it would be permissible to go behind them — by resort to cross-examination if necessary. There are good grounds for concluding that protection of a particular religion, and personal animosity are irrelevant considerations, and possibly evidence of bad faith and improper purposes. This also means that the decision was flawed.

Problems arise, however, in relation to the order that the court should make. Neither the quashing of the decision to refuse, nor a declaration that it was of no legal effect, would do much to assist Mr Knox. His legal position would be more or less the same as before, except in so far as he would be entitled to have the matter reconsidered. However, once again, the problem is that the only person who is empowered to reconsider the matter is the Attorney-General. If he were, on reconsideration, to make the same decision, all that Knox could do would be to make a further judicial review application. Even if this were to succeed, all it would mean would be that the matter would be referred back to him yet again. However, ministerial obduracy might have political costs. To have one decision quashed is a misfortune; to have two quashed is carelessness.

The decision to issue a certificate precluding AAT review

The decision to issue a certificate precluding AAT review may attract a duty to afford procedural fairness, albeit an attenuated one, and in any case is reviewable on other grounds: *Shergold v Tanner* (2001) 188 ALR 302; [2002] HCA 19. While the power to issue certificates is broad, there are limits to the Attorney-General's powers, and I think he has exceeded them. The fact that the Attorney-General must certify that it is in the public interest that the decision be the responsibility of the

Attorney-General rather than the AAT implies that a certificate may be issued only if the Attorney-General has addressed his mind to whether this is the case and only if his satisfaction is reasonable. It also implies that the power is to be used only in the public interest. Indeed, this would have been the case even if the subregulation had made no reference to public interests.

It follows that the power is not to be used in furtherance of longstanding vendettas. If the certificate was refused out of vengeance, this would involve the use of a power for an improper purpose (or, alternatively, the taking into account of an irrelevant consideration — it does not matter which). It is also arguable that the power has been exercised for the purpose of protecting the Attorney-General's faith, although a more charitable interpretation is that it is being used for the less objectionable (and possibly unobjectionable) purpose of discouraging the dissemination of offensive literature.

To rely on the 'improper purpose' grounds of review, Mr Knox would have to prove that the Attorney-General did indeed act to give effect to a long-standing vendetta or to advance the particular interests of his faith. Even if the person who overheard the 'vendetta' conversation were to give evidence, the Attorney-General might be able to argue that his decision was unaffected by his dislike of Knox, and he might be able to argue persuasively that his colourful statement to the talkback radio host was nothing more than a manifestation of his disgust that Knox should be trying to subvert the effect of an important piece of Commonwealth legislation.

In my opinion, Knox could succeed on the procedural fairness ground and possibly on the irrelevant considerations/improper purpose grounds. His application in relation to the certificate would be successful.

One problem which would face Mr Knox is that the Attorney-General would be free to reconsider the matter, and might well come to the same conclusion. But, pending reconsideration, there would be no operative certificate. Mr Knox could therefore appeal to the AAT. (It does not matter that the permission 'decision' is a nullity.) He should therefore do so immediately.

(iii) The AAT

Under the regulations, the AAT has the power to review a refusal to permit importation of a prohibited good in the absence of a certificate to the contrary. Here, the Attorney-General has purported to issue such a certificate. If the certificate is valid, the AAT does not have a review power: reg 4A(5). For the reasons given above, I do not think the certificate is valid. Accordingly, I think Mr Knox has the right to seek review of the decision to refuse permission. One course of action he could take would be to appeal immediately to the AAT and raise the validity of the certificate collaterally.

The AAT might be wary about determining the validity of the certificate, although it could do so. But it is empowered to refer questions of law to the Federal Court (AAT Act s 45), and if there were a dispute about its jurisdiction, it might well exercise that power.

If it were to take the latter course of action, the result would probably be a Federal Court ruling to the effect that the decision to refuse the certificate was flawed and that it did not operate to deprive the AAT of jurisdiction. The delay occasioned by the reference might give the government time to issue a new (and valid) certificate. This, however, would not affect Mr Knox's application, since the effect of a certificate is to preclude the making of an application, and not to deprive the tribunal of jurisdiction of an application which is already within its jurisdiction: see reg 4A(8).

If Knox were to appeal to the AAT only after a judicial review application had proved successful, his position would be weaker. He would be out of time, in that more than 28 days would long since have elapsed since the date on which he obtained reasons (assuming he obtained them) or the day on which he was given the terms of the decision: AAT Act s 29(1)(d), (2). The tribunal may, however, extend the time for making applications (s 29(7)), and in this case I am confident that it would, in so far as Mr Knox's delay could be explained by the flawed certificate, and given that the Commonwealth was clearly on notice as to Mr Knox's desire to challenge the decision. There is, however, a stronger reason for making an immediate application for review. If a successful judicial review application was immediately followed by a second (valid) certificate, then unless he had already made an application, Knox would lose any right he might have had to appeal to the AAT.

Access to the AAT would not necessarily be of much assistance to Mr Knox, since the value of this access would depend on the likelihood that the tribunal would make a decision in his favour. This would depend on the merits of Mr Knox's case. The tribunal is required to have regard to the criteria set out in reg 4A(2AA). In my opinion, the tribunal would be reluctant to allow importation. While the tribunal might regard the exposure of religious evils as a legitimate reason for allowing the importation of an otherwise prohibited work, it would, I think, be disinclined to accept that a work of pornographic fiction could truly be said to throw much light on this question. (Its views might be different if the reason for seeking to import the book was the light it might throw on the way in which the church was viewed and portrayed.) Further, while I am confident that Mr Knox views his activities as being activities which would fall within subreg (2AA)(b), I would need more material before I could advise that the AAT would agree with this assessment. Similar problems arise in relation to subreg (2AA)(c), depending on whether Mr Knox's activities had attracted adverse comment, as I could imagine they could. Given current sensitivities about overly frank expressions of hostility to others' religions, I would not be surprised if Mr Knox's application were not to succeed.

Mr Knox's application might have a better chance of success if he could frame it as a civil libertarian issue. Pornography may be more acceptable than what some might regard as religious bigotry.

(iv) Politics

It would help if PACSA had *three* Senators, since it could offer the government the votes it needs for the passage of pieces of legislation dear to its heart. Even two can constitute an invaluable bargaining tool, since it only needs two to block unpalatable motions from the opposition (including motions to disallow regulations). Moreover, if the regulation which removed the right to appoint authorised persons has not been before the Senate for the requisite number of sitting days, the two senators and the opposition could block it, thereby ensuring that, if the permission decision were quashed, it could possibly be reconsidered by an unbiased decision-maker. However, Mr Knox needs to recognise that, if the government starts doing deals with him, it may alienate other Senators with whom it might also want to strike deals. He also needs to ask how much this issue matters to him. Does he really want to engage in politics which could involve him being perceived as a defender of the right to import pornography?

(v) Conclusions

In short, Mr Knox has the choice between seeking judicial review, AAT review, and a political solution. An application for judicial review would probably succeed, but it would achieve little. Despite the certificate, I think that the AAT has jurisdiction to hear an appeal, although I am not sure that the outcome of the appeal would be a satisfactory one from Mr Knox's perspective. I think that PACSA has considerable political clout which it could use, so long as the bargaining was done with subtlety and as much out of public view as is possible.

I do not advise an application for judicial review. I think that Mr Knox should initiate an AAT application immediately. This will safeguard his procedural rights as at the time of application. Even if the AAT is found to have no jurisdiction, Mr Knox would not be much worse off than he would have been had he made a judicial review application, since the lack of jurisdiction could flow only from a finding that the certificate was valid. True, in the absence of judicial review there will be no authoritative finding in relation to the legality of the refusal of permission. But it is hard to see how even a finding in Mr Knox's favour could be of any assistance to him.

Mr Knox should recognise that, even if his appeal is heard by the AAT, he is likely to face an uphill battle persuading the tribunal that permission should be granted. If his reasons for seeking to import the book had been different, he might have been able to persuade the AAT to grant permission, but if at this stage he were to seek to rely on different purposes, his bona fides could — and would — be questioned before the tribunal, and I suspect that such questioning would succeed. The question for Mr Knox to consider must therefore be whether he wants to make a financial outlay of thousands of dollars on the off-chance that he might succeed. It may be that he could use the occasion of his AAT appearance to receive media coverage for his views. I am not sure of the wisdom of this, but I am sure that PACSA will give thought to this.

One course of action which might be worth pursuing is this: Customs is notorious for its porosity. Banned books sometimes find their way to public libraries. I haven't checked to see whether the work in question is already available in Australia. But Mr Knox might wish to have a look. It might save him a lot of money.

Examiner's Comments

This turns out to be a very challenging question. It not only requires students to consider the question of whether Mr Knox would be formally successful in his application for judicial review; it also requires recognition of the fact that formal success may turn out to represent a pyrrhic victory. While this is not usually the situation (see, for example, R Creyke and J McMillan, 'Judicial Review Outcomes — An Empirical Study' (2004) 11 *Australian Journal of Administrative Law* 82), cases such as *Attorney-General (NSW) v Quin* are a reminder that formal success may yield nothing except the satisfaction of winning one round in an ongoing contest. This answer recognises this, and attempts to come to grips with how the victim of administrative unlawfulness can achieve substantively satisfying outcomes.

One of the merits of this answer is that it recognises that the best (legal) course for Mr Knox to follow is a course which at first seems closed to him: applying for AAT review.

The assessment of whether judicial review would prove successful, and why, is answered reasonably well, although there are places where the argument is loosely developed. The answer does not address the significance of the Minister's observations about Mr Knox's having been denied entry to several European countries. It does not discuss whether the making of the certificate decision was subject to a duty to afford procedural fairness. However, these omissions are excusable given time constraints, and in any case, the discussion of the certificate issue recognises that the procedural fairness issue is difficult, and that in the circumstances, it is not necessary to resolve it.

The answer also recognises that success in the AAT in this case is going to turn largely on questions of fact and value. It attempts to predict how the tribunal would react to Mr Knox's application, and reaches a conclusion which is probably correct. It is important to note, however, that it makes a variety of assumptions about the way in which the case will be presented and assessed. In real life the person advising Mr Knox would (one hopes) have been presented with a comprehensive file, and would have met and talked with him.

The answer does not discuss the possibility of pursuing both a judicial review and an AAT application simultaneously. This is no doubt because the writer knows that this course of action would probably not be permitted. Told that an applicant for judicial review was simultaneously pursuing an AAT appeal in relation to the same decision, a court would almost certainly dismiss the application. Not told, it would almost certainly exercise its discretion to dismiss the application as an abuse of process, once it was informed of the parallel proceeding: see *R v Galvin* (1979) 2 NTR 9. I think this is a justifiable approach, but if the answer had addressed the issue, and handled it well, I would have given some credit for this.

There are times at which the answer may seem unduly sympathetic to Mr Knox. This, however, is as it should be. You are asked to advise PACSA. You can assume that PACSA is likely to show your advice to Mr Knox. Even if you think that Mr Knox is a nasty piece of work who needs the services of a psychiatrist rather than a lawyer, you should not say so in print. It would be unprofessional; it will probably lose you a client, and you may find yourself sued for libel. Your job is to advise PACSA to the best of your abilities, or to decline altogether to act (which you can do here only at the cost of receiving no marks for your answer).

The question does not expressly ask you to advise on non-legal avenues, but a conclusion which recognises that there may be attractive alternatives to the formal processes demonstrates a sound grasp of the realities of administrative review. This answer includes one suggestion. An alternative approach (which is suggested by the 'fact' that PACSA has two Senators) would be to discuss political avenues for redress. Given the complexity of the question, and the paucity of information relating to alternative courses of action, such considerations can at best involve speculation. This should be brief, but it can demonstrate awareness of the importance of considering non-legal solutions to 'legal' problems.

Common Errors to Avoid

- Failure to consider whether the Ombudsman has jurisdiction to entertain a complaint about the Attorney-General's conduct. (Note that in this case the Attorney-General acted personally and not through an authorised person.)

- In discussing judicial review, it is important to differentiate between the two decisions: the decision to refuse permission, and the decision to issue a certificate. The two decisions are governed by different legal regimes, and the effects of a finding as to their invalidity are different.

■ In discussing judicial review, you should consider not only what orders might be made, but the utility to Mr Knox of those orders. You are, after all, being asked to advise as to the course of action he should take.

■ In discussing merits review, it is important to consider not only whether the AAT has jurisdiction, but how it would be likely to exercise that jurisdiction. This involves recognising the degree to which AAT decisions can depend not only on law, but on facts and on the values which members bring to bear in the exercise of their discretion.

QUESTION 49

Rubens' *Massacre of the Innocents II* is probably his most chilling painting. Depicting the killing of children at Herod's orders, it shows soldiers engaging in a horrifying orgy of mayhem, using almost every conceivable means to discharge their orders. They are performing their task with undisguised enthusiasm, and obviously intend to turn their attentions to the mothers of the deceased once they have finished their immediate task. So horrified was the Duke of Roma-Tiburtina (who commissioned the work) that he hid the work behind his own painting of St Francis feeding birdseed to pigeons, and there it stayed until it was discovered by the executor of the estate of the late Major Major, whose World War II career included service in Italy. On sale, the painting yielded $138 million, just enough to cover the fees charged by the lawyers involved in determining its ownership.

The buyer was Midas Trumpeter, an art collector and misanthrope whose cynicism about human nature has been the basis for his huge private fortune. He tells you that he bought it because it was probably Rubens' greatest work. In addition, its theme appealed to him. He only wished that there had been a Herod around shortly after the birth of his appalling children Gieison and Gezzobelle. In the course of arranging to have the work air-freighted to Australia, he learned that Customs might well regard the work as a prohibited import under reg 4A(1A)(a) of the Customs (Prohibited Imports) Regulations 1956 (Cth). His response was to phone the Attorney-General and ask if he could import it, on the basis that it would be kept locked up in his well-secured study, to be shown to no one except himself and guests approved by the Attorney-General.

The Attorney-General referred the application to an authorised person, who concluded that the work was so horrifying that it should not be allowed into Australia. Trumpeter instructs you as follows:

> I want this matter resolved as quickly as possible. I want nothing to do with courts. In my experience, appointment to the bench strips people of what little common sense they might once have had. If I thought my case was devoid of merit, I'd obviously want the matter litigated, but I actually think I have right on my side, so I'd prefer to steer clear of the courts if you ➤

don't mind. I don't care what happens to the painting after I die. The only thing I care about is that it not fall into the hands of my children.

I want your advice. You should note that there is to be a federal election within six months.

Give that advice in a letter to Mr Trumpeter. Include references to relevant legislation and legal authorities.

Time allowed: 40 mins

Answer Plan

Summary and evaluation of options:

(i)   A complaint to the Ombudsman.

(ii) An application to the AAT.

(iii) Political pressure.

(iv) Do nothing.

(v)   Conclusion.

 ## Answer

Dear Mr Trumpeter,

Your reluctance to involve yourself in litigation precludes availing yourself of such remedies as you might enjoy under the Customs Act 1901 (Cth). It also makes it unnecessary to consider whether you could or should seek judicial review of the decision to refuse permission to import. Broadly, your options then are as follows:

- a complaint to the Ombudsman;
- an application to the AAT for review of the authorised person's decision;
- political pressure; or
- do nothing.

Each of the first three courses of action has something to commend it, but for reasons which will become apparent, I am inclined to favour option 2, possibly in conjunction with, or to be followed by, option 3.

(i)   A complaint to the Ombudsman

While the Ombudsman may not inquire into actions taken by a Minister (Ombudsman Act s 5(2)(a)), the Ombudsman may inquire into actions of an authorised person or authorised person: Ombudsman Act 1976 (Cth) s 5(3). However, s 6(3) provides that the Ombudsman may decide not to investigate a complaint where the relevant action could have been the subject of an application for judicial review, or an application to a tribunal if of the view that it would have been reasonable for the complainant to have exercised their right of review or appeal.

I think it is likely that the Ombudsman would conclude that it would have been reasonable for you to have appealed or to have sought judicial review. Even if he shared your views about the judiciary (and I have no reason to believe he does), he would point out that you have the alternative of seeking review by the AAT (which is not a court). He would further point out that this is a case where the stakes far outweigh the costs you would be likely to incur.

(ii)   An application to the AAT

I assume that if you wished to avoid both courts and tribunals, you would have instructed me accordingly. I should point out that there is the possibility that if your case were to be heard by the AAT, it would be heard by a tribunal composed of, or including, a judge. The likelihood of this is small, however, and there are several reasons why I would strongly recommend an immediate application to the AAT for review of the decision.

The tribunal has jurisdiction: reg 4A(4). You should apply immediately, because if you delay, there is a danger that the Attorney-General will issue a certificate depriving you of your right to do so: reg 4A(5), (8). To keep your options open, then, you should apply forthwith. Your application does not need to give anything away. It is enough that your grounds for objecting to the decision are that it is wrong. There is a filing fee and likely legal representation to be budgeted for, which I think lie within your resources.

The tribunal is not concerned with whether the original decision is correct, but with what, on the basis of the material and arguments presented to it, is the 'correct or preferable decision': *Drake v Minister for Immigration and Ethnic Affairs* (1979) 24 ALR 577. Even if you presented the same material to the tribunal as you presented to the authorised person, it is possible that the tribunal would reach a different decision. It might, for instance, react differently to the painting. That said, I would advise you to try to present as strong a case as possible to the tribunal. I would advise you not to joke about your empathy with Herod. The tribunal might not be impressed by the suggestion that a purpose for importing the goods was to feed filicidal fantasies. I would emphasise the extent to which you engage in artistic and cultural activities, and your reputation in this respect. (Your collection is testimony to this.) I have little doubt that there are many in the Australian and international art world who have welcomed your custom and patronage and who would be delighted to give evidence on your behalf.

As for conditions (reg 4A(3)), I have some reservations about what you originally proposed. It seemed too defensive, and it also would have involved unwelcome work for the Attorney-General. Prior to — and, if necessary, at — the hearing, the Commonwealth should be asked whether there are any conditions subject to which it would agree to importation. Rather than undermine its case by appearing totally unreasonable, it might in the end make a proposal which would prove acceptable to you.

I cannot predict the outcome of an AAT hearing, but I think it might well prove favourable.

(iii) Political pressure

However, I think that this is a matter best handled politically. There are various courses of action open to you. One would be to suggest to the Attorney-General that it had been your intention that the painting become part of the national collection on your death, and that he might wish to change his mind if this were to be formalised. Out of courtesy you could inform the Arts Minister of this. If I am correct in assuming that the matter has not yet become the subject of public controversy, this might be enough to resolve the problem. The Attorney-General would not run the risk of being seen to have made an about-turn. Honour would be left intact. And even if the Attorney-General was reluctant to agree to grant the relevant permission, I think you would have the Arts Minister on side. Moreover, implicit in the proffered carrot would be the threat of what would happen if the offer were to be turned down. The Attorney-General would then have to accept responsibility for having lost the chance to acquire a masterpiece for the nation.

If this failed, you could retain a life-interest in the painting and give the interest in remainder in the painting to one of the State art galleries, conditional upon immediate importation being approved, possibly with a gift-over to a person or body which the government would prefer not be enriched by your bounty. You would then, I think, have a State government on side. New South Wales and Victoria would be best, depending on which has more marginal seats inhabited by politically wavering art lovers. You might also leak news of the 'fact' that, given Australia's apparent cultural philistinism, you are rethinking your plans to leave your art collection to the nation.

You might wonder whether the government has the power to change its mind, once it has made a decision. There are three answers to this question. First, it can do so if the earlier decision is legally flawed: *Minister for Immigration and Multicultural Affairs v Bhardwarj* (2002) 209 CLR 597. (I have no information to suggest that it is.) Second, even if the government does not have the power to reconsider, I doubt that anyone would be in a position to challenge its decision if it did so. Their interest would normally be insufficiently direct. Third, if the matter is before the AAT (as is likely to be the case for the next 12 months), it is accepted that the government can settle the matter. This is one reason why it makes sense to initiate AAT proceedings.

In a worst case scenario, you could sell the interest in remainder and use the income from the invested capital to fund a handsome home in Europe or North America where the painting could be stored, and where you could visit it from time to time.

(iv)   *Do nothing*

I am not in favour of this. Other avenues (and in particular the political avenue) have definite promise. Doing nothing will simply give satisfaction to your children, and that is the last thing you want.

(v)   *Conclusion*

I am inclined to think that this is a matter which can probably be settled politically.

Just in case this is not possible, I would advise making an AAT application before the Attorney-General issues a certificate. Try to keep the application secret so that the Attorney-General can retreat gracefully in the event of your offer proving attractive. If the Attorney-General rejects the offer, go public. You might also suggest to the AAT that you would accept importation subject to a condition that your interest in remainder be transferred to a State gallery. This would strengthen your overall claim by enabling you to present yourself as a patron of the arts. I assume you would prefer this term to 'philanthropist'.

There will probably be an election before the AAT makes a decision. If, as is quite possible, the election means a new Attorney-General, you will have a fresh chance to negotiate. Even if this is not the case, the AAT might find in your favour.

Examiner's Comments

Midas' aversion to courts is extremely convenient, since it absolves you of the obligation to consider the operation of the seizure and forfeiture provisions of the Customs Act 1901 (Cth) (which are not set out for you). It also absolves you of the need to discuss the relationship between these and judicial review procedures. You are left with a question which does not require much knowledge of law, but which does require some basic problem-solving skills.

That said, the question does require some familiarity with law. Examinees need to know the limits of the Ombudsman's power to conduct investigations. They need to know that the AAT is not a court. (Yes, this seems obvious, but a Queensland Supreme Court judge, no longer serving, was alleged to believe that it was a travel company.) They also need to know that AAT proceedings can be settled by compromise. One of the strengths of this answer is that it gives good advice based on familiarity with the workings of the AAT. It recognises both the kinds of considerations that need to be taken into account by a person who is seeking a favourable outcome in the AAT, and the way in which AAT proceedings can be used to provide a backdrop against which ongoing negotiation may take place.

Examinees may have different ideas about political solutions to this problem. Obviously the advice which would be given to a real life Midas would be given on the basis of knowledge of the idiosyncrasies of the Attorney-General and other key political actors, and different answers are likely to proceed from different assumptions. It would not be reasonable to require that examinees articulate all their assumptions. However, they should present a plausible argument, and one which shows a degree of political awareness. This answer does so. It demonstrates awareness of the importance of preserving the appearance of honour. It is aware of the role of inducements, while recognising that it would be unwise to resort to bare-faced bribery. It includes contingency plans just in case some strategies fail. It also demonstrates awareness of the legal problems that could arise when a Minister proposes to override a delegate's arguably lawful decision.

I am a little unhappy about the suggestion that Midas should misrepresent his reasons for wishing to import the painting in order to improve his chances before the AAT. However, the answer does at least pay lip service to legal ethics by the pretence that the person giving the advice believes that Midas' comments about Herod were only a joke.

 ## Common Errors to Avoid

- Discussing judicial review, contrary to instructions.
- Failure to consider whether the Ombudsman is empowered to investigate the complaint, or would do so.
- Failure to recognise the importance of an expeditious application for AAT review.
- Failure to discuss the kinds of arguments which might improve Midas' prospects before the AAT.
- Lack of imagination in relation to possible political strategies.

 ## QUESTION 50

When Christian fundamentalists stormed the National Centre for Socio-Legal Studies (CSLS) in Dipodium, the capital of the Caledenian province of Glossodia, they seized files and documents, including one euphemistically entitled *Effective Interviewing Techniques: An Illustrated Manual for Social Researchers*. This book had been prepared for torturers, and included a DVD which showed people being subjected to various forms of torture, and included graphic images of the many ways in which the CSLS killed opponents of the regime. One of the insurgents sent an e-mail to an Australian supporter, Professor Rose Greenhood, and suggested that she might like a copy. She was delighted. She had heard rumours of the existence of this document (a guide for torturers) from human rights activists, but had treated them with scepticism, taking the slightly arrogant attitude that torturers tended to be illiterate and, in any case, didn't need to be able to read books in order to learn how to torture. The realisation that there was actual documentary evidence of the practices of the dreaded CSLS was therefore exciting. Aware that ➤

the document might fall foul of the Customs (Prohibited Imports) Regulations 1956 (Cth), especially given the photographs illustrating techniques for extracting information, and the sickening DVD, she asked for special permission to import the volume and the disk.

For the purposes of considering the proposal, the Attorney-General authorised Cynthia Prasophyllum, a secretary in the Australian Consulate in Dipodium. Ms Prasophyllum had majored in Caledenian Studies at Sydney University, and had taken a one unit course in Low Glossodian, the everyday language of the Glossodians. However, recognising that the document was written in High Glossodian, she asked for assistance from a local employee of the consulate who she believed to be fluent in High Glossodian, a language characterised by multiple meanings, evasiveness, the use of negatives to denote positives, and conventions whereby lies should be used in preference to the truth in contexts where they could be recognised as such by people in direct (but not indirect) communication. On the basis of the translations and their accompanying explanations, Ms Prasophyllum recommended that permission should not be granted.

Following refusal, Professor Greenhood sought access to the relevant file and discovered that there were several respects in which Ms Prasophyllum appeared to be acting on the basis of a misunderstanding of the contents of the book. Instead of forming her own views about the photographs, she had acted on the basis of their cultural significance from the perspective of a Glossodian. It looked as if she had sometimes relied on the views of the local employee rather than forming her own views. Moreover, to judge from the employee's name, he was a Minor Glossodian rather than a Major Glossodian, and would therefore not understand some of the subtleties of High Glossodian. She says that she cannot be confident that the decision would have been different had these errors not been made. The copy of the file did not, for some reason, include a copy of the book. The Attorney-General has not issued a certificate precluding AAT review.

Professor Greenhood is anxious to import the book and wants to know what to do. Should she seek judicial review or should she go the AAT? What should she do if these avenues fail? You are briefed to advise on these matters.

Time allowed: 1 hour

Answer Plan

(i)   Advantages and disadvantages of judicial review.

(ii) Advantages and disadvantages of AAT review.

(iii) Alternatives to judicial and tribunal review.

(iv) Conclusion.

Answer

In my opinion, Professor Greenhood could either seek judicial review or apply to the AAT. The latter option appears to me to be the preferable one. In the event of her AAT application proving unsuccessful, she should investigate the feasibility of examining a copy of the book in a country which has approved its importation.

(i)   Advantages and disadvantages of judicial review

On the basis of the information before me, it is clear that Professor Greenhood could seek judicial review of the authorised person's decision. The decision is clearly reviewable. It is a decision of an administrative character, made under an enactment. It is therefore reviewable under s 5 of the ADJR Act. It would also be reviewable under s 39B of the Judiciary Act 1903 (Cth).

It also seems to me that it would be possible to make out grounds for review, although I am by no means confident that this is the case. If there is a ground for review, it would be that the authorised person has failed to exercise the discretion conferred upon her: ADJR s 5(1)(e), (2)(e). This would be the case if she effectively acted at the behest of the employee. I am inclined to doubt that this was so, however. She certainly relied on advice from the employee, but to my mind this does not amount to a failure to exercise her powers under the regulation. Indeed, her conduct seems to have been calculated to yield a better-informed decision than would have been the case if she had sought to rely on her own limited expertise. It is hard to imagine that the regulation should be read so as to require less well-informed decision-making.

I am also advised that there are translation errors. It is unlikely that these can be said to constitute errors of law, or that they mean the decision is unreasonable in the *Wednesbury* sense. The ordinary meaning of a word is a question of fact and not of law: *Collector of Customs v Agfa Gevaert Ltd* (1996) 186 CLR 389 at [395]–[396]. Moreover, it seems apparent that even if there were errors, they were not unreasonable errors. It is unlikely that s 5(1)(h), (3)(b) of the ADJR Act would provide relief since there seems to be no suggestion that any particular error of fact was the basis for the decision. In any case, it is not even clear that there has necessarily been material error of fact. I shall not develop these arguments, given my belief that, in any case, an application for judicial review would be unwise.

One reason why I believe that an application would be unwise is that I think that this is a case where a court would dismiss the application. The ADJR Act expressly provides that a court may decline to exercise its ADJR Act jurisdiction on the grounds that adequate provision is made for an alternative form of review: s 10(2)(b)(ii). Here, there is an alternative form of review, namely the AAT, by virtue of reg 4A(4). Moreover, while the possibility of AAT review is not, of itself, grounds for a court declining to exercise its jurisdiction, this appears to be a case in which the court would consider that the AAT should hear the case. If the case involved a simple question of law which could dispose of the dispute, a court would not exercise its discretion to refuse to hear the case: *Mercantile Credits Ltd v Federal Commissioner of Taxation* (1985) ALN N192. However, where the case involves mixed questions of fact and law, and where a decision is unlikely to resolve the underlying dispute, courts are more inclined to decline jurisdiction in favour of a merits review tribunal: *Anderson v Commissioner for Employees' Compensation* (1986) 12 ALD 612; *Du Pont (Australia) v Comptroller-General of Customs* (1993) 30 ALD 829.

Here, the judicial review application would require consideration of questions of fact. In particular, it would require consideration of the degree to which the authorised person acted independently of the consulate employee. Any dispute about the reasonableness of the decision or about the existence or materiality of factual errors would require extensive evidence in relation to the correct translation of the documents in question. In any case, even if the decision were quashed, the question of whether permission to import should be granted would remain unresolved, and the person considering the application for permission would receive little or no guidance in relation to the handling of the matter from any decision a court might hand down. I think it is almost certain that a court would decline to exercise its review jurisdiction. Similar considerations would apply if the matter were to be brought under the Judiciary Act rather than the ADJR Act: *Du Pont (Australia)*.

Moreover, even if these hurdles could be overcome, the gain would be of limited value. It is likely that more than a year would have elapsed, and Professor Greenhood would still not have a decision in her favour. Reconsideration would take time. By the time a decision was made (and it might not be a favourable one), there might be little point in being granted permission. The document might well have already entered the country, and someone other than Professor Greenhood might have gained kudos from having publicised its content.

(ii) Advantages and disadvantages of AAT review

In my opinion, the AAT would be a more appropriate forum for handling the matter. The AAT may hear an appeal against a refusal to issue permission: Customs (Prohibited Imports) Regulations 1956 (Cth), reg 4A(4). It would be able to examine the questions of fact which bear on this issue. It would probably be more dispassionate than a person holding a sensitive post in Glossodia. Unfortunately, it is unlikely to handle the application with the speed that Professor Greenhood would wish. The hearing is likely to be a long one, and will involve a considerable amount of time devoted to the hearing of expert witnesses arguing about the meaning of a language whose meaning appears to be notoriously contestable. It will not be cheap, especially if Professor

Greenhood is legally represented (as I think she should be). However, it may all be worthwhile. The papers produced by the Commonwealth will have to include a copy of the book, and Professor Greenhood will have access to the file (in the absence of an objection under s 36B of the AAT Act). This access will, of course, only be temporary, but it may provide her with some of the information she is seeking. On the basis of the material before me, I am not sure what the outcome will be. I think, however, that Professor Greenhood should be able to satisfy the requirements implicit in the regulation. One condition which she should be prepared to contemplate would be the excision of particularly nasty photographs, and possibly that she forgo the DVD.

(iii) Alternatives to judicial and tribunal review

Since I assume that Professor Greenhood would like access to the book as quickly as possible, I think alternatives should be explored. One possibility is that the matter could be resolved by negotiation. The Commonwealth may well be receptive to this, since it may be reluctant to incur the expense and publicity associated with a long, drawn-out hearing. To facilitate negotiation, it will be necessary to find out what concessions Professor Greenhood would willingly agree to in exchange for access to the book. There may be issues about which she is indifferent and about which the Commonwealth cares strongly. If so, a basis for settlement may exist.

Alternatively, there may be other ways in which Professor Greenhood might be able to gain access to the book. I can understand that Professor Greenhood is reluctant to go to Glossodia in the hope of being able to see one of the copies of the manual there, but are there no copies anywhere else? Her Christian friends should be able to point her in the right direction. I'm sure that her university is badgering her to use accumulated leave entitlements. Perhaps she should use them; while travel can be expensive, stressful and time-consuming, the same could be said of a full-scale AAT application.

I have recommended that she pursue this option as soon as possible. It is also one which will probably continue to remain open, and she could avail herself of it if negotiation and the AAT application were to fail.

(iv) Conclusion

In my opinion, there is little to be gained from a judicial review application. Even if there were a real possibility that the application would result in reconsideration, and even if there were a distinct likelihood that reconsideration would yield a favourable result so that it was unnecessary to resort to the AAT, I would advise against judicial review. It would probably delay the decision-making process, and might not obviate the need for a further application to the AAT. Since I doubt that it would result in a favourable outcome, and since I doubt that reconsideration would produce a different result, I am even more confident in my advice that judicial review should not be sought in this case.

I think Professor Greenhood should appeal to the AAT. One reason for this recommendation is that I think she should keep her options open while she explores potentially more attractive alternatives. I think she may well be able to get her way without relying on a favourable AAT outcome, but, should these alternatives prove unsatisfactory, it would be as well that the AAT option were kept open. While an AAT decision is unlikely to be made quickly, it would be made eventually, and it might well turn out to be in her favour. An AAT application would also create a formal framework for negotiation, and is to be recommended on that ground too. I think that at the same time, she should explore the possibility of a negotiated settlement.

But I find it hard to believe that there are not easier ways of getting access to the document, and would recommend that these be pursued at the same time as the AAT proceedings.

Examiner's Comments

This question requires attention both to law and to practicalities. It requires attention to the relative advantages of judicial review, tribunal review, and other strategies. In considering the advantages of judicial review, examinees should discuss whether judicial review is available; whether it would be likely that one or more grounds of review could be made out; whether the court might dismiss the application; and whether, even where an application would likely prove successful, it would make sense in the circumstances. Given that there is a very strong likelihood that a court would dismiss the application in the circumstances of this case, examinees could be excused for not devoting much time to considering whether a ground for review could potentially be made out. Nonetheless, some attention should be given to this question. The answer addresses each of these issues, although its canvassing of the 'grounds made out' issue is not as detailed as one might expect in a question which focused solely on this issue, where the time allotted was enough to allow it to be canvassed more thoroughly.

In considering the advantages of AAT review, examinees should consider whether it is available, whether it would be likely to yield a favourable outcome, and the costs associated with an AAT application. Given the limited facts which have been provided, it would not be easy to predict the likely outcome of the application. It is therefore enough to point to matters which might prove relevant. In discussing the costs associated with an AAT application, examinees should show some awareness of how someone in Professor Greenhood's position would have to go about making a case. Examinees should also show that they are aware of the papers that the Commonwealth must produce to the AAT. This answer shows awareness of these issues. It recognises that AAT applications can take a considerable time to be completed. It also notes the irony that, in this case, the application would give Professor Greenhood much of what she wants, regardless of the outcome.

Given the problems associated with both judicial review and applications to the AAT, examinees ought to consider alternative courses of action. These include settlement of the AAT application, and getting access to the book outside Australia. It is clearly improper to recommend illegal courses of action (such as simply arranging to have the book posted to Professor Greenhood in Australia). In any case, it is notorious that parcels posted in Caledenia are stolen before reaching their destination, and the stamps torn off for re-use. The answer makes some suggestions. They do not exhaust Professor Greenhood's options. What is expected here is that examinees recognise the problem and approach it with some imagination.

 # Common Errors to Avoid

- Failure to recognise the likelihood that courts would dismiss the application in this case.
- Assuming that the decision to refuse could be reviewed on the basis of errors of fact or unreasonableness.
- Failure to recognise that even a successful application for judicial review would leave the applicant without a substantive decision in her favour.
- Failure to address the practical *disadvantages* of AAT review.
- Failure to consider non-legal strategies that might give Professor Greenhood much of what she wants.